L. Michael \

SAMS
Teach Yourself
Visual InterDev™ 6
in 21 Days

SAMS

A Division of Macmillan Computer Publishing
201 West 103rd St., Indianapolis, Indiana, 46290 USA

Sams Teach Yourself Visual InterDev™ 6 in 21 Days

Copyright © 1998 by Sams Publishing

International Standard Book Number: 0-672-31251-4

Library of Congress Catalog Card Number: 98-84621

Printed in the United States of America

First Printing: August, 1998

01   00   99   98   4   3   2   1

Trademarks

Warning and Disclaimer

EXECUTIVE EDITOR
Bradley L. Jones

ACQUISITIONS EDITOR
Kelly Marshall

DEVELOPMENT EDITORS
Linda Richmond
Matt Purcell

MANAGING EDITOR
Jodi Jensen

PROJECT EDITOR
Dana Rhodes Lesh

COPY EDITOR
Kate Givens

INDEXER
Kelly Talbot

TECHNICAL EDITOR
Sunil Hazari

SOFTWARE DEVELOPMENT SPECIALIST
Andrea Duvall

INTERIOR DESIGNER
Gary Adair

COVER DESIGNER
Aren Howell

TEAM COORDINATOR
Carol Ackerman

PRODUCTION
Marcia Deboy
Jennifer Earhart
Cynthia Fields
Susan Geiselman

Overview

	Forward	viii
	Introduction	1
WEEK 1 AT A GLANCE		**5**
Day 1	Presenting Visual InterDev 6	7
2	Creating Your First Visual InterDev Project	39
3	Creating the Content for Your Application	63
4	WYSIWYG Editing with Visual InterDev	83
5	Enhancing Your Web Page Through Client-Side Script	103
6	Extending Your Web Page Through Server-Side Script	136
7	Integrating Objects into Your Applications	155
WEEK 1 IN REVIEW		**179**
WEEK 2 AT A GLANCE		**181**
Day 8	Communicating with a Database	183
9	Using the Visual Data Tools for Maximum Productivity	211
10	Managing Your Database Components	239
11	Fundamentals of Active Server Pages	263
12	Extending Web Pages Through Design-Time Controls	297
13	Unleashing the Power of the Visual InterDev Programming Model	317
14	Building a Database-Driven Web Application	341
WEEK 2 IN REVIEW		**357**
WEEK 3 AT A GLANCE		**359**
Day 15	Building an Integrated Solution with Components	361
16	Managing Your Web Site with Visual InterDev	381
17	Debugging Your Applications with Visual InterDev	403
18	Exploring the Working Modes of Visual InterDev	425
19	Effective Team Development with Visual InterDev and Visual SourceSafe	445

20 Designing an Effective Site with the Site Designer   467

21 Making a Difference with Dynamic HTML   497

WEEK 3 IN REVIEW   **517**

APPENDIXES

A   Additional Resources   519

B   Answers   523

Index   551

Contents

INTRODUCTION   1

WEEK 1 AT A GLANCE   5

DAY 1 PRESENTING VISUAL INTERDEV 6   7

What Is Visual InterDev? 8
Visual InterDev 6—New and Improved 9
    A More Visual Experience 9
    WYSIWYG Editing..12
    Programming Support 12
    End-to-End Debugging 14
    Support for Development Teams 14
    Support for the Latest Web Design Technologies.....................................15
Radically Integrated 16
    The Visual InterDev 6 Development Environment 17
    Visual SourceSafe Integration 20
    Browser Integration 20
Taking a Closer Look at the Components 21
    The Views of Visual InterDev 21
    ActiveX Controls and Java Applets..25
    Design-Time Controls 25
    Active Server Pages 26
    The Script Outline 26
    File Management Components 31
Exploring the Database Integration 32
    The Data View 32
    The Query Designer 33
    The Database Designer 34
    The Stored Procedure Editor/Trigger Editor...34
    ActiveX Data Objects 34
    Database Design-Time Controls 35
    Database Wizards 35
How Should You Use Visual InterDev 6?..36
Summary...36

Q&A 37
Workshop 38
    Quiz 38
    Exercises 38

DAY 2 CREATING YOUR FIRST VISUAL INTERDEV PROJECT   39

Exploring a Standard Project 40
Creating Your First Visual InterDev Application 41
    Overview of the Application 41
    Creating the Project..42
Analyzing the Results...49
    Analyzing the Server 49
    Analyzing the Client 50
    Analyzing Visual InterDev 6 52
Creating the Content..53
Summary..59
Q&A 60
Workshop 60
    Quiz 61
    Exercises 61

DAY 3 CREATING THE CONTENT FOR YOUR APPLICATION   63

An Integrated Approach to Editing Content..64
Exploring the New Integrated Development Environment 64
    Adding Text with Design View 66
    Working with Tables 67
    Adding Controls and Objects 68
    Working with Code and Script 73
    Getting Around with the Outline Windows..76
    Customizing Your Development Environment 78
Choosing the Right Editor for the Job 78
    Using Other Editors..78
Previewing the Results 79
Summary..80
Q&A 81
Workshop 82
    Quiz 82
    Exercises 82

DAY 4 WYSIWYG EDITING WITH VISUAL INTERDEV   83

The Benefits of a Visual Environment 84
Exploring the Design View Features 85
    Formatting Web Pages in Design View..86
    Working with Lists 91

Working with Tables 91
Working with HTML Features in Design View 93
Positioning Objects on Your Pages 96
Adding User-Defined Styles to Your Web Pages 97
Creating a New Style Sheet...97
Working with the Cascading Style Sheets Editor 98
Customizing Your Toolbox 99
Changing the Toolbox Tabs...99
Adding Controls to the Toolbox 100
Summary 100
Q&A 101
Workshop 102
Quiz 102
Exercises 102

DAY 5 ENHANCING YOUR WEB PAGE THROUGH CLIENT-SIDE SCRIPT   103

Scripting for Success 104
The Marriage of HTML and Scripting Languages.............................105
What Is VBScript? 106
What Is JScript/JavaScript? 107
Creating a Web Page with Client-Side Script.....................................108
VBScript Basics 113
Understanding Procedures...114
Using VBScript to Extend Your Web Page..131
Summary 134
Q&A 134
Workshop 135
Quiz 135
Exercises 136

DAY 6 EXTENDING YOUR WEB PAGE THROUGH SERVER-SIDE SCRIPT   137

What Is Server-Side Script? 138
Exploring the Capabilities of Server-Side Script 139
Exploring the Client/Server Picture 140
Understanding Active Server Pages 141
Creating Your First Active Server Page 142
Adding the Content and Server Script 144
Using Server Script in Your Application 146
Creating the Form 146
Creating the Active Server Page 149
Taking a Closer Look at the Process...150

Integrating Client and Server Script 150
Summary 152
Q&A 152
Workshop 153
    Quiz 153
    Exercise 153

DAY 7 INTEGRATING OBJECTS INTO YOUR APPLICATIONS   **155**

Defining Objects 156
Introduction to Java Applets 156
    How Do Java Applets Work? 157
    Understanding Java Applets 158
ActiveX Overview 160
    Understanding ActiveX Controls 160
    Using the Attributes to Define an ActiveX Control 163
ActiveX Versus Java 163
    Exploring the Qualities of ActiveX 164
    Examining the Drawbacks of ActiveX 164
    Exploring the Qualities of Java 165
    Examining the Limitations of Java 166
Inserting an ActiveX Control into a Web Page 166
    Editing the Properties of an ActiveX Control 168
Manipulating Methods to Achieve the Right Behavior 169
    Using Methods in Your Application 170
Making Objects Come Alive with Script 172
    Reviewing the Script Editor 172
    Reviewing Statement Completion 173
    Scripting the Timesheet Application 174
Summary 176
Q&A 176
Workshop 177
    Quiz 177
    Exercise 177

WEEK 1 IN REVIEW   **179**

WEEK 2 AT A GLANCE   **181**

DAY 8 COMMUNICATING WITH A DATABASE   **183**

Leveraging Visual InterDev to Access Your Data 184
The Benefits of Database Integration 184

Integrating the Data 185
Comparing the Options 185
Visual InterDev Benefits 186
Seeing Clearly with the Data View..188
Exploring the Data View 188
Building a Connection with a Database Wizard..190
Selecting the Data Source 190
Creating a New Data Source 192
Analyzing the Results 197
Understanding the Query Designer 198
Understanding the Query Designer..198
Query Designer Features 199
The Query Designer Workspace 199
The ActiveX Data Object 201
Exploring ADO 202
Understanding ADO Objects..204
Understanding ADO Collections and Properties..207
Database Design-Time ActiveX Controls..207
Summary..208
Q&A 209
Workshop 209
Quiz 210
Exercises 210

DAY 9 USING THE VISUAL DATA TOOLS FOR MAXIMUM PRODUCTIVITY   211

Getting Started with the Query Designer 212
Using the Query Designer to Generate Your SQL 212
Using the Query Designer Toolbar 215
Creating a Query..218
Selecting the Tables..218
Using the Query Designer to Customize Your Queries 224
Adding and Deleting Columns for the Query 224
Changing the Column Order 225
Changing the Names of the Columns 225
Specifying the Output 226
Searching for Particular Rows..226
Grouping the Results 228
Creating an Update Query 232
Selecting the Table to Update 233
Adding the Values for the Update Query 233
Entering and Modifying Data 234
Adding New Data 235
Changing the Data..235
Deleting the Data..236

Summary 236
Q&A 236
Workshop 237
    Quiz 237
    Exercises 237

DAY 10 MANAGING YOUR DATABASE COMPONENTS   239

Introduction to Database Objects 240
    Tables..240
    Relationships 240
    Constraints 243
    Indexes 243
Getting Started with the Database Designer......................................243
Visualizing Your Database 244
    Exploring a Database Diagram 245
    Understanding Database Diagram Properties 246
Creating and Editing SQL Server Objects 250
    Creating a Database Diagram 250
    Creating a New Database Table 251
    Working with Diagrams and Tables 255
    Modifying Objects Within the Design View 255
Using SQL Scripts 256
    Saving the SQL Script..256
Creating and Editing Stored Procedures..258
    Creating a Stored Procedure 258
    Executing a Stored Procedure 259
Summary 261
Q&A 261
Workshop 262
    Quiz 262
    Exercise 262

DAY 11 FUNDAMENTALS OF ACTIVE SERVER PAGES   263

Making the Server Come Alive 264
What Makes Active Server Pages So Dynamic? 264
    Taking a Closer Look at the Process..265
Exploring the Client/Server Picture 266
Understanding Active Server Pages 267
    Working with Transactions 268
    Working with the Scripting Object Model 269
The Active Server Page Object Model 269
    The Request Object...270

The Response Object 279
The Session Object 285
The Application Object 288
The Server Object 290
Summary 294
Q&A 294
Workshop 295
Quiz 295
Exercise 295

DAY 12 EXTENDING WEB PAGES THROUGH DESIGN-TIME CONTROLS **297**

Defining Design-Time Controls 298
Design-Time Controls Versus ActiveX Controls 299
Design-Time Controls Make Effective Parents..............................299
The Origin of Design-Time Controls 301
Understanding Design-Time Controls 302
Inserting a Design-Time Control..302
Working with Design-Time Controls 303
Examining the Structure of a Design-Time Control 305
Editing the Script for a Design-Time Control................................306
Creating Database-Driven Forms with Design-Time Controls 307
Selecting the Target Scripting Platform 307
Adding the Database Connection 308
Using Design-Time Controls to Create the Page 308
Analyzing the Results 312
Summary 314
Q&A 315
Workshop 316
Quiz 316
Exercise 316

DAY 13 UNLEASHING THE POWER OF THE VISUAL INTERDEV PROGRAMMING MODEL **317**

The Document Object Model 318
DHTML and Client-Side Scripting Overview 318
An Overview of Scriptlets..321
DHTML Scriptlets...321
The Scripting Object Model 325
Design-Time Controls and Script Objects 326
The Page Object 327
How Does the Scripting Object Model Work? 331
Enabling the Scripting Object Model 333
Using the Scripting Object Model...334

The Data Environment Object Model..336
Summary...338
Q&A 338
Workshop 339
    Quiz 339
    Exercise 339

DAY 14 BUILDING A DATABASE-DRIVEN WEB APPLICATION   **341**

The Northwind Foods Case Study at a Glance 342
The Home Page..344
The Order Search Page 345
The Order Listing Page..347
The Order Details Page..350
Summary...355
Q&A 355
Workshop 356
    Quiz 356
    Exercise 356

WEEK 2 IN REVIEW   **357**

WEEK 3 AT A GLANCE   **359**

DAY 15 BUILDING AN INTEGRATED SOLUTION WITH COMPONENTS   **361**

Introduction to COM and DCOM 362
Examining COM and DCOM..363
    Understanding COM 363
    Benefits of COM 365
    Understanding DCOM..366
    Benefits of DCOM 367
Developing Components...369
    Integrating Components into Your ASP Code...370
Creating a Component with Visual Basic 6 371
    Step One: Creating the Project 371
    Step Two: Compiling Your Component 373
Building a Web-Based Application..373
    Constructing the Web Application..374
Integrating the Component into Your Application 376
    Analyzing the Results 377

Summary 378
Q&A 379
Workshop 379
   Quiz 379
   Exercises 380

DAY 16 MANAGING YOUR WEB SITE WITH VISUAL INTERDEV   **381**

Getting a Handle with the Link View 382
   Exploring the Link View Features.....................................382
   Opening a Link View 383
Using the Link View to Manage Your Site 387
   Opening the Link View Diagram for Your Application 387
   Filtering Your Link View 388
   Working with Objects 389
Leveraging Your Web Site for the Future 393
   Reaping the Benefits Within a Project 393
   Reaping the Benefits Across Multiple Projects..................394
   Copying a Web Site 395
Repairing the Links...398
Summary 400
Q&A 401
Workshop 401
   Quiz 401
   Exercises 401

DAY 17 DEBUGGING YOUR APPLICATIONS WITH VISUAL INTERDEV   **403**

Types of Errors 404
   HTML Errors..405
   Component Errors 405
   Database Errors 406
   Script Errors..406
Presenting the New Visual InterDev Debugger 406
   Starting the Debugging Process 408
Debugging Your Script on the Client and Server 410
   Working with Variables 411
   Controlling the Execution of Your Script 414
   Working with Your Processing Environment 417
Using Error-Handling Routines 419
   Resolving Errors with a Statement 420
   Resolving Errors with an Object......................................420

Common Consideration About Bugs 421
Summary 422
Q&A 423
Workshop 423
    Quiz 423
    Exercises 424

Day 18 Exploring the Working Modes of Visual InterDev   **425**

Choosing a Development and Deployment Platform 426
    Scalability 426
    Development Tools 426
    Standards 427
    Architecture 427
    Database...428
Using Windows 95 as Your Client and Server 429
    Client/Server Model on the Windows 95 Platform 429
    Database...430
Combining Windows 95 and Windows NT 430
    Client/Server Model on a Windows 95/Windows NT Mixed Environment ..431
    Database...431
Isolating Your Developers for the Best Results 431
Understanding the Visual InterDev Project Model............................432
    Master Mode 432
    Local Mode 434
    Offline Mode 434
    Establishing the Working Mode for the Project 435
Using the Different Project Modes Effectively 436
    Working in Isolation 436
A Practical Scenario 439
    Development 439
    Testing 441
    Production 442
Summary 442
Q&A 443
Workshop 443
    Quiz 444
    Exercises 444

Day 19 Effective Team Development with Visual InterDev and Visual SourceSafe   **445**

Visual InterDev Team Support Features...446
    FrontPage and Visual InterDev 446
    Visual SourceSafe and Visual InterDev 448

Integrating Visual SourceSafe with Visual InterDev 448

    Installing Visual SourceSafe 449

    Placing a Project Under Its Spell 451

    Determining the Characteristics of the Project 453

    Adding Files to a Source Controlled Project 454

    Disabling Source Control 454

Unleashing the Power of Visual SourceSafe 455

    Using the Library Functions 455

    Checking Out Your Files 456

    Checking In Your Files 457

    Discarding the Changes..458

Using Advanced Features of Visual SourceSafe 459

    Exploring the Visual SourceSafe Environment...459

    Viewing the History of a File 461

    Seeing the Differences...461

Further Integrating the Features of Visual SourceSafe....................................462

    Examining the Remnants of Visual SourceSafe 463

Summary..463

Q&A 464

Workshop 465

    Quiz 465

    Exercises 465

DAY 20 DESIGNING AN EFFECTIVE SITE WITH THE SITE DESIGNER 467

Effective User Interface Design 468

    Define a Purpose for the Interface 468

    Identify the Users' Needs and Expectations 469

    Design the User Interface 469

    Conduct Usability Testing 473

    Incorporate the Feedback into Your Interface 475

Construct Your Web Site with the Site Designer 476

    Creating a Site Diagram 476

    Creating New Pages for the Site 478

    Adding Existing Pages to the Site Diagram 481

Designing Effective Navigation for the User 485

    Establishing the Page Hierarchy 485

    Using the PageNavBar Design-Time Control 487

Leveraging Layouts and Themes 490

    Applying a Layout...490

    Applying a Theme 490

Reviewing HTML Form Design..491

    Designing an Effective Form...491

    Using the Proper Name 492

Considerations Checklist 492
Summary 493
Q&A 494
Workshop 494
    Quiz 494
    Exercises 495

DAY 21 MAKING A DIFFERENCE WITH DYNAMIC HTML   **497**

What Is Dynamic HTML? 498
The Components of Dynamic HTML 499
    Document Object Model 499
    Dynamic Styles 499
    Dynamic Positioning 500
    Dynamic Content 500
    Data Binding 500
Manipulating the Content of Your Web Pages 500
    Creating the Base Content 500
    Unleashing the Power of Dynamic Content 502
    Extending the Concept of Dynamic Content 504
Unleashing the Power of Data Binding 508
    Adding Some Smart Content 509
    Interacting with the Auction Page 509
    Analyzing the Code 510
Considerations Checklist 514
Summary 514
Q&A 515
Workshop 515
    Quiz 516
    Exercises 516

WEEK 3 IN REVIEW   **517**

APPENDIXES

A ADDITIONAL RESOURCES   **519**

MCP Home Page 519
Microsoft Home Page 520
Microsoft Visual InterDev Home Page 520
Microsoft Visual Studio Home Page 520
VBScript Home Page 520
Microsoft SiteBuilder Workshop 520
Microsoft Data Access Home Page 521
Microsoft Usenet Newsgroups for Data Access 521

Gamelan EarthWeb 521

JavaSoft Home Page 521

Java Boutique 522

World Wide Web Consortium..522

Microsoft Internet Information Server Home Page 522

Microsoft Visual Basic Home Page for Web Developers....................522

B ANSWERS   523

INDEX   551

Foreword

The Web provides a plethora of opportunities, especially for developers wanting to capitalize on this exciting and innovative technology. With all the excitement surrounding the Web, tools and technologies are maturing at an ever-increasing pace. Organizations are seeking to capitalize on these new technologies to gain a competitive advantage, be it decreased costs, increased customer satisfaction, or even increased sales.

The challenge for developers is choosing the right tool to build their Web-based solutions. Developers have spent several years accumulating their own favorite set of tools for traditional client/server development. In the last two years, we've seen the emergence of tools designed for Web designers and site managers. Until now, though, these tools have focused more on the visual aspects of designing pages, and less on the aspects of programming the server. Visual InterDev was designed to fill this need and is the first tool designed exclusively for the professional Web *developer*.

In designing this latest version of Visual InterDev, we listened to the cries of the developers who wanted a comprehensive, integrated development tool that would give them the ease of use of Visual Basic, the extensibility of Visual C++, and the database functionality of Microsoft Access—all within a single integrated development environment. We have provided a full set of tools that enable the professional developer to design, build, debug, and deploy database-driven Web applications faster than ever before.

Visual InterDev 6 is a member of the Visual Studio family of development tools and is designed to be used in conjunction with other Microsoft development tools such as Visual Basic, Visual C++, Visual J++, and Visual FoxPro. Used in conjunction with these other tools, Visual InterDev enables developers to build extremely high-volume, scalable Web applications based on the Windows DNA architecture.

Just as Visual InterDev provides you with the right tool for your Web-based development efforts, this book empowers you with the knowledge you need to take advantage of our new tool. Mike has been working with the Visual InterDev design team since the early alpha testing of the first version of the product. In addition, Mike has been a valued contributor to the success of the latest version: Visual InterDev 6. I know that you will enjoy this book as the key to unleashing the power and capabilities of Visual InterDev. I am very proud of our latest product and this book and hope that you thoroughly enjoy them both.

Garth Fort
Visual InterDev Product Manager
Microsoft Corporation
July 1998

About the Authors

L. MICHAEL VAN HOOZER is a director for BSI Consulting and has ten years of system development experience. His responsibilities include leading performance development and learning practice, providing leadership to application development projects, and directing the efforts of BSI's learning culture and research and development initiatives. Mike formerly worked for Andersen Consulting in three different areas of the practice, including business process, organizational and instructional design, and client/server and Internet technology. For the last six years, Mike has focused solely on client/server and Web-based application development. Mike has strong ties to Microsoft in that he has been very involved with the alpha and beta testing of products including Visual Basic, Visual InterDev, and the rest of the Visual Studio suite of tools. Mike has also implemented solutions for his clients based on these tools using his strong application development and user interface design skills.

Mike is a contributing author for *Visual Basic 4 Unleashed* (Sams Publishing, 1995) and has written articles for *Information Week*. Mike is the sole author of *Sams Teach Yourself Microsoft Visual InterDev in 21 Days* (Sams.net Publishing, April, 1997), and he contributed several chapters to *Visual InterDev Unleashed* (Sams.net Publishing, August, 1997). He has also designed, developed, and conducted training courses on both technical and leadership development topics. Mike is a regular speaker at Microsoft Tech-Ed conferences both in the United States and abroad and is sought out as a speaker for organizations and businesses in the Houston area. Mike graduated from Baylor University in 1988 with a B.B.A. in Finance, Economics, and Information Systems. Mike has volunteered much of his time to Child Advocates, Inc., serving as an outspoken advocate for abused and neglected children. He has served in various capacities with Child Advocates since 1989, including chairman of the board of directors in 1996. He currently volunteers as the Recruitment, Training, and Retention committee chair for Child Advocates, where he actively speaks to organizations, businesses, and civic groups about the issue of abuse and the need for quality volunteers. When he is not working or volunteering, Mike enjoys spending time with his wife, Gina, and their three children, Drew, Will, and Kyle.

MATT WATSON is a senior manager for BSI Consulting, a Houston-based information technology consulting firm that specializes in Internet and client/server consulting expertise. Matt has over eight years of experience in the information technology consulting industry and has worked on a number of client/server engagements in a variety of industries. Recently, Matt has focused his efforts on electronic commerce, Web application development, and Internet security. Matt is a contributing author of *Visual InterDev Unleashed* from Sams Publishing. Matt holds a B.S. in Computer Science from Baylor

University and lives in Houston with his wife, Chris, and their two children, Taylor and Travis. Matt wrote Chapters 3, 4, 11, and 17.

DOUG MCCLUNG is a technical consultant for BSI Consulting, a Houston-based information technology consulting firm. Previously, Doug worked as a systems analyst for Transco, and he has over two years of experience in information technology. Doug holds a B.B.A. in MIS from the University of Houston and is a Microsoft Certified Professional. On a lighter note, Doug is an Aquarius who spends his free time sailing, biking, and relaxing with his girlfriend, Heather Holcombe. Doug wrote Chapter 7, "Integrating Objects into Your Applications," and Chapter 11, "Fundamentals of Active Server Pages."

SCOTT SHANNON is a manager at BSI Consulting in Houston, Texas. He has over eight years of application development experience and currently focuses on Internet and intranet development for business applications. Scott wrote Chapter 10, "Managing Your Database Components," and Chapter 14, "Building a Database-Driven Web Application."

Dedication

To my wife, Gina, who complements, supplements, and completes my life; and to my sons,
Drew, Will, and Kyle, who provide an inspiration for my life.

Acknowledgments

First, I would like to thank my BSI coworkers—Matt Watson, Scott Shannon, and Doug McClung—for contributing to this book. I have truly enjoyed working with each of you on this project as well as our other endeavors. I think we created a great product! I would like to thank all the great people at Sams for the opportunity to write about such a revolutionary product for the Internet. Specifically, I want to thank Kelly Marshall, my acquisitions editor, who worked with me on this book and encouraged me every step of the way to ensure its success. I also truly appreciate the efforts of Matt Purcell and Brad Jones, along with the team of editors who worked diligently to develop a quality product. Sams is an excellent publisher, and I sincerely enjoyed working with everyone associated with the Macmillan family.

I truly appreciate the willingness and support of BSI Consulting, where I perform my day job, for giving me the chance to dedicate time to write this book. I have truly benefited from my experiences and association working with some really great people. I also appreciate the support, inspiration, and input from all my colleagues, friends, and mentors I have encountered over the years. Specifically, I want to thank Terrence Gee, my mentor and friend, who has truly affected my personal and professional life.

Many thanks to my good friends at Microsoft, including the Visual InterDev development team. I especially appreciate the support of Greg Leake, the Visual Studio product manager, as well as Garth Fort, Dennis Bye, and David Lazar, the Visual InterDev product managers. Thanks for all the information and guidance you provided during the creation of my second book on Visual InterDev. This version is totally RAD!

On a personal note, thanks to all my friends and colleagues who encouraged and prayed for me during the writing of this book. I would like to thank my eleventh grade English teacher, Carol Ramsey, who enriched and molded my writing abilities and taught me the importance of a good vocabulary. Carol, all those ultra-marathon vocabulary tests paid off. I also would like to sincerely thank Dr. Jim King who taught me about systems analysis while I was at Baylor University and inspired me to pursue consulting as a career. Dr. King is one of those rare professors who transcends theory and allows you to truly learn.

Most importantly, I thank my wife, Gina, and our three boys, Drew, Will, and Kyle, who supported and encouraged me throughout this exciting journey. Thanks for the sacrifices, again, that you made to allow me to continue my dream of writing. I also appreciate my mom and grandparents for their interest, support, and prayers along the way. I especially thank Mom, a former English teacher, for raising me and inspiring me to write.

Tell Us What You Think!

As the reader of this book, *you* are our most important critic and commentator. We value your opinion and want to know what we're doing right, what we could do better, what areas you'd like to see us publish in, and any other words of wisdom you're willing to pass our way.

As the executive editor for the Advanced Programming team at Macmillan Computer Publishing, I welcome your comments. You can fax, email, or write me directly to let me know what you did or didn't like about this book—as well as what we can do to make our books stronger.

Please note that I cannot help you with technical problems related to the topic of this book, and that due to the high volume of mail I receive, I might not be able to reply to every message.

When you write, please be sure to include this book's title and author as well as your name and phone or fax number. I will carefully review your comments and share them with the author and editors who worked on the book.

Fax: 317-817-7070

Email: adv_prog@mcp.com

Mail: Executive Editor
           Advanced Programming
           Macmillan Computer Publishing
           201 West 103rd Street
           Indianapolis, IN 46290 USA

Introduction

A famous saying used for a popular soap opera states, "Like sands through the hourglass, so are the days of our lives." This quote definitely applies to the evolution of Internet tools and technologies. Web-based development tools have been springing onto the scene at a rapid pace. Internet time has far surpassed dog years in terms of exponential growth. 1996 represented the year of the turnaround for Microsoft as it rapidly moved to Internet-enable all its products. From a development standpoint, 1997 reflected the year of the introduction for Microsoft, as it brought us Visual InterDev 1, which gave us the ability to create dynamic, database-driven applications from within a single integrated development environment. 1998 could be termed the year to be "RAD-ically different," as Microsoft introduces the next evolution of Visual InterDev—version 6.

You might be wondering why Visual InterDev jumped in version numbers from 1 to 6. Although Visual InterDev 1 was a great tool, Visual InterDev 6 represents such a quantum leap in features and capabilities that it justifies the skip in version numbers. Visual InterDev 6 still provides a robust, integrated development environment that includes all the necessary tools to develop and deploy applications for the Web. Developers no longer have to use multiple tools and environments to build their applications and distribute them to the world. Visual InterDev also provides tools to build dynamic Web-based applications through the use of Active Server Pages. Active Server Pages include components and scripts on the server machine that provide a dynamic experience for the user. The user can maintain an interactive session with the server instead of passively viewing static information. Finally, Visual InterDev includes very powerful tools for building robust database applications that connect to desktop as well as high-end database management systems. The tools are graphical and provide an easy-to-use interface that significantly enhances a developer's productivity. Comprehensive site management tools are also included for the deployment of your completed applications. To summarize, the main design goals of Visual InterDev 6 focus on the following concepts:

- A rapid application development (RAD) tool for Web developers
- An integrated database design and development tools
- An improved programming model for Web development
- Increased support for team development
- Support for enterprise application development

The idea is to provide a comprehensive, integrated development environment that supports all the current Web technology. By using Visual InterDev, a developer can perform WYSIWYG HTML editing with the Design Editor and can use technology such as

VBScript, JavaScript, ActiveX controls, Java applets, Active Server Pages, and ODBC and OLE/DB to build dynamic applications for the Web. Visual InterDev allows for the creation of effective, multitiered applications by supporting the use of HTML, controls, components, and services. Its tight integration with Visual Studio allows developers to build robust, enterprisewide applications.

Hopefully, you are already familiar with developing content for the Web. Maybe you have been juggling multiple tools while building applications for the Web. Regardless of your experience level, you have chosen this book to learn more about Visual InterDev and how you can create dynamic Web-based applications. This book will guide you through a step-by-step process of learning all the powerful features of Visual InterDev. This book takes you on a journey and teaches you how to integrate HTML, scripting languages such as VBScript and JavaScript, ActiveX controls and Java applets, Active Server Pages and components, and database connectivity to build rich and robust applications. Upon completion of this book, you will be able to unleash the power of Visual InterDev and take full advantage of its capabilities.

Who Should Read This Book?

You have chosen the right book if you are in one of the following categories:

- You have experienced the Web and now want to contribute.
- You are tired of using multiple tools to create a single application for the Web.
- You want to create dynamic applications for the Web instead of publishing static documentation.
- You want to enhance your productivity through the use of graphical database tools.
- You want to create a dynamic experience for your users.
- You have used FrontPage and now want to migrate to a higher-end development tool.
- You have used Java tools and now want to try a more comprehensive and integrated tool.
- You have developed client/server applications using tools such as Visual Basic and now want to try your hand at Web application development.

What This Book Contains

This book is intended to be completed in 21 days—a chapter each day. The book is designed in such a way that you determine the pace. Some readers might spend more time than 21 days, based on their proficiency or schedule. Other readers might choose to approach the book at a more rapid pace.

Reading this book is similar to taking a self-paced course. I begin the book by talking about the basics and build on these concepts as the weeks go on. By the end of the second day, you will have created your first Visual InterDev project. You will continue to build your skills through the second and third weeks and will develop more advanced applications. Throughout the book, I provide many examples and relevant exercises for you to try. Through reading and applying the material, you will become very proficient in using the tool. At the end of each chapter, I provide you with a chapter summary and a question and answer section based on topics covered in that chapter. Be sure to study hard during each chapter, though, because you will be tested on the material with an end-of-chapter quiz. I don't know about you, but I always read material more closely when I know I will be tested on it.

- During Week 1, you will receive an overview of the features of Visual InterDev. On the second day, you will get a chance to create your first Visual InterDev project. You will learn how to use the editors within Visual InterDev, including the new WYSIWYG Design Editor, to create the right content for your application. Toward the end of the first week, you will learn how to extend your Web-based application through the use of objects such as Java applets and ActiveX controls as well as client-side script, Active Server Pages, and Dynamic HTML.

- In Week 2, you are introduced to database connectivity and communication. You learn all the aspects of using a database, from inserting a simple connection to using the Visual Data Tools in Visual InterDev to gain maximum productivity and features. You also take a journey through the world of server-side scripting and experience its capabilities. Finally, you will build a database-driven application from start to finish.

- During Week 3, you learn how to integrate business objects into your applications. You will learn how to extend the application that you build at the end of Week 2 through the use of components. You will also learn how to implement some of the more advanced features of Visual InterDev in your application, such as Dynamic HTML. You will also learn how to use Visual InterDev to manage your Web site files. You will be exposed to other topics to consider when building a Web-based application, such as working in teams, source code control, debugging your application, and designing your site using the Site Designer.

By reading, studying, and applying this book, you will become extremely proficient with Visual InterDev. You will instantly begin developing and deploying robust applications and will gain the confidence that you need to master the Web. Just think, if you start right now, you could be a Webmaster in 21 days or less!

What You Need to Begin

Based on your purchase of this book, I assume that you already have Visual InterDev and have installed it on your PC. This book is a hands-on course, and you will need to try out the examples as you go along. To get the full use out of the tool, you should also have an ODBC-compliant database installed on either your desktop or a server machine to which you have access. Database connectivity is one of the key features for you to learn to provide dynamic applications for your users. My assumption is that you're familiar with HTML and have at least developed some kind of Web page or application. You don't need to be an expert in all the technologies supported by Visual InterDev; I'll introduce each of these in due time. If you're familiar with these technologies, the discussion can serve as a refresher—or you can skip to new or more advanced topics.

You're now ready to learn about a tool that is worth waiting for. I'm elated to present the radically new version of the Microsoft visual tools family. Let's begin the exciting expedition.

WEEK 1

At a Glance

This book teaches you how to use Visual InterDev 6 to develop powerful Web-based applications. During Week 1, you will learn about the plethora of features Visual InterDev 6 has to offer. You will also get a chance to build your first Visual InterDev project. The first week focuses a lot of attention on the client side of the application equation. By the end of the week, you should have a good feel for how Visual InterDev addresses this piece of the puzzle.

Where You Are Going

At the beginning of Week 1, you will learn about all the new features contained within Visual InterDev 6. On the second day, you will develop your first Visual InterDev project. The next two days show you how to use the various Visual InterDev editors, including the new WYSIWYG Design Editor. Toward the end of the week, you will learn how to use client-side script, server-side script, and ActiveX controls to enhance your application.

1

2

3

4

5

6

7

DAY 1

Presenting Visual InterDev 6

Dating back to 1996, developers were clamoring for an integrated development tool that provided comprehensive support for the various tools, languages, and technologies for creating Web applications. In March 1997, Microsoft introduced Visual InterDev 1.0 to address the urgent void of application development tools. For a version 1.0 product, Visual InterDev made great strides in addressing many of the concerns of Web developers.

Now, Microsoft has dramatically improved a very good product by creating Visual InterDev 6. Today, you will have an up close and personal tour of Visual InterDev and see its fascinating new features. You also will learn the answers to the following questions:

- What is Visual InterDev?
- How should I use Visual InterDev?

Today's objective: exploring the integrated development environment of Visual InterDev and discovering how the tool can immediately begin enhancing your applications and productivity.

Note   Although the version number on Visual InterDev is now 6, it is really only the second version!

What Is Visual InterDev?

The World Wide Web (WWW) has made the Internet come alive for many new users. Some companies have built Web-based applications that enable you to buy their products and services electronically over the Internet. Other companies enable you to fill out registration information to begin receiving certain services. The key point is that applications enable the user to act on the knowledge they have gained. Businesses can capitalize on opportunities sooner by becoming closer to the customer through a virtual marketplace. Visual InterDev provides all the necessary tools to build these vital applications for the Web.

Visual InterDev is a comprehensive, Web-based application development tool. It provides an integrated environment that brings together various technologies to work toward a common goal of building robust and dynamic applications for the Web. Visual InterDev achieves this integrated development environment through the use of its Microsoft Development Environment, also employed by Visual J++. You can open and work on Visual J++ projects while simultaneously creating your Visual InterDev project. This feature greatly enhances productivity, especially when you're building components using the Microsoft Component Object Model (COM) and incorporating these objects into your Visual InterDev application. You can also open multiple Visual InterDev projects within the same workspace.

Visual InterDev enables the developer to build applications that are dynamic and interactive. Visual InterDev enables the developer to build dynamic Web pages through the use of client- and server-side script. By default, Visual InterDev supports the use of VBScript and JScript. You can also use other scripting languages such as PerlScript, given that you have the appropriate scripting engine for the language.

Note   JScript is Microsoft's implementation of the ECMAScript scripting language, formerly known as JavaScript. JScript is a full implementation of the ECMAScript scripting language with some additional enhancements implemented for Internet Explorer 4.0. You will learn more about the different scripting languages on Day 5, "Enhancing Your Web page Through Client-Side Script."

Database integration is vital to any application. Visual InterDev provides a rich and robust set of visual database tools to immediately enhance your productivity. Visual InterDev supports the major ODBC-compliant databases, both on the desktop and the server.

Managing your Web site once it has been developed is a very crucial function. Visual InterDev provides a set of tools to view and maintain your site. These tools are similar and compatible with the site management tools found in Microsoft FrontPage.

Visual InterDev supports the major object-based technologies that exist for developing Web-based applications, including ActiveX controls and Java applets. You can also transform script code into "object-based" functions such as scriptlets and use them within your Visual InterDev project. Visual InterDev supports the use of third-party ActiveX controls and enables you to integrate your own custom ActiveX controls. Visual InterDev also provides design-time controls that enable you to visually set control properties when you're designing your application and then use this functionality at runtime without the overhead of a typical ActiveX control.

In a nutshell, Visual InterDev is an exciting tool that significantly augments a Web developer's productivity. In this next section, you will learn why you should use Visual InterDev instead of other development tools.

Visual InterDev 6—New and Improved

The basic premise behind the creation of Visual InterDev 1.0 was to provide a tool that enabled developers to build dynamic and interactive applications for the Web. The major design goals behind the creation of Visual InterDev 6 focused on extending and enhancing these features to provide a great experience both for the developer and the end user. The result is that developers have in Visual InterDev a new and improved tool that enables them to create a unique experience for the users of their applications. Why should you use Visual InterDev 6? The following sections briefly touch on some of the exciting features of Visual InterDev 6 to help you answer this question.

A More Visual Experience

The thing that immediately comes to mind when you open Visual InterDev 6 for the first time is the new and improved user interface (see Figure 1.1).

Figure 1.1.

The new and improved interface of Visual InterDev 6.

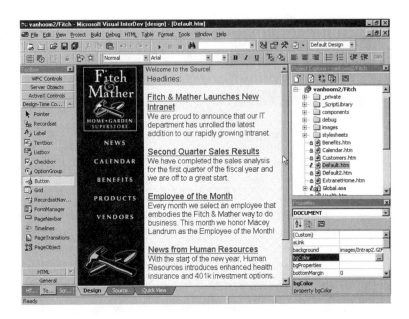

As you can see, Visual InterDev 6 contains a greatly enhanced integrated development environment (IDE). Visual InterDev employs a tab metaphor to enable you to easily transfer between different views of your project components. These views include Design, Source, and Quick View. Each of these views will be covered later today in the section "Taking a Closer Look at the Components," as well as on Day 3, "Creating the Content for Your Application."

The designers of Visual InterDev 6 have adapted many of the user interface features of Visual Basic and incorporated them into the Visual InterDev 6 development environment. For example, Figure 1.2 illustrates the ability to see the properties of an object.

In the example in Figure 1.2, the properties of the HTML Web page are displayed in the Properties window located in the lower-right corner of the screen. The Properties window displays the properties for any object in your Visual InterDev 6 project including HTML Web pages, Active Server Pages (ASP), ActiveX controls, and Java applets. This window enables you to visually inspect the properties that have been set for an object and customize them to meet the needs of your application.

FIGURE 1.2.

Visualizing the properties of an HTML page.

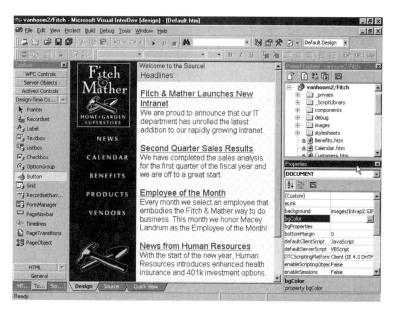

Visual InterDev 6 provides a RAD-like experience for Web development similar to other client/server development tools. RAD, or Rapid Application Development, in this context refers to the capability of a tool to provide a visual and productivity-enhancing experience for the developer. Two key RAD-like features include drag-and-drop capability and statement completion. Similar to the functionality of Visual Basic, Visual InterDev enables you to drag and drop objects such as ActiveX controls onto a Web page for faster and more intuitive development. Additionally, you can take advantage of the statement completion feature, which was first introduced in Visual Basic 5.0, to significantly improve your productivity. This feature provides a list of items from which to choose based on your code entry. For example, Figure 1.3 demonstrates the use of the statement completion feature to choose a method for a typical Visual InterDev object.

The statement completion feature, also called Intellisense, saves precious development time by providing a selectable list of items that are related to the object. In the example above, a list of methods is displayed. This feature reduces the time it takes to remember as well as type the appropriate method.

FIGURE 1.3.

*Using the statement
completion feature.*

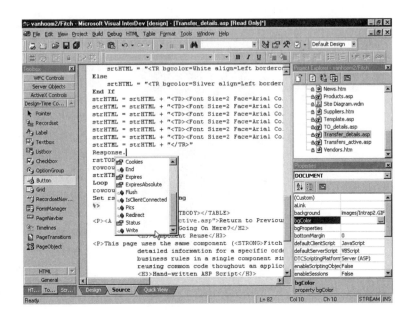

WYSIWYG Editing

The WYSIWYG editing capabilities have been significantly improved in Visual
InterDev 6. A very rich and robust WYSIWYG editor exists within the confines of the
Visual InterDev IDE that enables you to visually create and edit your Web pages at
the click of a tab and the drag and drop of an object. Figure 1.4 demonstrates the
enhanced Design Editor.

Programming Support

Visual InterDev 6 provides a plethora of programming features for developers at all levels.
First, you can treat Active Server Pages as objects. This feature enhances your ability
to refer to objects on other pages, thereby creating a truly integrated application. Also,
because your ASP pages are now considered objects, you can use the statement completion feature to customize methods and properties for the page. Moreover, the object capability of Active Server Pages enables you to create a shared state between the client and
server portions of your application.

FIGURE 1.4.

Editing made easy.

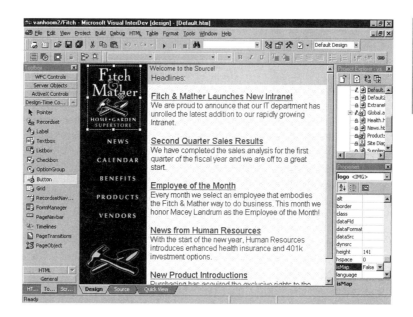

As you journey into the second week of learning Visual InterDev 6, you will discover all the capabilities of ASP page objects. Specifically, on Day 11, "Fundamentals of Active Server Pages," you will learn about the basics of treating ASP pages as objects. Then, on Day 13, "Unleashing the Power of the Visual InterDev Programming Model," you will learn how to unlock the potential of ASP objects within your applications.

Another programming support feature is the design-time control (DTC) Scripting Object Model (SOM). This model describes runtime methods, properties, and events that you can employ within your application. At design time, you can use these methods, properties, and events of the DTC to extend the logic and functionality that it provides in the form of HTML, script, and text. Again, because this model is an object model, you can use the statement completion feature to provide a list of choices regarding the method, property, or event that you want to use. You will learn more about design-time controls and the Scripting Object Model on Day 12, "Extending Web Pages Through Design-Time Controls," and on Day 13.

End-to-End Debugging

One of the biggest enhancements Visual InterDev 1.0 developers were clamoring for involved improved debugging tools, including the ability to debug server-side code. Visual InterDev 6 proves the old adage, "Ask and you shall receive." Visual InterDev 6 includes the standard debugging features that you have come to know and love in RAD client/server tools like Visual Basic, such as the ability to set breakpoints, the ability to step through code, and the ability to see the value of variables. You can also debug both client- and server-side logic. Yes, you now can discover what is happening in the black hole called the server. This improvement is monumental. Before remote debugging, we all experienced the joys of requesting a page and never knowing what exactly was happening on the server. Many developers used the very scientific testing strategy of praying and hoping for the best. Those days are behind us now in that you can truly perform the same debugging tasks on the server as you can on the client. You will have to wait until Day 17, "Debugging Your Applications with Visual InterDev," to see this dramatic new feature in action.

Support for Development Teams

Visual InterDev 6 has significantly improved support for development teams. For example, several development modes are included to support both individual and team development. Master mode enables you to read and maintain files from the central Web that is shared by a team on the server. Visual InterDev also supports the new Local mode that enables an individual developer to interact with files on the server while creating and maintaining files on his or her local workstation. Using Local mode, a developer can create and maintain parts of the application and then migrate these files to the master application once they have been individually tested.

Visual InterDev 6 also supports another new mode of Web development called Offline mode. This mode enables a developer to work on files while disconnected from the main Web server. A common example of this kind of computing is a developer who copies files from the Web server to a laptop to work on while disconnected from the master Web server.

Visual InterDev 6 also increases its integration with Visual SourceSafe for source control of your application by allowing you to use more Visual SourceSafe commands from within the Visual InterDev development environment. With Visual InterDev 1.0, you could only execute a couple of source control commands, such as enabling your Web project for source control and performing routine check-in/check-out commands. With Visual InterDev 6, you can now execute other Visual SourceSafe commands such as merging files, checking the history of a file, and comparing the differences between

1

multiple versions of a file. This functionality now brings Visual InterDev in line with the other Visual Studio tools such as Visual Basic and Visual C++ that already possess these abilities.

Support for the Latest Web Design Technologies

Visual InterDev 6 includes support for the latest Web standards and technologies, including cascading style sheets (CSS) and Dynamic HTML. An editor is included that enables you to construct your own cascading style sheets. You can then preview the style sheet from within the development environment to determine the look and feel of your new creation.

Support for Dynamic HTML (DHTML) in Internet Explorer 4.0 is also provided. The DHTML technology supported in Internet Explorer 4.0 extends the capabilities of standard HTML by providing more processing power on the Web client. By supporting this new technology, Visual InterDev 6 enables you to take advantage of the Dynamic HTML object model and events to provide a richer client experience that lightens the load on the Web server. You can also use Visual InterDev to target the browser platform that best suits your audience of end users.

For example, your application may need to support a number of browsers including Internet Explorer versions 3 and later and Netscape versions 3 and later. For this kind of audience, Visual InterDev enables you to target a "maximum reach" platform. In this case, the client portion of the application renders standard HTML 3.2 and incorporates other standard Web technologies such as JavaScript for scripting and Java for any client-side objects.

Visual InterDev 6 also enables you to take advantage of the latest in Microsoft technologies when you are certain that your user audience will be using the Internet Explorer 4.0 browser. For this kind of audience, Visual InterDev enables you to target what it calls the "best experience" platform. The Web client in this scenario renders DHTML, or HTML 4.0, and cascading style sheets. Both VBScript and JavaScript are used for the scripting languages, and a combination of DHTML, ActiveX, RDS, JavaScript, and Java objects are integrated into the client-side portion of the application.

Another Visual InterDev 6 feature is the Site Designer tool. This tool should greatly enhance the initial design phases of your Web site layout and structure. Using a drag-and-drop interface, the Site Designer enables you to create a logical view of the overall Web site, including the individual Web pages and their links. Figure 1.5 provides an initial view of this new tool.

FIGURE 1.5.

*The Site Designer at
work.*

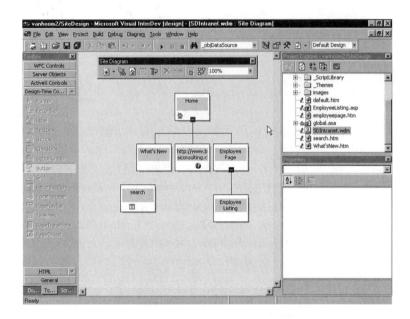

The site diagram shown in Figure 1.5 depicts a typical Web site with a home page and
several Web pages linked to the main page. After you create the pages for your Web site
and save the site diagram, the proper files related to each of the pages in the diagram are
created and added to your Visual InterDev project with their associated navigational
links. You can explore the capabilities of the Site Designer tool on Day 20, "Designing
an Effective Site with the Site Designer."

Radically Integrated

Visual InterDev 6 provides the tools to take advantage of the Web-based model of computing. Some development tools focus on supporting a single Internet technology. Others
support several technologies for Web-based development but don't provide visual tools to
accomplish these tasks. Visual InterDev exceeds existing Web development tools by
providing a way to integrate multiple technologies and supplies visual tools to greatly
enhance a developer's productivity. Visual InterDev also surpasses and extends the reach
of client/server tools to the Internet and the Web.

The *American Heritage Dictionary* defines the word integration in the following manner:

> "1. To make into a whole; unify.
> 2. To join with something else; unite."

Truly, Visual InterDev unifies and unites the technologies of the Web through its integrated development environment. You can use the environment to rapidly build a robust application. You have at your disposal all the tools necessary for Web-based application development in one integrated package. In this sense, the whole really is greater than the sum of its parts.

The Visual InterDev 6 Development Environment

Visual InterDev 6 provides an integrated container for a variety of visual tools. The integrated development environment is like a house with many rooms. Each room has its own specific function that contributes to the overall purpose of the house. Similar to the rooms of a house, each function contributes to the well-being of the developer or resident. No single tool is more important than the other, just as no room is more important than another. In a typical house, you can eat, sleep, and take care of your personal hygiene all under the same roof. With Visual InterDev 6, you can develop your Web pages, connect them to a database, and deploy your Web site all within the confines of the same development environment.

The development environment uses the new Microsoft Development Environment that will be used in the future as the IDE for the entire Visual Studio suite of tools. By using the IDE, multiple projects and tools can be supported. The IDE allows more efficient construction of components that can be integrated to create a truly effective solution.

The advantage of this integrated support is found in using multiple applications to provide a robust solution. You can build a Java applet using Visual J++, incorporate the applet into your Visual InterDev Web application, and test and debug the application all within the same environment. The same holds true for building an ActiveX control using Visual C++. Again, *integration* is the key word. Figure 1.6 illustrates the ability to open multiple types of projects from within the Visual InterDev 6 integrated development environment.

FIGURE 1.6.

Opening projects with Visual InterDev 6.

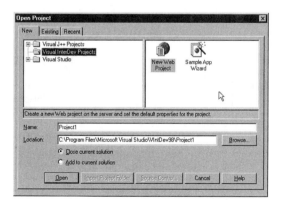

Figure 1.6 shows the Open Project dialog box. This dialog window is like the Open Project dialog box in Visual Basic. There are now three tabs located at the top of the dialog box: New, Existing, and Recent. These tabs enable you to shift between new, existing, and your most recently opened projects. This kind of interface enables you to quickly access your projects. Also, you can easily create new projects from the same dialog box without having to switch to another window.

When you open your project, you're viewing your actual Web site. The development environment uses the Explorer interface to view and manage your Web site files and folders. This interface simplifies the task of creating and maintaining your Web site files and folders. Also, the interface enables you to fully organize the construction of your Web-based application. The integrated development environment enables easy site creation through the use of wizards and enables developers to reuse files from other sites.

Visual InterDev 6 enables you to easily import existing files into your Web site structure. The Explorer interface enables you to accomplish this task through a point-and-click metaphor, just as you copy and paste files and folders on your PC. You can also use the menu commands. Figure 1.7 displays the contents of a project within the new development environment.

FIGURE 1.7.

A typical Visual InterDev 6 project.

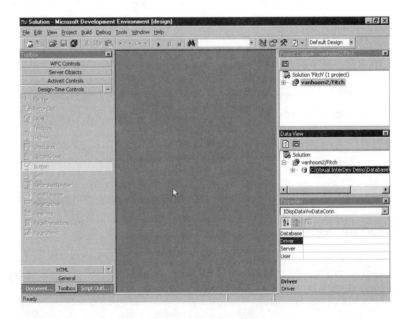

As you can see from Figure 1.7, the development environment includes several dockable windows. For previous users of Visual InterDev, you will notice a subtle but significant change to the project environment of Visual InterDev 6. The concept of the File, Data, and Info view has been removed. Instead, the project workspace window has been given a new name of Project Explorer. The tabs have been removed to reflect a true Windows Explorer–like control. The Data view has been moved as a tab to the Properties dialog box. The Info view tab has been removed, and its contents can now be accessed through the Help menu.

> **Note**
>
> The Data view tab only appears as an option for Web projects after you have inserted a database connection. The Data view also is displayed for database projects. The process of integrating database connectivity into your application will be covered on Day 8, "Communicating with a Database."

The Project Explorer

The Project Explorer is the central hub for a typical Visual InterDev 6 project. The Project Explorer enables you to see the structure of your Web site including files and folders. This view displays the entire contents of your site, including HTML pages, images, controls, applets, Active Server Pages, and other files. The Project Explorer employs a tree view control that enables you to expand and collapse folders within your project as well as open and view the contents of these files.

The Properties Dialog Window

The Properties dialog window displays properties for the components of your project— that is, any file that is located in the Project Explorer. If you have used a tool such as Visual Basic, you are probably already familiar with the use of this window. I have already explained that the Data view tab appears next to the Properties tab if a valid database connection has been added to your project.

This view shows all your database objects, including tables, views, stored procedures, and triggers. The Data view provides a direct connection to your ODBC datasource to enable remote configuration and maintenance as well as interaction with the database objects. Figure 1.8 demonstrates the Data view showing a sample Access database.

FIGURE 1.8.

The Data view.

Visual SourceSafe Integration

Visual InterDev supports integration with Visual SourceSafe to provide version control capabilities such as check-in/check-out. Similar to any application development effort, source code control becomes a big issue when you're building a site with multiple team members. Developers can check out their portion of the site, make the appropriate changes, and send the file back to the server to be incorporated with the other developers' files. The biggest improvement to the integration with Visual InterDev is the ability to execute more of the Visual SourceSafe commands from within the IDE. I will cover effective team development in more detail on Day 19, "Effective Team Development with Visual InterDev and Visual SourceSafe."

Browser Integration

Another integration feature is the inclusion of a browser within the development environment. An implementation of the Microsoft Internet Explorer 4.0 browser is included that enables you to preview your Web pages. This implementation supports all the same features of the commercial version of Internet Explorer, including Java applets, ActiveX controls, ActiveX documents, VBScript and JavaScript, style sheets, and HTML 3.2 features such as frames and tables. The browser also supports Microsoft's version of Dynamic HTML (HTML 4.0). By using the Preview pane, you don't have to use one tool to build the application and another tool to browse it. The Internet Explorer 4.0 browser integration is demonstrated in Figure 1.9.

FIGURE 1.9.

The Quick View pane.

With browser integration, you can build your Web-based application and view the results all from within one development environment. This feature adds to the speed with which a developer can create and update applications and Web sites.

You do have the option of using your commercial browser by executing the Browse With function to view your Web site from within the browser's native window. For example, you could configure Internet Explorer or Netscape Navigator and view the site from within the production browser environment. You probably will want to use this feature during final testing of your Web site. If you're deploying your site for use with the Netscape Navigator browser, you have to use this feature.

You can use either of these features by selecting an HTML file and right-clicking the mouse to display the shortcut menu. Figure 1.10 shows the View in Browser and Browse With menu options on the shortcut menu for an HTML file that has been selected.

FIGURE 1.10.

Browser viewing options.

Taking a Closer Look at the Components

The previous section discussed how Visual InterDev 6 provides an integrated development environment from which to work. You saw the Visual InterDev 6 workspace and the different options that are available. In this section, I will provide an overview of each of the features and components that make up Visual InterDev 6. This discussion will lay the groundwork for the remaining lessons over the next 20 days.

The Views of Visual InterDev

Visual InterDev 6 provides four main views to support your application development effort. These views provide the main tools for you to construct your Web pages and scripts as well as integrate the proper objects and components. Each view provides a different perspective regarding your project files. These views can be thought of as different modes of operation based on what you are trying to accomplish. The following list outlines the main views within Visual InterDev 6:

- Design view
- Source view
- Quick view

The Design View

The Design view is the default for HTML files and provides a WYSIWYG approach for developing HTML Web pages. With this approach, you can add HTML features to your Web page through a graphical, point-and-click metaphor. For example, to add a table, select Table | Insert Table and then visually set the parameters, such as number of rows and columns. Using the Design view, you can visually work with objects instead of the underlying HTML to construct your Web pages. These objects include images, HTML controls, ActiveX controls, and Java applets. This method can substantially save development time. After you have constructed a Web page using the graphical editor, you can access and manipulate the generated HTML code and add your own custom HTML. You can use the Properties window to set the attributes for each element on your page. Figure 1.11 highlights the WYSIWYG nature of the Visual InterDev Design Editor.

FIGURE 1.11.

The Visual InterDev editor using the Design view.

Note   You can use the commercial version of FrontPage 98, which is compatible with Visual InterDev 6.

The Source View

Using the Design Editor, you can create and edit your HTML and script code with a color-coded, visually appealing syntax. You can maintain the raw HTML and scripting logic behind your Web page, thereby giving you more precision and control. Source view uses a color-coded syntax to help you distinguish between the various tags, text, elements, attributes, and comments that exist in your code. You can also use Source view to view any script code that you have incorporated into your file. In Visual InterDev 6, the script tags <% and %> are highlighted. The script is color-coded to allow you to distinguish between reserved script words, text, variables, and so on, thereby enabling you to more easily understand the code logic.

Note

In Visual InterDev 1.0, all the script was highlighted in yellow. This rendered the code unreadable at times and somewhat annoying. The yellow highlight color has been replaced in favor of specific color within the code.

You can also incorporate many objects and controls, such as HTML controls, ActiveX controls, and design-time controls using the Source view. Figure 1.12 highlights standard HTML code using the Visual InterDev Source Editor.

FIGURE 1.12.

The Visual InterDev editor using the Source view.

> **Tip**
>
> You can use the Toolbox to insert ActiveX and design-time controls in your Web pages. The controls that appear on the Toolbox window are enabled only when you are using the Design or Source views. You cannot access these controls from the Script and Preview views. You will learn how to fully use the Toolbox on Day 7, "Integrating Objects into Your Applications."

When you view your file using the Source view, the Document Outline window changes to display an outline of the scripts, objects, and events for both the client and server portions of the selected page. This outline is called the Script Outline. You can either enter the scripting logic directly using Script view, or you can use the Script Outline to construct your code. The Document Outline window and the Script Outline are covered later in their respective sections.

The Quick View

The final view is the Quick View pane that enables you to preview the Web page using an implementation of Internet Explorer 4.0. Because the Quick View feature is contained within the development environment, you can develop and view your Web page using a single tool, thereby reducing the time it takes to develop your application. Figure 1.13 depicts the Quick View pane found in Visual InterDev 6.

FIGURE 1.13.

The Visual InterDev Quick View pane.

As you can see, there are several editors that you can choose, based on the task that you're trying to accomplish. These editors are covered in-depth later in the week, especially on Day 3, "Creating the Content for Your Application." You also will have a chance to learn about and use each of these editors to experience their features firsthand and to see how they can significantly enhance your development efforts.

ActiveX Controls and Java Applets

Visual InterDev 6 includes and supports the use of ActiveX controls. ActiveX controls are the next generation of OLE controls, or .ocx files. These controls use less overhead and memory and are perfect for transporting over the Internet. These controls also can be used with other client/server development tools, such as Visual Basic and Visual C++. ActiveX controls extend the reach of HTML controls and enable you to create effective user interfaces. Visual InterDev 6 also supports the use of Java applets to spice up your Web pages. You can integrate these controls with your Web pages using the Design and the Source views. After you have inserted them into your page layout, you can visually set the properties for the ActiveX control using the Toolbox and Properties windows.

Note As discussed earlier today, you can use the Design view editor to properly place and position ActiveX controls onto your Web page.

Design-Time Controls

Visual InterDev 6 uses design-time controls to provide similar functionality to regular ActiveX controls without the visual display of a runtime control such as a pushbutton or a text box. Design-time controls enable you to visually set properties for the control at design time. The design-time control then generates a combination of HTML, text, and scripting code based on the properties that you select. Regular ActiveX controls differ in that they include a runtime component that executes within the context of the browser.

Design-time controls don't have the overhead of a visual, runtime component such as an ActiveX control. Their script is processed on the server, and the HTML and results are returned to the client. Visual InterDev 6 provides many design-time controls, including some very powerful controls for building database connectivity. You can also build your own design-time controls with tools such as Visual Basic and Visual C++.

On Day 12, you will see how to extend your Web-based applications through the use of design-time controls.

Active Server Pages

Visual InterDev 6 enables you to add powerful processing for your application on the server through the use of Active Server Pages. If you have used Active Server Pages in the past, you know that they are a combination of HTML and scripting code that reside on the server. All the server-side script is processed on the server before the resulting Web page is returned to the client machine. Some common uses of Active Server Pages include interacting with a database and performing loop operations on a Web page. Active Server Pages are a great way to combine HTML, client-side, and server-side script all in one file to produce dynamic Web pages for your application.

Active Server Pages seamlessly integrate with your HTML files. These pages remove the need to link separately compiled programs to accomplish robust application tasks. The other benefit to using Active Server Pages involves the use of ActiveX Server Components. You can build an ActiveX Server Component with tools such as Visual Basic and Visual C++ to handle additional application processing.

In a distributed environment, ActiveX Server Components can be used to spread the processing across several application servers. Scripting code is very useful but has its limitations, like the inability to perform file I/O or provide access to system resources. ActiveX Server Components extend the limitations of scripting code by providing these features as well as other robust features.

 Tip

You should use a combination of Active Server Pages and ActiveX Server Components to provide the best solution for the server side of your application equation. In this way, the ASP can serve as a central hub that calls the ActiveX Server Component to execute the business processing logic.

The Script Outline

After you have created your basic HTML page and included a few objects, you will want to make your objects come alive. The Script Outline enables you to accomplish this task, providing a method for adding script to enhance your objects such as ActiveX controls. When you view your page using the Script view, the Script Outline appears as demonstrated in Figure 1.14.

FIGURE 1.14.

Viewing the main folders of the Script Outline.

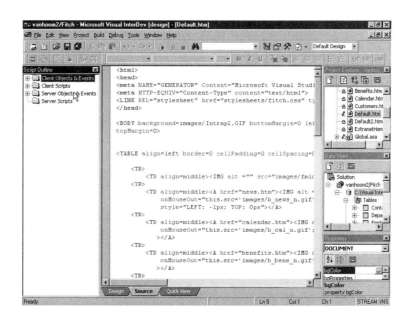

As you can see from Figure 1.14, there are four basic folders contained within the Script Outline:

- Client Objects and Events
- Client Scripts
- Server Objects and Events
- Server Scripts

Client Objects and Events

This folder contains all the client-side objects that are a part of the Web page and their associated events. This view provides easy access to all the objects that are contained in the Web page. After you double-click an object, the view expands to reveal all the events for the selected object. Figure 1.15 displays this expanded view.

FIGURE 1.15.

Viewing the list of events for a client-side object.

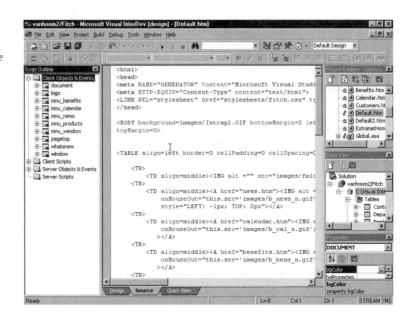

From this expanded view, you can scan the list of events and add the appropriate script-ing logic. You can accomplish this task by double-clicking the event, which automatically adds the appropriate tags and formatting for you to be able to add your scripting code. The Script Outline also automatically places the cursor at the correct insertion point for you to add your code. Figure 1.16 illustrates adding script for an object and event using the Script Outline.

Client Scripts

The Client Scripts folder displays a list of object events for which scripting code exists. This feature enables you to get a quick view of which events have associated script, as shown in Figure 1.17.

You can double-click any object-event combination, and the Script Outline will move your cursor to the script definition for that event. In the previous example, a function has been defined for the `onclick` event. The next step would be to add the logic for the defined function.

FIGURE 1.16.

Adding script for an object event.

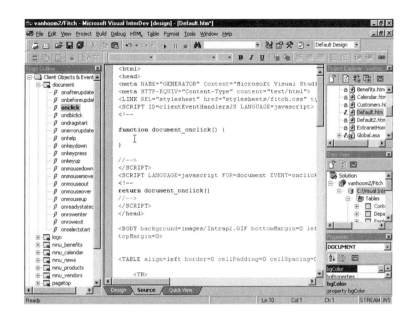

FIGURE 1.17.

Reviewing the event scripts.

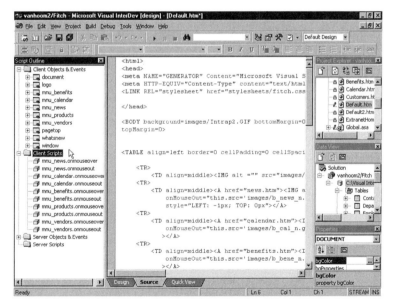

Server Objects and Events

The Script Outline also enables you to view any server-side objects associated with your page in the same way that you can see the objects for the client. The Server Objects & Events folder provides a list of all the server-side objects and their associated events for the selected page. By default, the standard ASP objects are displayed in this folder as shown in Figure 1.18.

FIGURE **1.18.**

Viewing the server-side objects and events for your page.

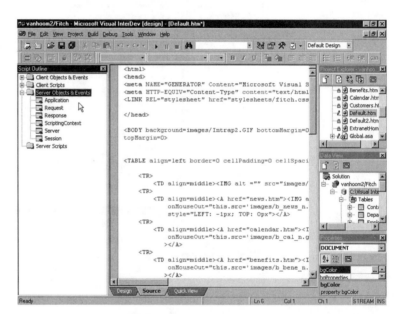

FIGURE 1.18.

Viewing the server-side objects and events for your page.

Server Scripts

The Server Scripts folder enables you to access any scripts that have been created for the server-side objects and their associated events. After you add your script for the function, a subfolder will appear within the Client Scripts folder based on the type of script language that is used for that object and event. In other words, if you create a function that is based on the VBScript language, a new VBScript subfolder will be created. This folder behaves similarly to the Client Scripts folders and is depicted in Figure 1.19.

FIGURE 1.19.

Viewing the server-side scripts.

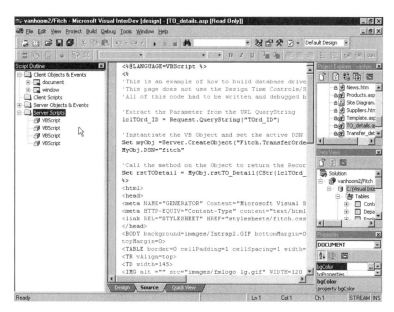

File Management Components

Visual InterDev 6 provides comprehensive site and file management tools to help maintain your components during every phase of development and deployment.

The Project Explorer enables you to view and manage all the file types located in your project. You can easily execute many of the same functions found in the Windows Explorer such as the ability to drag and drop files. Full right-mouse button functionality is also provided. The shortcut menu makes it easy to change the names of files, to move files within your Web site hierarchy, and to copy files to other Visual InterDev 6 projects. You can create folders that represent the subdirectories for your Web site. You can copy the subdirectories, including all the files, to another Web site. Another powerful feature is the Copy Web command. This feature enables you to copy an entire Web site from one place to another. This can save time when preparing your site for deployment. By using this command, you can migrate your site from a development server to a testing server and, eventually, to a production server.

Visual InterDev 6 can automatically verify links between pages and ensure that no links have been changed or broken. Upon detection of a broken link, Visual InterDev is able to repair these broken links. For example, if you changed the name of a file that was used by a Web page in your project, Visual InterDev 6 would detect the link and prompt you to update the Web page reference to the file.

The Link View provides a powerful tool for viewing the entire structure of your Web site. With this tool, you can graphically see the content of your Web site, how each object is related, and the filename and property information of each object. This view is similar to using an entity relationship diagram to graphically view a database. You can double-click any item in the view to use the appropriate editor to manipulate the object. You also can select parameters to view only certain objects or files. Figure 1.20 illustrates the power of the Link View.

FIGURE **1.20.**

The Link View.

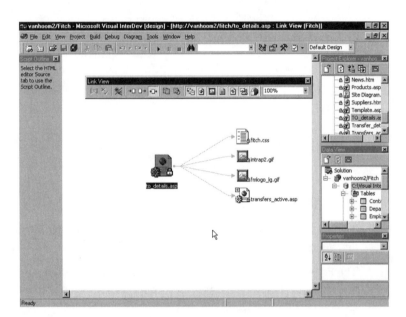

Exploring the Database Integration

Database connectivity and integration is another important component of Web-based development. Visual InterDev 6 helps significantly augment a database programmer's capabilities and productivity.

The Data View

With the Data view, which you saw earlier today in Figure 1.8, you see all the database components contained within your database. These components include tables, fields, views, stored procedures, and triggers. Using this view, you can directly manipulate the objects in your database.

The Query Designer

The Query Designer enables you to visually build SQL queries for your application. The Query Designer uses a very visual interface similar to Microsoft Access, which significantly improves development time for building database interaction. Similar to the Access interface, you can drag and drop objects onto the SQL design pane area. You can then construct your query by associating various tables and fields. As you build your query, the results are displayed in the design pane. You can view the SQL as it's constructed as well as the query criteria for the SQL statement. The Diagram, Grid, SQL, and Results panes can be stacked for simultaneous access. For example, you might want to view the tables, SQL statement, and results, all within the design pane area. Using this layout, you can manipulate your SQL statement while validating the results, all within the confines of the design pane. Figure 1.21 demonstrates the graphical nature and power of the Query Designer.

FIGURE 1.21.

The Query Designer.

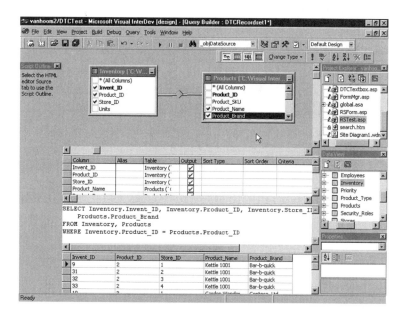

As you can see from Figure 1.21, the Query Designer visually displays your database objects. Figure 1.21 illustrates how you can stack a diagram of the tables, the query criteria, the constructed SQL, and the query results all in the design pane display.

The Query Designer saves an inordinate amount of time in building your SQL statements. You may choose to manipulate the generated SQL or build SQL statements on your own. Visual InterDev 6 enables you to easily accomplish all these tasks.

The Database Designer

The Database Designer helps you design and implement your SQL database. In Visual InterDev 1.0, this tool only supported Microsoft SQL Server. In Visual InterDev 6, the Database Designer also supports Oracle 7.x. The Database Designer provides a visual tool for creating and maintaining your database. You can directly manipulate the properties of your database objects, or you can generate the necessary Data Definition Language (DDL) scripts to execute against the database.

One of the most laborious tasks for database administrators (DBAs) is changing a field type for a table that has existing data. I remember how cumbersome this process was from my early Microsoft SQL Server DBA days. First, you had to back up the existing data. Then, you had to execute a DDL script that would drop the table and create a new table with the revised field type. Finally, you restored the data back into the revised table.

The Database Designer enables you to change field types for your database table by selecting the type from a drop-down combo box. The Database Designer handles the data type conversion for you. Again, the visual interface has been used to make cumbersome administrative tasks relatively easy.

The Stored Procedure Editor/Trigger Editor

The Stored Procedure Editor/Trigger Editor enables you to create and maintain stored procedures and triggers for your application. Stored procedures are SQL statements that are precompiled in the database. You call a stored procedure by name from your application, passing it the appropriate parameters. Stored procedures are more efficient than dynamic SQL because they reduce the number of steps to execute the SQL call. A trigger is a special type of stored procedure that executes based on some event that occurs in the database. For example, you might create a trigger to execute whenever a row is deleted in an Order Header table, ensuring that referential integrity is maintained and no Order Detail records exist for the deleted Order Header.

 Note

Visual InterDev 6 enables you to create, view, and maintain stored procedures for Microsoft SQL Server 6.x and Oracle 7.x databases. You also can establish who has permission to execute this stored procedure or trigger. You can debug your stored procedures through the use of the Visual InterDev debugger.

ActiveX Data Objects

Visual InterDev 6 achieves database integration through the use of the ActiveX Data Objects (ADO) model. The ADO model has been specifically designed for database connectivity over the Web. These database objects are more efficient than previous database controls used with existing client/server tools. Also, ADO easily accommodates the management of binary objects such as images and other multimedia objects. The ADO model supports the use of stored procedures and cursors for robust database access.

Database Design-Time Controls

Visual InterDev 6 includes several database design-time controls. These controls enable you to easily establish database connections for your applications by setting database connection properties for the particular control. After you have set these properties, the design-time control automatically generates all the necessary scripting and connection information for you. Examples of database design-time controls include the Data Command control and the Data Range Header and Data Range Footer control. With these powerful controls you can construct a Web page that interacts with a database and displays the results with little or no programming. You will get a chance to use these controls on Days 12 and 13.

Visual InterDev 6 also introduces support for Dynamic HTML (DHTML) through the use of design-time controls. These new data-bound design-time controls enable you to generate DHTML database logic through the use of Remote Data Services (RDS) for the client portion of your Web-based application. You will get a chance to experience the support for DHTML on Day 5, "Enhancing Your Web Page Through Client-Side Script."

Database Wizards

Visual InterDev 6 provides several database wizards that significantly reduce the time for developing database connections for your Web pages. These wizards guide you through the process of establishing connectivity with your database. Examples of database wizards include the New Database Wizard and the Data Form Wizard. The New Database Wizard guides you through the process of creating a new SQL Server database. The Data Form Wizard enables you to create related forms that are database-enabled. In other words, these forms can execute all the relevant database functions including inserting, selecting, updating, and deleting information.

Note   The Data Form Wizard creates an Active Server Page, or .asp, file to execute the database calls. This .asp file must reside on a server that supports the ActiveX Server framework.

How Should You Use Visual InterDev 6?

With all the features introduced today, you may be wondering where to begin. Also, you may be asking questions about how to use these features when building your Web-based application. Visual InterDev 6 should be used as a high-end development tool for building applications for the Web. The key words in the last sentence are *high-end* and *applications*. If all you want to do is publish basic information on the Web, you might want to consider another tool such as an HTML editor or Microsoft FrontPage. This prior example would be synonymous to having the U.S. President carry the suitcases for his entourage on all his travels. He could do it, but there are people better suited for this task.

Visual InterDev 6 is specifically designed to meet all your application development needs while providing compatibility with other tools such as FrontPage. In fact, for your development team, you may want to include functional members such as a marketing person to construct the content for the various Web pages, using a tool such as FrontPage. Then, application developers can incorporate that content into Visual InterDev and build a robust Web-based application.

The following is a checklist for deciding how to use each of the features of Visual InterDev 6:

1. Define what are you are trying to accomplish.
2. Identify the alternatives for accomplishing this task.
3. Assess the strengths of each method.
4. Choose the best alternative.
5. Implement to perfection.

Visual InterDev 6 incorporates many components and exciting features to provide a very robust and powerful development platform. You will have a chance to use each of these components in due time.

Summary

You have been given a taste of the features and components that make Visual InterDev 6 such a powerful application development tool for the Web.

When the day began, Visual InterDev 6 was described, and the question of why you should use this exciting new tool was answered by presenting some of the exciting new features. An in-depth discussion of its components and features followed. You learned about the powerful integrated development environment, which can significantly enhance

1

your productivity and make Web programming fun again by enabling you to build your applications within the confines of a single tool. You then learned about each of the major Visual InterDev 6 components. In reading about the components, you saw how their features could be used to develop your application.

Database integration is one of the most significant features of Visual InterDev 6. For this reason, this topic was saved for the end of the day to keep your attention. Visual Data Tools that enable you to use an intuitive, visual environment while constructing and executing powerful database commands were discussed, as were database wizards, which can make your life easier by guiding you through complex processes.

Remember, this material is just scratching the surface of the power of this tool. Over the next few weeks, you will be exploring and learning about the power of Visual InterDev 6. You should set a goal to learn how to incorporate each of these features into building more robust and powerful Web-based applications. Your overall goal, however, should be to learn to use Visual InterDev 6 to its fullest capacity. Your users will thank you for it when they interact with your applications.

This lesson has set the stage for tomorrow when you will build your first Visual InterDev 6 project.

Q&A

Q What is the biggest difference between Visual InterDev 6 and Visual InterDev 1.0?

A The biggest difference found in Visual InterDev 6 is the RAD-like development environment. Visual InterDev 6 provides a much more visual experience for the developer while still maintaining and extending the features that were introduced in Visual InterDev 1.0.

Q Why did the version number go from 1 to 6?

A You could argue that a leap from version 1 to 6 was warranted based on the tremendous new features found in Visual InterDev 6. The main reason that the second version is called version 6 has to with providing a consistent version number across all the tools in the Visual Studio suite.

Q Does Visual InterDev 6 support Java?

A Yes. Visual InterDev 6 supports the incorporation of Java applets and Java components.

Q How can I get ActiveX controls for my applications?

A Visual InterDev includes many ActiveX and design-time controls. You also can choose from over 1000 third-party controls on the market. Finally, you can create your own ActiveX and design-time controls with tools such as Visual Basic and Visual C++.

Workshop

The Workshop provides quiz questions to help you solidify your understanding of the material covered. The exercises provide you with experience in using what you've learned. You can find the answers to the quiz questions and exercises in Appendix B, "Answers."

Quiz

1. What is the main benefit of Web-based applications over typical client/server applications?
2. What is the purpose of the Design view?
3. What is the difference between Active Server Pages and ActiveX Server Components?
4. What is the difference between an ActiveX control and a design-time control?

Exercises

1. Install Visual InterDev 6 (if you have not already done so).
2. Make sure that you have an ODBC database to use with Visual InterDev 6, preferably Microsoft SQL Server or Microsoft Access.
3. Prepare to learn!

DAY **2**

Creating Your First Visual InterDev Project

Yesterday, you discovered many of the new and exciting features of Visual InterDev 6. Today, you will get a chance to experience some of these features for the first time by creating a Visual InterDev project.

You will get the most out of this lesson if you practice using the tools as you go along. Make sure that you have Visual InterDev up, running, and ready to go. Upon completion of this lesson, you will be able to

- Create a Visual InterDev project.
- Build a simple Web-based application using Visual InterDev.
- Understand the different parts of a Visual InterDev project.
- Navigate through the Visual InterDev integrated development environment (IDE).
- Use the basic features of Visual InterDev to create Web-based applications.

This lesson should be a very good introduction to the Visual InterDev 6 development experience. Get a refill on that cup of coffee, and let's begin.

Exploring a Standard Project

At this point, you have read a lot about the features of Visual InterDev as well as the various technologies that it supports. This lesson focuses on assimilating what you've read into a Visual InterDev project. If you have participated in any type of development effort, you are familiar with the concept of a project. You know that a project usually consists of various files that come together to build an application.

Developing an application is like making pancakes. When you're making pancakes, you have to add specific ingredients that include the pancake mix, eggs, oil, and milk, into a bowl. The ingredients symbolize the technologies such as HTML, ActiveX, and VBScript. The bowl symbolizes the project that provides a workspace for you to work with the ingredients. When you have mixed the ingredients in a bowl, you cook the results to produce the finished product. Likewise, when you have finished cooking up your Web pages with Visual InterDev, you will deploy them for display on your Web server.

A Visual InterDev project consists of multiple files that integrate to form your Web site and Web-based application. During development, you can install both the client and server portions on the same machine. Yesterday, you learned about the advantages and disadvantages of this approach. A more typical configuration enables the Visual InterDev development environment on the client machine to access all the files on a central Web server. These files are downloaded from the server to your machine in a local working directory so you can make any changes to your code. Possible project files include HTML files, Active Server Pages, images, and other components that make up your Web site.

When you create a new Visual InterDev project, Visual InterDev builds a subdirectory for your Web within the root directory of your Web server. Your project files will be stored within this subdirectory. The name of this subdirectory assumes the name of your project. For example, if you named your project MyFirstProject, a folder would be created within the root directory of your Web server called MyFirstProject.

You also can create subdirectory folders from within Visual InterDev to organize your files within your project directory. An example would be the Images subdirectory that's created by default when you create a Visual InterDev project. This directory structure contains all the master copies of your files. A virtual root directory for your Web site also is created on your Web server. This virtual root directory takes on the name of your project and points to the files within your project subdirectory. The virtual root represents the directory that contains all the files for a project on your Web server. The virtual root is comprised of the Web server name and the virtual root directory for your project. The Web server name also is referred to as the domain name. The following example shows a virtual root for a sample project:

```
Http://MyServer/MyFirstProject
```

In this example, you see how the name of the Web server, MyServer, and the name of a project, MyFirstProject, join together to form a virtual root for your application. You can see the virtual root for your application from within Visual InterDev, using the Project Explorer. Visual InterDev saves you time by handling the creation of this virtual directory structure.

The advantage of the virtual root is that users can access your files through a Uniform Resource Locator (URL) instead of having to search through your project file directory structure. Taking this example a step further, a sample URL for your project might consist of `http://MyServer/MyFirstProject/Default.htm` where `Default.htm` is the name of a Web page in your project.

By default, a global file (`global.asa`) and a search file (`search.htm`) are created. These files are placed in the root of your Web project directory. The global file enables you to place server-side script for initialization and termination routines for your session and application. The search file adds full text searching capabilities to your Web pages. Visual InterDev also creates a local working directory on your client machine. This working directory serves as a placeholder for the server files as you access them.

Creating Your First Visual InterDev Application

It's Day 2, and you are already developing your first application. You will have this tool mastered in no time at all. Throughout the lesson, I will provide insight into how a typical project is organized as well as how to utilize the features of Visual InterDev. You will be provided with a list of tasks and steps to accomplish as well as all the code examples you need to add. Make sure that you pay attention to the steps and code examples, and think about the tasks as you do them so that you understand what you're doing each step of the way. Remember, there will be a quiz at the end of the chapter, and you may be asked to accomplish additional tasks on your own during the workshop at the end of the day.

Overview of the Application

You need to see an overview of the application before you can begin the development process. You are going to create a basic application that will give you an introduction to using the Visual InterDev development environment. Although creating the application is simple, you will be learning the basic building techniques and how best to accomplish those tasks using Visual InterDev. The tenets that you learn in this lesson will serve as the foundation for every other application that you construct.

The application consists of a default home page as well as a page that provides a template table that can be used to display product orders for a fictional company. Figures 2.1 and 2.2 illustrate these pages.

FIGURE **2.1.**

The main Web page.

FIGURE **2.2.**

*The Order Reporting
page.*

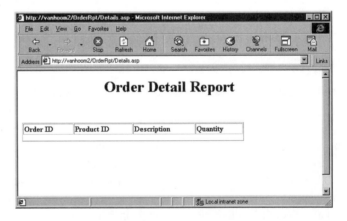

As you can see from Figure 2.2, the Order Reporting page provides a table with headings that can be used to display a list of orders.

These two pages demonstrate how to create a default HTML page that links to an Active Server Page. You will learn how to add static data to the table during today's exercise.

Creating the Project

Now that you have a blueprint of the application, you can begin the construction. First, if you haven't already opened Visual InterDev, you need to do so now. You should be looking at a window like the one shown in Figure 2.3.

FIGURE 2.3.

The New Project dialog box.

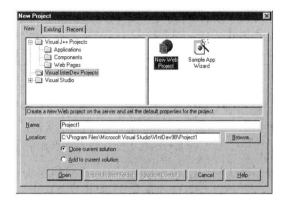

This window enables you to create new projects as well as open existing projects. This dialog box is the same interface used in Visual Basic, providing consistency across the Visual Studio developer tools. You can also access this dialog box by selecting File | New Project. The New tab, shown in Figure 2.3, enables you to create new Visual InterDev projects, including Web and database projects as well as Visual J++ and other types of projects.

 Note

A database project enables you to manage your database objects in the context of a specific project. A live connection to the database is maintained, and you can use the Visual Data Tools to create, edit, and manage your data and objects in the database.

If you want to open a project from this dialog box, you can click either the Existing or Recent tabs. The Existing tab displays a tree view of all the existing projects on the Web server. The Recent tab reveals the most recently accessed projects that you have opened. These tabs are displayed in Figures 2.4 and 2.5.

Because you are creating a new project, click the New tab and choose the Web Projects folder. The Web Projects folder will open and display several objects to the right of the tree view folder, including the New Web Project and Sample App Wizards.

The Sample Application Wizard enables you to install sample applications on your Web server and database server, including data that is needed by the sample application. You have the option of installing a Visual InterDev application or a custom application. The Web Project Wizard enables you to create a new Visual InterDev Web project. You will become very familiar with this wizard and use it often to create your new projects. Choose the New Web Project Wizard as shown in Figure 2.6.

FIGURE 2.4.

Viewing the existing projects.

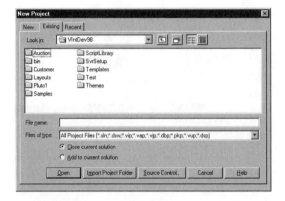

FIGURE 2.5.

Viewing the most recently opened projects.

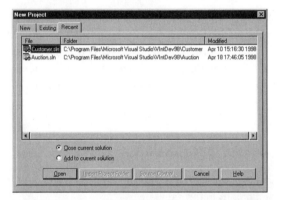

FIGURE 2.6.

Choosing a name and location for your new Web project.

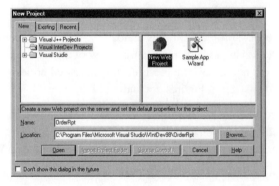

A default name and location should appear in the project Name and Location fields. In the example above, the default name is Project1, and the default location for your project is C:\My Documents\Visual Studio Projects. You can change the location if you want to place your projects in another directory.

Note	The project location that you select is your working directory where all files that you retrieve from the server are placed. After you make changes to the local copy, these files can be returned to update the master copy on the server.
	With Visual InterDev 6, you can choose to either automatically or manually update the master Web server files based on the mode of operation that you choose. I will provide in-depth coverage of this topic on Day 18, "Exploring the Working Modes of Visual InterDev," and Day 19, "Effective Team Development with Visual InterDev and Visual SourceSafe."

For the Name field, type OrderRpt and click Open. Notice that as you type the name of the project, the Location field changes to match what you are typing. The Web Project Wizard will use this information to create a subdirectory on your local machine with the same name as the project name.

Once you click Open, the Web Project Wizard will begin allowing you to select the Web server for your application, as shown in Figure 2.7.

FIGURE 2.7.

Step 1: Selecting a Web server.

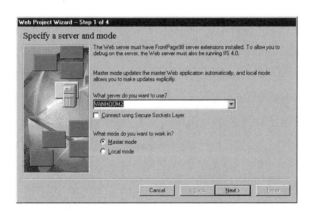

For Visual InterDev 1 users, you will probably notice that the steps for creating a new Web project have increased from two to five. I think you will find that the extra steps provide some very good additional options. First, you must specify the target Web server for the project.

You must select or enter the name of your Web server in the Server Name combo box. The name of the Web server is also referred to as the domain name. If you're connected to a Web server through a network, you should enter the name of that Web server. If you're running a local configuration on a standalone machine, you should enter the name of the Web server on your local machine. If you are using a local Web server, you can also refer to it as localhost.

Tip

If you don't know the server name, you can discover it by identifying the computer name for the Web server. For example, you can identify the computer name for a standalone Web server configuration by right-clicking the Network Neighborhood icon on the desktop and selecting Properties from the shortcut menu. Choose the Identification tab. This dialog box will then display the computer name for that computer, which is also the name of the Web server.

You also have the option of selecting the Connect Using SSL check box. SSL stands for Secure Sockets Layer from Netscape and enables you to connect to the server through this Netscape standard. SSL is a protocol that protects and secures all HTTP transmissions from unwanted visitors. When a Web site uses SSL, all HTTP requests and replies are encrypted before transmission and decrypted after message receipt. You must install an SSL certificate on your Web server to initiate SSL connections.

An additional option to the Web Project Wizard is the ability to work in isolated mode. Isolated mode enables you to make changes to the files you are working on and save them to your local development machine without saving them to the master Web server. The implication is that you can update and test your files and then migrate them to the master Web server when they have been fully tested. For your first project, select the name of your Web server without any options selected and click Next. The Web Project Wizard contacts the Web server and retrieves a list of the current Webs on the server.

Caution

You may get the Cannot Contact Server error message if the Web Project Wizard cannot contact the Web server. Click OK on this dialog box, and you will be taken back to the Web Project Wizard. Verify that you entered the correct server name. If the name is correct, verify that the server is running and then click Next to advance to step 2.

In step 2, the Web Project Wizard prompts you to either create a new Web for your project or connect to an existing Web on the Web server. As you can see from Figure 2.8, the Create New Web option is selected by default on the dialog box for step 2 of the Web Project Wizard.

FIGURE 2.8.

Step 2: Specifying a Web.

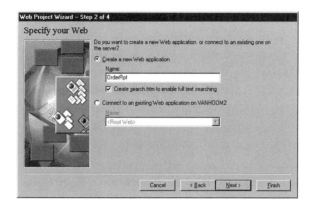

The Web Project Wizard displays a Web name that is the same as your project name in the Name field under the Create New Web radio button. For this example, the name for the new Web should display `OrderRpt` as seen in Figure 2.8. The check box that enables full text searching of the Web pages within this site is typically selected by default.

The other option on this dialog box enables you to create a project as part of an existing Web site. Use this option if you want to add new applications to your current Web site. If you select this radio button, the Name combo box will enable you to choose from the list of Web sites on your server. Choosing the root Web option places the project in the root of your Web server.

For the purposes of this project, make sure that the Create New Web radio button is selected and that the name of the Web site is OrderRpt. Accept the default to enable full text searching for pages in the Web site and click the Next pushbutton.

Note

Internet Information Server (IIS) 4 introduces the ability to create applications on either a physical directory or a virtual directory. This feature is a significant enhancement to IIS 3, which only allowed you to create applications for virtual directories. You will learn how to take advantage of this feature on Day 16, "Managing Your Web Site with Visual InterDev."

Step 3 of the Web Project Wizard enables you to select a layout for your Web pages. You can choose from a list of predefined layouts that allow you to design how users will navigate your Web site. Accept the default of <none> and click Next (see Figure 2.9).

FIGURE 2.9.

*Step 3: Selecting a
layout.*

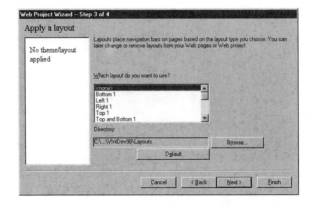

FIGURE 2.9.

*Step 3: Selecting a
layout.*

Visual InterDev provides many predefined layouts that you can experiment with and use.
After you click Next, the dialog box for step 4 of the Web Project Wizard appears, as
shown in Figure 2.10.

FIGURE 2.10.

*Step 4: Choosing a
theme.*

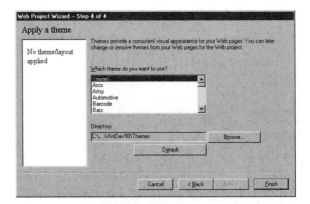

Step 4 of the Web Project Wizard enables you to select a theme for your Web pages from
a predefined list. Themes help define the look and feel of your Web-based application by
applying a set of consistent graphics, fonts, and page elements. By using themes, you can
create a consistent page design across your application for your users. Accept the default
of <none> and click Finish to complete the process of creating the Order Reporting
application.

Note

While Visual InterDev 6 comes with many predefined themes and layouts,
you can create your own themes and layouts to apply to your Web-based
applications.

Analyzing the Results

After you have clicked the Finish pushbutton, the Web Project Wizard will create the basic project structure and files including global.asa and search.htm. You should now be looking at your project within Visual InterDev. The following sections help you analyze the results of your actions.

Analyzing the Server

The Web Project Wizard created a new Web and a directory (both named OrderRpt) for your project files on the server. Your project directory and project files are contained within the root directory for the Web server. For example, if you're using Microsoft Internet Information Server, the folder OrderRpt is located within the wwwroot directory. Using the Windows Explorer, Figure 2.11 shows the file directory structure for the OrderRpt Web site.

FIGURE 2.11.

The OrderRpt server files.

In Figure 2.11, the global.asa and search.htm files have been created in the root of your Web directory. Also, an images folder has been created by default as well as two additional folders that are new in Visual Studio 6—the private folder and the ScriptLibrary folders. These folders will be described later today. You can create additional folders to further organize your files from within the Visual InterDev development environment.

Analyzing the Client

The Web Project Wizard also created an OrderRpt directory on your client machine. This working directory serves as the placeholder for server master files that you retrieve from your Web project directory. When you retrieve these files, Visual InterDev 6 places these files into a local working directory on your machine. This directory structure is the same as the directory structure on the Web server. A copy of global.asa is copied from the server. Also, several additional project files are generated in the client working directory. Figure 2.12 shows the OrderRpt file structure for a client machine.

FIGURE 2.12.

The OrderRpt client files.

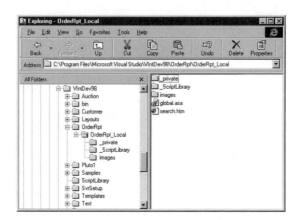

These are the project files for your application. The file extension for Web projects has been renamed in Visual Studio 6 to .vip. As you can see in Figure 2.12, the name of your new Web project is OrderRpt.vip. The concept of a workspace still exists in Visual Studio 6. This idea has been expanded to reflect the concept of integrated solutions that may contain HTML, scripts, and components. The integrated solution idea directly supports Microsoft's vision for Visual Studio—a set of tools to build integrated client/server and Web-based applications. Given this expanded nature of the Visual Studio development environment, the workspace has been renamed to adequately reflect this vision from a suffix of .dsw to .sln.

A Visual InterDev 6 solution can have multiple projects, but a project can have only one solution. In other words, a solution has a one-to-many relationship with a project, and a project has a many-to-one relationship with a solution. You could have a database project and a Web project all contained within one solution.

After you have created a project, you will begin to work with the files within that project. Some files will be created for you. You will add other files as you design and develop your application and use the Project Explorer to interact with your project files. The Project Explorer provides a Windows Explorer–like interface, enabling you to create and maintain your files and folders effectively. The Project Explorer supports most Windows

Explorer functions like drag-and-drop support for moving files and right mouse button support for accessing the shortcut menu for a particular file. You can add files and create new folders for existing files.

The Data view enables you to view all your database objects from the database server, and it becomes accessible when you add a database connection to an Active Server Page within your project. You can interact with each object and display the results to the right of the project workspace pane. This view is very similar to the Project Explorer. The only difference is that you are manipulating objects in your database as opposed to files on your Web server. You will learn more about the Data view on Day 8, "Communicating with a Database."

You can open a file with its native editor by double-clicking the file. You also can select the file and right-click the mouse to display the shortcut menu. Then, you can select Open to open the file with its default editor. You also can choose the Open With menu option to open the file with another application, as long as the selected program supports the file type. When you open a file in your project, the client first attempts to get the file from the working directory on the client machine. If no working copy exists, the client machine requests a working copy from the server. The server machine sends a copy of the master file to the client and places the file in the working directory of the client machine.

Visual InterDev provides visual cues to indicate the status of the file. The icon for a file that has a working copy resident on the client machine is colored, and the icon for a file type that doesn't have a working copy resident on the client machine or that is read-only is grayed.

You can request a working copy from the server by selecting the file and choosing the Get Working Copy option from the shortcut menu. This command retrieves the file from the server.

If you have already retrieved a working copy and made changes to the file, a warning message is displayed, indicating that you already have a working copy of the file. The message asks whether you want to use the local file or the copy from the server as your working copy. The dialog box displays the file statistics for both the server master copy and the local file, including the name, date, and time of each. You then can choose to use the existing local file, use the master copy from the server, or cancel the action.

After you have made changes to a file, you choose the Save, Save As, or Save All option to save your changes. This action updates the master copy on the server. The Save command saves the current file, whereas the Save As command enables you to save the file with another name. The Save All option saves all the files in your project.

Analyzing Visual InterDev 6

Now that you know what the Web Project Wizard has created behind the scenes, it's time
to take a look at these files through the eyes of Visual InterDev 6. Within the Visual
InterDev 6 development environment, you should see the OrderRpt solution that you just
created. The Project Explorer displays the project files and folders, including the virtual
root for this project as the top node. Your virtual root should be similar to the one created
in Figure 2.13.

FIGURE 2.13.

*Looking at the project
through the eyes of the
Visual InterDev IDE.*

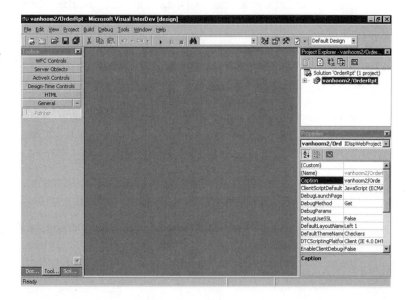

Remember that the virtual root is the combination of your server name and the name of
your Web site. In this example, the name of the server is Vanhoom2 (the name of my
Web server machine), and the name of the project is OrderRpt. These names combine to
form the virtual root of //Vanhoom2/OrderRpt. The + sign to the left of the virtual root
indicates that there are files and folders located within this directory. Click the virtual
root to expand the directory structure and view your project files.

You should now see the global.asa and search.htm files as well as the _private,
_ScriptLibrary, and images folders. Each of the files that are contained within your
project will have specific icons to the right of the file to indicate its meaning.

Note The meanings of these file icons take on a different context based on the working mode that you choose for your project.

In order to become familiar with the different statuses of your project files, select the `global.asa` file and click the right mouse button. From the shortcut menu, choose Get Working Copy. This command will create a write-enabled copy of the file and place it in your working directory on your local machine. The name of this directory in your file system consists of the project name, an underscore (_), and the word *Local*. For this example, the local directory is named `OrderRpt_Local` and can be found within the `OrderRpt` project directory.

2

Tip You can also use the Open command to obtain a copy of the file from your local working directory. If a working copy doesn't exist, this command executes the Get Working Copy command to retrieve the file from the server. The Get Latest Version command retrieves the latest copy of the file from the master Web server.

The Open With menu option enables you to open the file with another application, given the program supports the selected file type.

You should now see the contents of the `global.asa` file in Source view, which is the default editor for Active Server Pages (ASP). Remember, the `global.asa` file is a special kind of ASP.

Creating the Content

Now that you have examined the initial files for your project, it's time to construct the main Web page using basic HTML. The following instructions will guide you through the process:

1. Select the virtual root and click the right mouse button to reveal the shortcut menu.
2. Choose Add | HTML Page from the shortcut menu.
3. Select the HTML Page option and type the name `Default.htm` in the Name field.
4. Click the Open pushbutton to create the new HTML page and add it to the current project.

Visual InterDev 6 creates a basic HTML page named `Default.htm` and adds this file to your project workspace.

Tip

> Visual InterDev automatically adds the correct file extension to the filename based on the file type that you select. In the preceding example, you chose to create an HTML file. Based on that selection, you could have just entered Default. Visual InterDev would then have added the .htm extension to your file.

You should now be looking at the Default.htm file in Design view, the default editor for HTML files, as shown in Figure 2.14.

FIGURE 2.14.

A newly created HTML Web page.

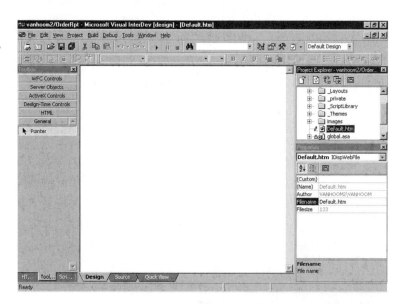

Visual InterDev created a basic template for you to use while constructing your HTML Web page. The Design view enables you to utilize a WYSIWYG editor to graphically create and construct the layout and content of your Web page. Although you can always use Source view to add native HTML tags and scripting code, Design view enables you to build a Web page quickly without having to remember the HTML language. An overview of the Visual InterDev 6 content editors is provided on Day 3, "Creating the Content for Your Application." On Day 4, "WYSIWYG Editing with Visual InterDev," you will learn in detail how to effectively use the Design view editor.

Tip

> You should use Design view to get a jump-start to constructing the basic content and layout for your Web page.

Using Design view, follow these instructions to create the content for the main Web page:

1. Place your cursor on the first line of the Web page and enter the words Order Reporting Web Site, as shown in Figure 2.15.

FIGURE 2.15.

Entering the title for the default Web page.

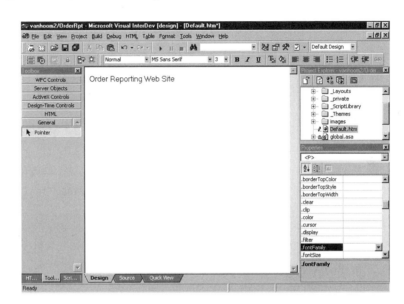

2. Highlight the newly created title and choose Times New Roman and 6 from the Design toolbar for the font style and size.
3. Click B from the Design toolbar to change the text to bold.
4. Create two blank lines by pressing the Enter key twice.
5. Change the font size to 3 and type Order Detail Report.
6. Highlight Order Detail Report and click the Link button on the toolbar, as shown in Figure 2.16.
7. Enter the following name for the URL link: http://<name of your Web server>/OrderRpt/details.asp and click OK. You will create the details.asp page in the next set of instructions.
8. Save the Web page by selecting File | Save.

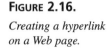

FIGURE 2.16.

Creating a hyperlink on a Web page.

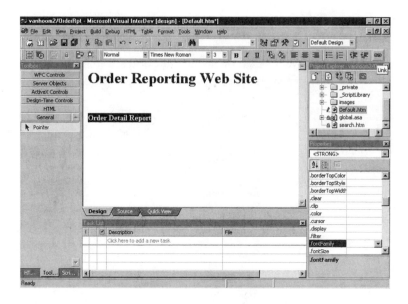

You have now created the content for the main Web page of the application. Click the Quick View tab to see what the Web page will look like in a browser.

You now need to create the second page of the application—the Order Detail page. To accomplish this task, complete the following steps:

1. Select the virtual root and click the right mouse button to reveal the shortcut menu.

2. Choose Add | Active Server Page menu option from the shortcut menu.

3. Select the ASP Page option and type `Details.asp` in the Name field.

4. Click the Open pushbutton to create the new ASP page and add it to the current project.

As you learned yesterday, Active Server Pages enable you to combine HTML, script, and component integration to create a dynamic Web page. By default, ASP pages are opened in the Source view, as shown in Figure 2.17.

FIGURE 2.17.

*Viewing a newly
created ASP page.*

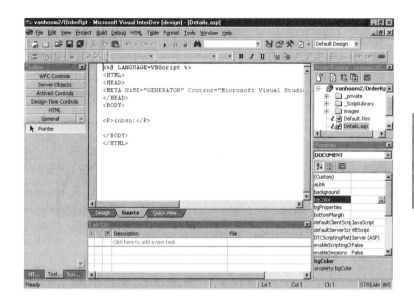

2

Complete the following steps to further develop the Order Details page:

1. Click the Design view tab and enter `Order Detail Report` on the first line of the Web page.

2. Highlight the newly created title and choose Times New Roman and 6 from the Design toolbar for the font style and size.

3. Click B from the Design toolbar to change the text to bold and the Center text icon to center the text on the Web page.

4. Create two blank lines by pressing the Enter key twice.

5. Click the Left Align icon to move your cursor to the left side of the page and choose Table | Insert Table to insert a table on the Web page.

6. Enter 5 for the number of Rows and 4 for the number of Columns and click OK.

7. Enter `Order ID`, `Product ID`, `Description`, and `Quantity` for the respective column titles.

8. Highlight the column titles and click B on the Design toolbar to change the text to bold. Your Web page should now resemble the page depicted in Figure 2.18.

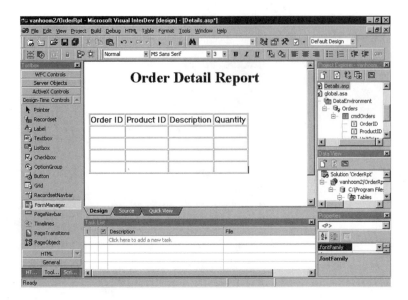

Now that you have entered your HTML code, you're going to preview your results in a browser. You first need to save your project. To do this, choose File | Save All. This option saves all the files in your project.

You can view your Web pages in one of two ways. First, you use the View in Browser function, which will activate Internet Explorer (IE). You can also choose the Browse With command and select a browser. Both options are available from the shortcut menu when you select a file from within the Project Explorer (see Figure 2.19).

Select the `Default.htm` file and right-click the mouse to display the shortcut menu. Choose the View in Browser (or Browse With if you do not have IE) option. Figure 2.20 shows what your Web page should look like using this option.

From this page, you can navigate to the Order Detail Report Page by clicking the URL link on the default Web page. Although this application doesn't include server-side script, database integration, and so on, today's lesson has taken you through the steps of creating your first Visual InterDev project. During the rest of the lessons this week as well as the following two weeks, you will learn how to use the robust features of Visual InterDev to create dynamic, database-driven Web applications.

FIGURE 2.19.

Choosing to browse the Web page.

FIGURE 2.20.

Viewing the Web page.

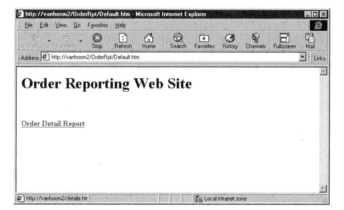

Summary

Congratulations! You've finally had a chance to interact with Visual InterDev and develop your first application. As you can tell, Visual InterDev is very easy to use once you get a feel for the features.

Early in today's lesson, you explored a standard project, learning about the different files and components. You learned about the concept of a Visual InterDev project by comparing it to making pancakes, and then about the virtual root and how Visual InterDev builds the virtual root based on your project name. Next, you read about working with Visual

InterDev files and learned some of the more common files within a Visual InterDev project. During the middle part of the day, the Visual InterDev development process was discussed. You learned how Visual InterDev facilitates each phase of this process from development to deployment.

The final part of the day was spent developing your first project. You received a hands-on approach to development through each step involved in building this application. Throughout the day, you saw the Visual InterDev development environment, including pertinent dialog boxes and menu options. The lessons you learned today will prove invaluable as you delve deeper into Visual InterDev's features and capabilities.

Q&A

Q What is the difference between a workspace and a project?

A A project is a collection of files that join together to accomplish some specified purpose. For example, a Web project is made up of HTML files, Active Server Pages, and ActiveX Layout files that work together to build a Web site and application. Another example is a database project, which is comprised of database objects that enable a programmer to manipulate a database. The project operates within the confines of a workspace. A workspace allows the project or projects to accomplish their mission. Going back to the pancake example, the kitchen or house is analogous to the workspace. A workspace can contain multiple projects.

Q How can I create additional folders for my project?

A You can create new folders for your project within the confines of the Visual InterDev development environment. Right-click the mouse on the virtual root in your project workspace to display the shortcut menu. Choose the New Folder option from the menu, enter a name for your folder, and click OK.

Q Can I configure my Netscape Navigator browser to work with Visual InterDev?

A Yes. Visual InterDev includes Microsoft Internet Explorer. You can, however, add another browser, including Netscape Navigator or Communicator, from the Browse With dialog window.

Workshop

The Workshop provides quiz questions to help you solidify your understanding of the material covered. The exercises provide you with experience in using what you've learned. You can find the answers to the quiz questions and exercises in Appendix B, "Answers."

Quiz

1. What two components make up the virtual root?
2. What is the purpose of the virtual root?
3. What is the default editor for HTML pages?

Exercises

1. In today's exercise, you get to create your own application. Use today's lesson as a guide to create several HTML and ASP pages that relate to each other. You should practice using the various concepts that you learned about today. Start a new project and walk through the whole process. Also, use Windows Explorer to view the file structures and files as they are created. You should understand the basic building blocks by using Visual InterDev to produce your application. Practice makes perfect!

2. Using the information in Table 2.1, change the details.asp page to display a list of orders. This information is provided as static text— that is, not from a database. You will learn how to create dynamic, database-driven applications during the second week of this book.

TABLE 2.1. DATA TABLE FOR THE details.asp TABLE.

Order ID	Product ID	Description	Quantity
100	1-111	Basketball	10_
101	1-112	Baseball	30
102	1-113	Softball	30_
103	1-114	Football	10_

DAY 3

Creating the Content for Your Application

On Day 2, "Creating Your First Visual InterDev Project," you had the opportunity to create a Visual InterDev project. While creating your project, you had the opportunity to work with the basics of Visual InterDev's integrated development environment. Today, you are going to take a closer look at the features of Visual InterDev's integrated development environment and how you can use this environment to create content for your Web site or application.

Most first generation Web development tools offered little more than a text editor to create content. Then came specialized editors that created interactive objects and HTML layouts. Although developers have had the tools to create all kinds of Web sites and applications, productivity and efficiency have suffered because of the lack of an integrated development environment. As Web sites and applications have become more complex, the need for tools with robust, full-featured development environments has become a necessity. Visual InterDev gives developers several ways to create and edit HTML and Active Server Pages for Web sites and applications. Each Visual InterDev editor serves a particular purpose. Today, you'll learn about each of the editors available in Visual InterDev. In addition, you'll learn a few tips on how to select the proper editor for your Web authoring task.

An Integrated Approach to Editing Content

Visual InterDev provides several different editors to create content for Web sites. Most Web sites created today consist of different types of content. Your Web pages might contain HTML code, a scripting language such as VBScript or JavaScript, and objects such as ActiveX components or Java applets. Visual InterDev provides several different options for creating these and other types of content. Best of all, Visual InterDev provides this capability in an integrated environment that is easy to use and powerful. In addition, you can open your Web pages with other editors, such as FrontPage 98, that you are comfortable with.

 Note

Many times you'll see the acronym IDE associated with application development tools. IDE stands for integrated development environment. Here I am discussing Visual InterDev's IDE. I will also refer the IDE as simply the development environment.

Exploring the New Integrated Development Environment

Visual InterDev provides several views of the Web page that you are working with. These views serve as your mechanism for creating and editing content for your Web site or application. Figure 3.1 shows what the Visual InterDev development environment looks like with the editor view visible.

Now is a good time for you to go ahead and take a look at the Visual InterDev editor. Simply right-click your project in the Project Explorer window and choose Add. From here, you can add an HTML page, style sheet, site diagram, or an Active Server page. You add a new HTML page to your project with the dialog box shown in Figure 3.2.

FIGURE 3.1.

The Visual InterDev editor.

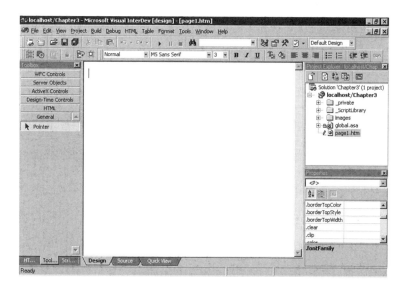

FIGURE 3.2.

Adding a New HTML Page.

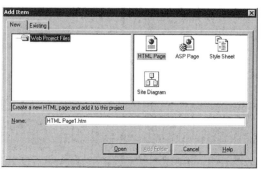

Adding the HTML page will invoke the Visual InterDev editor. Later, you will add content to your new Web page using the features and views of the Visual InterDev editor. You'll notice that the editor window has a tabular interface with three tabs located at the bottom of the window. Each tab represents a view of your Web page source. The following table summarizes the uses for each of these editor views.

TABLE 3.1. VISUAL INTERDEV EDITOR VIEWS.

View	Purpose
Design view	Default view for editing pages in Visual InterDev. Enables you to work with pages as they appear in a Web browser.
Source view	View that enables you to edit and create HTML source or script code.
QuickView	View that displays your HTML or Active Server Page content as it will appear in a Web browser.

Today you are going to walk through an example of creating Web content using each of the Visual InterDev editor views. Day 4, "WYSIWYG Editing with Visual InterDev," will focus even more on the WYSIWYG capabilities of the Design view. For now, let's start exploring the features of Visual InterDev's integrated development environment.

 Note

A quick note on the term WYSIWYG—it stands for What You See Is What You Get. For Visual InterDev, it means that when working in Design view, your Web page will look like it does in a browser.

Adding Text with Design View

Using Design view, you can type text directly onto your Web page in the same way that you would use a popular word processor such as Microsoft Word or Corel WordPerfect. Using the HTML toolbar, you can apply a number of formatting options to your typed text.

The HTML toolbar enables you to change the style and layout of your text as well as change the text's font and font size. Other options include applying bold, italic, or underline format to your text. In addition, you can change both the foreground and background color of your text, create bulleted or numbered lists, and indent your text.

Let's add some text to the new Web page that you added to your project. You might also want to apply different types of formatting to your text using the HTML toolbar. Figure 3.3 shows an example of a Web page with formatted text in Design view.

FIGURE 3.3.

Adding text in Design view.

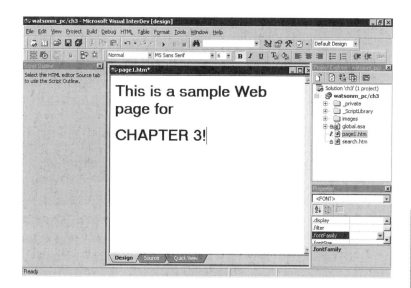

Working with Tables

Using tables is a common technique that adds a consistent and uniform layout to a Web page. In addition, you can use tables in the traditional sense to display rows and columns of data. Visual InterDev makes adding tables to your Web page easy in Design view. By using Design view, you don't have to worry about typing the proper HTML tags for tables into the editor. To add a table to your Web page, select the Table menu and choose Insert Table. This action will display the Insert Table dialog box.

This dialog box enables you to add a table of any size to your Web page. In addition, you can customize how the table looks on your Web page. You can set items such as table alignment, background color, and border width to your own specifications. Using the dialog box, add a table with 2 rows and 2 columns to your Web page. After you have added the table, type some text in the cells. Figure 3.4 shows a table that has been added to a Web page.

After a table has been added to your Web page, the Table menu gives you options of adding or deleting table rows and columns. In addition, you can add or delete individual cells in the table. To get an idea of the effort saved by creating your table visually in Design view, take a look at the HTML code in Source view for the added table. Select the Source view tab with your mouse. You should see something similar to Figure 3.5.

FIGURE 3.4.

Adding a table to a page.

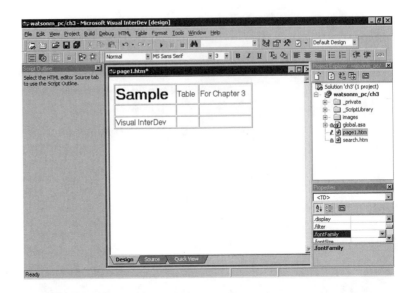

FIGURE 3.5.

A table in Source view.

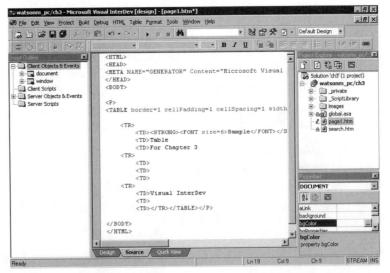

Adding Controls and Objects

You can really spice up your Web page by adding visual controls and objects to your page. Objects enable you to capture input from users of you application as well as convey information to your users in interesting ways. The overall effect of using controls and objects on your Web page is providing the user with a rich graphical environment similar to typical Windows-based applications.

Visual InterDev provides a visual Toolbox that simplifies adding controls and objects to your Web page. The Toolbox enables you to drag and drop objects onto your Web page. All you have to do is select the object you want, hold down the left mouse button, and move the object to your Web page. To view the Toolbox, select the View menu and choose the Toolbox menu item. When visible, the Toolbox contains tabs for each of the following:

- ActiveX Controls
- Design Time Controls
- HTML
- Server Objects
- General (User Defined)

Each tab can be expanded to display the controls of that type that are available on your computer and have been added to the Visual InterDev development environment. To expand a Toolbox tab, click the tab you want to work with.

The controls listed can be added to your Web page in Design or Source view by dragging the control on top of your Web page.

ActiveX Controls

You can add ActiveX controls to your Web page by accessing the ActiveX tab in the Toolbox. Let's add an ActiveX control to your page by dragging the ActiveX calendar control onto your Web page.

 Note
> Currently, Microsoft's Internet Explorer is the only browser that natively supports ActiveX controls. The current release of Netscape Navigator can support ActiveX controls through the use of a purchased plug-in. Keep your target audience and their browser in mind when designing your Web application.

Access the ActiveX tab, select the calendar control, and drag it onto the Web page. Figure 3.6 shows how the Web page looks with the calendar control in Design view.

FIGURE 3.6.

*Design view with an
added ActiveX control.*

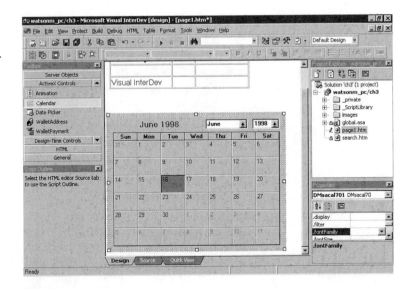

After the control is on your page, you are free to modify its behavior through the
Properties window. To access the Properties window in Design view, select the control
and click the right mouse button. Next, choose the Property Pages option from the displayed pop-up menu. The Property Pages dialog box displays the custom properties that
can be set depending on the object or control selected.

You might want to experiment with the Property Pages dialog box for the ActiveX calendar control. Using the dialog box, you can customize the appearance of the ActiveX
calendar control. Take a look at the Source view to see how your added control is displayed. Click the Source view tab. After you scroll through the HTML code, you should
see the visual control embedded in your HTML source. Figure 3.7 shows how the
ActiveX calendar control looks in Source view.

Note   In Day 7, "Integrating Objects Into Your Applications," you'll get another,
more detailed, opportunity to work with ActiveX objects and their properties and behaviors.

FIGURE 3.7.

Controls in Source view.

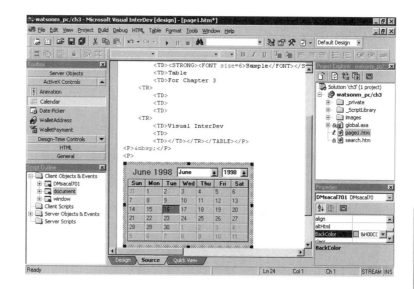

HTML Controls

You can add HTML intrinsic controls to your Web page in much the same way that you added an ActiveX control to your page. Simply select the HTML control that you want to add to your page and drag it onto your page. To see the available HTML controls available in the Visual InterDev development environment, select the HTML tab in the Toolbox. Let's add the Horizontal Rule HTML control to the Web page. Select the control from the Toolbox and drop it on the Web page. To modify properties for the Horizontal Rule, first select the control in Design view. Next, choose the Properties Window option from the View menu. You should see a Properties window like the one shown in Figure 3.8.

FIGURE 3.8.

Properties for HTML controls.

You'll probably notice that modifying control properties via this dialog box isn't as user friendly as the Property Pages dialog box that you use for ActiveX controls. HTML Intrinsic controls don't expose their properties visually the way that ActiveX controls or design time controls do. However, the Properties window is still a better alternative than remembering the various tags for setting HTML properties. Java applets also use the same property window as HTML Intrinsic controls.

Design Time Controls

Visual InterDev introduces the concept of design time controls. A design time control is actually an ActiveX control that enables you to add rich functionality and behavior to your Web pages. Simply insert the design time control onto you Web page by dragging it from the Toolbox. Design time controls place instructions or script code into your Web page and enable you to set custom properties for the inserted instructions. You can think of design time controls as a kind of helper or wizard that facilitates the construction of your Web page or application. Design time controls are especially helpful when adding database connectivity to your Web application. Insert a design time control onto your Web page from the Toolbox. Select the DTC Text Box control from the Toolbox and drop it on your Web page in Design view. Note that DTC stands for Design Time Control. To see the source code for the DTC control, select View All Controls as Text from the View menu. Figure 3.9 shows what the JavaScript code for the DTC Text Box looks like in Source view.

FIGURE 3.9.

A design-time control in Source view.

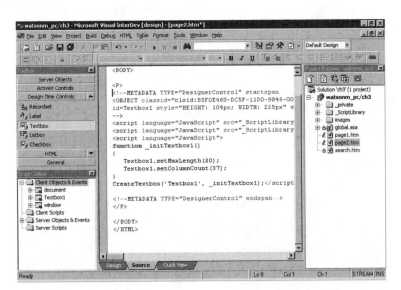

> **Note**
>
> In Day 8, "Communicating with a Database," you'll have the opportunity to explore the many features of database-oriented design time controls.

> **Note**
>
> You can use the Customize Toolbox window to add any additional ActiveX and design time controls that are installed on your computer to the Visual InterDev toolbox. You can find the Customize Toolbox menu item under the Toolbox menu.

Working with Code and Script

So far, you've seen how you can create basic Web content using the Visual InterDev editor views. I have focused primarily on working with Design view. However, to add full functionality and user interaction to your Web application, you'll probably end up working with actual HTML and script code. The two most popular scripting languages for Web development are VBScript and JavaScript. VBScript is a subset of the popular Visual Basic programming language and is interpreted at runtime. JavaScript is a subset of the Java language and is also interpreted at runtime. The choice of scripting language is entirely up to you. You should work with the language that you or your development team is most comfortable with. Visual InterDev provides a great environment for working with HTML code or script.

Adding HTML Code

You can use the Source view to modify the HTML code that is created in Design view or you can use Source view to create all the content for your Web page. However, working with just HTML code can be tedious and time consuming, so a combination of working with Design view and Source view is probably best. To work with HTML code in Source view, simply select the Source view tab and start typing. You'll notice that the Visual InterDev Source view editor uses color to make editing the HTML code easier. Later, I'll discuss how you can customize the colors used by the Source view editor.

Adding Custom Script

You can also use Source view to add either VBScript or JavaScript to your Web page. Let's use Source view to modify the behavior of the ActiveX calendar control that you added to your Web page earlier. Select the Source view tab to expose the code behind your Web page. You are going to add two behaviors to the ActiveX calendar control on your Web page. The first behavior will enable the user to click anywhere on the calendar and see the month for the previous year. The second behavior will enable the user to return to the current year by double-clicking anywhere on the calendar. Although this example is fairly simplistic, it should give you an idea of some of the script editing features of Visual InterDev. Listing 3.1 shows the JavaScript code to add the event behavior to the Web page.

LISTING 3.1. ADDING EVENT BEHAVIOR TO AN OBJECT.

```
 1: <HTML>
 2: <HEAD>
 3: <META NAME="GENERATOR" Content="Microsoft Visual Studio 98">
 4: <META HTTP-EQUIV="Content-Type" content="text/html">
 5: <TITLE>Document Title</TITLE>
 6: <SCRIPT LANGUAGE=javascript FOR=Calendar1 EVENT=Click>
 7: <!--
 8: Calendar1.PreviousYear()
 9: //-->
10: </SCRIPT>
11: <SCRIPT LANGUAGE=javascript FOR=Calendar1 EVENT=DblClick>
12: CurrentYear = new Date()
13: Calendar1.Year = CurrentYear.getYear() + 1900
14: //-->
15: </SCRIPT>
16: </HEAD>
17: <BODY>
18: <OBJECT classid=clsid:8E27C92B-1264-101C-8A2F-040224009C02 height=183
19: id=Calendar1 style="HEIGHT: 183px; WIDTH: 310px" width=310></OBJECT>
    ➥</P></FONT>
20: </BODY>
21: </HTML>
```

Note Your ActiveX controls will appear as graphical objects in Source view unless otherwise directed. To view the HTML object tag for your ActiveX controls, select View All Controls as Text from the View menu. To switch back to a graphical view, select View All Controls Graphically from the View menu.

Visual InterDev simplifies working with objects and controls in Source view through a feature known as statement completion. You can set *properties* to modify the appearance and behavior of a control. *Methods* are predefined procedures or functions that you can use with controls in your Web page. Each control or object has a defined set of properties and methods that can be used programmatically in your VBScript or JavaScript code. Using methods, you can extend the functionality of the control or object. Statement completion automates the process of using these predefined properties and methods in your script code. The following syntax is used to call a control's methods:

```
ControlID.MethodName
```

When you type `ControlID.` in Source view, a drop-down list box appears with the control's available methods and properties. Figure 3.10 shows what this drop-down list box looks like in Source view.

FIGURE 3.10.

Statement completion.

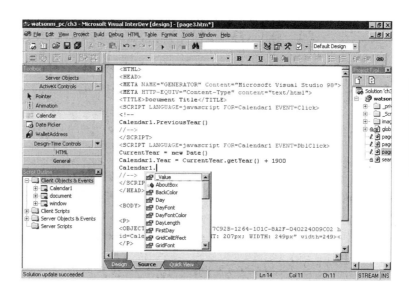

Furthermore, if the method needs any parameters to perform its function, the Source view editor displays the method's arguments. Day 7, "Integrating Objects into Your Applications," will cover in detail working with an object's properties and methods.

Working with Scraps

You can also use the Toolbox to save sections of HTML code, script code, or text from the Visual InterDev editor. Simply highlight the section of code, script, or text that you would like to save and drag it on top of the tab where you would like to store it. In Visual InterDev, these pieces of code are referred to as *scraps*. After the scrap is in the Toolbox, you can rename it by selecting the scrap with the right mouse button and choosing Rename from the pop-up menu. You can also use this pop-up menu to delete the item from the Toolbox. In addition, I would recommend creating a new tab for storing your scraps. By doing this, you'll separate your additions to the Toolbox from the development environment defaults.

Tip

When working in team environments, many times it is a good idea to share common pieces of code or programming templates. One way to facilitate this in Visual InterDev is to place common pieces of code in an Active Server Page. By doing this, each member of the team can copy the file into their environment and drag the individual code blocks onto their Toolbox window.

Getting Around with the Outline Windows

One problem area in working with any programming language is editing your source code. Visual InterDev's integrated development environment helps alleviate this problem through the Document Outline and Script Outline windows. To access these windows, select View | Other Windows. Two of your choices are Document Outline and Script Outline. The Document Outline window enables you to quickly navigate through your HTML source code in Design or Source view. The Script Outline window allows you to visually see and navigate through objects and events on both the client and server. Figure 3.11 shows what the Document Outline window looks like in the Visual InterDev IDE.

FIGURE 3.11.

The Document Outline window.

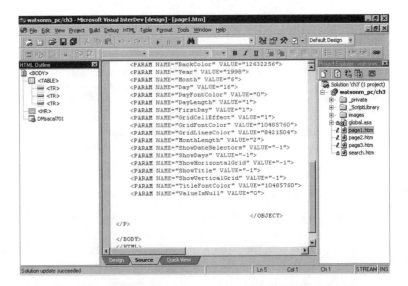

Using the Document Outline Window

When using Design view, the HTML Outline window displays a hierarchical view of the HTML elements and other components in your page. When selecting an element in the HTML Outline pane in Design view, the corresponding HTML control, ActiveX control, and so on is selected in the Design view window. This gives you a fast way to select any

HTML element on your page. If your page is large or has many controls and objects, this navigation feature is especially helpful. The same holds true for using the Document Outline window with Source view.

Using the HTML Outline Pane with Source View

When editing script code with Source view, the Script Outline window displays a tree view of all the objects, events, and scripts in your Web page for both the client and server. The following lists the top-level folders displayed in the Script Outline window when using Source view:

- Client Objects and Events
- Client Scripts
- Server Objects and Events
- Server Scripts

You can use the Script Outline window to easily navigate to the script sections of your HTML code. After you move to a section of script code, you can perform your editing tasks. In addition, you can use the Script Outline window to insert basic script code for a particular object's events. To add the basic code for an event to your script, simply double-click the appropriate event from the client or server objects folder. On Day 5, "Enhancing Your Web Page Through Client-Side Script," you'll learn more about creating scripts for your Web application. Figure 3.12 shows what the Script Outline window looks like while in Source view.

FIGURE 3.12.

Using Script Outline with the Source view.

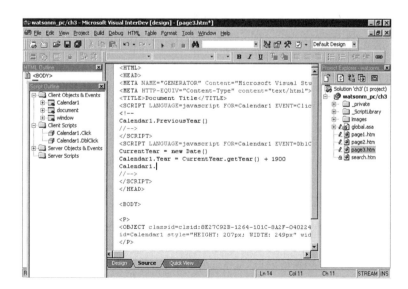

Customizing Your Development Environment

Visual InterDev enables you to modify the development environment to suit your individual preferences. This is accomplished via the Options window. To modify your development environment, select the Tools menu and choose Options.

From this window, you can set many options that effect the Visual InterDev development environment. For example, you can change the color-coding scheme that is used in Source view. In addition, you can set language-specific options for HTML, Java, Text, or SQL. You might want to experiment with the various settings in the Options window to customize your own development environment.

Choosing the Right Editor for the Job

It's nice to have options in life, and Visual InterDev doesn't disappoint with its multiple editor views. Having multiple options also means that you have decisions to make as to which editor you should use to develop the content for your Web pages and applications. The real answer is that you should use a combination of each of the editors in developing your content. Design view is better suited for working with items such as visual controls and tables. Design view also gives you a good idea of what the page will actually look like as you are developing it. This visual feedback can enhance the initial design experience and get your development efforts started quickly. Source view is great for working with the intricate details of HTML and script languages such as VBScript and JavaScript. You might want to customize how the visual controls on your page interact with users and with one another. Using the source and script views, you can easily add this custom logic and test the results using the preview capabilities of the Visual InterDev editor. Other factors involve the complexity of your efforts and your own individual skill level in working with HTML and scripting languages. The Visual InterDev development environment is flexible and offers enough options to meet any of your development needs.

Using Other Editors

Although Visual InterDev defaults to use its own editor for creating Web content, you have the option of using other editors that you are comfortable with to create and edit content. To open a Web page with another editor, right-click the filename in Project Explorer. You'll see the pop-up menu in Figure 3.13.

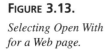

FIGURE 3.13.

Selecting Open With for a Web page.

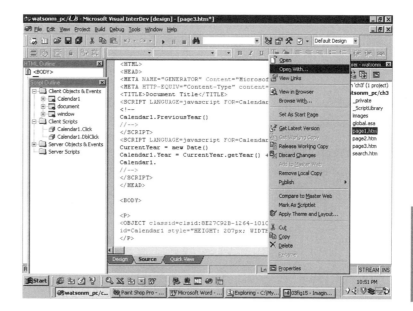

Next you'll see a dialog box like the one in Figure 3.14 that displays other editors to use for this file type.

FIGURE 3.14.

Choosing another editor for a Web page.

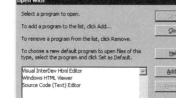

From this dialog box, you can select the editor of your choice from the displayed list. You can also add and remove editors from the list using the corresponding Add and Remove buttons.

Previewing the Results

You can view how your Web page will look throughout the editing process by using the QuickView tab in the Visual InterDev editor. QuickView enables you to see how your HTML or Active Server Page will appear in a Web browser like Internet Explorer. By having preview capability built into Visual InterDev as opposed to using a separate browser, you should save time testing the look of your Web application. The QuickView tab also enables you to interact with your Web page just as a normal user would. Figure 3.15 demonstrates the use of the QuickView tab to view your Web pages.

FIGURE 3.15.

Using QuickView.

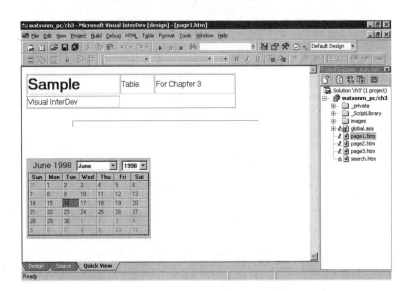

> **Note**
>
> You can rely on QuickView to see how your Web pages will look in Internet Explorer 4 from Microsoft. However, some Web page elements might appear differently, if at all, in Netscape Navigator. Keep this in mind when designing your Web pages and applications.

You can also preview your Web pages with an external browser. To choose another browser, select the Browse With menu option from the View menu.

From this dialog box, simply select the installed browser to view your pages. You can also change the default browser from the Preview view in the Visual InterDev editor to an external browser of your choice.

Summary

Today's lesson covers the basic aspects of creating content for Web pages and applications. You learned how to add various types of content—text, tables, ActiveX objects, Java applets, and HTML controls—to your Web page using the Visual InterDev development environment.

You learned about each editor view offered by the Visual InterDev development environment. You learned how each editor serves a purpose to enable you to create rich, robust, and interactive Web pages. You gained hands-on experience using Design view to place text, objects, and controls on Web pages. In addition, you learned how to use Source view to create and modify HTML and script code in your Web application. You also saw how Visual InterDev eases the process of working with an object's properties and methods via the statement completion feature. You learned how to use the HTML Outline pane to easily navigate through the objects and code that make up a Web application. The final editor view that you learned about was Quick View. Quick View enables you to preview how your Web page will look in a browser.

Finally, you saw how to customize the Visual InterDev development environment to meet your own personal preferences. In the next lesson, you'll get a chance to gain even more experience working with Design view.

Q&A

Q Does Visual InterDev have its own editor that is part of the integrated development environment?

A Yes. Visual InterDev contains an editor that supports three different views of a Web page. The three editor views are Design view, Source view, and Quick View. Visual InterDev offers the developer a powerful development environment through the use of these three views.

Q What is the best way to navigate through your HTML or script code in Visual InterDev?

A You can use Visual InterDev's HTML Outline pane to quickly navigate through HTML source or script code. You can also use the HTML outline pane to work with objects and events in your script code. The HTML Outline pane also works in Design view as a means of quickly selecting a particular element on your Web pages.

Q How does Visual InterDev ease the task of working with an object's properties and methods?

A Visual InterDev has a feature called statement completion that displays the defined properties and methods for an object after the object's ID is typed in Source view.

Workshop

The Workshop provides quiz questions to help you solidify your understanding of the material covered in this chapter. The exercises provide you with experience in using what you've learned. See Appendix B, "Answers," for answers.

Quiz

1. Name the tabs that are present in the Visual InterDev Toolbox.
2. What are the two things that you can modify in relation to an object?
3. What does the term IDE stand for?
4. How do you customize the Visual InterDev development environment?
5. When working with script, which folders are present in the HTML Outline pane?

Exercises

Now that you are familiar with the Visual InterDev development environment, you are going to create a Web page using each of the three editor views. This exercise should give you more experience developing Web pages with Visual InterDev. You have the freedom to select the idea and content for your pages as long as they contain the following:

- Formatted text
- ActiveX controls or HTML controls
- Custom scripts that manipulate your ActiveX or HTML controls
- Tables

DAY **4**

WYSIWYG Editing with Visual InterDev

In yesterday's lesson, you had the opportunity to work with Visual InterDev's integrated development environment, specifically the Design and Source editors. Today I'll focus in detail on the Design view editor. As you learned yesterday, Design view provides a powerful way to construct your Web pages visually.

Before you start learning the finer details of constructing Web pages with Design view, you'll learn about the benefits of working in a visually oriented development environment—especially in relation to creating content for the Web. Then you take a look at each feature of the Design view editor. You'll learn how these features can enhance your abilities to create dynamic and compelling Web pages. Towards the end of the day, you'll have the opportunity to reinforce your familiarity with these features by creating a sample Web page with the Design view editor.

You will cover the following key Design view topics today:

- Working with text and paragraphs
- Working with tables

- Inserting images
- Inserting links and bookmarks
- Absolute positioning
- Customizing the Visual InterDev Toolbox
- Working with Cascading Style Sheets

The Benefits of a Visual Environment

When working with Visual InterDev's Design view, the Web pages that you create truly represent the final product. The Design view editor is just like using a word processor such as Microsoft Word to format a document. If you have used Microsoft's FrontPage, the features of Design view should be very familiar to you. Design view enables you to set the font type, font size, and character formatting such as bold and italics. Printing in Design view also works the same way as it does in a word processor. That is, when you print your Web page from Visual InterDev, the pages that you create are printed exactly as you designed them. In addition, when you design a Web page with Design view, the position of any objects, controls or text is exactly as you see it. In other words, what you see is what you get.

Also, the Design view editor automates the time-consuming and painstaking process of HTML character formatting. With the earlier generation of HTML text editors, a developer had to code the format of your text with HTML tags and test the results in a separate Web browser application. With Visual InterDev's Design view, you visually select the format of your text as you would in popular Windows-based word processors.

As you learned yesterday, you can also see the results of your design within Visual InterDev's development environment with Quick View. With this, you receive immediate feedback on the look and feel of your design, saving valuable development and testing time.

The main benefit of working in a visual environment like the Design view editor is the automation of repetitive tasks. For example, when inserting a table, you insert the table using Design view's Table menu. Design view enables you to design the layout of the table, including the number of rows and columns. Design view saves you the trouble of having to code a series of HTML tags that tell a browser how to display a table. Instead, the Design view editor creates the HTML tags for you.

Figure 4.1 shows a sample Web site displayed in Visual InterDev's Design view editor. As you can see, the Design view editor displays the images, text, tables, and graphical controls that make up the design of the Web page. It's a safe bet that creating this page with a text editor would take you much longer than with Design view. Now think about the great graphical and interactive Web pages that you have seen or used on the Internet. Development tools such as Visual InterDev enable developers like you to visually construct Web pages and applications with great content and without all the fuss.

FIGURE 4.1.

Visual InterDev's Design view.

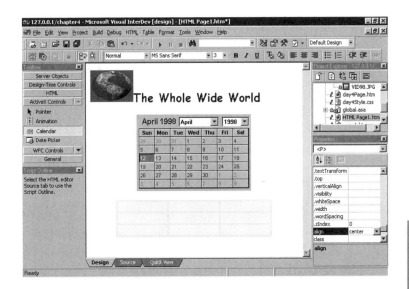

Exploring the Design View Features

As a developer, the Design view editor gives you many features to construct major portions of your content visually. Furthermore, Design view's WYSIWYG capabilities enable you to see a more than fair representation of your Web page as it is being designed.

Let's start by adding an HTML page to the current project. To add an HTML page to your current project, choose the Add HTML Page menu option from the Project menu. You should see a dialog box like the one in Figure 4.2.

From the dialog box, select the New tab and choose the New HTML Page icon. You can use the Name text box to give your new Web page a meaningful name. Let's name our page day4Page. You can also select the Existing tab to browse your computer for existing Web pages. You can add Web pages from other projects or sites to your current project.

When the new page is added to your current project, the Visual InterDev editor appears. The Design view editor is the default tab selected in the Visual InterDev editor.

Tip

Working with Web pages visually in Design view is a powerful way to develop content for your Web applications. However, if you are familiar with HTML tags, you may prefer to work with the native HTML language as a starting point. You can choose to have the Source view editor as the default tab selected in the Visual InterDev editor. Select Tools | Options; a window will appear with multiple setting for your Visual InterDev environment. Select the HTML/Forms option. You should see a Start HTML Pages In option followed by two radio buttons—one for Source view and the other for Design view. If you would like to start your pages in Source view, select the Source view radio button. Of course with Visual InterDev, you can easily switch between the Source view editor and Design view editor.

You can set properties for your newly added Web page by clicking anywhere on the page with the right mouse button. This will display a pop-up menu with a Property Pages choice. The Property Pages dialog box enables you to change several visual attributes on your Web page. For example, you can modify the background image and color for your new page. You can also modify the default colors for text and HTML links on your page. To get a feel for setting properties for your page in Design view, use the right mouse button to display the Property Pages dialog box. Choose your favorite color as the background color for the Web page you created earlier.

FIGURE 4.2.

Adding an HTML page.

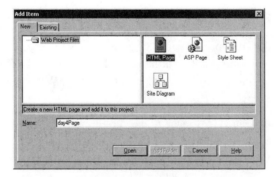

Formatting Web Pages in Design View

To create a compelling Web page, you must use the formatting capabilities of HTML. As stated earlier in the day, working with formatting tags in HTML can be a tedious process. Design view provides assistance with formatting your Web pages through the HTML toolbar and Format menu. When you add or create a new Web page in your project, the HTML toolbar appears. The HTML toolbar enables you to quickly format any text that you type into Design view. Figure 4.3 displays the HTML toolbar.

FIGURE 4.3.

The HTML toolbar.

The HTML toolbar enables you to use several formatting options including the following:

- Paragraph Styles
- Font Type
- Font Size
- Font Format
- Font Foreground Color
- Font Background Color
- Paragraph Justification
- Bulleted and Numbered Lists
- Paragraph Indention
- URL Links

You can also use the Format menu in Visual InterDev to apply some of the same formatting features as the HTML toolbar. Moreover, you can apply superscript and subscript formatting to text in Design view. To apply any of the styles in the Format menu, select the text you would like to apply the format to and then select the appropriate menu option. Figure 4.4 displays the Format menu in action.

FIGURE 4.4.

The Format menu.

You might have noticed that the Format menu has a few other options that I didn't discuss. These options are used when working with images on your Web pages. You'll have the opportunity to explore these options later today in the section titled "Making Your Web Snazzy with Images."

Next, you'll learn how to use each of these formatting features to liven up the text in your Web pages.

Working with Paragraphs

The HTML toolbar enables you to work with and apply paragraph styles to text that you add to your Web page in Design view. Visual InterDev enables you to apply any styles that are supported by the HTML standard. For example, six levels of headings are supported in HTML. Each of these heading styles has a different size font than the other heading styles. To apply a style, select the text that you want to format and then select a paragraph style from the HTML toolbar's pull-down menu. Selecting paragraph styles from the pull-down menu is analogous to using the <H1>, <H2>, <H3>, and so on tags in HTML. Figure 4.5 shows the HTML toolbar with the paragraph style drop-down selected.

FIGURE 4.5.

Selecting a paragraph style.

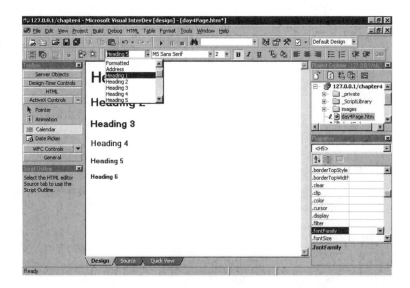

Figure 4.5 also displays a sample Web page with paragraph heading styles applied. When creating a text-oriented site, you may want to experiment with the various paragraph styles offered by Visual InterDev.

> **Tip**
>
> You can use the heading styles to organize your Web content. For example, you could use the heading styles to organize your content in the form of an outline or a book's table of contents. This is especially useful when the information you are conveying to the users is hierarchical in nature.

In addition, you can justify paragraphs and blocks of text by using the paragraph justification buttons on the HTML toolbar. The HTML toolbar supports standard left, center, and right justification. To use the justification features of the HTML toolbar, select the appropriate text block or paragraph in Design view and push the button corresponding to the justification you desire.

You can use the paragraph indention feature to quickly indent paragraphs and blocks of text. The HTML toolbar has two buttons for indenting paragraphs—one to increase the indention and one to decrease the indention. Like the other formatting features, paragraph indention can be used to make your content more readable. Paragraph indention also enables you to separate blocks of text from the rest of the paragraph and makes the selected text stand out.

Working with Fonts

Like most Windows-based word processors, Design view enables you to easily change the font for your typewritten text. You can change the font in Design view by selecting the text you want to change and then selecting font type from the HTML Format toolbar. Using different font types can give your Web page a distinctive look. However, keep in mind that the chosen font must be installed on your user's computer in order for the page to display in the correct manner. Most browsers use a default font if the specified font isn't available on the user's computer. Although the default fonts will work for most content, there are times when this replacement can severely impact the look of your pages. An example of this is using a font from a third-party provider or a font that is intended for specialized use. For example, you may choose a font that resembles text created with a can of spray paint. If your content depends on these types of fonts for its impact on the user, that impact will be lost if the default font is used in the user's browser. Figure 4.6 displays the Font Type drop-down list box on the HTML toolbar. Also, notice the various font types applied on the Web page.

FIGURE 4.6.

Modifying font types.

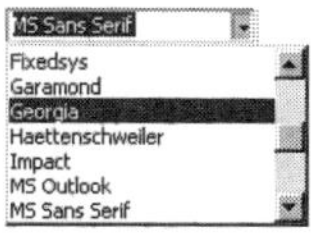

Changing Font Sizes

Just as you change font types with the HTML toolbar, you can also change a font's size. In the HTML specification, font size values are between 1 and 7. The font size 1 represents an 8-point font size value and the font size 7 represents a 36-point font size value. To modify a font size, select the text you want to modify and change the font size using the

Font Size drop-down list box. Figure 4.7 displays the Font Size drop-down list box and text on a Web page with various font sizes.

FIGURE 4.7.

Modifying font sizes.

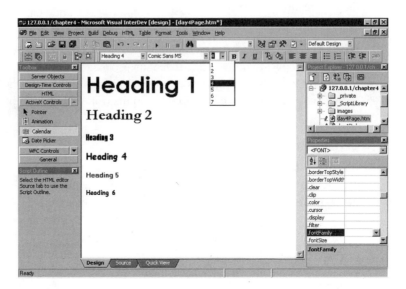

Adding Style to Your Text

There are three basic font styles that you can apply to text on your Web pages. Each is useful for helping you as a developer create Web page content that is distinctive and grabs the attention of the user. The three basic styles should be familiar to you—**bold text**, *italicized text*, and underlined text. To apply a particular font style to your Web page, select the text that you want to change and push the appropriate push button on the HTML toolbar.

Tip

When working with font formats, try not to use too many different formats on a page within one paragraph. Too many different font formats in one place are difficult to read. Use the formats for effect and emphasis on certain words on the page. For example, bold text is often used on heading items. Italicized text is often applied to a single word in a sentence to place emphasis on that word for the reader.

Adding Color to Your Text

Adding both foreground color and background color to the text on your Web page can make your Web pages visually appealing to the user. In addition, color can be used to draw the user's attention to certain parts of the Web page. However, you should use caution and restraint when applying color to the text on your Web page. Too much color can make the information on your Web page difficult to read. To change the color of text on the Web page, select the text and use the Background and Foreground Color buttons on the HTML toolbar. Figure 4.8 shows the Color Picker dialog box that appears when one of the color buttons is selected on the HTML toolbar.

FIGURE 4.8.

Changing a font's color.

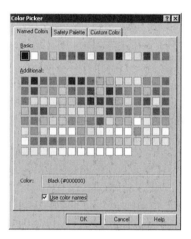

Working with Lists

You can create bulleted and enumerated lists using the HTML toolbar. Lists in HTML are often used to provide an outline for your ideas or content. They also provide structure to your content and make your pages easier to read. To experiment with the list features of the HTML toolbar, type your three favorite colors on the day4Page you added to your project earlier. Type each color on a separate line. Next, select the text and click the Bulleted List button on the HTML toolbar. Visual InterDev will add bullets in front of each line of selected text.

Working with Tables

Tables are often used in Web sites to organize information in an effective and eye-pleasing manner. For example, you could use a table to place "menu" items on the left side of your pages and content in the middle of your page. This type of format gives your pages an organized and uniform layout. Your pages could utilize the same "menu" options on each page with the placement of the items consistent from page to page.

In Visual InterDev, you can add tables to your Web page by using the Table menu option in Design view. Let's place a table on our day4Page:

1. Place the cursor on the page where you want to insert the table.

2. Select the Insert table option from the Table menu.

The Insert Table dialog box should appear (see Figure 4.9).

FIGURE 4.9.

The Insert Table dialog box.

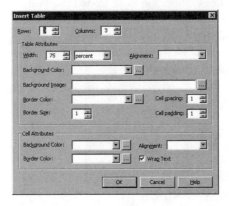

With the Insert Table dialog box, you can specify many of the attributes for your new table. Not the least of these attributes is the number of rows and columns in the table. Other table attributes that you can set pertain to the width and alignment of the table on your Web page, background colors and images for the table, and table border properties.

Tip

When working with the width of the table, you can choose to assign the width as a percentage or as pixels. When using pixels, the width of the table is absolute, regardless of your current window size. The Percentage option assigns the width of the table relative to the current window size. This is useful because your Web pages may be viewed by users with different screen resolutions. Using the Percentage option enables the table to resize according to the current screen resolution or window size.

You can apply color and alignment options to cells in your table using the Cell Attributes section of the Insert Table dialog box.

Let's insert a table with 6 rows and 4 columns on the day4page HTML page. Let's make the background color of the table blue and the cell border yellow:

1. Using the Insert Table dialog box, enter the number of rows and columns in the appropriate drop-down list box.

2. Select blue from the background color drop-down list box.

3. Select yellow from the border color drop-down list box.

You may want to go ahead and work with some of the other table formatting options. When you have inserted the table, you can use the Table menu to add and delete from your table. Figure 4.10 displays the Table menu options.

FIGURE 4.10.

The Table menu.

If you want to modify the attributes of the table, select the table with the right mouse button and select the Property Pages item from the pop-up menu. This dialog box enables you to change the options that you set when the table was inserted in Design view.

Working with HTML Features in Design View

The HTML menu enables you to work with many of the familar features of HTML. The HTML menu enables you to add the following to your Web pages in Design view:

- Links
- Bookmarks
- Images
- Scrolling Marquees
- Dividers

Now, you'll take a look at each of these HTML features and how you can use the HTML menu to add them to your Web pages.

Adding Links to Your Page

To create a link to another Web page, first select the text or image you want to add the link to. Next, select the HTML menu and choose the Link menu item. A dialog box should appear in which you can enter the type of link (http, ftp, and so on) and the location of the file to which you want to link. In addition, you can select the linked text with the right mouse button to view the link's Property Pages. From here, you can make changes to the link such as the page or file location.

Working with Bookmarks

A bookmark is simply a link within the same document. You can use links to enable your Web pages views to jump from place to place in your content. You can create bookmarks in Design view by selecting the text you want to bookmark. Next select the Bookmark option from the HTML menu. Bookmarks are referenced by links in the Web page containing the bookmark or by other Web pages. Use a # sign in front of the bookmark name to reference it. The following example references a bookmark named section1 on the myPage.htm page:

```
MyPage.htm#section1
```

Making Your Web Snazzy with Images

As long as you take into account the bandwidth issues of the Internet, the strategic use of images and graphical content can enhance the appearance of your Web pages. To insert an image onto your Web page, select HTML | Image. You should see a dialog box like the one in Figure 4.11.

FIGURE 4.11.

Inserting an image.

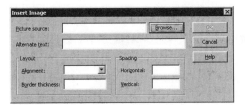

From here you can specify an image to place in your Web page. You can also specify alternative text for the image as well as the alignment of the image. Alternative text refers to text that appears when the user places the mouse over the image.

> **Tip**
>
> To add an image to your Web page, you must add the image to your project first. To add an image, use the Add Item menu option from the Project menu. Use the Existing tab to locate the image on your computer and add it to the project. You might want to store the images you want to use for your Web application in a central location.

When the image has been inserted into your Web page, you can modify its properties by selecting the image with the right mouse button and choosing the Property Pages menu item. The Property Pages dialog box enables you to modify the location of the image, the alternative text, and the size of the image. In addition, it enables you to add image map information to the inserted image. Image maps enable you to specify areas of an image that serve as links to other Web pages. These areas of the image are *hotspots*.

Earlier today, I mentioned that you could use the Format menu to work with images. The Format menu contains a Z Order menu item. This menu item enables you to control the order of images on your Web pages. With this feature, you can control stacking images and text on top of one another. If you want to type on top of an inserted image, you can use Z Order to send the image behind the typed text. You can also stack images on top of each other to create a collage effect on your page.

Scrolling Text with the Marquee

The Marquee menu item under the HTML menu enables you to insert a running marquee of text on your Web page. Place the cursor where you want to have the marquee inserted in Design view. Next, select the Marquee menu item from the HTML menu. This will insert a text box on your Web page design. Type the text you want to have run in the marquee in the text box. You can also use the mouse to select the marquee text box and resize it to your specifications.

Tip

Use caution when working with marquees in your Web pages. A marquee can be a distraction to your Web page users and take away from the overall impact of the page. Marquees should be used in situations where marquees are used in the everyday world. For example, advertisements often appear on an electronic billboard or marquee. In addition, the marquee may not work with all browsers, including versions of Netscape Navigator.

4

Adding Dividers to Your Page

You can also add dividing lines to your Web pages using the HTML menu. Dividing horizontal lines are useful in separating header and footer information on your pages from the body of the page. To add a dividing line to your page, place your cursor in the appropriate location in Design view and add the line by choosing HTML | Div (see Figure 4.12). Let's add a horizontal line to the top of our day4Page HTML page:

1. Position the cursor at the top of your page in Design view.

2. Select the Div option from the HTML menu.

3. When the dividing line is inserted onto your page, use the mouse to resize the horizontal line to your specification.

FIGURE 4.12.

*Horizontal divider
added to a page.*

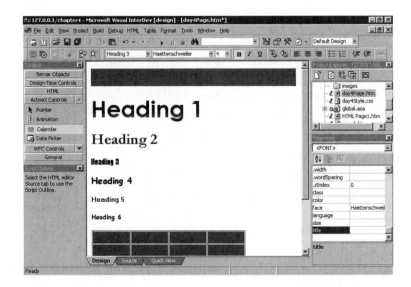

Positioning Objects on Your Pages

When working with visual objects such as images and controls on your Web pages,
placement of the objects is key to the overall impact of your page. Design view has some
nice features that enable you to visually control the placement and layout of such objects
on your Web pages. Let's take a look at these features.

Placing Objects Absolutely

In the past, HTML developers were limited when it came to positioning objects on a
Web page. In general, when working in WYSIWYG editing environments, objects were
placed on a line within a Web page or within a cell of a table. The position of the object
could be only left, center, or right justified. Visual InterDev enables you to position
objects absolutely on a Web page by simply moving the objects around on the page with
the mouse. With this feature, you can place objects literally anywhere, both vertically and
horizontally, on your Web page. To enable this feature, absolute positioning mode must
be selected within Visual InterDev. From the Format menu, select Absolute Positioning.
When this mode is turned on, you are free to move images and controls around on your
page as you want.

When you have the image where you want it on the page, you can also use the Format
menu to lock the position of the image on your page. Select the image and choose the
Lock menu item from the Format menu.

You can turn off absolute positioning mode in the same manner that it was turned on—via the Format menu. Absolute positioning in Visual InterDev is a powerful way to control the overall layout of your Web pages.

Positioning Objects Using a Grid

Although absolute positioning gives you the ability to move objects around on your Web pages with abandon, you may want to impose a little order on the situation by using the Snap to Grid feature under the Tools menu. This feature places objects on a predefined grid within Design view. You can use the Snap to Grid feature to line up objects on your pages. For example, you may have several images that you would like to use as a sort of visual menu bar. You can use the absolute positioning feature together with the grid feature to place and line up the images on your Web page.

Adding User-Defined Styles to Your Web Pages

Cascading style sheets (CSS) enable Web page developers to specify design and layout properties for every element in an HTML page. These properties override the browser's normal methods for displaying HTML to the user. Style sheets enable you to control properties for all the HTML elements discussed so far today.

Style sheets make it easy for developers to give their pages a unique and consistent design. In general, both Internet Explorer 4.0 and Netscape Navigator 4.0 support the cascading style sheets standard. Older browser versions may not support the current style sheet standard. Keep this in mind when creating style sheets for your Web pages. Overall, cascading style sheets give you more control over the layout of objects and text on your Web pages.

Visual InterDev provides an integrated cascading style sheets editor that enables you to create style sheets for your projects. Let's take a look at this editor and how you can use it to add some style to your pages.

Creating a New Style Sheet

To create a new style sheet, select your project in the Project Explorer window and choose Add Item from the Project menu. Select the New Style Sheet icon from the displayed dialog box and type in a name for your new style sheet. After you click the Open button, Visual InterDev's style sheet editor appears. Figure 4.13 displays the style sheet editor.

4

FIGURE 4.13.

The style sheet editor in Visual InterDev.

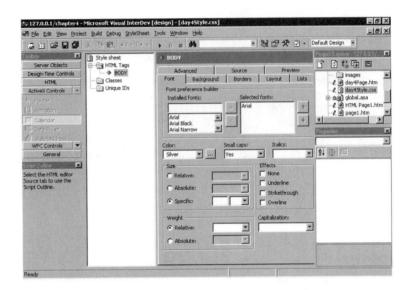

Now you can begin creating a style sheet that can be applied to pages throughout your Web site.

Working with the Cascading Style Sheets Editor

The cascading style sheet editor contains several tabs that enable you to create your own customized styles for elements on your Web page. To create a new style, select the tab that corresponds to the element you want to modify. Next, use the controls in the tab to define the elements of your new style. Table 4.1 summarizes the name and function of each tab.

TABLE 4.1. CASCADING STYLE SHEET EDITOR TABS.

Tab	Purpose
Font	Enables you to set font properties such as type, size, color, and so on.
Background	Used to set background colors and images for a Web page.
Borders	Enables you to format borders and margins for a Web page.
Layout	Enables you to set spacing between characters, alignment, indention, and other formatting related to text.
Lists	Enables you to format bullet styles and images for your pages.
Advanced	Controls the positioning of images and objects on your pages.
Source	Displays the HTML style code for the new style sheet that you created.
Preview	Enables the previewing of the style against a default page or a page of your choice.

When you are satisfied with your style, close the cascading style sheet editor. The new style sheet is now a part of your project. Keep in mind that style sheets have a file extension of `.css`.

Create a cascading style sheet and apply it to the day4Page:

1. Select Project | Add Item.

2. Select Style Sheet from the New tab of the Add Item dialog box.

3. Name your new style sheet day4Style.

4. Using the displayed style sheet editor in Visual InterDev, set the background color to your favorite color.

5. Select your favorite fonts for the style sheet and apply the formatting of your choice.

6. Use the Preview tab in the style sheet editor to see how your new style looks.

7. Save the changes you have made to the style sheet.

8. Apply the style sheet to your day4Page HTML page. Use the following HTML tag between the `<HEAD>` and `</HEAD>` tags:

```
<LINK REL="stylesheet" TYPE="text/css"
➥HREF="YourStyles/day4Style.CSS">
```

4

Save your day4Page and check out the results in the QuickView preview tab. As you can see, style sheets are a powerful way to customize HTML for you own personal use. You may want to study style sheets at a detailed level to realize their full benefit.

Customizing Your Toolbox

In yesterday's lesson, you had the opportunity to explore the features of the Toolbox in Visual InterDev. To refresh your memory a bit, the Toolbox is a visual container for objects such as ActiveX controls, Design Time controls, and HTML controls. Visual InterDev is flexible in that it enables you to customize the Toolbox to suit your development needs. By customizing the Toolbox, you have the ultimate control over your WYSIWYG editing environment. Let's take a look at some the ways you can modify the Toolbox.

Changing the Toolbox Tabs

You can display a pop-up menu that enables you to add, delete, or rename a tab in the Toolbox by selecting a tab with the right mouse button. You can also modify the order of the tabs with the same pop-up menu.

Note

You can only delete a tab from the Toolbox that you added. You cannot delete the tabs for ActiveX Controls, Design Time Controls, or HTML Intrinsic Controls.

Adding Controls to the Toolbox

Visual InterDev enables you to add any ActiveX, Design Time, Windows Foundation Class (WFC) or Applet controls on your computer to the Toolbox. This is accomplished via the Customize Toolbox window (see Figure 4.14).

FIGURE 4.14.

The Customize Toolbox dialog box.

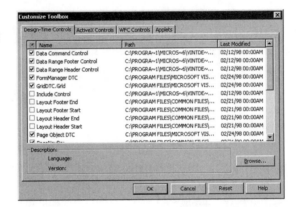

To view this window, click the Tools button and choose the Customize Toolbox menu option. You can also access this window by right-clicking in the Toolbox window and selecting Customize Toolbox from the pop-up menu. When you have the Customize Toolbox window displayed, simply scroll through the list of available controls and select the check box for the control that you would like to add to your Toolbox. Conversely, you can remove a control from the Toolbox by clearing the check box. You can also use the Browse button to search your computer or network for controls that are not listed.

Summary

In today's lesson, you studied the benefits and features of working with Visual InterDev's WYSIWYG editing capabilities. By creating your Web pages in a visual environment, you receive instant feedback on how your page will look to your end users. In addition, being able to see how the elements on your page relate to one another enhances the overall design process. Contrast this with working in source code–only HTML editing tools.

You focused on the Design view editor and its word processor-like capabilities related to formatting text on your Web pages. In regards to text formatting, you learned about each of the features of the HTML format toolbar. In addition, you learned how you can apply these features to enhance the appearance of your Web content. Tables are extremely useful when designing the layout for your Web pages. You learned about the Table menu and how Visual InterDev automates much of the process of creating tables of any size and format in your Web pages. You learned how you can use the HTML menu along with Design view to add links, bookmarks, images, scrolling marquees, and dividing lines to your Web pages. Design view also gives you the ultimate in control when working with images and objects on your Web pages. Using the absolute positioning mode and grid features in Visual InterDev, you can place images and objects anywhere on your Web pages.

Finally, you looked at the cascading style sheet editor and its features. Style sheets give you the ability to define and apply a set of consistent formats to elements on your Web pages. In the next lesson, you'll learn how to use client-side script to enhance your Web pages and applications.

Q&A

Q Can you open Web pages created in other editors and modify them in Visual InterDev's Design view?

A Yes, Visual InterDev enables you to edit HTML source files created from any editor. Choose Project | Add Item; then you can choose to add existing HTML files to your projects.

Q If Design view is so powerful, why would you ever want to use Source view?

A Although Design can handle almost any task related to creating your Web pages, it cannot handle adding custom script code to your Web pages. Source view is excellent for adding VBScript or Javascipt to your Web pages.

Q Should I always create cascading style sheets to format my Web pages?

A Cascading style sheets are a great way to add consistent formatting and style to multiple Web pages. One style sheet can be used by many Web pages. However, if your site is small and doesn't require a consistent look and feel for the user, cascading style sheets may not be necessary.

Workshop

The Workshop provides quiz questions and exercises to help you solidify your understanding of the material covered and to provide you with experience in using what you've learned. You can find the answers to the quiz questions and exercises in Appendix B, "Answers."

Quiz

1. What are two ways that you can format text in Design view?
2. Name the menu items under the HTML menu option.
3. How can you control the order of images and objects on your Web pages?
4. How do you turn on the absolute positioning mode in Design view?
5. Name three elements that you can format with the cascading style sheet editor.

Exercises

Now that you are familiar with the Visual InterDev's Design view, you are going to create a Web page using the WYSIWYG editing capabilities that you learned today. First, create a new Web page with text and images. Use the formatting techniques described today to add some excitement to your text. Next, add a link to another page in your project with the HTML menu. Add other elements such as a scrolling marquee or dividing lines. Finally, create a new cascading style sheet in Visual InterDev and apply it to your page.

DAY 5

Enhancing Your Web Page Through Client-Side Script

Most of the focus for the week has been on the client. You have learned the basic building blocks of building a better client Web page. Today, you will learn a final piece to the client side of the application puzzle. Client-side scripting can provide a dynamic experience for the user if used in the right manner.

Upon completion of this lesson, you will be able to

- Explain the concept of using client-side scripting within a Web page.
- Understand the benefits and pitfalls of using client-side script.
- Explain the relationship of HTML and client-side script interaction.
- Explain the difference between VBScript and JavaScript.
- Utilize VBScript in your Web-based applications.

Scripting for Success

HTML provides a standard method for Web browsers to render Web pages but at the same time it lacks the power to interact with the user. Scripting languages were created to provide a method for the user to interact with the Web page. The user metaphor for the Web has gone from information gathering to true interaction. For example, many companies publish Web sites that not only provide information about their company, but also allow you to purchase their products and services. Web-based applications must have a way to interact with the user. HTML does a fairly good job of formatting documents for the Web but can't handle application processing.

The first applications for the Web used the server to execute special instructions and application logic. Program interfaces on the server like CGI have provided this processing in the past. This model is very inefficient because the information and logic that could be verified and processed on the client is constantly passed back and forth between the client and the server. This situation creates more traffic across the network and additional processing for the server machine.

Client-side script can help alleviate this inefficient process. With the advent of scripting languages, the Web browser can process certain functions on the client through the use of script code embedded in the HTML. Script is normally used for user-initiated events like form activities or mouse events. For example, you can use client-side script to verify that a user entered the right type of information into a field on a form. A user who clicks the mouse or moves the mouse over a certain area of the Web page could also trigger the execution of client-side script.

 Note   All references to script in this chapter pertain to the implementation of script within an HTML Web page on a client machine unless noted otherwise. Day 6, "Extending Your Web Page Through Server-Side Script," covers the concepts of implementing script on the server.

The advantages of using client-side script in your HTML Web page include

- Increased interaction with the user
- Shared processing of simple tasks with the server
- Integration of multiple objects like ActiveX controls and HTML form controls
- More responsive Web pages

There are some limitations to executing script on your client. First, security models are still being developed for the different scripting languages. Some people might argue that there is no definitive model. Most scripting languages were specifically designed with limitations that prevent the code from performing destructive actions on the client machine like destroying files. For instance, scripting languages cannot perform file I/O.

Another limitation to scripting languages is the lack of support for defining different data types. For example, VBScript only supports one data type. If you want to use a different data type, you have to change the type programmatically. The key point is that you must be careful in coding your client-side script. Both Microsoft and Netscape have attempted to implement security measures for their languages. You should, however, be cognizant of the fact that this code is still executing on an unsecured client machine.

You should definitely implement client-side script as a part of your Web-based application. The benefits far outweigh the limitations as long as you construct your code in the right manner. In this respect, a Web-based application is analogous to a movie. A movie must contain a good script no matter how good the actors are. Likewise, your applications must contain effective script to produce the desired results for your applications. You will learn how to implement effective script throughout the day.

The Marriage of HTML and Scripting Languages

Scripting code is embedded within the confines of an HTML page. The <SCRIPT> and </SCRIPT> tags separate the script from the rest of the HTML. Listing 5.1 demonstrates the structure of an HTML document that contains scripting code.

LISTING 5.1. VBSCRIPT CODE EXAMPLE.

```
 1: <HTML>
 2: <HEAD>
 3: <TITLE>VBScript Page </TITLE>
 4: </HEAD>
 5: <BODY>
 6: <P>HTML Paragraph Text
 7: <SCRIPT LANGUAGE = "VBScript">
 8: <!--
 9: ...VB Scripting Code is here
10: !-->
11: </SCRIPT>
12: </BODY>
13: </HTML>
```

5

In this example, the HTML document uses VBScript as its language. You can see the type of scripting language in the following line:

```
<SCRIPT LANGUAGE = "VBScript">.
```

The next line contains a comment tag that denotes the beginning of the scripting code. A comment tag is used for those browsers that can't execute script. Scripting code is hidden from these browsers and treated as if the code were comments. The next line contains the actual script. Your scripting code extends for multiple lines within your document. A closing comment tag is placed at the end of the script. This tag is followed by an ending </SCRIPT> tag.

 Note
Script can be displayed in the <HEAD> and <BODY> sections. If the script is included in the <HEAD> section, the code is interpreted before the page is fully downloaded. Page objects, therefore, are not necessarily recognizable if referenced in this section of the code.

Scripting languages like VBScript and JavaScript are interpreted languages. An interpreted language must be translated by another program at runtime to be able to execute. This interpreter program performs the same duties as a person who acts as a translator between people who speak different languages. The interpreter listens to the speech of one person and translates those words into words that the second person can understand. In a similar fashion, an interpreter program must translate the language of a scripting program to a language that the client machine can understand. Given the code in Listing 5.1, the VBScript interpreter looks for the <SCRIPT> tags and processes all the code in between.

For browsers that can read and support client script, the integration and marriage of HTML and script can be quite harmonious. You will definitely see the benefit of using scripting code on the client machine when you're building an application for the Web. Client-side script can significantly enhance the use of objects like Java applets, ActiveX controls, and HTML form controls.

You're probably wondering about the different scripting languages that are available. The next two sections provide a definition and overview of the two most widely used scripting languages.

What Is VBScript?

VBScript is a subset of the Visual Basic language and is Microsoft's entry into the Internet scripting languages arena. For developers who are familiar with Visual Basic, you will recognize much of the VBScript language and syntax. VBScript is very easy to learn and implement. Microsoft has created and optimized this scripting language specifically for the Internet. Microsoft's Internet Explorer 4.0 supports the use of VBScript by providing the VBScript runtime interpreter.

VBScript uses procedures and functions to process your application needs.

What Is JScript/JavaScript?

JavaScript performs the same type of scripting extensions as VBScript. Netscape collaborated with Sun Microsystems to develop JavaScript as a scripting language to accentuate the Java programming language. Like VBScript, JavaScript is interpreted at runtime. You must use a browser that includes a JavaScript runtime interpreter. You also should be aware that some browsers allow the user to turn JavaScript off for all pages.

Microsoft has reverse engineered the JavaScript code into its own implementation called JScript. Both implementations are pretty much the same, although peculiarities do exist. Microsoft and Netscape agreed in November 1995 to define a single specification for JavaScript that will be managed by the European Computer Manufacturers Association (ECMA) standards body. This single specification hopefully avoids the problem that people have experienced with other "open" technologies, such as the UNIX operating system.

Note

Visual InterDev natively supports the use of JScript with its editors and tools. When you choose a scripting language for your projects, you must either choose VBScript or JScript. You can, however, create a Web page containing JavaScript with another editor, such as Notepad, and insert this file into your project.

The terms JavaScript and JScript are used interchangeably throughout this book to refer to fully compatible implementations of ECMAScript.

5

Many publications use the terms JavaScript and Java interchangeably. JavaScript is not Java. The Java programming language enables you to create applets and applications. These programs are precompiled programs that execute specific functions. You can insert Java applets into your Web page. You also can call Java programs on the server to process more extensive application logic. In summary, Java is an object-oriented language much like C++.

JavaScript, on the other hand, is an interpreted scripting language that resides within the context of an HTML page. The browser, with the help of a JavaScript runtime interpreter, translates the script along with the rest of the HTML when the Web page is downloaded from the server. JavaScript, by nature, doesn't possess the strength or robustness of the Java programming language. JavaScript borrows much of its syntax from the Java language. Listing 5.2 demonstrates the format for JavaScript code within an HTML document.

LISTING 5.2. JAVASCRIPT CODE EXAMPLE.

```
 1: <HTML>
 2: <HEAD>
 3: <TITLE>JavaScript Page </TITLE>
 4: </HEAD>
 5: <BODY>
 6: <P>HTML Paragraph Text
 7: <SCRIPT LANGUAGE = "JavaScript">
 8: <!--
 9: ...JavaScript Scripting Code is here
10: // -->
11: </SCRIPT>
12: </BODY>
13: </HTML>
```

In Listing 5.2, notice the closing comment tag is different than the closing comment in the previous VBScript example. For JavaScript, a closing comment tag is denoted by two forward slashes. Also, the <SCRIPT LANGUAGE> tag set to "JavaScript" indicates that the scripting language is JavaScript.

VBScript and JavaScript are similar in coding structure. JavaScript, like VBScript, doesn't support specific type casting of variables. An integer is represented in the same way as a string. Also, JavaScript makes use of functions, methods, and properties, similar to VBScript, to accomplish its tasks. Functions are defined in the following section, "VBScript Basics." Methods and properties are defined on Day 7, "Integrating Objects into Your Applications."

Creating a Web Page with Client-Side Script

Now that you have a feel for how HTML and client-side script can be integrated, let's create a simple Web page that contains some client-side script. The following steps will guide you through this process:

1. Create a Visual InterDev project named ClientScript.

2. Add an HTML page and name it HelloWorld.

3. Using the Design editor, add several paragraph breaks by pressing Enter three times.

4. Drag and drop two HTML pushbutton controls from the Toolbox onto the Web page. Your page should now look like the one shown in Figure 5.1.

FIGURE 5.1.

Designing your page.

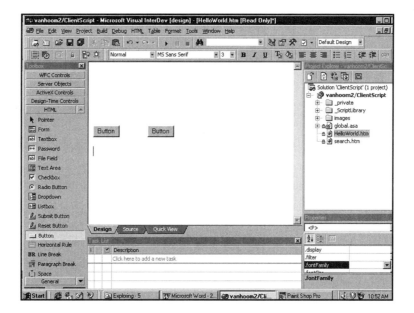

Tip

After you add the first pushbutton, press the Spacebar to add spaces between the first and second button. You can then drag and drop the second pushbutton control.

5

5. Select the first pushbutton and use the Properties window to change the `value` property to `Use VBScript`. This action will change the text that appears on the button. Remember, once you select the pushbutton, the properties for that object will be displayed in the Properties window.

6. Change the Name and ID properties to `btnVBScript`.

7. Select the second pushbutton control and change the `Value` property to `Use JScript`. You need to also change the Name and ID properties to `btnJScript`. Figure 5.2 reflects the changes you have made so far.

Now you are going to add the client-side script that will process when the buttons are pressed.

8. Click the Source tab to switch to the HTML Source editor. Make sure your cursor is at the top of the `<BODY>` section.

FIGURE 5.2.

*The VBScript and
JScript buttons.*

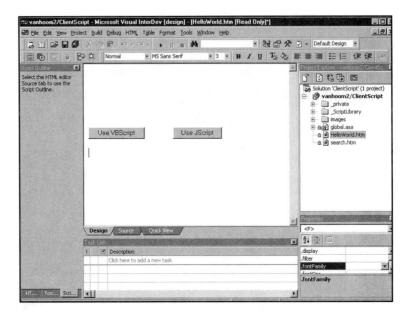

9. Click the Script Outline tab. If it is not shown within your current development environment, choose View | Other Windows | Script Outline windows from the Visual InterDev menu items. The Script Outline reveals all the client- and server-side objects, events, and scripts for both HTML pages and Active Server Pages. Also referred to as the ScriptBuilder, this feature helps you build scripting logic for your pages.

10. If necessary, open the Client Objects & Events folder to display all of the client-side objects and their associated events.

11. Click the btnVBScript button to display its events.

12. Double-click the `onclick` event. This action will create a sub procedure within the HTML page enabling you to enter you script code for this event. Figure 5.3 displays the results of this action.

13. Add the following line of code for this procedure:

```
MsgBox "Hello world!", 0, "VBScript"
```

14. In the Properties window, change the default `ClientScript` property to `JavaScript`.

FIGURE 5.3.

The procedure shell for the VBScript button.

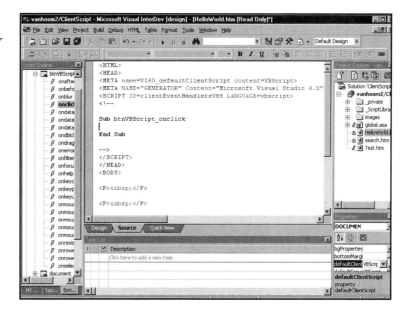

> **Note**
>
> This page serves only as an example of comparing how the two languages appear on a page. You should typically adhere to one scripting language for your client-side script. An exception would be if you were using a combination of client-side script for something like validation logic and design-time controls (DTC) for your database logic. In this scenario, you could use VBScript for your validation logic, and the DTC would use JavaScript. If you are not sure about which browser you are targeting, you should typically use JavaScript, which is more widely supported by a range of browsers at this time. You will learn more about DTCs on Day 12, "Extending Web Pages Through Design-Time Controls," and on Day 13, "Unleashing the Power of the Visual InterDev Programming Model."

15. Click the btnJScript button to display its events.

16. Double-click the `onclick` event.

17. Add the following line of code for this function:

    ```
    alert("Hello world!");
    ```

    Figure 5.4 displays the results of this action.

18. Save the file and click Quick View to view your results.

When you click the Use VBScript button, you will get a message box like the one shown in Figure 5.5.

FIGURE 5.4.

The procedure for the JavaScript button.

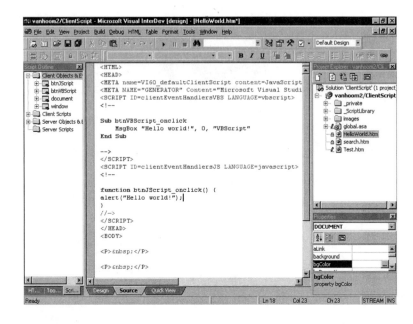

FIGURE 5.5.

Using VBScript to generate a message box.

A similar reaction happens when you click the Use JScript button except JavaScript is used instead.

Listing 5.3 shows the same sample code for the page implemented with VBScript and JScript.

LISTING 5.3. HELLO WORLD WITH VBSCRIPT AND JAVASCRIPT.

```
 1: <HTML>
 2: <HEAD>
 3: <META name=VI60_defaultClientScript content=JavaScript>
 4: <META NAME="GENERATOR" Content="Microsoft Visual Studio 6.0">
 5: <SCRIPT ID=clientEventHandlersVBS LANGUAGE=vbscript>
 6: <!--
 7:
 8: Sub btnVBScript_onclick
 9:     MsgBox "Hello world!", 0, "VBScript"
10: End Sub
11:
12: -->
```

```
13: </SCRIPT>
14: <SCRIPT ID=clientEventHandlersJS LANGUAGE=javascript>
15: <!--
16:
17: function btnJScript_onclick() {
18: alert("Hello world!");
19: }
20: //-->
21: </SCRIPT>
22: </HEAD>
23: <BODY>
24:
25: <P> </P>
26:
27: <P> </P>
28:
29: <P> </P>
30:
31: <P><INPUT id=btnVBScript name=btnVBScript type=button value="Use
➥VBScript">         
➥      
32: <INPUT id=btnJScript name=btnJScript type=button value="Use JScript"
➥LANGUAGE=javascript onclick="return btnJScript_onclick()"></P>
33:
34: </BODY>
35: </HTML>
```

This code example shows some differences between VBScript and JavaScript. The first difference is the format of a JavaScript function. The syntax is very similar to the C++ language, which uses braces to organize a block of code statements and semicolons to signify the end of a statement.

Another difference is the method that is used to call a JavaScript function. Notice in the JavaScript example that the word onclick is used to call the function. In the VBScript code, the word NAME is used to activate the procedure. If you aren't familiar with C++ or Java, VBScript may seem like the more intuitive language. Both languages support your needs for providing robust, client-side functionality.

VBScript Basics

Now that you have a feel for how to create client-side script, this part of the lesson will concentrate on teaching you the basic building blocks for creating VBScript code. In the section "Using VBScript to Extend Your Web Page," later in this chapter, you apply these lessons and discover how to integrate VBScript into a Web page.

Understanding Procedures

VBScript uses procedures to provide a home for its code. You're probably familiar with the concept of using procedures. Most programming environments, regardless of the language, use procedures as their basic foundation. Procedures provide a logical container for groups of related code.

A procedure is a logical grouping of code statements that works together to complete a specific task. Procedures can be called from within your application and also can call other procedures.

VBScript contains three types of procedures:

- Sub procedures
- Functions
- Event procedures

Sub Procedures

A sub procedure is a group of related VBScript code statements that complete a task but don't return a value to the calling program. A procedure is called from your application or another procedure. When a program or procedure calls a sub procedure, the caller asks the procedure to perform a task. The calling program isn't interested in receiving anything in return. This process is analogous to a person calling a restaurant for carry-out food. The person calls the restaurant to prepare the food, and the person then drives to the restaurant to pick up the food. I will contrast this process with that of a function in the next section, so keep the food analogy fresh on your mind.

When a sub procedure is invoked, program control is temporarily passed to the called procedure. A sub procedure is denoted by the Sub and End Sub keywords. You can think of these keywords as tags that signify the beginning and ending of the procedure. They are similar in nature to HTML tags that mark the beginning and ending of an HTML element. The following code segment illustrates the basic structure of a sub procedure:

```
Sub CalculateTotal (A,B)
Total=A*B
MsgBox "The total is " & Total
End Sub
```

In this example, CalculateTotal is the name of the sub procedure. A and B refer to arguments that are passed by the calling program. These arguments are optional. You can pass up to n arguments to the called sub procedure. You also may develop procedures that don't need parameters to be passed. For those sub procedures, the parentheses are optional.

An argument is a variable that a procedure needs to complete its task. You can specify a number of arguments to be passed to the procedure.

You can pass arguments by value to the procedure. You specify an argument to be passed by value by placing `ByVal` in front of the argument.

By value means that a copy of the variable's value is passed to the procedure. The procedure can use this value as well as make changes to it within the scope of the procedure. Because the variable is passed as a copy, changes that are made by the procedure to the value of the variable don't affect the original variable.

The following code segment demonstrates how to pass a variable by value:

```
Sub CalculateTotal(ByVal A, ByVal B).
```

Arguments also can be passed by reference. This method is the default method of passing a variable. This method differs from the traditional way that other development tools such as Visual Basic construe passing a variable by reference. By reference in VBScript means that a variable's value is passed to the procedure as read-only. The procedure can read the value but can't make any changes to it.

In Visual Basic and other tools, passing a variable by reference enables you to access the storage of the original variable and changes the contents of the original variable. After the procedure has completed, the variable reflects the changes when the calling program tries to access its contents. VBScript doesn't enable you to alter the contents of the original variable.

You don't have to explicitly state that you're passing a variable by reference. The following code example shows how to pass a variable by reference:

```
Sub CalculateTotal(A, B).
```

You should develop descriptive names for your sub procedures so that anyone who uses the procedure will know what it does. I prefer to name my procedures using a verb-object nomenclature. For example, if I developed a procedure to format a date to display to the user, I would name that procedure `FormatDate`. `Format` is the verb that tells what the procedure is doing, and `Date` represents the object that is the object of the action. The preceding example multiplied two numbers to calculate a total, hence the name `CalculateTotal`. Valid characters to include in your procedure name include letters and numbers as long as the first character is not a number. You can't use symbols in your procedure name. VBScript performs error checking on your names to validate their syntax.

To call a sub procedure, you simply enter the name of the procedure. You also can use the optional `Call` keyword to activate a procedure. The following examples demonstrate

5

how to call a sub procedure. The first example uses the `Call` keyword whereas the second example only states the name of the procedure. To call the `CalculateTotal` sub procedure, you can use

```
Call CalculateTotal(A, B)
```

or

```
CalculateTotal(A, B)
```

If the procedure that you're calling requires arguments, place the arguments within optional parentheses after the name of the procedure. To call the `FormatDate` procedure that doesn't require parameters, enter

```
FormatDate()
```

or

```
FormatDate
```

VBScript provides you with a lot of flexibility when calling a sub procedure. You may want to explicitly call procedures with the `Call` keyword so that you can distinguish the difference between a sub procedure and other elements within your code, such as variables.

Functions

The second type of procedure is a function. Similar to a procedure, a function is a collection of VBScript statements that work together to perform a task. The difference between a procedure and a function is that a function can return a value.

A function is a group of code statements that collaborate to accomplish a task. A function is similar to a procedure in that a function can accept arguments and be called from the application and other procedures. A function can return a value to the calling program. A function is denoted by the `Function` and `End Function` keywords.

The following code example demonstrates the structure of a function.

```
Function Function Name(Argument 1, Argument 2,..., Argument n)
...Function Code
End Function
```

The structure of a function is very similar to the structure of a sub procedure. The same rules concerning sub procedure names and arguments apply to functions. I stated that the distinguishing factor concerning a function was the ability to return a value to the calling function.

When I explained the concept of a sub procedure, I used the analogy of calling a restaurant to order carry out. You call the restaurant, order the food, and pick it up from the restaurant. Extending the analogy, the function represents a person who calls and orders food to be delivered. You call the restaurant and ask for a mushroom pizza to be delivered to your house. The restaurant informs you that they need to cook the pizza, and it will be delivered in 30 minutes. The delivery person drives to your house and delivers the pizza. You can then use the pizza to feed yourself and your family. Similarly, a program makes a request of a function expecting to get something in return. When the function finishes executing its code, it sends a value back to the calling program. Listing 5.4 illustrates how a procedure can call a sample VBScript function and receive a value in return.

LISTING 5.4. RETURNING A VALUE.

```
 1: <SCRIPT LANGUAGE="VBScript">
 2: <!--
 3: Sub ConvertTemp()
 4: temp = InputBox("Please enter the temperature in degrees Fahrenheit:",
➡1)
 5: MsgBox "The temperature is " & Celsius(temp) & " degrees C."
 6: End Sub
 7:
 8: Function Celsius(fDegrees)
 9: Celsius = (fDegrees - 32) * 5 / 9
10: End Function
11: !-->
12: </SCRIPT>
```

In this code example, the sub procedure prompts the user to enter a temperature in degrees Fahrenheit. After the user enters the number, the function is called to convert the temperature to Celsius. Notice that the function variable, `Celsius`, which captures the converted temperature, is the same as the name of the function. In order to return a value back to the calling program, you must specify a variable to have the same name as the function. By design, the function returns a value through the use of its own name as the variable.

The function in Listing 5.4 contained only one line of code. Most of your functions will contain multiple lines of VBScript code. For this reason, you should make it a practice to populate the function variable in the last line of the function code. Listing 5.5 shows a sample function that contains multiple lines of code.

5

LISTING 5.5. FORMATTING THE FUNCTION VARIABLE ON THE LAST LINE OF CODE.

```
1: <SCRIPT LANGUAGE="VBScript">
2: <!--
3: Function CalculateAverage(A,B)
4: Dim Total
5: Total = (A*B)/2
6: CalculateAverage = Total
7: End Function
8: !-->
9: </SCRIPT>
```

In this example, a temporary variable, Total, is established to hold the value of the calculated average. On the last line of the function, CalculateAverage is set to the value that is stored within the Total variable. Although this is a simple example, I think you can extrapolate the significance if your function code has many lines. Using this standard can provide meaning to your functions. You will always know to look at the last line of the code for the value that is being returned to the calling program. Assigning the function variable on the last line of the function also prevents this statement from getting lost in the shuffle of your code.

Calling a function is different from calling a procedure. Because a function returns a value, you must be prepared to do something with the value when it returns from the function. The syntax for calling a function is

```
Return_Variable = Function Name(Argument 1, Argument 2,..., Argument n)
```

where Return_Variable is the name of the variable that will store the value that is returned from the function. To call the CalculateAverage function, you could enter either

```
Average = CalculateAverage(A,B)
```

or

```
Average = CalculateAverage A,B
```

Notice that the parentheses are optional. For a function that doesn't require arguments, you can enter either

```
Date1 = FormatDate()
```

or

```
Date1 = FormatDate
```

Notice again that the parentheses are optional.

Functions are very useful when you need to complete a task and then return the results back to the calling program.

Event Procedures

The first two procedures that you learned about are procedures that you can create. The event procedure is different from sub procedures and functions in that it is constructed automatically for you by the objects and controls that you use to build your application. Event procedures also differ from sub procedures and functions in the manner that they are initiated. The browser calls event procedures automatically, based on user actions and requests. With sub procedures and functions, you must call them within the context of your program.

An event procedure is a group of code statements activated by a user-initiated event. This action could be the result of a user action such as clicking a button. An event procedure also could be triggered by a system action where the user has made a request of the system and the system needs to respond.

When you use objects such as ActiveX controls to create your application interface, standard events are associated with these controls. For example, a user can click a button; therefore, a standard event for a button is the `On_Click` event. This event is triggered and its code is executed any time the user clicks the button. The structure for your event procedure code is constructed automatically based on the controls that you select. You must fill in the blank with any code that you want processed when the event is initiated.

You don't have much choice in naming your event procedures. Most of the time this name is generated for you. The standard naming convention for an event procedure is as follows:

```
Sub ControlName_EventName()
```

`ControlName` is the name of the control and `EventName` refers to the name of the event. For example, an event procedure for a click event associated with the Submit button might be called

```
Sub cmdSubmit_OnClick
```

 Note
> The control name is based on the ID property value that you establish when you place the control within your application. In the line of code above, I placed a button on a Web page and changed the value for the ID property to `cmdSubmit`.

5

Event procedures are preconstructed programming shells that a control provides for you. Each control will have a different set of events associated with it. Event procedures serve as a helpful reminder to think about the various user and system actions that can occur within your application. Based on these actions, you can then provide the logic process and handle the application requests.

Procedures and HTML

As you can see, procedures provide the foundation and residence for your VBScript code. Although you can place script outside the confines of a procedure, most of your application logic resides within a procedure. You should generally place your VBScript code within the <HEAD> section of an HTML document for readability. You may be tempted to separate your procedures into different script sections as in Listing 5.6.

LISTING 5.6. SEPARATING THE SCRIPT.

```
 1: <SCRIPT LANGUAGE="VBScript">
 2: <!--
 3: Function CalculateTotal(A,B)
 4: Total = A+B
 5: CalculateTotal = Total
 6: End Function
 7: !-->
 8: </SCRIPT>
 9: <SCRIPT LANGUAGE="VBScript">
10: <!--
11: Function CalculateAverage(A,B)
12: Dim GradeAverage
13: GradeAverage = (A*B)/2
14: CalculateAverage = GradeAverage
15: End Function
16: !-->
17: </SCRIPT>
```

Although VBScript enables you to divide your script into separate sections, as shown in Listing 5.6, it isn't a good habit to develop from a maintainability and readability standpoint. You should instead make it a habit to place all of your code into one script section. This practice enables you, as well as others who may use your code, to easily understand and locate your scripting code as demonstrated in Listing 5.7.

LISTING 5.7. PROVIDING THE RIGHT ORGANIZATION FOR YOUR SCRIPT.

```
 1: <SCRIPT LANGUAGE="VBScript">
 2: <!--
 3: Function CalculateTotal(A,B)
```

```
 4: Total = A+B
 5: CalculateTotal = Total
 6: End Function
 7:
 8: Function CalculateAverage(A,B)
 9: Dim GradeAverage
10: GradeAverage = (A*B)/2
11: CalculateAverage = GradeAverage
12: End Function
13: !-->
14: </SCRIPT>
```

Summarizing Procedures

Although this section on procedures may have been refresher for some of you, I hope
you have gained a better understanding of the basic building block for your code.
VBScript procedures are very similar to Visual Basic and other development tools. Table
5.1 summarizes the three types of procedures and provides a description of each type.

TABLE 5.1. VBSCRIPT PROCEDURES.

Procedure	Description
Sub Procedure	Processes a group of related code statements
Function	Processes a group of related code statements and returns a value to the calling program
Event Procedure	Control-specific procedure that processes user or system events

5

I have mentioned the term *variable* several times today. I'm sure that you have used variables to develop your applications, but I did want to define the term and outline how you
can use variables within the context of VBScript.

A variable serves as a placeholder for some type of information. You can use variables to
store information that your application logic will need at some point in time. You can
access the value of the variable as well as modify its contents.

Types of Variables

There is only one data type for a VBScript variable. The variant serves as the data type
for all the variables that you create within your VBScript code. A variant is very flexible
in that it can hold almost any type of information.

A variant is a special data type that can store all types of information, including strings,
numbers, dates, and objects such as ActiveX controls.

When you define a variable, you don't have to state an explicit data type. In other programming languages, you must specifically define a data type for the variable such as an integer or a date. All variables in VBScript are defined as variants.

You don't have to worry about specifying a data type for your variables. When you assign a value to a variable, VBScript stores additional subtype information about the data that's being held in the variable. This subtype, or category, information helps VBScript determine the usage of variants based on the variable's context. For instance, if you want to add two number variables that are stored as variants, VBScript assumes that the variables are numbers and treats them as such. Textual information is handled in a similar manner, based on the internal subtype of the variable. Table 5.2 describes the different subtypes for a variant data type.

TABLE 5.2. VARIANT SUBTYPES.

Subtype	Description
Boolean	Contains a value of either True or False
Byte	Stores integers between 0 and 255
Integer	Contains a number between -32,768 and 32,768
Long	Contains an integer between -2,147,483,648 and 2,147,483,647
Single	Contains single precision, floating point data with a range from $-1.4E^{-45}$ to $-3.4E^{38}$ for negative numbers and $1.4E^{-45}$ to $3.4E^{38}$ for positive numbers
Double	Contains double precision, floating point, or decimal data with a range from $-4.9E^{-324}$ to $-1.8E^{308}$ for negative numbers and $4.9E^{-324}$ to $1.8E^{308}$ for positive numbers
Date/Time	Contains a date including time information between January 1, 100, and December 31, 9999
Empty	Contains 0 for numbers and " " for strings; represents a variable that hasn't been assigned a value
Error	Contains a VBScript error number
Null	Variable that contains no data; represents a variable that has been assigned a value of nothing
String	Contains alphanumeric information up to 2 million characters
Object	References an object like an ActiveX control

Exposing the Variable's Data Type

You can determine and change the subtype that VBScript selects for your variable. There are two ways to discover the subtype. First, you can use the VarType function. This function enables you to request the subtype of a variable. The syntax for this function is as follows:

```
VarType(VariableName)
```

VariableName is the name of the variable that you are inquiring about. Listing 5.8 illustrates the use of the VarType function.

LISTING 5.8. DETERMINING THE SUBTYPE OF A VARIANT.

```
 1: <SCRIPT LANGUAGE="VBScript">
 2: <!--
 3: Function DisplaySubtype(TestVariable)
 4:
 5: Dim VariableSubtype
 6:
 7: VariableSubtype = VarType(TestVariable)
 8: 'Determines the variable subtype
 9: MsgBox "The subtype for the variable is " & VariableSubtype
10: 'Displays the subtype
11: DisplaySubtype = VariableSubtype 'Assigns the value of the subtype
12: 'to the function variable
13:
14: End Function
15: !-->
16: </SCRIPT>
```

You can use this function to determine the subtypes of variables within your application. This function requires that a variable be passed as an argument. The function determines the subtype for this variable and passes the value back to the calling program. I created it as a function that displays a message box as well as returns the value of the variant subtype.

The VarType.htm file contains the entire Web page that calls the function. To test the function, I populate the argument TestVariable before it's passed to the function. When the Web page is loaded, a message box displays the value of the subtype. I used the message box for testing purposes only, as well as the hard-coding of the TestVariable. To use this function with your application code, you should copy the function code and insert it into your <SCRIPT> section. Also, if you want to use the return variable but not display the message box, remove the MsgBox line of code.

The second method to determine the subtype of a variant is to use some special functions provided with VBScript. These functions perform a check for a specific data type. After the check is performed, the functions return a value of True or False, indicating whether the variable matches the specific data type of the function. The following list shows the type of VBScript functions that are available:

- IsArray
- IsDate
- IsEmpty
- IsNull
- IsNumeric
- IsObject

The syntax for each function is as follows:

```
FunctionName(VariableName)
```

For example, to call the IsDate function, you would enter

```
IsDate(TestDate)
```

Remember that these functions return a value of either True or False. For this reason, the most typical use of these functions is in the context of testing whether the return value of the function is True or False. This test can be performed using an If...Then...Else statement, which is covered in a later section.

Changing the Variable's Data Type

VBScript also supplies functions to alter the internal data type of a variable. You can use these functions to specifically change the variable subtype that is assigned by VBScript for the variant. For example, you may want to explicitly define a variant to be represented as a certain variable subtype such as a string or integer. Table 5.3 displays the available VBScript functions to change a variant's subtype.

TABLE 5.3. VBSCRIPT SUBTYPE CONVERSION FUNCTIONS.

Function Name	Description
CBool	Converts subtype to Boolean
CByte	Converts subtype to Byte
CDate	Converts subtype to Date
CDbl	Converts subtype to Double
CInt	Converts subtype to Integer
CLng	Converts subtype to Long
CSng	Converts subtype to Single
CStr	Converts subtype to String

The syntax for calling these functions is similar to the functions that determine the sub-type for a variant. For example, to call the CInt function, you would enter

```
CInt(OriginalVariable)
```

This function converts the data to the integer format. For all these functions, you need to assign the return value to a variable:

```
ChangedVariable = CInt(OriginalVariable)
```

Defining the Scope of a Variable

Variables can be used within the context of a procedure. You also can share variables across all of procedures. The scope of a variable determines its availability to your code.

Scope refers to the ability of a code statement to access a certain variable's contents. The scope of a variable determines the context for usage by your application.

Variables consist of two types of scope—procedure-level and script-level. Procedure-level scope, sometimes called local scope, refers to variables that are declared within a procedure. Procedure-level variables can only be used and accessed within the context of that procedure.

Script-level scope refers to variables that are defined outside your procedures. Script-level variables can be recognized across all your procedures. The lifetime of your variable signifies the length of time that the variable exists. Lifetime and scope are closely tied together. Whereas scope determines what code statements have access to the variable, lifetime indicates how long the variable exists in memory. For procedure-level variables, the variable exists only for the life of the procedure. When the procedure ends, the variable no longer exists. Script-level variables exist until the script finishes processing.

You will constantly have a need to use variables. They are a powerful part of any programming language. As you progress through the next few weeks, the proper use of variables will become very evident.

So far, you have learned about structuring your code through the use of procedures. You also have recognized that variables are a necessary component of any set of code statements. With all this capability, how do you control your program's flow while unleashing the potential of your code?

VBScript, like other programming languages, provides control structures that enable you to designate how your script is executed. Control structures are analogous to highway signs that direct you to the right place. You make decisions, based on these signs, about where to turn and which direction to drive. Similarly, control structures help your code make decisions about which logic to execute. This section covers the basic control

5

structures that are available within VBScript. This section serves as a refresher for those experienced Visual Basic programmers.

If...Then...Else

This control structure is used to evaluate whether a condition is `True` or `False` and compares the values of variables. The following code example demonstrates the use of this control structure:

```
If RoundWorld = True Then
MsgBox "Sail around the world!"
Else
MsgBox "Don't go! You'll fall off the earth!"
End If
```

Notice the structure of the `If...Then...Else` statement. You're basically telling your program to evaluate whether a condition is true. If it is, you want to execute one piece of code. If the condition isn't true, you want to execute another piece of code. There are several variations to this control structure. The first variation involves only executing a piece of code if a situation is true. You don't care if the situation is false. For this situation, you would enter the following:

```
If RoundWorld = True Then MsgBox "Sail around the world"
```

Another variation that is similar to the preceding example is if you want to run multiple lines of code when a situation is true. For this scenario, you would enter

```
If RoundWorld = True Then
PackedBags = True
lblHouse.Caption = "Gone Sailing"
MsgBox "Sail around the world!"
End If
```

The `End If` statement is used in this example to signify the end of the code. You must include this statement when executing multiple lines of code within an `If...Then` statement.

You also can use this control structure to evaluate and compare the values of variables. For this kind of comparison, you need to use the VBScript comparison operators.

 Note

VBScript contains comparison, arithmetic, and logical operators. Comparison operators, as the name states, enable you to compare variables. Arithmetic operators enable you to perform mathematical operations between numbers and variables. Logical operators assist you in testing the validity of one or more variables.

The following code example demonstrates the use of a comparison operator within an `If...Then...Else` statement:

```
If Age >12 Then
MsgBox "You are a teenager."
Else
MsgBox "You are not a teenager."
End If
```

A final variation includes the ability to construct multiple tests. You can use the `ElseIf` statement to construct another test within your `If...Then...Else` statement. The most common use of this structure is when you have multiple comparisons to perform. The following code example illustrates the use of this construct:

```
If Age <= 12 Then
MsgBox "You are a not a teenager."
ElseIf Age < 20 Then
MsgBox "You are a teenager."
ElseIf Age > 40 Then
MsgBox "It's all downhill from here."
End If
```

Notice from the previous example that you can construct multiple `ElseIf` statements within an `If...Then...Else` statement.

Select Case Statements

`Select Case` statements are similar in function to the `If...Then...Else` statement. `Select Case` statements enable you to execute code based on the value of an expression. You will want to replace an `If...Then...Else` statement with the `Select Case` statement when you have multiple conditions to test.

How many `ElseIf` statements are too many? I usually start to consider a `Select Case` statement after the third test of a variable. In other words, Listing 5.9 would be a good candidate for a `Select Case` statement.

LISTING 5.9. UNWIELDY `If...Then...Else` STATEMENT.

```
1: <SCRIPT LANGUAGE="VBScript">
2: <!--
3: Sub DisplayName(Name)
4:
5: If Name = "Bob" Then
6: MsgBox "Your name is Bob."
7: ElseIf Name = "Mike"
8: MsgBox "Your name is Mike."
9: ElseIf Name = "Gina"
```

continues

LISTING 5.9. CONTINUED

```
10: MsgBox "Your name is Gina"
11: ElseIf Name = "Steve"
12: MsgBox "Your name is Steve"
13: End If
14:
15: End Sub
16: !-->
17: </SCRIPT>
```

Listing 5.10 shows what the previous listing would look like as a `Select Case` statement.

LISTING 5.10. PROVIDING STRUCTURE THROUGH A `Select Case` STATEMENT.

```
 1: <SCRIPT LANGUAGE="VBScript">
 2: <!--
 3: Sub DisplayName(Name)
 4:
 5: Select Case Name
 6: Case "Bob"
 7: MsgBox "Your name is Bob."
 8: Case "Mike"
 9: MsgBox "Your name is Mike."
10: Case "Gina"
11: MsgBox "Your name is Gina"
12: Case "Steve"
13: MsgBox "Your name is Steve"
14: Case Else
15: MsgBox "You don't have a name"
16: End Select
17:
18: End Sub
19: !-->
20: </SCRIPT>
```

The first statement in the `Select Case` statement provides the expression to be tested. This expression must have a distinct value. In other words, you can't use a `Select Case` statement to make comparisons between variables. The lines denoted by the `Case` statement signify the comparison value for each set of code statements. VBScript traverses the list of `Case` statements, comparing each value to the test expression. If it finds a match, the code for that `Case` statement is executed. If no match is found, the code within the `Case Else` statement is executed.

Note

It's a very good programming practice to use the `Case Else` statement even if you think you have covered all of the possible values in the `Case` statements. Your code will crash if you don't provide a parachute for the script to execute in case of emergency.

The function below determines the type of conversion that you want to perform and then converts the variable subtype. This function demonstrates the use of a `Case` statement in combination with some of the previous functions you learned about earlier today. Listing 5.11 displays the code for this function.

LISTING 5.11. CHANGING A VARIANT'S DATA TYPE.

```
 1: <SCRIPT LANGUAGE="VBScript">
 2: <!--
 3: Function ConvertSubtype(ConversionType,OriginalVariable)
 4:
 5: Dim ChangedVariable
 6:
 7: Select Case ConversionType
 8: Case "Boolean"
 9: ChangedVariable = CBool(OriginalVariable)
10: Case "Byte"
11: ChangedVariable = CByte(OriginalVariable)
12: Case "Date"
13: ChangedVariable = CDate(OriginalVariable)
14: Case "Double"
15: ChangedVariable = CDbl(OriginalVariable)
16: Case "Integer"
17: ChangedVariable = CInt(OriginalVariable)
18: Case "Long"
19: ChangedVariable = CLng(OriginalVariable)
20: Case "Single"
21: ChangedVariable = CStr(OriginalVariable)
22: Case "String"
23: ChangedVariable = CStr(OriginalVariable)
24: Case Else
25: ChangedVariable = ""
26: End Select
27:
28: ConvertSubtype = ChangedVariable
29:
30: End Function
31: !-->
32: </SCRIPT>
```

5

For...Next Loops

The For...Next loop is a widely used method to control the flow of your code. You can use a For...Next loop to execute a group of code statements a specified number of times. A counter is used to control the number of times that the code is executed. By default, the counter is increased by one for each iteration of the loop. You can set the starting value of the counter as well as the value of the increment. You also can specify that the counter be decremented with each loop iteration. The format of a For...Next loop is as follows:

```
For counter = beginning to end Step increment
Execute Code segment
Next
```

counter represents the variable that is going to be incremented, beginning signifies the beginning number of the counter, end represents the ending value for the counter, and increment specifies how much to increase or decrease the counter after each iteration of the loop. The Step statement is optional.

Do Loops

The Do loop provides another popular way to execute your code multiple times. The Do loop can be implemented in a variety of ways. You can use the While keyword to execute a block of code as long as a condition is true. The behavior of the loop changes based on where the While keyword is placed in the loop. If the While keyword is placed in the opening line of the loop, VBScript first checks to see if the condition is true before executing the code segment. The syntax for the Do...While loop is

```
Do While condition
...block of code statements
Loop
```

You also can place the While keyword at the end of the loop to execute the code at least once before exiting the loop. The syntax for the Do...Loop...While is

```
Do
...block of code statements
Loop While condition
```

You also can use the Until keyword to execute a block of code until a condition becomes true. The same rules for the While keyword concerning placement within the loop apply to the Until keyword.

Using VBScript to Extend Your Web Page

Now that you have learned some of the basics of VBScript, I want to walk you through two examples of using VBScript to extend and enhance the functionality of your Web page.

The first example uses VBScript code to validate an input field for a form. The script validates that the user enters a numeric value between 1 and 10. The application displays a different message box based on a correct or incorrect entry. To create this Web page, complete the following steps:

1. Create a new HTML form and name it `ValidInput`.
2. Enter the text `Validating The User Input` at the top of the page. Highlight the text and make it bold and size 6 font.
3. Add a paragraph break by pressing Enter once and then drag and drop a horizontal rule from the HTML Toolbox.
4. Add another paragraph break and then change the font size to 3 and enter the text `Enter a value between 1 and 10:`.
5. Add two spaces to the right of the text.
6. Drag and drop a Textbox control from the HTML Toolbox to the right of the second space. Resize the text box to be just big enough to handle a double-digit number.
7. Drag and drop a Button control to the right of the text box.
8. Change the Value property of the button to `Verify`. Your page should now look similar to the one displayed in Figure 5.6.
9. Change the `ID` and `Name` properties of the Verify button to `btnVerify`.
10. Change `ID` and `Name` properties of the text box to `txtNumber`.
11. Using the Source editor and Script Outline, add the following code for the `onclick` event procedure:

```
Sub btnVerify_onclick
Dim EntryNumber
    EntryNumber = window.txtNumber.value
  if IsNumeric(EntryNumber) then
    if EntryNumber < 1 or EntryNumber > 10 then
       MsgBox ("Please enter a number between 1 and 10.")
    Else
       MsgBox ("Your entry was valid.")
    End If
  Else
     MsgBox ("Please enter a numeric value.")
```

5

```
        End if
   End Sub
```

12. Save the file and view the page using Quick View.

FIGURE 5.6.

*Designing the page to
validate the input.*

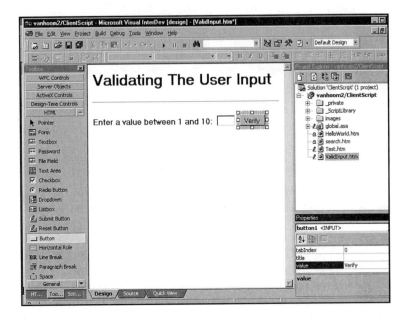

Listing 5.12 shows the Web page and the VBScript code for this example.

LISTING 5.12. VALIDATING USER INPUT.

```
 1: <HTML>
 2: <HEAD>
 3: <META name=VI60_defaultClientScript content=VBScript>
 4: <META NAME="GENERATOR" Content="Microsoft Visual Studio 6.0">
 5: <SCRIPT ID=clientEventHandlersVBS LANGUAGE=vbscript>
 6: <!--
 7:
 8: Sub btnVerify_onclick
 9:    Dim EntryNumber
10:       EntryNumber = window.txtNumber.value
11:    if IsNumeric(EntryNumber) then
12:       if EntryNumber < 1 or EntryNumber > 10 then
13:          MsgBox ("Please enter a numnber between 1 and 10.")
14:       Else
15:          MsgBox ("Your entry was valid.")
16:       End If
```

```
17:    Else
18:        MsgBox ("Please enter a numeric value.")
19:    End if
20: End Sub
21:
22: -->
23: </SCRIPT>
24: </HEAD>
25: <BODY>
26:
27: <P><STRONG><FONT size=6>Validating The User
➥Input</FONT></STRONG></P><STRONG><FONT size=6>
28: <HR>
29:
30: <P><FONT size=3>Enter a value between
31: 1 and 10:  
32: <INPUT id=txtNumber name=txtNumber style="HEIGHT: 22px; WIDTH: 39px"
➥value=15>  <INPUT id=btnVerify name=btnVerify style="HEIGHT: 24px;
➥WIDTH: 56px" type=button value=Verify></FONT></P>
33:
34: <P> </P>
35:
36: <P> </P></FONT></STRONG>
37:
38: </BODY>
39: </HTML>
```

Figure 5.7 displays what happens when the user types in an incorrect entry.

Although this example is simple in nature, you should be able to get a feel for how to

FIGURE 5.7.

An invalid entry.

5

integrate the power of VBScript into your HTML code. At the beginning of the day, I explained that user input validation was an important capability of client-side script. If you didn't use scripting code on the client, you would have to pass the entry and validate the information with a program on the server. If the input is wrong, you have to send a message back down to the client informing the user to enter the data again. This process could be repeated several times before the user enters a correct value for the field.

In Listing 5.12, you see the value of having the script resident within the Web page on the client. After the user enters a value and clicks the Verify button, the input is instantly validated on the client machine. For the purposes of this example, a message box is displayed informing the user whether the entry was valid or not. Figure 5.8 shows the results of typing a correct value and clicking the Verify button.

FIGURE 5.8.

A valid entry.

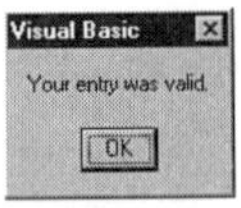

In the context of a more robust application, you might pass a valid entry on to the server for further processing. This example should provide a good understanding of the benefits of client-side script.

Summary

Hopefully, some of this information served as a refresher for you. If you have used Visual Basic before, you should notice the glaring similarities it has with VBScript. These similarities are only natural because VBScript is a subset of the Visual Basic language. This lesson focused on the advantages of using a language like VBScript to enhance the functionality of your Web page from a client perspective. During tomorrow's lesson, you will discover the power of applying these concepts on the server side of the equation.

Today you received an overview of how to use scripting code on the client, discovering both the power and some of the drawbacks of client-side script. Next, you learned about VBScript and JavaScript—two of the most widely used and popular scripting languages today. The lesson presented a brief introduction and definition for each of these languages. You were able to walk through the process of using the Script Outline to add VBScript and JavaScript to your Web page.

The latter part of the lesson provided you with some of the basics of VBScript. This part of the lesson taught you some of the more robust features and capabilities of the VBScript language. Finally, you created a specific example that demonstrated the impressive capabilities of VBScript and Web page interaction.

Q&A

Q Can I use JavaScript and VBScript within my Web page?

A For client-side scripting, you should typically use only one scripting language per page. A common scenario of using two different scripting languages on a page

might be where you incorporate design-time controls into your application that utilize JavaScript and you provide client-side validation of controls with VBScript.

Q What is the difference between VBScript, VBA, and Visual Basic?

A Visual Basic is the parent language for both VBA and VBScript. Visual Basic provides both a robust language and development environment for client-server development. VBA and VBScript are subsets of Visual Basic. VBA stands for Visual Basic for Applications and is geared toward the power user. VBA is the programming language for the Microsoft Office suite of applications. VBScript is yet another derivative that is geared specifically for HTML Web pages. VBScript can be used both on the client and the server side of a Web-based application.

Q What is a variant?

A A variant serves as the lone data type for all variables in VBScript. The variant can handle multiple data types, including numbers, text, dates, and objects. VBScript categorizes the data that is stored within a variant through the use of subtypes. These subtypes help VBScript to classify and perform operations on a variant.

Workshop

The Workshop provides quiz questions to help you solidify your understanding of the material covered. The exercises provide you with experience in using what you've learned. For answers, see Appendix B, "Answers."

Quiz

1. What is the difference between Java and JavaScript?
2. What is the difference between a function and a sub procedure?
3. What is the difference between `Null` and `Empty`?
4. What does the `ByVal` statement do?
5. Given the following code segment, how many times will the code within the loop execute before the loop terminates?

```
Sub cmdCalculate_OnClick()
Dim A, B, C
A = 10
B = 20
Do While A > B
C = A - B
A = A - B
Loop
End Sub
```

Exercises

Create a Web page that includes several HTML text box controls including name, address, city, and state. Provide a Submit button for the user. Add client-side validation logic that verifies each of the fields have been filled in when the user clicks on the Submit button.

DAY 6

Extending Your Web Page Through Server-Side Script

Now that you have learned the virtues of Dynamic HTML and client-side script, turn your attention to how you can extend your application even more through the use of server-side script. Upon completion of this lesson, you will be able to

- Explain the concept of server-side script and Active Server Pages.
- Create an Active Server Page (ASP) from within the Visual InterDev environment.
- Understand the relationship between client- and server-side script.
- Create a Web-based application that incorporates client- and server-side script and ASPs.

What Is Server-Side Script?

Server-side script enables you to execute scripting logic on the server that manipulates your Web page in some way. This script can be used to retrieve rows from a database as well as dynamically create content that is then sent to the browser as HTML. Visual InterDev provides an excellent way for you to incorporate server-side script into your application through the use of Active Server Pages.

Active Server Pages add an intriguing alternative to your choices for server-side development. You can design and develop Active Server Pages in a way similar to the process that you use for your Web page development. Active Server Pages consist of HTML and script that reside on the server. Active Server Pages support the same popular scripting languages that you use on the client, including VBScript and JavaScript. The main benefit is that you can leverage the investment you make learning HTML and a scripting language on the client to your development for the server.

The Web has been transformed into a place of interaction. Users don't just want to browse a Web page; they want to experience and interact with a Web site. Using the server to provide this interactive experience for your users is a very important concept to master. Active Server Pages enable you to easily integrate server-side logic into your application. In the past, you may have used CGI or APIs to provide this logic. With both of these methods, you have to create an executable program on the server that involves a development process different from your Web page development. Figure 6.1 depicts the history of server-side logic.

FIGURE 6.1.

The evolution of server-side logic.

Evolution Of Web Technologies

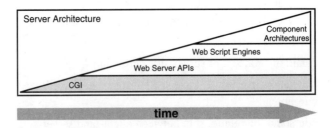

From Figure 6.1, you can see that CGI was the first common language for building interactive functionality into your Web pages. CGI provided a general way to respond to requests from the browser but was somewhat cryptic to use. A CGI program also is not very efficient in that it opens up a process in memory for each client request.

The creation of application programming interfaces, or APIs, opened more possibilities over the traditional use of CGI programs. APIs were more efficient than CGI programs because APIs execute processes in the same memory address space, eliminating the overhead of separate executing processes on one machine.

The main disadvantage to APIs was that they were proprietary in nature and harder to program. Scripting languages such as VBScript and JavaScript were developed to address the ease-of-use issues. With these languages, developers could quickly and easily build dynamic functionality and content into their applications. The tradeoff was performance, which created the answer that we have today—component-based architectures. With the advancement of tools such as Visual Basic, you can now place more robust business logic in components that are called from your server-side script. Components provide a robust and developer-friendly way to create a scalable application.

 Note
You will learn more about the use of components on Day 15, "Building an Integrated Solution with Components."

Exploring the Capabilities of Server-Side Script

Active Server Pages can be used as the main hub to control your server activity. You can code application-specific logic directly into an Active Server Page. This logic could be HTML as well as script code that changes the format of your Web pages.

Within an Active Server Page you can also include ActiveX and design-time controls that are built specifically to execute on the server. Active Server Pages can be integrated with objects on the server to provide robust application processing on the server. For example, you might interface with an object on the server that processes financial data and then returns the results through an Active Server Page. You also can place your database connections in Active Server Pages.

The development paradigm for Active Server Pages differs slightly from programming script on the client. If you remember from the lesson on client-side script on Day 5, "Enhancing Your Web Page Through Client-Side Script," the script that you develop for the client is embedded within the Web page that is sent to the browser. The browser executes the script based on system and user events. The browser must support the use of the particular scripting language to execute the code. If the browser doesn't recognize the script language, it will ignore the code.

6

In addition, not all Web servers support Active Server Pages. Of course, Microsoft's Internet Information Server (IIS) does support Active Server Pages. In fact, Active Server Pages were first introduced with IIS version 3. IIS contains a scripting engine that processes embedded Active Server script on the server. The results are returned to the client in a standard HTML format that is universally recognized by the browser. Because results are returned to the browser in standard HTML, any browser can read Active Server Pages. This powerful feature enables you to develop and deploy applications with Active Server Pages to all users on the Internet or intranet, regardless of browser type.

Exploring the Client/Server Picture

Active Server Pages are an important part of your application. You can use Active Server Pages to create more intelligent server-side processing that handles the specific needs of your application. Active Server Pages are a central piece of the Web-based client/server model for your application. Figure 6.2 demonstrates the role of an Active Server Page in the overall scheme of a Web-based application.

FIGURE 6.2.

Playing an active part in the client/server picture.

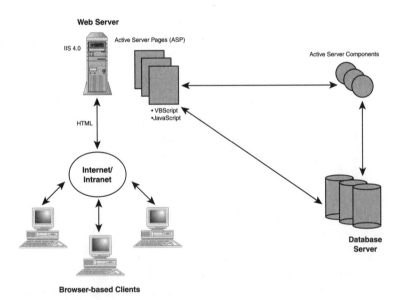

Active Server Pages reside on the Web server and play an active part in the functionality of your application. First, you can return dynamic Web pages to the client based on the preferences entered by the user. The ASP also can interface through the Component Object Model (COM) with Active Server Components. These components are applications that you develop using a more robust language such as Visual Basic, Visual C++, or

Java. These components are compiled as executable (EXE) or dynamic link library (DLL) programs that handle the detailed processing of the application. You will learn more about working with and developing these components on Day 15.

Also in Figure 6.2, you should notice the database component of the application. You can use Active Server Pages to directly interface with the database. The other alternative is to use a COM-based component that is called from an ASP to handle the database processing. For database-intensive processes and transaction processing, you will probably want to use the power of a language such as Visual Basic or Visual C++ to build these middle-tier business objects to interface with your database.

Tip

When deciding whether to access the database directly from your Active Server Pages or from a component, you may want to use the following rule of thumb. If your database access and processing logic takes up more than 20-30 lines of script code, it's probably a good idea to create a separate Active Server Component to handle the database access and processing logic.

Note

The concepts presented in this lesson are sometimes referred to as *multitier architectures*. For example, in a classic client/server application, the user interface or presentation tier accessed a relational database or data service. This access normally occurred over a local network. You could say that this type of application uses a two-tier architecture. Web applications utilize HTML and ASP to present information to users, multiple Active Server Components to provide processing logic, and relational databases to provide data services. Usually, the public Internet or private intranet is used to connect the various tiers involved with the application.

Understanding Active Server Pages

6

Active Server Pages can contain both script and HTML. Visual InterDev includes scripting engines for both VBScript and JavaScript.

To select the default scripting language for your Active Server Pages, first open the property pages for your script page by selecting the Property Pages menu option from the View menu. You should see a dialog box like the one in Figure 6.3.

FIGURE 6.3.

Choosing a default scripting language.

In the Property Pages dialog box, you will see a Default Scripting Language section with two drop-down list boxes. The Server list box represents the default language for your server-side scripts. The Client list box represents the default language for your client-side scripts. Select the drop-down list box for the Server, and you will see two choices in the list—VBScript and JavaScript (ECMAScript). At this point, you can select the scripting language that you are most comfortable with.

Note

You may be asking yourself, what is ECMAScript? ECMAScript represents the ECMA-approved standard for the JavaScript language. Microsoft's implementation of ECMAScript is known as JScript.

Visual InterDev formats a line of your ASP to denote the type of scripting language that is being used. This is similar to the way that client-side script is recognized in an HTML file. The following code example demonstrates an ASP that uses VBScript for the ASP scripting language:

```
<%@LANGUAGE="VBSCRIPT"%>
```

You can include both client- and server-side script in an Active Server Page. The client-side script is passed to the client along with the HTML and executes within the context of the browser. The HTML may also contain references to client-side objects such as ActiveX controls or intrinsic HTML controls.

Creating Your First Active Server Page

Your choices for scripting languages include VBScript, JScript, Perl, and other scripting languages. Active Server Pages enable you to interface with ActiveX Server Components and interact with your database.

You can use the HTML Source Editor in Visual InterDev to create and maintain these pages. To create an Active Server Page, complete the following steps:

1. Select the project name in the Project Explorer and click the right mouse button to reveal the shortcut menu.

2. Choose Add, Active Server Page. The project directory for your files also is displayed as the default location to place your new page.

3. Select ASP Page from the options and enter a name for the Active Server Page as demonstrated in Figure 6.4.

FIGURE 6.4.

Creating an Active Server Page.

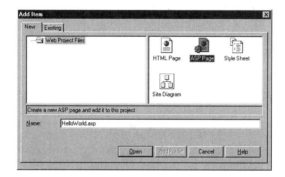

4. When finished, click Open to create your first Active Server Page.

You should now be looking at an ASP similar to the one shown in Figure 6.5.

FIGURE 6.5.

A sample Active Server Page.

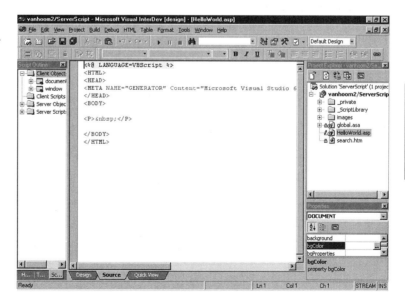

The format of this page is practically the same as an HTML page. The scripting language is denoted at the top of the document. The page contains a Header, Title, and Body section. Comments are included so that you know where to place your HTML code.

> **Tip**
>
> As a general guideline, you should not intersperse HTML with script code. In other words, try to uniquely group your script code and your HTML code.

Adding the Content and Server Script

Now that you have created the page, the next step is to add content and scripting logic so that the page can come alive. For your first ASP, you will build the classic Hello World application. The following steps will guide you through the process:

1. Enter `My first ASP` for the title of the page.

2. Enter the following code after the `<P></P>` tags:
   ```
   <%For i = 3 to 7 %>
   <FONT SIZE = <%=i%>>
   Hello World!<BR>
   <FONT>
   <%Next %>
   ```

3. Save the file by selecting File, Save `HellowWorld.asp`.

4. Click the file in the Project Explorer and choose View in Browser (or Browse With if you are using a browser other than Internet Explorer) to view the results.

You should now be looking at a page like the one displayed in Figure 6.6.

This ASP utilizes server-side script to create a dynamic rendition of Hello World. Listing 6.1 displays the source code that is sent to the client browser.

FIGURE 6.6.

A dynamic Hello World page.

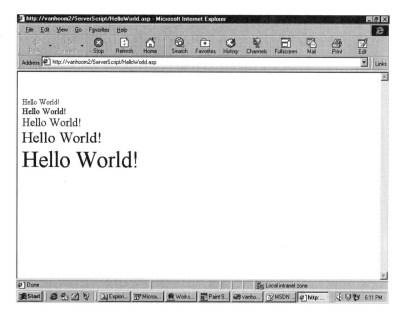

LISTING 6.1. VIEWING THE SOURCE FOR THE CLIENT.

```
 1: <HTML>
 2: <HEAD>
 3: <META NAME="GENERATOR" Content="Microsoft Visual Studio 6.0">
 4: </HEAD>
 5: <BODY>
 6:
 7: <P> </P>
 8:
 9: <FONT SIZE = 3>
10: Hello World!<BR>
11: <FONT>
12:
13: <FONT SIZE = 4>
14: Hello World!<BR>
15: <FONT>
16:
17: <FONT SIZE = 5>
18: Hello World!<BR>
19: <FONT>
20:
21: <FONT SIZE = 6>
22: Hello World!<BR>
23: <FONT>
```

6

continues

LISTING 6.1. CONTINUED

```
24:
25: <FONT SIZE = 7>
26: Hello World!<BR>
27: <FONT>
28:
29:
30: </BODY>
31: </HTML>
```

The interesting thing about the listing is that no script exists within the code that is sent to the browser. The server-side script manipulates the page dynamically, processes on the server, and then distributes pure HTML down to the client. In this way, you can create a dynamic Web page that is browser-agnostic—a Web page that is indifferent to and works with all browsers. The only requirement for this code to work is that you have a Web server that supports the appropriate scripting engine for the script language that you use in your application.

Using Server Script in Your Application

Now that you have created a simple ASP page with server-side script, let's see how you can employ these same techniques in a typical application. The next sections will walk you through the process of creating an HTML form that calls an ASP page to process its results.

Creating the Form

You will begin by creating an HTML form that enables you to enter your name and favorite basketball team. Complete the following steps to accomplish this task:

1. Create an HTML file named InputForm.

2. Using the Design Editor, drag and drop the HTML Form control from the Toolbox onto the page. The form control is located within the HTML section of the Toolbox.

3. Drag and drop the following HTML controls onto the page: Textbox, Listbox, and Submit Button. Your page should now look like the one picture in Figure 6.7.

FIGURE 6.7.

Viewing the basic HTML controls.

FIGURE 6.7.

Viewing the basic HTML controls.

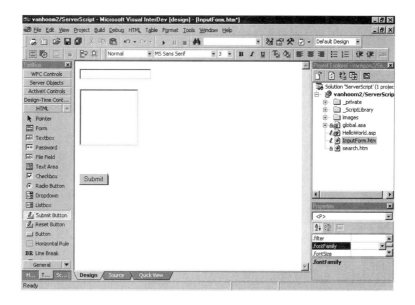

4. Right-click the mouse on the Listbox control and choose the Property Page for this control, thereby displaying the window shown in Figure 6.8.

FIGURE 6.8.

The Listbox property page.

This dialog box enables you to graphically set the properties for the Listbox, including the name of the control, the display size, and the items that will display in the list. You can also allow the user to select multiple items from the list.

5. Change the name of the control to lstTeams.

6. Click Insert. You can then enter the items and their values into the Options for the SELECT tag section. (See Table 6.1 for the items and values to enter.)

6

TABLE 6.1. PROPERTY TABLE FOR THE LISTBOX CONTROL.

Text	Value
Suns	Suns
Spurs	Spurs
Rockets	Rockets
Lakers	Lakers
Jazz	Jazz
Heat	Heat
Cavaliers	Cavaliers
Bulls	Bulls

Tip

After you enter the Text and Value, click Insert to add the item to the list. The arrows located to the right of the list box enable you to change the arrangement of the items in the list. The Delete button at the bottom of the dialog window enables you to delete an individual item from the list.

7. After you enter all the SELECT tag options, click OK. You will be returned to the Design Editor and see a list box full of the values that you entered.

8. Select the Textbox control and choose Properties from the shortcut menu. Your cursor will be placed in the Properties window, allowing you to change attributes of the control.

9. Change the Name and the ID of the control to txtName.

10. Switch to the Source editor and enter the name ProcessForm.asp for the ACTION attribute of the form. This tells the form which ASP file will be used to process the form.

11. Save the HTML file.

12. View the HTML page in your browser. You should see a Web page that looks similar to the one depicted in Figure 6.9.

From this page, you can enter your name and select a favorite NBA basketball team from the list. You now need to create the ASP to process this form.

FIGURE 6.9.

Viewing the HTML form in the browser.

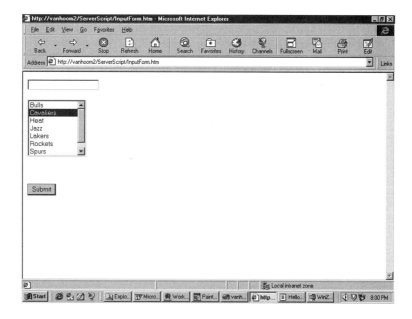

Creating the Active Server Page

The ASP in this simple application will process the values that are entered in the form and display them back to the user through a new page in the browser. To create the ASP, complete the following steps:

1. Create an Active Server Page as you did for the Hello World application earlier today. Enter ProcessForm for the name of the ASP.

2. Enter the following code within the ASP file:

```
Welcome, <%=Request.Form ("txtName")%>.
Your favorite NBA basketball team is <%=Request.Form
➥("lstTeams")%>!
```

Note   You will learn about the Request object as well as the other ASP objects on Day 11, "Fundamentals of Active Server Pages."

6

3. Save the file.

You are now ready to use the application. Select the input form in the Project Explorer and view it in your browser. Enter your name and select a team from the list. If your team is not listed, choose my favorite team—the Rockets. You can then click Submit to process your selections. You should see a page similar to the one shown in Figure 6.10.

FIGURE 6.10.

Viewing the results of your choices.

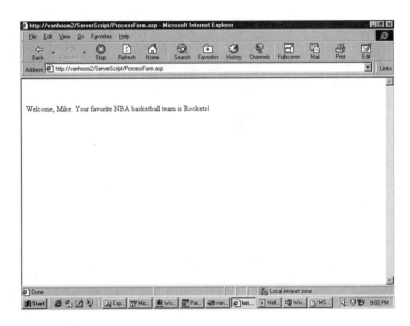

Taking a Closer Look at the Process

This section explores how a browser interacts with an Active Server Page. First, the Web page references an Active Server Page within the context of the application. Active Server Pages contain the filename extension of `.asp`. The following line of code demonstrates an example of calling an Active Server Page:

```
<FORM METHOD= "POST" ACTION="ProcessForm.asp">
```

When the browser requests the ASP, the file is first processed by the server. The ASP may contain both HTML and scripting code. Any HTML code is passed directly to the browser as well as any client-side script. The server then searches for any server-side script. Similar to script on the client, server-side script is denoted by the symbols <% and %>. Upon locating the server-side code, the server processes the script and returns the results to the browser in the form of HTML. The server processes the script based on the current conditions and events. This model gives your application its unique and dynamic nature. The Web page that is formatted is based on conditions that are dynamic and changing, instead of a static HTML file that resides on the server. These conditions could be based on user input as well as information that is contained in a database.

Integrating Client and Server Script

In order to create a complete application, you should incorporate both client- and server-side script. Yesterday you learned how to use client-side script to perform validation routines for fields and controls on your Web page. You will use these principles and apply them to our input application to make it complete. You will use the Script Outline to add the necessary client-side script. The following steps will guide your through this process:

1. Open the `InputForm.htm` file in the Source Editor.
2. Click the Script Outline to view the client and server objects and scripts.
3. Open the Client Objects and Events folder.
4. Click the `Form1` object to expand its objects and events.
5. Click the `Submit1` object to expand its events.
6. Double-click the `onclick` event. This action will create a function shell for the event as shown in Figure 6.11.

FIGURE 6.11.

Adding event code for the Submit pushbutton.

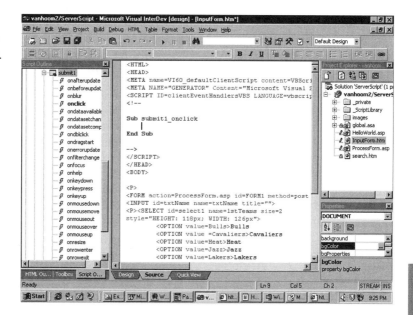

7. Add the following code for the `onclick` event to make sure that the user enters a name into the text box:

```
If FORM1.txtName.value = "" Then
MsgBox "Please Enter Your Name"
End If
```

8. Save your changes to this file.
9. Switch to Quick View to see how the new client-side script works.

10. Select a team without entering a name and click Submit. You should see a message box prompting you to enter a name, as illustrated in Figure 6.12.

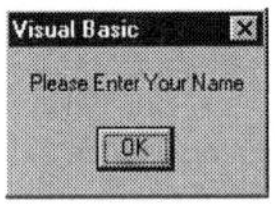

FIGURE 6.12.

Validating that the user entered a name.

Summary

Today's lesson has provided a good introduction into the world of server-side script. Combined with yesterday's lesson, you are now armed with some basic fundamentals that will serve you well throughout the rest of this book.

Let's review some of the basic concepts that you learned today. First, you learned what server-side script is and how it can be used within an Active Server Page. You gained a historical perspective on the evolution of Web server technologies and how ASPs and component-based architectures are crucial to the success of your application. You also learned how ASPs execute within the context of a Web-based application.

Next, you created your first Active Server Page—the Hello World application. This example gave you a perspective on how server-side script can be used to dynamically generate HTML that is then sent to the browser.

Toward the end of the day, you learned how to create a basic input form and use an ASP page to process the user's input. You also learned how to combine client- and server-side script into the application. The rest of the lessons will build on these foundational concepts and allow you to build more robust applications.

Q&A

Q Can I view Active Server Pages with my Netscape browser?

A Yes. Because Active Server Pages distribute only standard HTML to the browser, you can use any browser, including Netscape, to view an Active Server Page. If you choose to send client-side script within an ASP, you need to make sure that the browser supports the scripting language that you are using.

Q Can I include HTML and script within an ASP page?

A Yes. Active Server Pages support the inclusion of HTML objects and forms, client- and server-side script, ActiveX objects and components, Java applets, and text. During today's lesson, you learned how to call an ASP from an HTML form. During Weeks 2 and 3, you learn how to create ASPs that include all these objects.

Q Which scripting languages does Visual InterDev support?

A Visual InterDev supports the generation and use of JScript and VBScript. You can also obtain other scripting engines for languages such as Perl to use in your Active Server Pages.

Workshop

The Workshop provides quiz questions to help you solidify your understanding of the material covered. The exercises provide you with experience in using what you've learned. You can find the answers to the quiz questions and exercises in Appendix B, "Answers."

Quiz

1. What is the difference between client- and server-side script?
2. What are some advantages of Active Server Pages?
3. What is the default editor for Active Server Pages?
4. What is the name of the Visual InterDev feature that helps you build the script for your objects and events?

Exercise

Change the input form application so that the message displays not only the user preferences but also the date and time.

6

DAY 7

Integrating Objects into Your Applications

Today you explore more advanced objects and controls. The objects and controls that are discussed in this lesson enable you to build a more effective and interactive interface for the user. By using these objects on your Web pages, you can design a Web-based application that offers the interactivity and features (such as expandable and hierarchical Explorer-style menus and right-click context menus) that users expect from their non-Internet applications.

Some of the topics that you'll be covering today are

- An overview of objects.
- What is a Java applet?
- What is an ActiveX control?
- A comparison of the pros and cons of Java applets and ActiveX controls.
- Using ActiveX controls and Visual InterDev to create a Web application.

Defining Objects

A *programming object* is a set of computer code that contains both data and actions that affect that data. The data that an object contains is called *attributes* or *properties*. The actions that affect that data are called *methods*. For a real-world example, take a tree; a tree is an object. A tree has attributes, such as height. A tree also has actions that affect its attributes, such as growing. Similarly, in the programming world, a database recordset is an object. A recordset has attributes, such as the EOF (end of file) flag. It also has actions that affect its attributes, such as `MoveNext`.

In the programming world, objects facilitate interaction between the user and your application. You can use objects and controls to complement, supplement, and complete your application interface.

Note

During today's lesson as well as future lessons, I use the terms *objects* and *controls* almost synonymously to refer to items that are placed on a Web page to enable the user to perform some function. Where necessary, I explicitly cite items referred to solely as an object or a control.

Now that you understand the definition of an object, it's time to examine two of the most common types of objects, Java applets and ActiveX controls.

Introduction to Java Applets

Java applets are an important part of the Internet; they are everywhere and are an effective way of providing a useful and pleasing user interface for Web applications. Java applets are derived from the Java programming language developed by Sun Microsystems, Inc. The biggest benefit of the Java language is its support for cross-platform development. You can develop an applet or application with Java to support different client platforms. The Java program will, in theory, execute in the same manner on both the Windows 95 platform and an Apple Macintosh, for example.

Note

Today's lesson focuses on the explanation, use, and integration of objects such as Java applets and ActiveX controls into your Visual InterDev application. It's beyond the scope of this book to teach you how to build a Java applet.

How Do Java Applets Work?

Applets are embedded in a Web page and execute within the context of a browser. The browser must support Java to be able to execute the program.

First, a user requests a certain Web page. The HTML document is sent from the Web server to the browser on the client machine. If the browser detects a Java applet embedded in the document, the browser requests the individual applet from the Web server. The browser detects the applet by discovering the <APPLET> tag within the HTML document. The <APPLET> tag is covered in the next section.

The applet is distributed to the client machine in the form of bytecodes. Then the Java virtual machine (JVM) on the client interprets these bytecodes and executes the applet program. Figure 7.1 visually depicts this process.

FIGURE 7.1.

Executing a Java applet.

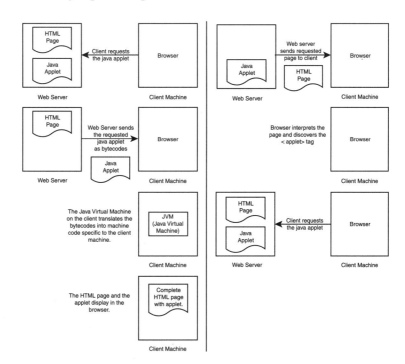

Note

Java bytecodes are a set of machine codes that are not specific to any particular processor or computer. The Java virtual machine, however, is specific to a particular type of processor. It interprets the generic bytecodes to processor-specific code.

7

Here are the steps to execute a Java applet embedded in a Web page:

1. The client requests an HTML page from a Web server.
2. The Web server sends the HTML page to the client.
3. The browser on the client interprets the HTML page and discovers the <APPLET> tag.
4. The client requests the applet referenced in the <APPLET> tag from the Web server.
5. The Web server sends the requested applet to the client in the form of Java byte-codes.
6. The Java virtual machine on the client translates the Java bytecodes into machine-specific code.
7. The HTML page is displayed and the Java applet is executed inside the client's browser.

Understanding Java Applets

The basic tag to define an applet is the <APPLET> tag. This tag is supported by the HTML 3.2 standard and enables you to insert an applet into an HTML document. The syntax for using the <APPLET> tag is as follows:

```
<APPLET [CODEBASE=URL] CODE=applet [ALT=alternate text]
[NAME=appletInstanceName] WIDTH=nPixels HEIGHT=nPixels
[ALIGN=alignment] [VSPACE=nPixels] [HSPACE=nPixels]>
```

As you can tell from the syntax, the only parameters required for inserting an applet into a Web page are the CODE, WIDTH, and HEIGHT attributes. The following sections explain each of these parameters.

 Note

The <APPLET> tag is the HTML standard for referencing Java applets. Microsoft's browser, Internet Explorer, supports the use of the <OBJECT> tag for inserting Java applets into a Web page. The <OBJECT> tag is covered in a later section titled "ActiveX Overview." Keep in mind that if you're using Internet Explorer, you can use either tag to insert a Java applet into a Web page.

CODEBASE

The CODEBASE attribute is an optional parameter that enables you to specify the URL location of the applet code. The browser uses the Web page document's URL by default if this parameter isn't included. The browser uses this parameter to locate the code for the applet after it realizes that the Web page document contains an applet.

CODE

The CODE attribute indicates the name of the compiled applet program to be used with the Web page. The syntax for referencing the applet is as follows:

```
<APPLET CODE=Applet.class>
```

Notice that the applet has a suffix of .class. This suffix is the standard naming convention for Java applets. In this example, Applet.class represents the applet code that will be executed within the context of the browser. The file must be located either in the same directory as the HTML document or in the URL directory that you specify using the CODEBASE attribute.

ALT

The ALT attribute enables you to provide alternative text to display for browsers that cannot execute Java applets. This attribute is an optional parameter for the <APPLET> tag. In these cases, the browser understands the <APPLET> tag and recognizes its inability to process the applet code. Given this scenario, the browser uses the ALT attribute to present the alternative text to the user. The value of this attribute is a string of text enclosed within quotes, as shown in the following line of code:

```
<APPLET CODE=Applet.class ALT=I'm sorry. I don't do JAVA!>
```

NAME

The NAME attribute is an optional parameter that enables you to specify an instance name for the applet. This attribute is useful for Web pages that include multiple applets on the same page. The instance name is used by scripting code to reference the Web page applet and its attributes.

WIDTH and HEIGHT

The WIDTH attribute is used to specify the width of the display area for the applet measured in number of pixels. The HEIGHT attribute indicates the height of the applet display area and also is measured in number of pixels. These parameters are required. The following line of code provides an example of specifying the width and height for an applet:

```
<APPLET CODE=Applet.class WIDTH=250 HEIGHT=200>
```

ALIGN

You can use the ALIGN attribute to indicate the alignment for the applet. This attribute is an optional parameter of the <APPLET> tag. The valid values for this attribute include left, right, middle, absmiddle, texttop, baseline, bottom, and absbottom. The ALIGN attribute and its alignment values are similar in nature to that of images. You can

7

use the ALIGN attribute to specify the layout and alignment of the applet in relation to the rest of the content for the Web page.

VSPACE and HSPACE

The VSPACE attribute defines spacing in terms of pixels above and below the applet. The HSPACE attribute defines spacing to the left and right of the applet. The HSPACE attribute also is measured in terms of pixels. These attributes are similar to their <IMG> tag brethren.

Using Parameters with Java Applets

Most applets use parameters to establish values for the applet's properties and attributes. You can supply these parameters when the applet is loaded into the Web page. The syntax for supplying applet parameters is as follows:

```
<PARAM NAME=appletParamName VALUE=appletParamValue>
```

appletParamName is the name of a parameter for the applet, and appletParamValue is the value to be supplied to the applet. The following code sample demonstrates an example of using parameters with an applet:

```
<APPLET CODE="MoreHelloApplet.class" WIDTH=200 HEIGHT=50>
 <PARAM NAME=name VALUE="Reader">
```

This example uses a hello world applet and defines the width and height to 200 and 50 pixels, respectively. The MoreHelloApplet applet contains the Name parameter, which is set to Reader in the example.

ActiveX Overview

You can use ActiveX controls to build a dynamic and interactive interface for your client/server or Web-based application. These controls are ideal for using over the Internet and the Web. ActiveX controls basically enable you to provide a dynamic interface for a user to interact with your application. ActiveX controls are similar in purpose to Java applets and HTML form controls. In fact, some ActiveX controls have the same name as the HTML form controls that you learned about yesterday. ActiveX controls are much more robust.

Understanding ActiveX Controls

Many ActiveX controls exist on the market. These controls have been developed by Microsoft as well as third-party software vendors. Independent developers such as yourself also have developed their own custom ActiveX controls and made them available for use by Web and client/server developers. ActiveX controls can be inserted into a Web page using the <OBJECT> tag. The attributes and parameters to include an ActiveX control into a Web page differ slightly for each control, but Table 7.1 outlines the basic attributes that can be used to define all ActiveX controls.

TABLE 7.1. THE <OBJECT> TAG ATTRIBUTES FOR ACTIVEX CONTROLS.

Attribute	Description
CLASSID	Unique identifier for the ActiveX control
ID	Instance name of the ActiveX control
HEIGHT	Specifies the height of the control
WIDTH	Specifies the width of the control
ALIGN	Specifies the alignment and placement of the control
HSPACE	Defines the left and right margin around the control
VSPACE	Defines the top and bottom margin around the control

The following sections explain each of the attributes for the <OBJECT> tag.

CLASSID

The CLASSID attribute represents the key to unlocking the power of an ActiveX control. The CLASSID, or class identifier, explains the implementation of the control to the browser. In other words, the CLASSID helps the browser identify the type of control contained within the Web page. After the ActiveX control has been identified, the browser realizes the characteristics and behavior of the control.

Every ActiveX control contains a unique class identifier. The CLASSID consists of characters and numbers. The following example displays the class identifier for a calendar control:

```
classid=clsid:8E27C92B-1264-101C-8A2F-040224009C02
```

You may be wondering how the browser can interpret these characters. The CLASSID is linked to an entry in the Windows Registry. The entry in the Registry, in turn, points to the code for the ActiveX control.

Tip

> You can locate the CLASSID by its filename in the Windows Registry under HKEY_CLASSES_ROOT. You also can look in the CLSID section of HKEY_CLASSES_ROOT in the Registry.

7

You also can use the CODEBASE attribute that was discussed in the previous section concerning Java applets to specify the location of an ActiveX control. Remember, this attribute enables you to indicate a URL address location for the object. In the case of ActiveX controls, the browser downloads the ActiveX control to the Web page. As the browser downloads the ActiveX control, the control automatically registers itself on the client machine.

 Note

> The more popular browsers enable you to designate what kind of controls and content can be executed on the client machine. These browser security options control the ability of an ActiveX control to register itself and run on the client machine.

ID

The ID attribute refers to the instance of the object. You use the ID attribute to refer to and access the properties and methods of the control within your code. The ID provides a name for you to use when communicating with the control.

HEIGHT and WIDTH

These attributes are similar to the HEIGHT and WIDTH attributes that are used with the <APPLET> tag. The HEIGHT and WIDTH attributes for the <OBJECT> tag enable you to specify the size for the ActiveX control. The area that you specify defines the size of the placeholder for the control on the Web page. You can designate the value of both the HEIGHT and WIDTH attributes in number of pixels as depicted in the following example:

WIDTH=240 HEIGHT=240

You also can specify the attributes as a percentage of the screen size, as denoted in the following example:

WIDTH=50% HEIGHT=50%

ALIGN

The ALIGN attribute enables you to design the alignment of the control in relation to the rest of the content on the page. You can use most of the same values that you used for the similar Java applet attribute. The valid values for this attribute include left, right, top, middle, absmiddle, texttop, center, baseline, bottom, and absbottom. The ALIGN attribute and its alignment values are similar in nature to that of images.

HSPACE and VSPACE

The VSPACE attribute defines spacing in terms of pixels above and below the ActiveX control. The HSPACE attribute defines spacing to the left and right of the control. The HSPACE attribute also is measured in terms of pixels. These attributes are similar in nature to their applet counterparts. You can specify the values for these attributes in terms of a percentage of the screen.

Using Parameters with ActiveX Controls

Just like Java applets, you can use parameters to specify certain values for an ActiveX control. The format for the PARAM attribute is the same as the syntax for the <APPLET> tag. The syntax for setting the value of ActiveX control parameters is as follows:

```
<PARAM NAME=objectParamName VALUE=objectParamValue>
```

objectParamName is the name of the parameter, and objectParamValue specifies the value for the parameter.

Using the Attributes to Define an ActiveX Control

Now that you have learned about the attributes for an ActiveX control, it's time to look at an example of a calendar control. The following example shows the definition for a calendar control:

```
<OBJECT classid=clsid:8E27C92B-1264-101C-8A2F-040224009C02 id=
➥Calendar1 style="LEFT: 0px; TOP: 0px">
<PARAM NAME="BackColor" VALUE="-2147483633">
<PARAM NAME="Year" VALUE="1998">
<PARAM NAME="Month" VALUE="2">
<PARAM NAME="Day" VALUE="22">
</OBJECT>
```

This example demonstrates an object declaration for a calendar control. You can see that the ID attribute is set to Calendar1. The first line of the declaration depicts the CLASSID for the calendar control. I think you'll agree that Calendar1 is much more intuitive than CLSID: 8E27C92B-1264-101C-8A2F-040224009C02. In this example, four parameters also are depicted for the calendar control. ActiveX controls can be implemented with a variety of parameters. You can assign values to these parameters, which supply attributes and characteristics that help define the appearance and behavior of a control.

ActiveX Versus Java

7

You'll probably use both technologies to develop your Web-based application. Both Java applets and ActiveX controls have a place and purpose in your application. Each technology offers important benefits, which you'll explore next.

Exploring the Qualities of ActiveX

ActiveX controls, which enable you to construct interactive Web-based applications, have two main strengths. First, there are many different types of ActiveX controls that give you unique, effective ways to distribute and gather information from the user. These controls range from standard GUI controls, such as the command button and text box, to the more robust Web-based controls, such as the RealAudio control. You can use these ActiveX controls to create an effective user interface and metaphor for your application. ActiveX controls offer more robust objects and features than intrinsic HTML controls, which are somewhat limited in capabilities.

The second main advantage of ActiveX controls is their ability to integrate with other components on the desktop and the server. This feature can also be a disadvantage, as I will discuss in the next section, "Examining the Drawbacks of ActiveX." Because ActiveX controls are built by using Microsoft's Component Object Model (COM), you can integrate the controls with other components, such as a Microsoft Word document, Excel spreadsheet, or any other component that supports COM. This feature opens up new possibilities when you're designing your Web-based application.

Many people are converting their document information produced with proprietary software to the open HTML format for publishing on the Web. With ActiveX controls, you can integrate these documents into your application and avoid the conversion process. Much as you can embed a spreadsheet into a Word document by using object linking and embedding (OLE), ActiveX controls give you a new model with less overhead to do the same task. You don't have to convert all the proprietary information. Instead, you can use ActiveX to embed this information into your Web-based application. The browser remains the universal client for your application. Your application interface incorporates the COM object into the Web page, enabling the user to interact with the spreadsheet, graph, or document within the browser.

Examining the Drawbacks of ActiveX

Drawbacks of ActiveX controls include

- Potentially high security risks
- Currently, client platforms limited to Microsoft Windows platforms

As already stated, one of the main benefits of ActiveX is also a potential disadvantage. The ability of ActiveX controls to interact with the file system and other components on the client and server machines is a potential security hazard for malicious controls.

ActiveX controls rely on neutral third-party services to verify their reliability, or trustworthiness. These services attach a digital certificate to ActiveX controls that they deem safe for download and use. Your browser can identify and read these certificates. If a certificate is present, the browser can download the ActiveX control with the assurance that it won't engage in some harmful activity, such as corrupting your file system.

With Microsoft Internet Explorer, you can set specific levels of Internet security for downloading ActiveX controls as an additional safeguard. Trust verification is a fairly reliable safeguard to ensure the reliability of ActiveX controls; however, it's not airtight and could result in a corrupt ActiveX control being downloaded to your system. If a malicious ActiveX control masks its way through the process, the potential damage can be disastrous, but the reliability of the verification process makes the chance of this happening very slim.

ActiveX controls are targeted toward the Microsoft Windows platform, which can be a disadvantage if your application is going to be used across multiple platforms. Microsoft has transferred the ActiveX specifications to the Open Group in an effort to make the technology more acceptable and compatible across multiple platforms. The Open Group will provide an impartial consortium of vendors to oversee the expansion of the ActiveX technology and help address the cross-platform issues surrounding ActiveX controls. Recently there have been reports that COM, which includes ActiveX, will soon run on UNIX.

ActiveX controls, because they are based on Microsoft-defined technology, are best supported by Microsoft Internet Explorer. However, third-party vendors, such as Ncompass, have ActiveX plug-ins available that allow other browsers to support and run ActiveX controls.

Exploring the Qualities of Java

Java offers the promise of a true cross-platform development language. Two main advantages of Java are its support for multiple platforms and its security. Java's multiple-platform support includes Microsoft Windows, Apple Macintosh, and Sun Solaris, to name just a few; this support is built into the language. In theory, Java executes the same way across all the supported platforms because of its neutral implementation design. This approach means that programs such as Java applets and applications behave in the same manner regardless of the platform. With this feature, you can create Web-based applications that use Java applets and applications and without worrying about different end-user machines.

Another advantage of Java is its security. Java applets downloaded to your browser have to "play within the sandbox." The sandbox is your browser; applets cannot access your file system or other objects on your computer without your explicit permission. You can use the Security Manager to manipulate the level of file access an applet can have, and

7

you can even choose to provide no file access at all. Also, the Java virtual machine offers a systematic bytecode verification process. The JVM makes sure that the language adheres to Java standards and that the program hasn't been altered since its compilation. These security measures help ensure the safety of your Java-based application.

Examining the Limitations of Java

Although Java touts itself as being more secure, it's definitely more limited than ActiveX controls in desktop integration. Java doesn't offer the same robust features that ActiveX does when it comes to integrating desktop applications such as Excel or Word. Java's security model contributes to its limited file system access.

Java's cross-platform support prevents it from taking advantage of platform-specific features in your applications. For instance, Java applets don't offer the same choices as ActiveX controls do for your application interface. In some ways, Java sacrifices capabilities for portability.

Another slight disadvantage of Java applets compared to ActiveX controls is that applets must be downloaded to the browser every time the page in which they are embedded is accessed. ActiveX controls have to be downloaded only once. After ActiveX controls are registered on your machine, they are available for quick and easy use. Pages containing many Java applets may download slower than a page containing many similar ActiveX controls.

If you want to build a Web-based application that can be easily executed across multiple platforms, you might want to use Java applets throughout your application. However, if you've decided that Windows will be your deployment platform of choice, you can then consider a more heavy dose of ActiveX. You'll probably use both technologies to construct your Web-based application.

It's beyond the scope of this book to go into detail about how to build your own ActiveX controls or Java applets. For the rest of the chapter, you will concentrate on ActiveX controls and how to integrate them into your Web page.

Inserting an ActiveX Control into a Web Page

So far, you have learned about the tags and attributes that enable you to define Java applets and ActiveX controls. The previous example demonstrated how to use the <OBJECT> tag to define an ActiveX control. You might be thinking, "Visual InterDev should provide an easier way to define a control rather than using tags and attributes.

After all, the name of the tool is VISUAL InterDev." Don't worry, Visual InterDev lives up to its name regarding the integration of controls into your Web pages. Visual InterDev has a very visual and intuitive method for placing controls on your Web page.

On the toolbox in Visual InterDev, you'll notice an ActiveX Controls tab. This tab lists all the ActiveX controls currently available for use in your workspace.

Note

Java applets are also listed on this tab of the toolbox. Java applets are distinguishable from ActiveX controls on this tab by their icon. The icon for all Java applets looks like the planet Earth behind a browser.

You can add registered ActiveX controls to your toolbox by right-clicking in the toolbox. Then select Customize Toolbox from the pop-up menu. Click the ActiveX Controls tab and check all the controls you'd like included in your toolbox. Click OK and the controls will be added to your toolbox.

Note

Follow the same steps listed above to add Java applets or design-time controls to your toolbox. Select Customize Toolbox from the pop-up menu. Then, to add applets, click the Applets tab; to add design-time controls, click the Design-Time Controls tab after.

You can insert an ActiveX control into a Web page by dragging the desired control from the toolbox onto your page (see Figure 7.2). When you insert a control onto your page, you probably won't see an object tag anywhere in the source code for your page. You'll see a visual representation of the control. You may find this visual representation more intuitive and easier to read than the HTML <OBJECT> and <PARAM> tags. If, however, you want or need to see the HTML tags associated with an object, right-click the object and select View Text to display the HTML. If you'd like to switch back to the visual representation of the control, you can right-click the word VIEWASTEXT found inside the <OBJECT> tag. Then select View Graphical from the pop-up menu.

Now you'll begin constructing the sample application. You'll build the front end of a Timesheet application that will enable users to enter the project they worked on, the date they worked on it, and the number of hours they worked on it. For this application you'll use a prebuilt ActiveX control, the Calendar control.

7

FIGURE 7.2.

Inserting an ActiveX control into your page.

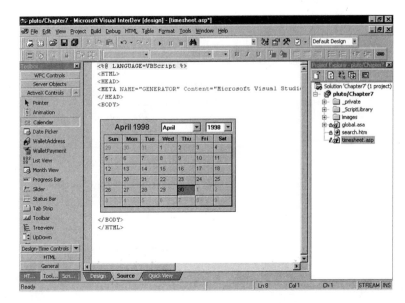

Here are the steps to begin building this application:

1. Create a new .asp page.
2. Select the Calendar control from the toolbox.
3. Drag the Calendar control from the toolbox onto your new ASP page.

Editing the Properties of an ActiveX Control

To edit the properties of an ActiveX control, right-click the mouse on that control. Select Property Pages from the shortcut menu. You can then change the properties for the control by changing values on the various property tabs and saving the updates. The changes that you make will be reflected in the Web page. Figure 7.3 shows the Property Pages dialog box for the Calendar control.

FIGURE 7.3.

Setting the properties for the Calendar control.

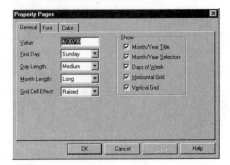

Continuing with the Timesheet application, edit the properties of the Calendar control. Follow these steps:

1. Right-click the Calendar control.

2. Select Edit Properties from the pop-up menu.

3. On the General tab, change the Month Length to Short. This will change the display from February to Feb.

4. Click the OK button to save your change and close the Edit Properties dialog box.

Manipulating Methods to Achieve the Right Behavior

A method is a predefined procedure you can call to execute a specific function on or by your control. Each control consists of associated methods inherent to the control that you can use in your application. The method contains prepackaged code that enables you to extend the control's power. Methods also save precious development time because you don't have to custom-develop the code carried out by the method.

This is the syntax for calling a control's method:

```
ControlID.MethodName
```

In this code line, `ControlID` is the ID for the control and `MethodName` is the name of the method you're calling. For example, one of the methods for the calendar control is `Click`. The following line of code demonstrates how to call this method for a pushbutton called `objCalendar`:

```
objCalendar.Click
```

If an application executes the `Click` method, the `Click` event is triggered, executing any code in the procedure for that event. Remember, the `Click` event is typically initiated by the user. This example demonstrates how you can use a predefined method for the calendar control to simulate the same behavior in your application code.

 Note

> The purpose of this part of the lesson is to teach you how to use methods in your application, but it's beyond the scope of this lesson to cover each and every method for all the different types of controls. You will, however, learn the purpose and basic concepts of using methods that you can apply to any control you integrate into your application. After you understand these concepts, you can research the product documentation for the ActiveX controls you're using to learn about their explicit methods.

7

Using Methods in Your Application

In this section, you learn how to use some of the methods associated with the controls to create intelligent logic for your application.

Now you'll continue the Timesheet application by adding other controls and using those controls' methods to add functionality to our application. In Figure 7.4, I've added an ActiveX combo box, an ActiveX text box, and an ActiveX command button to the ASP page.

FIGURE 7.4.

Building the Timesheet application.

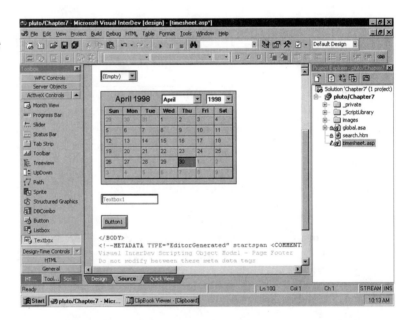

You might have noticed that although the basic combo box control has been constructed, there are no items in the list. The combo box control has a predefined method, AddItem, that you can use to populate its contents. This is the syntax for the AddItem method:

```
ComboBoxControlID.AddItem Item ¦varIndex
```

ComboBoxControlID is the ID, or name, of the control, Item is the information to be added to a row in the combo box, and varIndex specifies the row in the combo box to add the data. Both the Item and varIndex attributes are optional. You can enter a variable or a value enclosed in quotes for the Item attribute. If you don't specify a value for varIndex, the item is added to the last row of the combo box. The varIndex attribute for the beginning row of the combo box has a value of 0.

Listing 7.1 gives you the client-side code used by the Timesheet application to fill the contents of the combo box. Copy the following code into your ASP page.

Note

In this example you are using VBScript as the scripting language for your client-side script. It should be noted that Netscape browsers don't support VBScript. If you want your application to run on Netscape browsers or other browsers besides Microsoft Internet Explorer, all client-side script should be written in JavaScript or ECMAScript.

LISTING 7.1. POPULATING THE ITEMS IN THE COMBO BOX.

```
1: sub Window_Onload()
2: window.cmbProjects.AddItem "Acme",0
3: window.cmbProjects.AddItem "Blammo",1
4: window.cmbProjects.AddItem "MegaInc",2
5: end sub
```

This code example shows a procedure, Window_OnLoad(), that executes when the page is initially loaded. In this way, the user sees a list of items when the application opens, as shown in Figure 7.5.

FIGURE 7.5.

Giving the user choices.

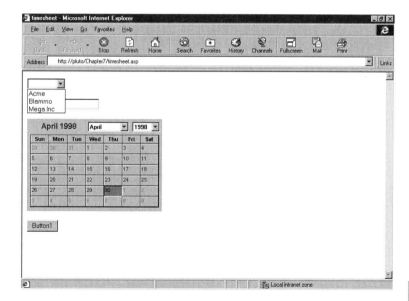

Note

You can also create an Active Server Page that creates the Web page and populates the contents of the combo box from rows in a database table.

7

Making Objects Come Alive with Script

Now that the control has been placed on the page, scripting code must be added to give the page its function. You can add scripting logic to both the client and server to meet your application's needs. Client-side logic can be used to provide user input validation and respond to user-initiated events.

For the purposes of this application, client-side script is used to validate the user input and to display a confirmation message to the user after the entry has been made.

This final part of today's material teaches you how to add more functions and features to the application by using client-side script. The Script Editor gives you a visual helper to implement scripting logic for your application.

Reviewing the Script Editor

For the purposes of the Timesheet application, client-side script needs to be added to supply user-entry validation and the code to display a confirmation message to the user. You can activate the Script Editor by selecting a specific control and right-clicking to open the shortcut menu. Next, choose Edit Script from the list of menu items. You can also activate the Script Editor by clicking the Script tab at the bottom of your workspace. Figure 7.6 shows the Script Editor open and ready for you to add your own scripting logic.

FIGURE 7.6.

The Script Editor.

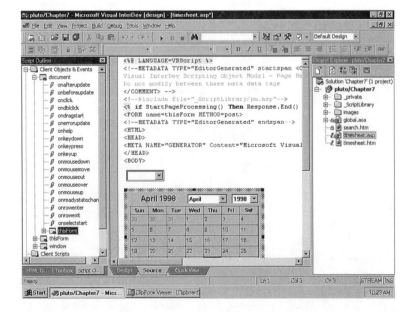

The Client Objects & Events folder in the Script Outline window displays all the objects and their events that are currently available for you to add code to. Expanding the listing for an object by clicking the plus sign next to an object causes the events contained by that object to be displayed. By double-clicking an event, you can add custom code that will be executed when that event is triggered.

The Client Scripts folder displays all the client-side scripts that are currently on your page. By double-clicking a script, you can edit it.

The preceding descriptions also apply to the Server Objects & Events folder and the Server Scripts. You'll recall our discussion of server-side scripts from Day 6, "Extending Your Web Page Through Server-Side Script." Server-side objects are described in detail on Day 15, "Building an Integrated Solution with Components."

Reviewing Statement Completion

A nice feature of the Script Editor, which you may already be familiar with if you've used Visual Basic lately, is Statement Completion. Statement Completion shows syntax tips as you type your script. It lists objects, properties, and methods available to an object you've just typed.

For example, if I type `window` on the page I've built, a pop-up list box will appear showing me all the objects and methods available under the `window` object. If I select my combo box from the list, its name is entered into my script for me. If I type a period after my combo box's name, a listing of available properties and methods, including syntax and parameter information, is displayed. Figure 7.7 shows Statement Completion in action.

FIGURE 7.7.

Statement Completion in action.

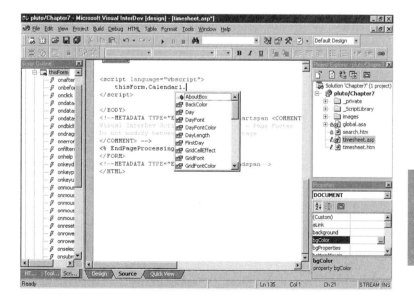

Note This feature works only when entering script through the Script Editor on the Script tab of the workspace.

Scripting the Timesheet Application

In this section, you use the Script Editor to add the scripting logic for this application. You need to add a validation function to make sure that the user enters a valid number of hours and that he picks a project from the list before the entry can be submitted. Then, scripting logic needs to be added to display a confirmation message when the user clicks the Submit button. Listing 7.2 displays the validation code for the Submit button's Click event.

LISTING **7.2.** VALIDATING THE HOURS WORKED FIELD.

```
1: if (window.txtHours.Text) > 8 then
2: window.alert("You work too hard.  Remove some hours")
3: elseif window.cmbProjects.Value = "" then
4: window.alert("You must pick a project from the list")
5:
```

The code in Listing 7.2 displays message boxes to the user if she entered more than eight hours into the Hours text box and if she didn't pick a project from the Project combo box.

The second piece of code that you need for your Timesheet application is a confirmation of the data entered by the user. In the real world, this would probably insert the data into a database or spreadsheet, but it's sufficient for this sample application to display the data the user entered in a message box. Listing 7.3 displays the confirmation code from the Submit button's Click event.

LISTING **7.3.** CONFIRMING THE DATA ENTERED.

```
1: window.alert("You've entered " & window.txtHours.Text & " hours on " &
➥Calendar1.Month & "/" & Calendar1.Day & "/" & Calendar1.Year &
➥" for the " & cmbProjects.value & " project")
```

By putting these two pieces of code together, you get an application that takes input from a user, validates that input, and outputs a confirmation if the user's input was valid. Listing 7.4 displays the code for the Submit button's Click event.

LISTING 7.4. VALIDATING AND CONFIRMING THE DATA ENTERED.

```
1: sub cmdSubmit_Click()
2: if (window.txtHours.Text) > 8 then
3: window.alert("You work too hard.  Remove some hours")
4: elseif window.cmbProjects.Value = "" then
5: window.alert("You must pick a project from the list")
6: else
7: window.alert("You've entered " & window.txtHours.Text &
➥" hours on " & Calendar1.Month & "/" & Calendar1.Day &
➥"/" & Calendar1.Year & " for the " & cmbProjects.value & " project")
8: end if
9: end sub
```

This code validates the information entered for the Hours Worked field and displays a message if the number of hours worked exceeds eight. (You don't want to work too hard now, do you?) It also makes sure that the user selects a project from the combo box.

To enter this code using the Script Editor, perform the following steps:

1. Click the plus sign to the left of cmdSubmit in the Script Editor's Client Objects & Events list to expand the events for the Submit button.

2. Double-click Click to display the procedure for the Click event in the Script pane.

3. Enter the script code in Listing 7.2 for the subprocedure.

After you have entered all the scripting logic, you're ready to run the application, as shown in Figure 7.8.

FIGURE 7.8.

*Entering your
Timesheet information.*

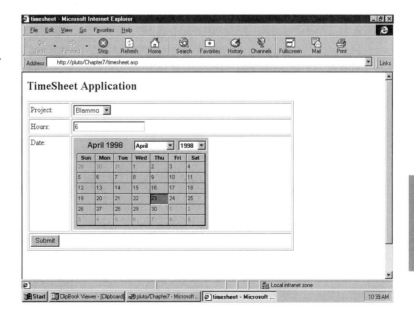

7

Summary

The Timesheet application demonstrates how to integrate ActiveX controls into your application. Today's lesson has focused on extending your Web pages with the power of ActiveX controls and Java applets. You should now understand the basic concepts and steps for integrating objects into your pages, and how to use control methods and script to extend the power of these controls. Although the debate will continue to rage over Java and ActiveX, the central premise of this lesson is that you should use both these robust objects in your application as complementary technologies.

The first part of today's lesson outlines the basic strengths, differences, and weaknesses of ActiveX controls and Java applets. Next, you learned how to use Visual InterDev to integrate a Java applet into your Web-based application. The lesson then focuses on integrating ActiveX controls into your Web pages. The Timesheet application is a good example of how to build an application based on ActiveX controls. The lesson guided you through inserting basic ActiveX controls and manipulating those controls' properties and methods to get the behavior you want for your interface. Finally, you learned how to extend the reach of your controls by using client-side script.

Now that you have finished today's lesson, you should have a thorough understanding of building the front end of a Web-based application. This knowledge, combined with your comprehension of server topics such as database integration and Active Server, will enable you to use Visual InterDev to create a killer application for the Web.

Q&A

Q With security concerns on the rise and the potential risks of using objects, should I use Java applets and ActiveX controls in my Web pages?

A Both Java and ActiveX have tried to define tight security standards for the implementation and use of objects. Moreover, browsers from Netscape and Microsoft have also implemented security controls for downloading these controls and objects. Finally, third-party vendors are building software to specifically monitor the activities of Java applets and ActiveX controls. One such company is Finjan Software, Ltd., which has developed a software product called SurfinGate that helps to keep these objects in check. This product is representative of some of the newer products being developed to further protect your Internet and intranet applications from the activity of rogue objects. The SurfinGate software analyzes and verifies the safety of Java applets and ActiveX controls and then provides a digital certificate of authenticity. Based on these safety measures, you should feel confident and secure about using ActiveX controls and Java applets in your Web-based applications. Remember, use only those objects and controls that have been digitally signed and authenticated.

Q What tools are available to build Java applets?

A Many tools already exist, or are being developed, to help you create Java applets and applications. Some of the more popular tools are Microsoft Visual J++ and Symantec Visual Café. If you're thinking of building your own custom Java applet, you should seriously consider Visual J++ because of its strong integration with Visual InterDev. The Developer Studio shell enables you to simultaneously open Visual J++ and Visual InterDev projects, reducing your development time and making it easier to integrate applets into your Web-based applications.

Q What tools can I use to develop ActiveX controls?

A You have several options for developing ActiveX controls, including Microsoft Visual C++, Visual Basic, and Borland Delphi.

Workshop

The Workshop provides quiz questions and exercises to help you solidify your understanding of the material covered and to provide you with experience in using what you've learned. You can find the answers to the quiz and exercises in Appendix B, "Answers."

Quiz

1. What is a method?
2. What method do you use to add items to a combo box?
3. What property enables you to define the text for the label control?
4. What exciting Visual InterDev feature automatically generates script code based on your input?

Exercise

Write a timesheet-type application. The timesheet should include a calendar control, a text box, a combo box, and two command buttons. All these controls should be ActiveX controls. Code the calendar control to make sure that the user can't pick a date that is in the future or that is more than two weeks old. Make one of the command buttons a

7

Submit button. Code the timesheet so that the user must select a project from the combo box and enter the number of hours worked (less than 24) in the text box. If the preceding criteria is met, a message box should pop up confirming the entered data. Make the other button a Cancel button that resets the other controls to their original state. Populate the combo box with the names of several projects when the page is loaded into the browser.

WEEK 1

In Review

The first week is filled with information about Visual InterDev. You discovered how this exciting new tool completes the application development puzzle. You learned about the features of Visual InterDev and had a chance to build your first project. You should now have a good feel for how Visual InterDev addresses the client side of the application equation.

Where You Have Been

At the beginning of the week, you were bombarded with an overview of all the new features of Visual InterDev 6. On Day 2, you developed your first Visual InterDev project. Next, you were introduced to the different editors within Visual InterDev, including the new WYSIWYG Design Editor. You discovered the joys of visual editing. Toward the end of the week, you learned the dynamics of using client-side script, server-side script, and ActiveX controls to enhance your application.

WEEK 2

At a Glance

Week 1 provides you with a solid foundation upon which to build and prepares you to take on more advanced Visual InterDev topics. In Week 2, you will learn more about the server side of the application equation. A majority of the week will focus on integrating a database with your application. You will also learn about some more advanced client-side topics, such as how to use objects and design-time controls to build your application.

Where You Are Going

At the beginning of Week 2, you will learn how to communicate with a database. You will discover how to use the power of the Visual Data Tools included with Visual InterDev to provide true database interaction in your application. On Day 10, you will learn how to administrate and manage your database components. In the middle of the week, you will discover how to create dynamic applications through the use of Active Server Pages. The last few days of the week focus on using design-time controls to rapidly build database integration into your application. The topics covered earlier this week prepare you for the last lesson of Week 2, in which you will assimilate all the concepts to build an application.

8

9

10

11

12

13

14

DAY 8

Communicating with a Database

The second week begins with a very exciting topic—database integration. Communicating with a database is an integral part of any application. For a Web-based application, it's essential to provide the users with a way to interact with data and information. This lesson begins a series of lessons on how to use the features of Visual InterDev to facilitate communication between the users and their data. Today's lesson provides an introduction to help you build database communication into your application. Day 9, "Using the Visual Data Tools for Maximum Productivity," extends the scope of today's lesson to show you how to use the Visual Data Tools to enhance your productivity. To round out the discussion of database integration, you will learn how to administer your database components on Day 10, "Managing Your Database Components."

Today you will receive an overview of how to leverage Visual InterDev to access your database information. In this overview, you are introduced to the benefits of database integration and how Visual InterDev seamlessly provides this essential component. The next part of the lesson explains the Active Data

Object model. Visual InterDev uses this model to provide controls for communicating with the database. The lesson also explains the different types of data sources that you can establish based on the open database connectivity (ODBC) standard.

The final sections introduce you to several database features of Visual InterDev. You will learn how to use the Data View to examine and interact with your database objects. The lesson also outlines the features of the Query Designer and how this tool can make your life easier. Lastly, you will see an introduction to special design-time ActiveX controls that are geared specifically to database integration.

Leveraging Visual InterDev to Access Your Data

A database provides the vehicle for storing information for future use. Whether you're building an electronic commerce application for the Internet or constructing an intranet to provide applications for your employees, you must enable the users to interact with the information. The application must support creating, storing, modifying, and, if necessary, deleting information to be considered valuable. But how do you develop applications that can access the database? Visual InterDev provides some very robust features for accessing the database from your application. You will be learning about a few of these features in today's lesson.

You can use Visual InterDev to rapidly build your application to include database connectivity. These features are intuitive, powerful, and easy to use. The word *leveraging*, used in the title of this section, refers to the use of a lever to provide an advantage in the accomplishment of a task. For example, you might use a physical lever to help you move some heavy object. You might capitalize on a friendship to get you into the door at some organization or business. Similarly, Visual InterDev provides the lever to accelerate your development of an interactive, database application. You will realize the power of the database features over the next few days.

The Benefits of Database Integration

Database integration is integral for creating a dynamic, interactive application. The benefits of database integration include not only being able to access a database from your Web page, but also using this connection to integrate the results to create a holistic application for the user. Visual InterDev provides a comprehensive development tool to produce these results.

Integrating the Data

A *holistic application* refers to an application that provides a complete experience for the user. If a user places an order for some items, the application should provide a way for that person to check the status of her order. Also, your application should integrate the use of the data to provide additional value to the different types of users.

For example, a customer supplies some customer information along with the order. This data is stored in different tables within your database. You should be able to provide a way for the business user in the sales department to locate information about the customer and her order information. The sales manager might want to explore the past buying habits of this person and determine if she is a repeat customer. In other words, you should use the data and integrate this information throughout your application to satisfy the request of both external and internal users.

Your requirements vary, however, depending on the type of application you're building. A public Internet site that provides electronic commerce is dramatically different from a private intranet application. Integration of the data is still the key for both types of applications.

Comparing the Options

There are many options for providing database connectivity to your Web page. These options range from simple solutions that don't contain much robustness to the very powerful tools that are difficult to use. The matrix in Figure 8.1 compares some of the many options that are available for connecting a Web page to a database.

The matrix in Figure 8.1 consists of two axes. The horizontal axis measures the capability of the features of the tool and ranges on a scale from Low to High. The vertical axis describes the ease of use and again ranges from Low to High. I have rated each tool in the comparison on both of these scales to determine its position in the matrix. As you can see from the comparison, Visual InterDev is very robust and easy to use. Java applications and applets rate slightly higher than Visual InterDev on the capability scale due to their portability across platforms. These same tools rate lower on their ease of use due to the nature of the Java programming language.

Java is very similar to C++ and is, therefore, a more complex language when compared to a tool like Visual InterDev. The database tools in Visual InterDev are very intuitive and easy to use because you can visually build your SQL statements.

Visual InterDev also receives high marks for its ability to provide a single environment for constructing both the Web page and the database calls for your application. With earlier database solutions such as Internet Database Connector (IDC), you had to create one file to handle your SQL information and calls and another file to process the formatted HTML page.

FIGURE 8.1.

Web-to-database connectivity comparison matrix.

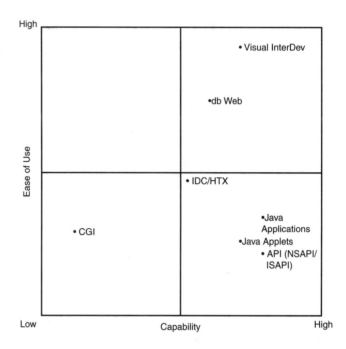

In the matrix, Application Programming Interface (API) programming receives a high rating on the capability scale but is more difficult to use than the other solutions. Those of you who were common gateway interface (CGI) pioneers are probably unhappy about the low rating of CGI in the comparison matrix. CGI will still be used as a solution for connecting to a database; however, with the advent of APIs that improve the performance of server connections as well as visual tools that significantly augment the time it takes to build your database application, CGI is now considered more of a legacy.

Visual InterDev Benefits

Now that you have seen where Visual InterDev compares with other database connectivity tools, let's look at some specific benefits of the database features included with Visual InterDev. The benefits of having an integrated development environment (IDE) to create your application can't be understated. You might be familiar with some of the tools listed in the Web-to-database connectivity comparison matrix. With many of these solutions, you have to use separate development environments and tools to accomplish database connectivity. Visual InterDev provides a comprehensive and integrated development environment that offers the following features and benefits:

- Ease of use
- A visual environment

- Rapid application development
- Robustness

These features are outlined in the following four sections.

Ease of Use

Visual InterDev offers a seamless environment that includes several database tools under one integrated roof. For this reason, Visual InterDev is very easy to use. You don't have to migrate between separate tools and environments to build your database connection and SQL calls as well as your formatted HTML Web pages. Also, the Visual InterDev development environment provides toolbar and menu options to guide you through the process of adding database functionality to your Web page.

A Visual Environment

Visual InterDev, as the name indicates, provides a visual environment in which you build your applications. This intuitive environment includes the Visual Data Tools, which you will learn more about tomorrow. These tools enable you to visually construct your SQL statements and immediately test the results. Microsoft Access users love the interface of the tools because of the similarities between the two environments. You discovered the benefits of a visual tool to build your HTML Web pages during the lesson on the Design Editor on Day 4, "WYSIWYG Editing with Visual InterDev." The Visual Data Tools provide the same type of benefits to your database calls. You don't have to know the details of SQL to construct your queries. For power SQL programmers, the visual nature of the tools saves you time from programming the mundane and routine queries and enables you to spend time on the more complex SQL calls.

 Note

> Some people think of the term *query* to denote the execution of an inquiry, or a SELECT statement against a database. In this book, I use the term *query* to refer generically to any SQL statement that you can execute against a database. I will specifically use the word *select* or the keyword SELECT when I am describing an inquiry against a database.

Rapid Application Development

Visual InterDev provides an environment that enables you to rapidly build database connectivity and integration into your application. Our modern age requests, and sometimes demands, instantaneous information all the time. With Visual InterDev, you can use the database tools to help meet the needs of your users. Visual InterDev promotes the theory behind rapid application development by supporting both PC desktop and server databases.

The database tools enable you to construct actual ODBC-compliant SQL calls that can eventually be used when you migrate the application to a more robust production database such as Microsoft SQL Server. This method can facilitate a very iterative and rapid cycle for your development process.

Robustness

So far, I have talked a lot about the ease of use of the Visual InterDev database features. Some people seem to think that a product has to be difficult to offer powerful features, and that a product that is easy to use can't possibly be very robust. Visual InterDev provides the best of both worlds—robustness and ease of use. You can program complex SQL directly from within the Visual InterDev environment. For some databases, you also can edit and manage your database components. Visual InterDev supports all the major ODBC-compliant databases including Microsoft SQL Server, Oracle, Sybase, Informix, IBM DB2/2, Microsoft Access, Microsoft FoxPro, and Borland Paradox.

Seeing Clearly with the Data View

Given the benefits of the Visual Data Tools, let's take a closer look at these features. The first feature that you will learn how to use is the Data View. You received an introduction to this feature during the first week on Day 1, "Presenting Visual InterDev 6." The Data View enables you to view all the database objects within a database. These objects include tables, fields, views, stored procedures, and triggers. You can use the Data View to access all these objects from your client machine. You also can use the Data View to examine detailed information about the database objects including field types, key structures, and table definitions.

Exploring the Data View

The Data View tab is a dockable window that appears in your project workspace after you have connected your project to a data source. You will learn how to use a wizard to walk you through this process in the next section, "Building a Connection with a Database Wizard." Visual InterDev uses a live connection to the database to present the Data View. This connection enables you to interact directly with the database objects. Figure 8.2 demonstrates the power of the Data View.

The best part about the Data View is that it provides a graphical tool for this interaction that is very intuitive. The Data View works in conjunction with the Query Designer and the Database Designer (which you will learn more about tomorrow) to provide a robust set of database tools for a developer. The Data View enables you to connect to any ODBC-compliant database. You can establish multiple connections to different databases.

FIGURE 8.2.

Using the Data View to see your database.

8

Table 8.1 examines the icons that are displayed within the Data View, as well as their meanings.

TABLE 8.1. DATA VIEW ICONS.

Icon	Folder Name	Description
	Database Project	Project that contains database connection
	Data Source	Identifies a data source connection
	Database Diagram	Indicates a database diagram
	Table	Represents a database table
	View	Represents a database view
	Stored Procedure	Indicates a stored procedure
	Parameter	Signifies a stored procedure parameter

The Data View provides a very intuitive method for examining your database and its contents. Moreover, you don't have to use a separate database administrator tool to view these objects. You can develop your application and manipulate your database objects all within the comforts of your own Visual InterDev home.

Building a Connection with a Database Wizard

You can connect to a database in several ways. The easiest method to add a database connection to your project is to use the Database Connection Wizard, described in the next section.

> **Note**
>
> Before you begin the next section, create a project using the Web Project Wizard. The name of the project isn't important for the purposes of these exercises.

Selecting the Data Source

There are several methods for adding a data source to your project. First, you can right-click the web root in Project Explorer and select Add Data Connection from the list of menu items. You can also right-click the `global.asa` file and choose Add Data Connection.

After you have added a data connection, the Select Data Source dialog box appears, enabling you to choose a data source. Figure 8.3 illustrates the available options in the Select Data Source dialog box.

FIGURE 8.3.

Selecting a data source.

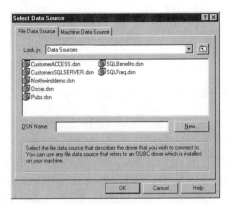

The File Data Source Tab

The File Data Source tab is shown in Figure 8.3. This display enables you to configure a file data source name (DSN) for your project. A file DSN enables you to set up a file-based connection that is dependent upon information stored in a file versus a specific machine's Registry. Multiple people using different machines can share this connection.

A file-based connection means that the information to connect to the database is stored in a .dsn file. When the database connection is created for your project, the information in the .dsn file is inserted into the connect string within your global.asa file. Because the information is stored in global.asa, you no longer need the .dsn file to use the connection information for your application.

A file DSN is sometimes referred to as a *DSN-less* connection because connection information is stored within your project—not a separate file. A file DSN provides portability and reduced ODBC maintenance. You don't have to copy or create a DSN file on the computer each time a user moves to a different machine.

The Look In combo box enables you to browse the file system for a data source. This combo box defaults to the ODBC\Data Sources\ directory on the computer. The File DSN list box displays all the available data sources within the specified directory. You can either double-click a data source within the list box or select the item and click OK to connect to the data source. The New button enables you to create a new data source.

The Machine Data Source Tab

The Machine Data Source tab enables you to establish a machine data source for your project. You can create two types of machine data sources. The first type is called a *user DSN*. This type of DSN can be used only by the designated user and is specific to a machine. A *system DSN* is the other type of machine data source. A system DSN is specific to a machine but can be shared by multiple users. This information is stored in the Windows Registry and must migrate with the application if it is moved to another machine. Figure 8.4 depicts the Machine Data Source tab.

FIGURE 8.4.

Specifying a machine data source.

This window contains a list of machine data sources that are available. You can select an item from the list and click OK to create a connection to an existing machine data source. You also can create a new machine data source by clicking the New button. You are prompted to indicate whether you're creating a user DSN or a system DSN.

The advantage of machine data sources is that they execute faster than file DSNs. When deciding between a file DSN and a machine DSN, you must make a choice between portability and maintenance versus speed.

Creating a New Data Source

I stated earlier that for both the file and machine data source you can choose an existing data source to insert into your project. The data source creates a connection, enabling you to interact with the database. This process is straightforward if you have already established the data source. What if you need to create a new data source? This section focuses on showing you how to create a new data source. I will continue to walk you through the Database Connection Wizard windows to create a new file DSN. The process for setting up a machine data source is very similar.

Selecting the Type of Data Source

When you click the New button from the Select Data Source window, the Create New Data Source dialog box is displayed. This window enables you to specify the database driver that will be used to create the new data source. Figure 8.5 demonstrates an example of how to specify the data source type.

FIGURE 8.5.

Selecting a new data source type.

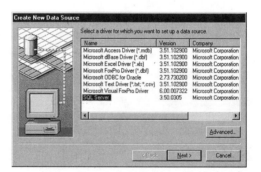

In Figure 8.5, a list box displays the available drivers for the data type. These items vary depending on what database drivers you installed on the machine when you originally installed Visual InterDev. The Advanced button enables you to view the driver information that will be created for the data source based on your selection. You can customize this information if you want to be very specific about the parameters that should be created for the data source. You can use the Create New Data Source window to enter this information directly into the list box. In this example, I'm going to select the SQL Server driver to create a new data source connection to Microsoft SQL Server.

Note   If you are using a different database such as Microsoft Access or Oracle, choose the appropriate driver for your respective database. You can still apply the concepts explained in the rest of today's lesson.

After you have made your selection, click Next to display the next window.

The next step involves entering a name for your data source.

The name that you enter is used to represent the underlying data source and database objects. Choose a meaningful name that accurately indicates to the user what kind of information the data source contains. For example, Orders is a more meaningful name than MyData. For this example, you can enter Pubs.

The Final Steps

After you have entered the name for the data source, a list box is displayed, indicating the choices that you have made. This window specifies the data source type, name, and driver. You can click the Back button to go back and change one of the parameters. Clicking Finish confirms the choices that you made and creates the new data source. You can also click Cancel to cancel this process.

After you click Finish, an additional wizard appears helping to further configure the ODBC data source, as shown in Figure 8.6.

FIGURE 8.6.

Creating a new data source for SQL Server.

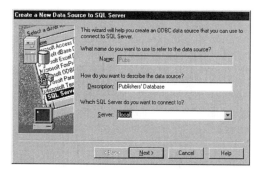

 Note   Figure 8.6 demonstrates a wizard that appears for configuring an ODBC data source for Microsoft SQL Server. Based on the database you are using, you might encounter a different dialog box.

The dialog box shown in Figure 8.6 enables you to specify a description of the database
and the database server to connect to. When you click Next, you advance to the next step
of the wizard, as shown in Figure 8.7.

FIGURE 8.7.

*Choosing the proper
security.*

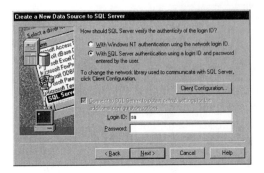

This window allows you to choose between Windows NT trusted security and SQL
Server authentication. Windows NT authentication allows the user to log in to the SQL
Server database using the same user ID and password they used to log in to the Windows
NT domain. If you choose SQL Server authentication, the user will need to be set up in
both the SQL Server database as well as the Windows NT domain. If you choose SQL
Server authentication, you will need to specify a user ID and password.

Tip

> You will typically use Windows NT trusted security when your database server
> is located on a separate machine from your Web server. In this scenario, you
> can choose to trust the connection between the two Windows NT domains,
> meaning that the NT database server "trusts" the connections that have
> already been verified by another NT domain. Another common scenario is
> where the database server and the Web server are on the same machine. In
> this case, using NT trusted security would allow you to rely on the ID and
> password that were supplied by the user when he logged into the domain.

Clicking Next takes you to the next step in the process, as illustrated in Figure 8.8.

From this window, you can choose a default database for the data source user. The default
behavior for this window is to accept the default database specified for the user in the
SQL Server database. From this window, you can override the default database for the
user by clicking the check box located at the top of the window and choosing the default
database from the database drop-down list box. Click the check box and change the
default database to Pubs. The other options allow you to further define the behavior of
the SQL Server database. Accept the defaults for the purposes of this example.

FIGURE 8.8.

Choosing the default database.

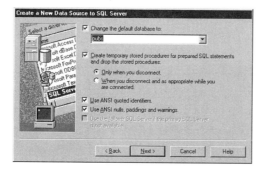

The next step in the wizard enables you to establish the character set translation for the database. The default selection is to enable the ODBC driver to choose the translation method.

The next window enables you to save long running queries to a log file. You can also save ODBC driver statistics to a special log file.

When you click Next, a dialog box appears that displays the results of your selections, as shown in Figure 8.9.

FIGURE 8.9.

Seeing the results of your actions.

From this window, you can test the connection to the data source as a final step in the process. Figure 8.10 demonstrates testing a connection to a sample SQL Server data source.

Clicking OK brings you back to the ODBC setup window, enabling you to click OK and complete the data source configuration. After the process is complete, you see the new data source in the Select Data Source window. From this window, you can select the data source as shown in Figure 8.11.

FIGURE 8.10.

Testing the data source.

FIGURE 8.11.

Selecting the right data source.

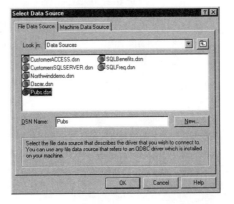

After you click OK, you might be prompted to log in to the SQL Server database, as shown in Figure 8.12.

FIGURE 8.12.

Logging in to the database.

The default user information should appear, enabling you to enter the appropriate password and to click OK. From this window, enter the server, user ID, and password. The Options button enables you to enter specific data source information like the name of the database and the application type. Figure 8.13 displays the Properties window for the data source.

FIGURE 8.13.

Viewing the properties for the data source.

When you click OK, Visual InterDev logs in to the database and establishes the database connection.

Analyzing the Results

The data source information is captured in the `global.asa` file. Listing 8.1 shows what happens to the `global.asa` file when a Microsoft SQL Server connection is inserted into a project.

LISTING 8.1. USING THE `global.asa` FILE TO CONNECT TO A DATA SOURCE.

```
 1: <SCRIPT LANGUAGE="VBScript" RUNAT="Server">
 2:
 3:  'You can add special event handlers in this file that will get run
 4: 'automatically when special Active Server Pages events occur.  To create
 5: 'these handlers, just create a subroutine with a name from the list
➥below
 6: 'that corresponds to the event you want to use.  For example, to create
➥an
 7: ' event handler for Session_OnStart, you would put the following code
➥into
 8: 'this file (without the comments):
 9: 'Sub Session_OnStart
10: '**Put your code here **
11: 'End Sub
12:
13: 'EventName              Description
14: 'Session_OnStart        Runs the first time a user runs any page in your
➥application
```

continues

LISTING 8.1. CONTINUED

```
15: 'Session_OnEnd        Runs when a user's session times out or quits your
➥application
16: 'Application_OnStart  Runs once when the first page of your application
➥is run
17:  'for the first time by any user
18: 'Application_OnEnd    Runs once when the web server shuts down
19:
20: </SCRIPT>
21: <SCRIPT LANGUAGE=VBScript RUNAT=Server>
22: Sub Application_OnStart
23:     '==Visual InterDev Generated - startspan==
24:     '— Project="Data Environment"
25:         Set DE = Server.CreateObject("DERuntime.DERuntime")
26:         Application("DE") = DE.Load(Server.MapPath("/Project8/_private/
➥DataEnvironment/DataEnvironment.dat"))
27:         Application("DE_DataEnvironmentUsage") = "page"
28:     '==Visual InterDev Generated - endspan==
29: End Sub
30: </SCRIPT>
```

You should be able to see that the Database Connection Wizard enables you to create a data source in a few simple steps. The data source is placed in the Visual InterDev project workspace, providing a live connection to your database objects. You can then use the Data View to access the objects.

Understanding the Query Designer

The Query Designer is part of the Visual Data Tools included with Visual InterDev. These tools definitely make the life of a database programmer easier, providing graphical tools to access the database objects. You will learn how to use the Visual Data Tools tomorrow, but the following section introduces you to some of the Query Designer's features.

Understanding the Query Designer

After you have created your data source, you're ready to access the data. The Query Designer helps you accomplish this task by enabling you to visually specify your SQL statements. You build your statements by selecting the tables that you want to use as well as the fields within those tables. As you make your choices, the SQL statement is constructed. You can view the statement as it is built and make any changes to the native SQL. You also can test and view the results of your query within another pane in the Visual InterDev development environment. The Query Designer can significantly enhance your database development effort. You can use the Query Designer to drastically reduce your database programming and testing cycle.

Query Designer Features

The Data View window enables you to access the features of the Query Designer. The Data View display tab enables you to see and access all the objects for the data source. You can use the Query Designer to execute queries against the database and to specify the tables, columns, and order of the query results. You can very easily create joins between multiple tables. In addition to queries, you also can insert, update, and delete data that is contained within the database. You also can use the Query Designer to execute stored procedures if you're using SQL Server or Oracle as your database. The following section examines the features of the Query Designer in a little more detail.

The Query Designer Workspace

The Query Designer contains four panes that you can use to interact with your data:

- The Diagram pane
- The Grid pane
- The SQL pane
- The Results pane

The Diagram Pane

The Diagram pane enables you to work with the database objects to construct a SQL statement. Using this pane, you can drag and drop tables and views into the workspace. Figure 8.14 depicts the layout of the Diagram pane.

FIGURE 8.14.

The Diagram pane.

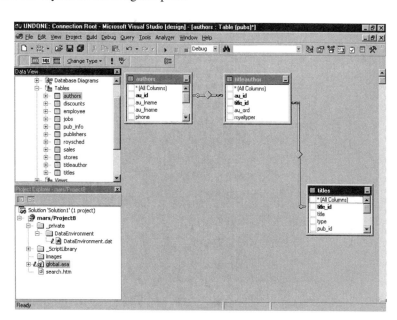

As you choose the tables, the Query Designer associates related tables and indicates table joins through the use of lines between the tables. You can select individual columns to be included in the SQL statement or select All Columns. For those SQL programmers, selecting the All Columns option performs a SELECT * to retrieve all the columns within the table.

The Grid Pane

The Grid pane provides a spreadsheet interface to customize the results of the query. You can designate which columns to show in the result set as well as how to order and group the results. Figure 8.15 shows the Grid pane for two sample tables.

FIGURE 8.15.

Customizing the results.

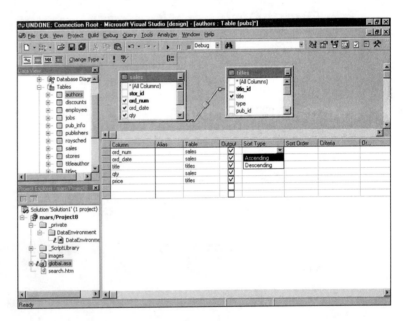

The SQL Pane

The SQL pane enables you to view the SQL statement for the tables and options that you have selected. You can use the SQL pane to view a SQL statement as well as to modify the statement. You also can use this pane to create your own SQL statements. Figure 8.16 displays a SQL statement within the SQL pane.

The Results Pane

You can use the Results pane to view the data that is returned from the SQL statement. Based on the query that you construct, this pane displays the results set of the current query. You can use the Results pane to add, modify, and delete data in the database. The effects are immediate because you're using a live connection to access the database.

FIGURE 8.16.

The SQL pane.

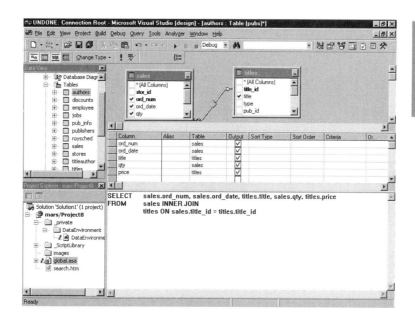

 Note   The actions that you can perform are limited to your access permissions on the database. Visual InterDev uses the access rights for your user ID and password to determine which commands you can execute.

Figure 8.17 shows the Results pane as well as the other three Query Designer panes.

The ActiveX Data Object

The ActiveX Data Object (ADO) provides database access for all the Visual InterDev database tools. ADO serves as the central model for you to build database interaction within your Web pages. ActiveX Data Objects can supply connections for your Web pages to any ODBC-compliant database. Microsoft implemented ADO specifically to provide data access across the Web. The main benefits of the ADO model include low memory overhead and high speed, which are ideal for Web-based applications.

ADO enables you to use ActiveX scripting to establish a connection to your data source. You also can use ActiveX scripting to customize the properties and methods of an ActiveX Data Object. ADO supports a variety of data types, including images and binary large objects (BLOBs). ADO supports transactions, cursors, error handling, and the use of stored procedures.

FIGURE 8.17.

Displaying the Results pane.

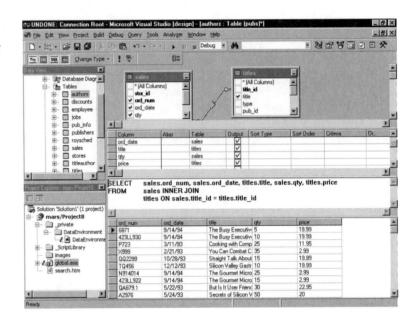

Exploring ADO

The following section provides a brief explanation of ADO. This overview provides a basic context for you to understand how Visual InterDev provides data access for your application through the use of ADO. This discussion isn't meant to be an exhaustive review of ADO and similar data access methods. For an in-depth discussion of these topics, I would suggest that you visit the Microsoft ADO Web site at www.microsoft.com/ado and the Microsoft OLE DB Web site at www.microsoft.com/oledb.

Microsoft designed ActiveX Data Objects to be language-independent objects for you to access a database from your Web pages. ADO is built on top of the OLE DB model from Microsoft. For Visual Basic programmers who are familiar with Data Access Objects (DAO) and Remote Data Objects (RDO), you might think that Microsoft is playing alphabet soup with so many standards and acronyms. ADO is the successor to both RDO and DAO. ADO combines the best of previous data access methods with an object-based standard, including the capability of RDO and DAO and extending their reach to provide data access for the Internet using the OLE model.

Note

Data Access Objects were first introduced with previous versions of Microsoft Visual Basic and Microsoft Access. DAO was developed to encapsulate database functions and operations within the context of an object. DAO provides access to ODBC-compliant databases.

8.

Remote Data Objects were the successor to DAO and were included in Visual Basic 4. RDO provided a better solution for ODBC database access and extended the reach of these objects to the server.

The benefit of using ADO over these two methods is that you can independently create objects. With RDO and DAO, you had to create a hierarchy for your objects. Also, ADO is faster and more efficient.

The idea behind ADO is to provide an object-based interface that makes remote objects appear as if they were local. You can see how this model would help you in your development. The goal is to enable you to access your database through helpful objects that provide seamless access to your database, which could reside on a remote server or locally on your machine. Figure 8.18 illustrates how ADO and OLE DB work together to provide database access for a SQL Server database.

FIGURE 8.18.

ADO and OLE DB.

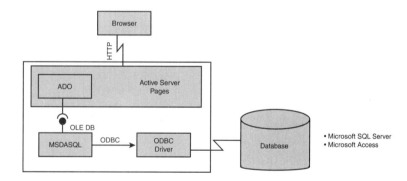

Figure 8.18 presents a configuration for a typical Web-based application built using Visual InterDev. You can see that the ActiveX Data Object resides within an Active Server Page (ASP) on the Web server. When the browser sends a request for database information, the Active Server Page is called, and ADO submits the request via OLE DB to the database server.

MSDA SQL is used to format the ODBC request for the database server. MSDA is an ODBC-specific SQL language, and both Access and SQL Server support the use of it to communicate with their respective data sources. The ODBC driver translates the MSDA SQL into a specific language for a particular database. The information is then passed back through this pipeline. The Active Server Page and ADO work together to format and send the results back to the browser.

Note

The previous illustration contained some components that are specific to SQL Server and Access. ADO works with any ODBC-compliant database. This illustration is provided as an example to understand the communication links and path from the browser to the database and back. Other database implementations of ADO might contain slightly different components, but the communication concepts are the same.

Understanding ADO Objects

I have mentioned that ADO is an object-based solution. The ADO model includes seven major objects:

- The Connection object
- The Command object
- The Recordset object
- The Field object
- The Parameter object
- The Property object
- The Error object

Figure 8.19 illustrates how each of these objects relate to each other.

FIGURE 8.19.

The ADO model.

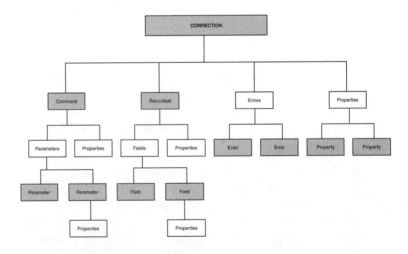

In this model, you see that the Connection object is the central object in the model. Every other object in the model is related to the Connection object. This hierarchy makes sense because the other objects can't exist without a connection to the database.

8

The ADO model isn't an autocratic hierarchy. In other words, you don't have to create the second tier of objects under a single Connection object. For example, you could create a Recordset object that is separate from a previously defined Connection object. The Recordset object that you define will exist under a newly created Connection object. Although you aren't confined to a strict hierarchy, you typically use the structured nature of the ADO model to provide organization for your objects and code.

Before I explain each of these objects, I need to explain the concept of how objects, properties, and methods work together. *Objects* contain certain characteristics, or attributes. These *attributes* help to define the behavior and composition of the object. *Methods* define certain commands that can be carried using these objects to accomplish some task.

The Connection Object

The Connection object controls your connection to the database. All the information about your connection is established with this object. You can customize the behavior of the Connection object. For example, you can set the timeout properties and default database for the connection, and you also can specify to open and close the connection to the database and manage its transaction properties.

Tip You should use the Connection object for executing multiple commands against a database.

The Command Object

The Command object enables you to specify a specific command that you are going to execute on a database. For example, you can use the Command object to call a stored procedure. You can create a Command without associating the object with a previously defined Connection object. This feature is an example of where ADO differs from previous database access methods. You don't have to use a hierarchy of objects to carry out your commands. You will want to organize your objects into a hierarchy, however, when you execute multiple commands against the same database connection.

Tip You should use the Command object for executing the same commands multiple times against a database.

The `Recordset` Object

You can use the `Recordset` object to manipulate the records or rows within your database tables. A recordset can contain all the rows within a base table. A recordset can also consist of the result set from a specific query. The `Recordset` object supports both immediate and batch updates. Immediate updates are executed against the database instantaneously. With batch updates, the changes are saved and then sent as a batch to the database. Most of the time, you will probably be using immediate updates.

The `Recordset` object supports the use of four different types of cursors. These cursors indicate how the user will interact with the information in your database. The type of cursor that you can use depends on what cursors your database supports.

A cursor establishes the navigation behavior for the data that is contained in a database. A cursor's relationship with a database is analogous to the mouse cursor's relationship with a document. The mouse cursor indicates where you are in a document and where you can go. Similarly, a cursor defines where you are in the database and where you can go.

Table 8.2 presents the four types of cursors that you can use with the `Recordset` object, along with a description of each.

TABLE 8.2. RECORDSET CURSORS.

Cursor Type	Description
Dynamic	View additions, changes, and deletions by other users
Keyset	View changes, but not additions and deletions
Static	View only a copy of the data; cannot view additions, changes, or deletions
Forward-only	Same as Static cursor but can only scroll forward through a table

Tip

> You should use the `Recordset` object for executing a single command against a database.

The `Field` Object

The `Field` object pertains to a particular column within a recordset. You can use this object to retrieve specific information about the field as well as change the contents of a particular field.

The `Parameter` Object

You can use the `Parameter` object to specify parameters for executing a command against the database. For example, you can use this object to designate the values for the parameters that are passed to a stored procedure on the database. This object is typically used with the Command object.

The Property Object

The Property object captures specific properties that are defined by the service provider. The service provider performs the specific services that enable you to access and query your data. OLE DB service providers can choose to present additional characteristics, or properties, to the ActiveX Data Object. You can then use these properties to implement further capabilities in your application. For example, you can use the Property object to determine whether a service provider supported transactions.

The Error Object

The Error object collects error information that is generated from the database. Any errors that are encountered when attempting to perform a database function are captured within this object.

Understanding ADO Collections and Properties

ADO provides collections and properties for the objects within the ADO model. Collections consist of a group of properties for an object. You use properties to customize the behavior of your objects. Table 8.3 lists the types of collections that exist for ADO objects.

TABLE 8.3. ADO COLLECTIONS.

Collection	Description
Fields	Collection of Field objects for a Recordset object
Parameters	Collection of Parameter objects for a Command object
Properties	Collection of Property objects for an instance of an object
Errors	Collection of Error objects for an ADO operation

Each ADO object consists of a distinct set of properties. Refer to the ADO help documentation within Visual InterDev for an alphabetical listing of all the ADO properties.

Database Design-Time ActiveX Controls

Visual InterDev includes several design-time controls for communicating with a database. You will see an in-depth lesson on these controls on Day 12, "Extending Web Pages Through Design-Time Controls." Design-time controls enable you to set properties and attributes at the time of design. At runtime, the properties that you set perform robust functionality without the overhead of an ActiveX control.

The Database design-time controls that are included with Visual InterDev are built on top of the ADO model. These controls generate much of the script that is necessary for connecting and executing commands against a database. A good example of a database design-time control (DTC) is the Recordset design-time control. You can insert this control into your application and then use the Query Designer to build your SQL statements. The Recordset DTC captures all the scripting that is necessary to execute your SQL statements and insert this logic into an Active Server Page.

Database design-time controls can provide a lot of power to your application. You can use these controls to significantly reduce the time that it takes to build database integration into your application.

Summary

This lesson provides you with an overview of how to communicate with a database from your Visual InterDev application, setting the stage for tomorrow when you discover how to use the Visual Data Tools.

First, the chapter centers on the benefits of database integration, explaining integration from a user and developer point of view. Visual InterDev can serve as a powerful lever for building database integration into your application. You then received an in-depth look at how to use the Data View to access your database objects. The Data View works in conjunction with the Visual Data Tools to provide some very robust features for interacting with the database.

Next, you learned how to build a database connection for your project using the Database Connection Wizard. The lesson provided a step-by-step tour of how to establish this connection. You also learned how to access your data using the Query Designer after the connection has been built. The lesson explains the basic Query Designer features and workspace.

Toward the end of the day, the lesson uncovers the mystery of the ActiveX Data Object model. The ADO model is explained so that you can understand what Visual InterDev uses behind the scenes to connect to and access the database.

The final section of the day focuses on Database design-time controls. The chapter presents an introduction to how these controls can be used at design time to provide robust functionality when your application is executed.

Q&A

8

Q **Does Visual InterDev connect to the database through the Web server via HTTP or directly to the database server via the LAN?**

A The answer to this question depends on your operating mode. At design time, you establish and utilize a connection directly to the database via your LAN using ODBC. At runtime, when a user is accessing your Web via a browser, the connection will be established through the Web server via HTTP.

Q **Are ActiveX Data Objects just a renamed version of Remote Data Objects?**

A ADO is the successor to RDO, but their models aren't identical. ADO extends the functionality of RDO to the Internet. ADO differs from RDO in that you don't have to create a hierarchy of objects to execute certain commands. All the objects within the ADO model can be instantiated as individual objects.

Q **How does ADO relate to OLE DB?**

A ADO is the abstracted object model that enables you to easily program over OLE DB. Whereas ADO provides an application programming interface, OLE DB provides a system-level interface that enables you to access various databases without having to know the underlying services. OLE DB is implemented using the Component Object Model (COM) and is Microsoft's key ingredient for universal database access.

Q **When I use the Data View, do my changes affect the database or am I using a copy of the database?**

A When you insert a database connection into your project, Visual InterDev creates a live connection to the database. Therefore, when you use the Data View to view and modify the objects and data, you're interacting with the actual database. Your changes have an immediate effect on the database.

Workshop

The Workshop provides quiz questions to help you solidify your understanding of the material covered and exercises to provide you with experience in using what you've learned. You can find the answers to quiz questions and exercises in Appendix B, "Answers."

Quiz

1. What are the four panes of the Query Designer?

2. What is the difference between a file data source and a machine data source?

3. Name the two types of machine data sources.

4. In the ADO model, what is the `Recordset` object?

Exercises

Create the data source that was presented in the lesson. If you're using a database other than SQL Server, create a data source connection to your particular database. After you have established the connection, practice using the Data View and the Query Designer so that you will be familiar with these tools when you put them to the test during tomorrow's lesson. Practice using all four of the Query Designer panes to produce the desired results from your SQL statements. Some things to practice include the following:

1. Selecting two (or more) related tables to perform a query.

2. Selecting the fields to perform the query on.

3. Entering parameters to further qualify the results.

4. Executing the query and displaying the results.

DAY 9

Using the Visual Data Tools for Maximum Productivity

The Visual Data Tools provide a rewarding experience for the developer who is building an integrated database application. (I bet you didn't think that "building a...database application" and "rewarding" could be found in the same sentence.) Visual InterDev makes this possible through the use of visual tools that simplify the process of creating database functionality in your application. You received an overview of the Visual Data Tools during the first week. Yesterday, the lesson presented the Query Designer as one of the Visual Data Tools. Today's lesson provides an in-depth look at several members of the Visual Data Tools family. The lesson focuses on how to use the programming aspects of the tools to provide database interaction within your application. Specifically, you learn the following concepts:

- How to use the Query Designer to build and construct SQL statements.
- How to construct queries within the context of your Web-based application.

- How to modify, extend, and test your query.
- How to integrate stored procedures into your application.
- How to enter and modify information in the database.

Getting Started with the Query Designer

On Day 8, "Communicating with a Database," the lesson walked you through an example of setting up a database connection. Today's lesson continues with that example to show you how to use the connection after it has been built. I hope that you had a chance to practice using the Query Designer on your own during yesterday's Workshop. In the following sections, you are guided through several examples of how to use the Query Designer to select, insert, modify, and delete your data. I will be using the data source that I established yesterday, which means the example will be using the sample Pubs database included with Microsoft SQL Server.

Note   If you are using Microsoft SQL Server and have installed this database, feel free to follow along with the example and execute the commands as they're presented in the lesson. I have also posted a Microsoft Access version of the Pubs database on the MCP Web site (http://www.mcp.com/info) named Pubs.mdb that you can use for today's lesson. If you're using another database, follow along with the example to understand the process. A good comprehension of the concepts enables you to apply the knowledge to other databases as well.

Using the Query Designer to Generate Your SQL

The Query Designer works in conjunction with the Data View to enable you to access your data. To use the Query Designer, you must establish a connection to a data source. Let's establish a connection to the Pubs database:

1. Create a new Web project and application named Customer, using the Web Project Wizard.

2. After you create the new project, you should see a project workspace that looks similar to the one shown in Figure 9.1.

FIGURE 9.1.

Viewing the new project.

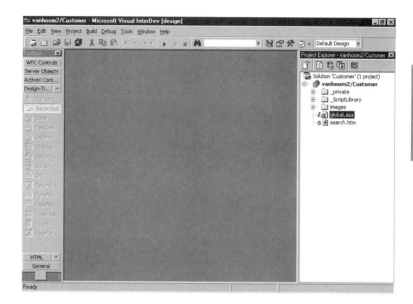

3. Right-click `global.asa` and select Add Data Connection to add a data source to your project. This option is also available from the Project menu.

4. From the File Data Source dialog box, choose the Publishers data source that you created during yesterday's lesson and click OK.

5. In the Properties dialog box, change the Connection name to **Pubs**.

6. Click the Miscellaneous tab and choose 3 - Use Client-Side Cursors from the Cursor Location combo box; then click OK.

Note

The selection of client-side cursors from this window refers to the Web server as the client, not the database server. This option caches information from the database server onto the Web server.

After you have established the connection, you're ready to begin communicating with your database. Figure 9.2 displays the tables, views, and stored procedures that are contained within the Pubs database.

FIGURE 9.2.

The Pubs database.

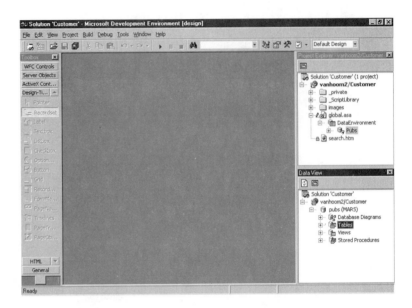

 Note

If you are using an Access database, you will not see the stored procedures folder.

Each folder represents a different type of database object. For example, database tables are displayed in the Tables folder. To view the data contained in the Authors table, right-click the Authors table from within the Data View. Choose Open from the shortcut menu and the entire contents of the table are displayed in the Results pane, as shown in Figure 9.3.

Tip

You also can double-click an object to reveal its contents. In the previous example, you could have double-clicked the Authors table to display the rows contained within the table.

After you have opened a table, you can use the Query Designer toolbar to create and view your queries, as well as to see the results.

FIGURE 9.3.

Opening the Authors table.

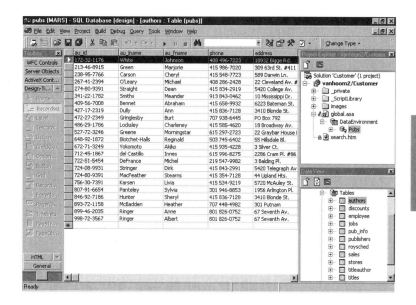

Using the Query Designer Toolbar

During yesterday's lesson, you learned about the four panes of the Query Designer—the Diagram pane, the Grid pane, the SQL pane, and the Results pane. Each pane is represented by a toolbar button that you can use to display a particular view. Figure 9.4 illustrates the available options of the Query Designer toolbar.

FIGURE 9.4.

The Query Designer toolbar.

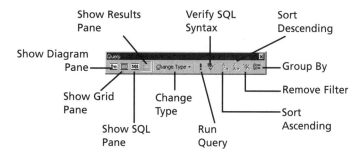

The following sections provide brief explanations of these buttons.

Show Diagram Pane

You can use the Show Diagram Pane option to display the Diagram pane. Remember, the Diagram pane enables you to work with specific tables and views to create your queries. This icon becomes enabled after you have opened a table or view. When you click this toolbar icon, the Diagram pane for that table or view is displayed. You can then work with that table, as well as drag and drop other tables into the Diagram pane.

Show Grid Pane

The Show Grid Pane icon displays a view of the Grid pane that enables you to customize the SQL statement. For example, you can choose the individual columns that you want to use in the query or select all the columns within a table. The columns that are involved in the query appear in the grid. The corresponding table for these columns also appears. You can enter search criteria for the query. For the rows that are returned from the database, you can designate ascending or descending order.

Show SQL Pane

You can use this icon to view the actual SQL statement for your query. From the SQL pane, you can modify the generated SQL statement, as well as create custom queries. The SQL pane automatically builds the SQL statement based on your choices in the Diagram and Grid panes. Any changes that are made to the Diagram and Grid panes are instantly reflected in the SQL pane. You may need to modify the SQL statement that is generated. For example, you may be a very proficient database programmer who can create a new query quickly by typing the SQL statement directly into the SQL pane. You might also want to extend the generated SQL statement to take advantage of some feature that's specific to the database you're using. Whatever the case, you can use the SQL pane to create new queries, as well as to modify existing queries.

Show Results Pane

When you click the Show Results Pane icon, the Results pane is displayed. This pane reveals the results from the database based on your query. From this pane, you can directly modify the database information. You also can add and delete database rows.

Change Type

The Change Type button/combo box enables you to change the type of query that you are defining. The following list outlines the different types of queries that you can define:

- Select—A query that returns a results set from one or more tables.
- Insert—A query that enables you to create a new row for a table by copying data from an existing row within the table. You also can create a new row for a table by copying a row of data from one table into another table. If you use this feature, you generate an INSERT INTO SQL statement.
- Insert Values—A query that inserts a new row into a table with specified values.
- Update—Enables you to update and change the values of a column or columns for one or more rows in a table.

- Delete—Enables you to delete one or more rows from a table.
- Make Table—Enables you to create a new table from an existing table, including all its data.

 Caution   When you establish a connection to a data source using Visual InterDev, all the actions that you take are live and automatic based on your security privileges. You need to establish the correct access privileges for each developer to ensure that your data remains reliable and accurate.

9

Run Query

The Run Query toolbar icon enables you to execute your query against the database. You can view the results of the query using the Results pane.

Verify SQL Syntax

You can use the Verify SQL Syntax option before you run your SQL statement to ensure that the syntax is correct. When you click this toolbar icon, the Query Designer tests your SQL statement against the data source. If the SQL syntax is accurate, you receive a confirmation message. If the SQL statement is incorrect, a message displays, indicating the syntax error as well as where the error is located.

Remove Filter

The Remove Filter option enables you to remove any special search criteria conditions that have been specified for the query. This option works in conjunction with the Diagram pane. After you select a field that contains a search criteria filter, the Remove Filter icon becomes enabled, allowing you to remove the conditions that have been created for this query.

Sort Ascending

You can click the Sort Ascending icon to view your results in ascending order. The Sort Ascending toolbar button works in conjunction with the Diagram pane. This icon becomes enabled after you select a field within a table that is displayed in the Diagram pane. After you click this icon, a SQL statement is created, sorting the query in ascending order for the field that you select. You can choose multiple fields to help construct the sort.

Sort Descending

You can use the Sort Decending feature to view your results in descending order. The Sort Descending toolbar button works in conjunction with the Diagram pane. This icon becomes enabled after you have selected a field within a table that is displayed in the Diagram pane. You can choose multiple fields to help construct the sort.

Creating a Query

Now that you have learned some of the basics about using the Query Designer, you're ready to create your first query. This part of the lesson covers how to combine features of the Query Designer panes and menu options to rapidly build queries for your applications.

Selecting the Tables

First, you need to select the tables that you're going to use to create the query. From the Data View, drag and drop the Titles table onto the Diagram pane. (The mouse pointer becomes a plus sign when you have reached a valid spot to place the table.) Repeat this step for the Sales table. Figure 9.5 shows these two tables within the Diagram pane.

FIGURE 9.5.

Selecting the tables.

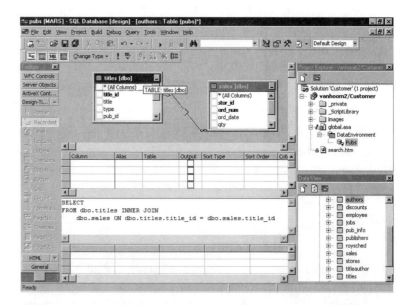

As you can see, the name of the table is displayed along with the fields. You can use the shortcut menu to display only the name of the table. A join line also is displayed, defining the relationship between the two tables. The join line is composed of two components—the join type and the join relationship.

Exploring Joins

Table 9.1 displays the possible types of joins and a definition of each type.

TABLE 9.1. DEFINING THE TYPES OF JOINS.

Icon	Description
	Inner join
	Inner join using the greater than sign
	Left outer join
	Right outer join
	Full outer join

9

Note

The join types illustrate how the tables are joined. A join based on the equal sign is the default. For this reason, the equal sign doesn't display in the middle of the icon for joins of this type. If the join is based on another type, such as greater than or less than, the symbol displays in the middle of the icon.

Table 9.2 shows the possible join relationships and their meanings.

TABLE 9.2. JOIN RELATIONSHIPS.

Icon	Description
	One-to-one relationship
	One-to-many relationship
	Undefined relationship

A brief explanation of joins is warranted here. By default, the Query Designer creates an inner join between the tables, if possible. An inner join only returns a related set of rows between the tables. In the example, you selected the Titles and Sales tables. The Query Designer created an inner join between these two tables and generated the following SQL statement:

```
SELECT titles.title, titles.price, titles.type, sales.ord_num,
sales.ord_date, sales.qty
FROM titles INNER JOIN sales ON titles.title_id = sales.title_id
```

Figure 9.6 shows the Diagram, SQL, and Results panes for an inner join between the Titles and Sales tables.

FIGURE 9.6.

An example of an inner join.

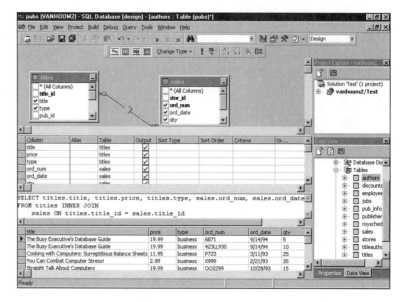

Notice that the inner join is based on the title ID field. If the title ID of the Titles table is equal to the title ID of the Sales table, the resulting row is displayed in the result set. Rows in either table that don't have the same title ID aren't returned from the database. In other words, sales information is displayed for each title that contains this information. If a particular title hasn't generated a sale, the title isn't displayed.

An outer join differs from an inner join in that an outer join can return rows that don't have related, or matched, rows in the joined table. The inner join displays only related rows between the tables. The outer join displays rows that fall outside the relationship based on the type of join. You can create three types of outer joins. The left outer join includes unmatched rows in the result set that are displayed in the left table, or the table that is specified first in the join statement. Right outer joins display all the rows that are included in the right table, or the table that is listed second in the join statement. The third type of join is the full outer join, which displays all rows of all tables whether the rows have matching data or not.

The Query Designer lives up to its visual nature by providing a way to easily designate the type of join you want to create. In fact, this visual feature enables you to create these joins without having to know the types of joins or their meanings. To change the type of join, click the mouse on the join line between the tables. The line becomes bold, indicating that this object has the focus of the mouse. You can then display the shortcut menu for the join line by clicking the right mouse button. Figure 9.7 displays the different options that you can select to change the type of join for the query.

FIGURE 9.7.

Displaying the shortcut menu to create a join.

In Figure 9.7, you should notice that there is no mention of the word "join" in the list of menu items. The options are in plain English and describe the type of action that you are trying to accomplish. In this example, you can choose to display all the rows from the Titles table (a left outer join). You also can choose to select all the rows from the Sales table (a right outer join). Notice that these menu items are not mutually exclusive. In other words, you can select both items at the same time, thereby creating a full outer join. This feature provides a very intuitive way to achieve the correct results for your queries.

Change the join relationship between the Title and Sales table by right-clicking the join type and choosing Select All Rows from Titles. This action will create a left outer join, as shown in Figure 9.8.

FIGURE 9.8.

An example of a left outer join.

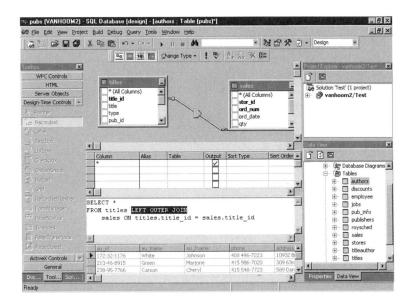

Choosing the Columns for Your Query

After you have selected the tables for your query, you need to choose the columns of the tables that will have an effect on the query. You may use these columns to display the results of the query in addition to specifying the parameters for your query. You can choose individual columns by clicking the box located to the left of the column name. Finally, you can select the All Columns option to include all the table columns in the query.

Tip   You should always try to specify only the individual columns that you need
for your query versus selecting all the columns. You will gain better performance from your queries.

All the choices that you make in the Diagram pane are immediately reflected in the Grid
and SQL panes. If you choose three columns from the Titles table and two columns from
the Sales table, these columns are reflected in the Grid pane and inserted into the SQL
statement.

A symbol visually indicates how the column is being used in the query. In Figure 9.8 in
the preceding section, the columns contain a check mark in the check box to the left.
Figures 9.9 through 9.11 demonstrate the indicators for the other types of queries.

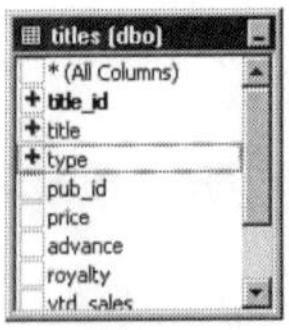

FIGURE 9.9.

*Indicating an insert
query column.*

FIGURE 9.10.

*Indicating an update
query column.*

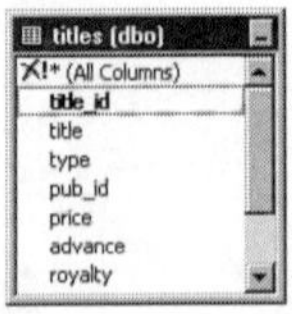

FIGURE 9.11.

*Indicating a delete
query column.*

 Note   The update query only pertains to one table. Also, the delete query relates
to all columns of a particular table; therefore, this indicator only appears by
the All Columns name in the table.

Several other symbols may display to the right of your column names. Table 9.3 illustrates these symbols and their meanings.

TABLE 9.3. OTHER COLUMN SYMBOLS.

Symbol	Meaning
 ![A Z ↓]	Sort column—Ascending (part of ORDER BY statement)
 ![Z A ↓]	Sort column—Descending (part of ORDER BY statement)
 ![▽]	Search criteria column (part of WHERE or HAVING statement)
 ![〔≡]	Groups the results (part of GROUP BY statement)
 ![Σ]	Summary column (used for aggregate functions such as SUM and AVG)

Continuing with the example, choose the Title, Type, and Price columns from the Titles table and the Ord_Num, Ord_Date, and Qty columns from the Sales table. Figure 9.12 displays these choices within the Diagram pane.

FIGURE 9.12.

Selecting the columns.

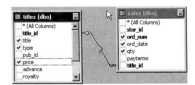

Executing the Query

So far, this lesson has taught you how to use the Diagram pane to construct a basic query. In the example, you created a query that displays the title, price, type of book, order number, order date, and quantity of the order. The next step runs the query. To execute the query, click the Run icon from the Query Designer toolbar.

> **Tip**
>
> You also can right-click in any of the four panes and then choose Run from the shortcut menu.

Figure 9.13 shows the rows that are returned from the database when you execute the query.

You can see from Figure 9.13 that several rows were returned from the database. The columns, however, aren't in the most intuitive order. For instance, the order number and order date fields are displayed too far to the right. A more useful way of organizing the data is to display the order information columns first and then the title information. You will discover in the next section how to further customize this initial query.

FIGURE 9.13.

Examining the results.

Using the Query Designer to Customize Your Queries

You received a brief introduction to the Grid pane yesterday. This pane enables you to work with the columns in the tables to further customize the query. Initial columns that you selected using the Diagram pane are displayed as rows within the grid. You can add to this list of columns as well as delete the columns that have been selected.

Adding and Deleting Columns for the Query

To add a column to the query using the Grid pane, place the cursor in the column named Columns on an empty row. You can then choose a column from the tables you have selected from a drop-down list box.

Tip

You also can drag and drop columns from the Diagram pane into the grid. Select a column from a table in the Diagram pane and hold down the left mouse button. Drag the field to the grid in the Grid pane. The mouse pointer changes to a plus sign, indicating that you're adding a column to the query. You can then insert the query anywhere in the list of columns. For instance, you can place the new column at the end of the list of columns. You also can choose to insert the new column before another column in the list.

To delete a row, click the box to the left of the Column name to select the row. The row is highlighted, enabling you to press the Delete key or to choose Delete from the Edit menu to delete the row. Deleting a row removes the column from the query.

Tip

You also can place your cursor in the Column Name field and select the contents of the field. With the column name highlighted, delete the contents of the field. This action causes the column to be removed from the query.

Any changes that you make to the query using the Grid pane are instantly reflected in the Diagram and SQL panes. The following sections outline the Grid pane options that you can use to customize your queries.

Changing the Column Order

The order in which the columns appear in the grid on the Grid pane determines the order that the columns will be displayed in the results for your query. This order is determined by the order in which you selected your columns in the Diagram pane. You can change the order of these columns by selecting a row and moving it to the new location within the rows in the grid. To move the order number and order date columns, complete the following steps:

1. Highlight the Ord_Num and Ord_Date rows by placing the cursor over the box located next to these columns, as shown in Figure 9.14.

FIGURE 9.14.

Highlighting the columns to move.

2. Next, move the cursor to the right of one of the highlighted boxes until it becomes the cursor arrow and drag the two rows to the top of the grid above the title row, as demonstrated in Figure 9.15.

FIGURE 9.15.

Moving the columns.

When you execute the query, the columns will display in the new order.

Changing the Names of the Columns

Many times, the name of the database column isn't very user-friendly. This is especially true if you have cryptic naming standards for defining your table columns that only a database administrator can understand. The Alias column within the Grid pane enables you to create a more intuitive alias name for the column that is displayed to the user with the result set.

You also can use an alias for columns that are computed based on the values within your table columns. For example, you may want to create a query that displays the price and quantity for certain book orders. Because the order total changes frequently, this value isn't stored in the database. You can create an alias column that computes the total value of the order from the Price and Quantity columns and displays this total for each row.

To enter an alias, type the new name in the Alias field next to the column that you want to rename. The alias that you enter is then used to display the results. In the example, the column names for the order number, order date, and quantity aren't very intuitive. Use the Alias column in the Grid pane to change the names of these fields to something more user-friendly, as shown in Figure 9.16.

FIGURE 9.16.

Providing more intuitive column names for the user.

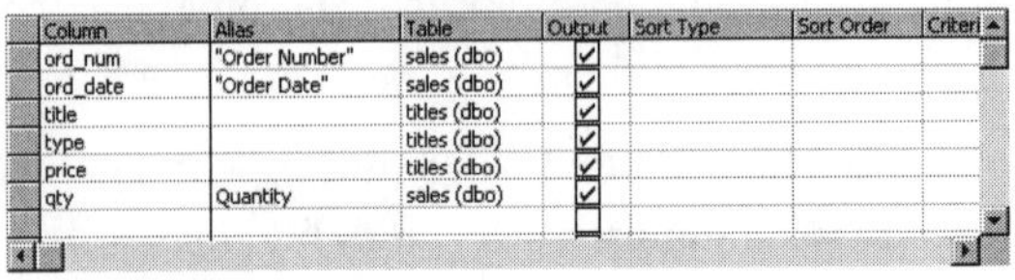

Column	Alias	Table	Output	Sort Type	Sort Order	Criteri
ord_num	"Order Number"	sales (dbo)	✓			
ord_date	"Order Date"	sales (dbo)	✓			
title		titles (dbo)	✓			
type		titles (dbo)	✓			
price		titles (dbo)	✓			
qty	Quantity	sales (dbo)	✓			

Specifying the Output

The Grid pane enables you to choose the results that you want the user to see when selecting information from the database. You can use the Output column to designate whether the column is displayed in the results for the query. This field is checked by default, meaning that the column is displayed in the query results. You may want to use columns in a table to construct a query but not display the columns in the query results. To change the Output column, click the field and the check mark is turned on or off, depending on its current status.

Note

The Output column pertains only to select queries. You use this column when you're inquiring on rows in a database and want to customize both the query and the results that are returned. This column is typically used with the Sort columns, which you will learn about next.

Searching for Particular Rows

You can further customize your query by using the following columns located in the Grid pane:

- Sort Type
- Sort Order
- Criteria
- Or

The Sort Type Column

The Sort Type field enables you to sort the query using that column. You can specify ascending or descending for the type of sort. To choose the sort type, place your cursor in the Sort Type field for a particular column. A drop-down list box is displayed, enabling you to pick a sort type from the list.

The Sort Order Column

The Sort Order indicates the priority of the columns to be sorted. This column is in conjunction with the Sort Type field. Whereas the Sort Type field indicates the type of sort that you want to use, the Sort Order field determines the order in which columns will be sorted. The first field that you select to sort is indicated by the number 1, the second field contains the number 2, and so on. For example, you may want to sort the sales data by order date and then order number. To create this sort, choose a sort type for the Ord_Date column first and then for the Ord_Num column.

The Criteria Column

The Criteria column enables you to enter special search conditions for the query. You can use this column to specify that you want the query to find only those columns that meet your search criteria. The default criteria condition is based on the equal (=) sign. If you enter a value into the Criteria field for a column, the Grid pane formats the condition using the equal sign. For this example, type the value $19.99 into the Criteria column for the price field. Figure 9.17 shows the Grid, SQL, and Results panes for this customized query.

FIGURE 9.17.

Searching for books that cost $19.99.

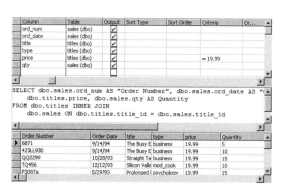

In this example, you entered the value into the field, and the Grid pane automatically inserted the equal sign into the Criteria field. If you want to enter other types of search conditions such as greater than or less than, you can manually enter these conditions, along with the search condition value. As you enter search condition criteria for multiple columns, these conditions are linked using the AND statement.

The Or Column

The Or column enables you to specify additional search conditions to a particular column. These conditions are linked together using the OR statement.

> **Tip**
>
> When you add a search condition value for the last Or column that is dis-
> played for a column, the Grid pane inserts an additional Or column. You also
> can add additional Or columns by pressing the Tab or right-arrow key in the
> right Or column.

You also can enter the logical operators directly into the Criteria column. Figure 9.18
shows an example of this method.

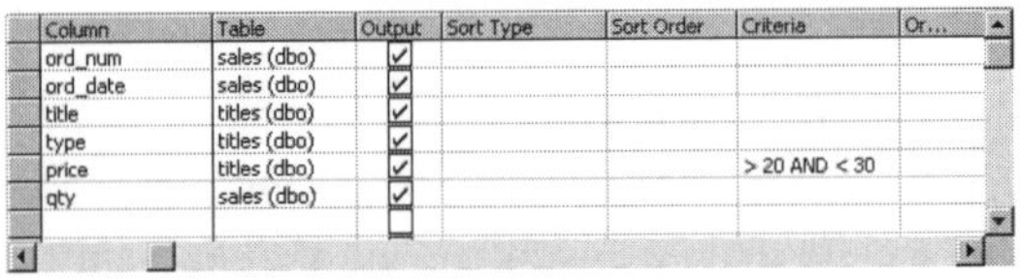

FIGURE 9.18.

*Using logical
operators to
create a query.*

Column	Table	Output	Sort Type	Sort Order	Criteria	Or...
ord_num	sales (dbo)	✓				
ord_date	sales (dbo)	✓				
title	titles (dbo)	✓				
type	titles (dbo)	✓				
price	titles (dbo)	✓			> 20 AND < 30	
qty	sales (dbo)	✓				

Notice in this example that the SQL pane creates the appropriate SQL statement, using
the AND logical operator statement based on the choices made in the Grid pane. The
Results pane displays the rows from the database based on this query. This example
demonstrates the interactive nature of working with the Query Designer to create and
construct queries that produce the desired results for your application.

Grouping the Results

You can use the GROUP BY statement to organize your rows into specific groups. For
example, you may want to create a query that returns the average book price for a certain
publisher. To create a query based on the GROUP BY statement, drag and drop the table
that you want to work with into the Diagram pane. For this example, use the Titles table.
Make sure that you have the Grid pane activated as well. You also can group the results
by selecting Group By from the Query menu. This adds a Group By column to the grid
in the Grid pane. Figure 9.19 shows what your Query Designer workspace should look
like so far.

FIGURE 9.19.

Selecting the table to group.

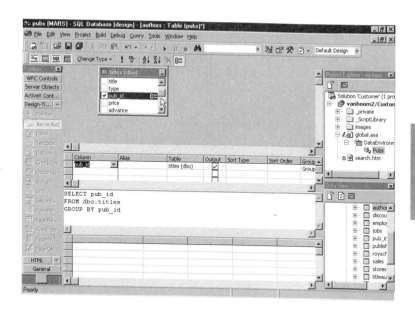

Next, add the column that you want to group by. You can perform this step in one of two ways. First, you can place your cursor in the Column field in the grid within the Grid pane and choose the column from the drop-down list box. You also can select the Group By field by using the Diagram pane. Using this method, click the box to the left of the column that you want to group by. The column displays a check mark next to its name in the Diagram pane. The Query Designer also inserts this column into the grid in the Grid pane and selects the Group By value for the Group By column. Figure 9.20 shows what the Diagram, Grid, and SQL panes look like as a result of choosing the Pub_ID column to group the results.

After you have chosen the column to group the results, you need to add the column that will average the prices of all the books for the publishers. This column will be a computed column that calculates the average based on information in the database. It displays the average price in the query results.

You can add the column in one of two ways. First, you can add the column to the Grid pane from the drop-down list box in the Column field. Place your cursor in the Column field for an empty row in the Grid pane. Choose the column that will supply the data for the computed column. Second, you can use the Diagram pane to add this column, similar to the method you used to add the Group By column in the preceding example. Click the column that you want to use. A check mark is placed next to the name in the Diagram pane, and the field is added to the Grid pane.

FIGURE 9.20.

*Choosing the column
to group the results.*

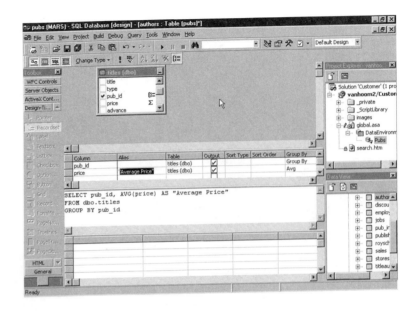

Tip

> You should always create an alias for computed columns. The alias name
> helps provide a useful and meaningful name for the column. If you don't
> supply an alias, the computed column's name is displayed as a generic name,
> such as Column 2. The reason for this generic name is that a computed col-
> umn isn't stored in the database and, therefore, doesn't have a column
> name.

For the purposes of this example, Average Price is used for the alias name of the computed column. After selecting the column that will be calculated, you need to select the
computation method. In this example, select the AVG function. This function calculates
the average price for a particular publisher's books, based on the individual book prices
for that publisher. Figure 9.21 depicts the choices you have made so far within the Query
Designer workspace.

You can now run the query to discover the results. Figure 9.22 displays the results of this
query example, using all four panes of the Query Designer.

In the previous example, you learned how to group your results and use the AVG function
to calculate an average. You can use the Query Designer to build other aggregate functions. Table 9.4 lists some of the available aggregate functions and their descriptions.

FIGURE 19.21.

Choosing the calculation method.

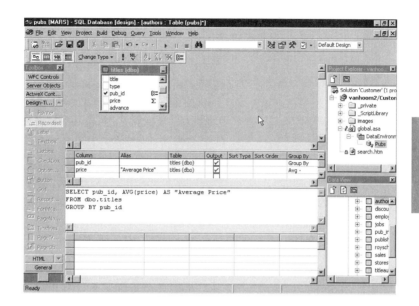

FIGURE 9.22.

Showing results of average price query.

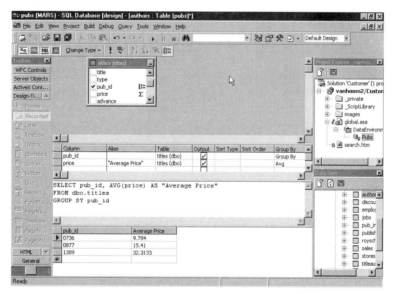

9

TABLE 9.4. GROUP BY AGGREGATE FUNCTIONS.

Function	Description
AVG	Calculates the average of numeric values in a column
MAX	Finds highest value for a numeric column, last value for an alphanumeric column; ignores null values
MIN	Finds lowest value for a numeric column, first value for an alphanumeric column; ignores null values
SUM	Calculates the total of numeric values in a column
COUNT	Counts the number of values in a column if column name is specified; ignores null values

You can use the WHERE and HAVING clauses to create specific criteria for your queries. You also can use expressions within your queries. For example, you might want to calculate the price of a book by a specific discount percentage. You can create an expression that multiplies the price times the discount percentage number to calculate the discount price. Figure 9.23 shows an example of calculating a discount of 20 percent on all the books in the Titles table.

FIGURE 9.23.

Using an expression to discount the price.

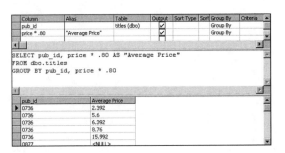

You can choose the WHERE clause and the Expression options from the drop-down list box for the Group By column in the Grid pane.

Creating an Update Query

So far, you have learned how to use the Diagram and Grid panes to construct a select query. You have used the individual features of both panes to create your query. You also have discovered how your choices in the Diagram and Grid panes affect the SQL and Results panes. In this section, you learn how to apply those techniques to create an update query.

An update query enables you to change the value of a column or columns in a row. You also can create an update query to make changes to multiple rows. The update query uses the UPDATE SQL statement to execute against a database. The update query can be very useful when you don't want to manually update individual rows within a database.

Selecting the Table to Update

To create an update query, you first need to select the table that you want to update. Select the table from the Data View and drag it over to the Diagram pane.

Next, choose the type of query that you're constructing. To create an update query, click the Change Query icon on the Query Designer toolbar.

Click the box to the left of each column that you want to use to create the update query. As in the previous example, these fields are displayed in the Grid pane in the order that you select them. A pencil indicator is displayed in the Diagram pane next to each column that you select.

For this example, use the Titles table and select several of the fields to use in the update query.

Adding the Values for the Update Query

Next, use the Grid pane to enter the new values for the columns that you want to change. The grid for an update query differs from the select query grid in that the update query grid contains a New Value column. You use this column to enter the new value for the column you're going to change. You can enter a value, a column name, or an expression in the New Value column.

After you enter the update value for the column, specify any special search criteria for the update query. For example, you can create a query that discounts the price for all books for a certain publisher by 10%. You need to enter an expression in the New Value column for this type of update. You also need to include a special search condition that only updates the rows for that particular publisher ID. You can enter the search conditions in the Criteria column. The same search condition rules that apply to the select query also apply to update queries. In this example, a condition is entered to discount the price by 10% for all books that have a publisher ID number equal to 1389. Figure 9.24 demonstrates how this is displayed in the Query Designer workspace.

FIGURE 9.24.

Entering the update parameters.

 Note

> In the previous example, the update query changed the value of a column for rows containing a publisher ID equal to 1389. The example accomplished this update by specifying a special search condition for the Pub_ID column. If you don't enter a condition in the Criteria field, all rows are updated with the new value for the column or columns that you select.

After you have entered the new values for the columns and specified a search condition, you can execute the query to update the database with new values. Figure 9.25 shows the results of the update query.

FIGURE 9.25.

Updating the database.

When you run an update query, the Results pane doesn't display any rows. Instead, a confirmation message indicates how many rows were affected by the update.

 Note

> Creating a delete query is similar to creating an update query. The delete query differs in function from the update query in that the delete query deletes all the rows for the conditions that you specify. Like the update query, a confirmation message displays after you execute the query, indicating how many rows were affected by the delete query.

Entering and Modifying Data

You can use the Query Designer to manually add, change, and delete data. You discovered in yesterday's lesson that the connection in your Visual InterDev project is a live connection to the database. Changes that you make manually or through your queries have an immediate impact on the information stored in the database. You can use the Results pane to manually update the database. Your ability to make updates to the database depends on your database permissions and any triggers that have been established to enforce referential integrity for the database.

Adding New Data

To add new data to a table, place your cursor in the first empty row in the Results pane. This row is denoted with an asterisk (*) in the box to the left of the Column field. When you begin to enter data for the row, the asterisk changes to a pencil indicator, signifying that you are editing the row. After you have finished entering the data for the last column, the Query Designer commits the information to the database. Figure 9.26 depicts a row that is being added to the Authors table in the Pubs database.

FIGURE 9.26.

Using the Results pane to add data.

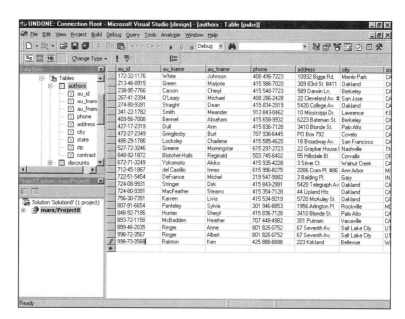

Changing the Data

To change the information stored in a database, place your cursor in the field you want to change and make the appropriate update. The change is confirmed when you exit the field. You can press the Esc key before you move the cursor to cancel changes for a field. To cancel changes made to a row, press the Esc key while the cursor is in a field that hasn't been changed.

Eventually, you may have to update a row that has already been updated by another user. In these situations, the Query Definitions Differ dialog box will display, indicating the conflict. You can choose to overwrite the other user's changes, cancel your changes, or return to the Results pane and run the query again to view the other person's changes.

Deleting the Data

You also can use the Results pane to delete rows within a database. Again, this ability is based on the permissions that have been established in the database concerning data deletion. To delete a row, select the entire row that you want to delete by selecting the box to the left of the Column field. When the row is highlighted, press Delete. For deletes, a warning message is displayed that enables you to confirm your delete.

Summary

Today's lesson provides a wealth of knowledge and instruction concerning the Visual Data Tools. You learned how to maximize your productivity by using these robust database programming tools that are included with Visual InterDev. Database programming is a big part of your application. By now, you can probably see the benefit to having visual aids to help you through this process.

First, you discovered how to use the Query Designer to generate your SQL statements. You spent the majority of the day learning how to work with the Query Designer workspace and features to visually construct your queries. The lesson provides an in-depth look at each Query Designer pane. You learned about the features of each pane and how to use these features to your advantage. Along the way, the lesson provides a guided tour through an example of how to use these features in a real-world situation. You should now have a very good understanding of the four panes of the Query Designer and feel comfortable using these panes to build queries and interact with the database.

You also learned how to manipulate the SQL statements that are generated by the Query Designer. For this part of the lesson, you used the SQL pane of the Query Designer to build custom SQL statements. The final lesson for the day taught you how to enter and modify information in the database, using the Results pane of the Query Designer.

You should feel very confident about using the Visual Data Tools to interact with the database. The Visual Data Tools can significantly boost your productivity and provide a great tool for working with the database.

Q&A

Q Do I have to use the Query Designer Diagram and Grid panes to construct my queries?

A No, you can develop your custom queries using the SQL pane. You may feel more comfortable typing in the SQL statement yourself. The Diagram and Grid panes serve as visual tools to help you quickly construct your queries. After you enter

your custom query using the SQL pane, the Query Designer attempts to construct the query in the Diagram and Grid panes.

Q Can I use the Visual Data Tool against any database?

A The Visual Data Tools enable you to access any ODBC or OLEDB data source. Almost all the major databases support these two standards.

Q How do the Query Designer panes relate to each other?

A The Query Designer consists of four panes—Diagram, Grid, SQL, and Results. The Diagram pane enables you to choose your tables and provides a starting point to construct your query. The Grid pane enables you to extend the construction of the query by defining search criteria and update values. The SQL pane shows the SQL as it is constructed and enables you to modify this statement. These panes work together to help you build your query. Any changes that you make in one pane are reflected in the other panes. The Results pane displays the results of your query. All four panes work together to help you create a query and instantly verify the results.

Workshop

The Workshop provides quiz questions and exercises to help you solidify your understanding of the material covered and to provide experience using what you've learned. You can find the answers to the quiz questions and exercises in Appendix B, "Answers."

Quiz

1. What is an update query?

2. What is a stored procedure?

3. What is a computed column?

Exercises

1. Use the Publishers database to create a query that displays the royalties and year-to-date sales for authors sorted by author last name.

2. Customize the query in exercise 1 to list just those authors that have royalties greater than 10 percent.

DAY 10

Managing Your Database Components

The proper administration and management of objects in your database isn't a rudimentary exercise. Yesterday, you discovered some of the Visual Data Tools that facilitate interaction with the database. Today's lesson demonstrates how you can create, organize, and maintain all the components within your database. Visual InterDev, again, is true to its name by providing visual tools that remove the difficulty from database administration. Some of the topics you'll be covering today are

- The types of objects that are contained in a database
- Maintaining database objects using the Database Designer
- Creating and modeling your database with database diagrams
- Creating and maintaining stored procedures and triggers

You might be thinking that this lesson is targeted at database administrators (DBAs) and not developers. Actually, the lesson is targeted at both. As a developer, you need to understand the principles of database administration so you can communicate your application needs to your DBA.

You might be a part of a development team that doesn't have the luxury of allocating a dedicated person to assume the role of DBA. This chapter reveals how the Visual Data Tools enable you to properly manage and administrate your database. You don't have to be a DBA to use these tools. The Database Designer is very intuitive and powerful. For DBAs, the Database Designer provides yet another set of tools to add to your toolbox. You might find that you like them much better than the typical database administration tools. Whether you are a developer or a DBA, this chapter is very important. The lesson helps you understand how you can use Visual InterDev to create and maintain the right type of database for your application.

Introduction to Database Objects

A database is composed of objects that define its behavior and use. You might be familiar with a lot of the terms in this section. By using the Database Designer, you can create and manage the following objects:

- Tables
- Relationships
- Constraints
- Indexes

Tables

Tables are the basic objects contained in a database. You use tables to store your information in the database. Tables are composed of columns, or fields, that help further define the attributes of the data. Each table must contain at least one column to be saved in the Database Designer. When you define a column for a table, you must specify the column name, length, and datatype.

Relationships

After you construct your database tables, you must define how they will interact, or their relationship to each other. Relationships help avoid redundant data by enabling you to relate two tables together instead of storing the same information in both tables. For example, you can create an order header table that contains basic order information and then relate an order detail table that contains multiple line items for each order header. Each order detail line item represents an item that has been ordered. By relating these two tables, you avoid having to store the order header information for each detail line item. For each order detail line item, you only need to store the order number from the order header table.

Relationships also help enforce referential integrity. The data contained in the database must be accurate and correct. Referential integrity means that everywhere the data is referenced in the database, the integrity of that data is maintained. Referring back to the order header and order detail example, an order detail line cannot exist without having an order header row. Conversely, an order header row that references order detail lines cannot be deleted without first deleting the order detail lines. Figure 10.1 shows an example of an order header and the relationship to multiple order detail items.

FIGURE 10.1.

An order header with multiple order detail lines.

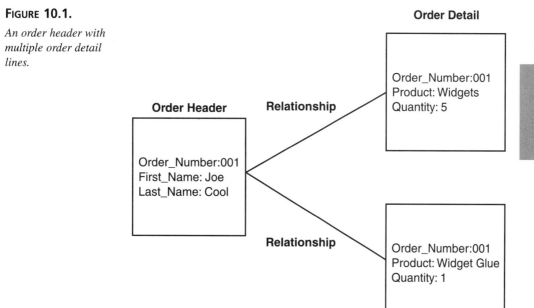

10

Defining Relationships

You define a relationship through the use of *keys*. A primary key is a column or set of columns that uniquely identifies a row in the table. For example, the order number is the primary key for the order header table in the preceding example. Likewise, the combination of the order number and order detail line number serves as the primary key combination for the order detail table. A foreign key is a column or set of columns that matches the primary key of another table. The order number that resides in the order detail table is referred to as a foreign key because its value matches the value of a column in the order header table.

There are three basic types of table relationships: one-to-many, many-to-many, and one-to-one.

One-to-Many Relationships

One-to-many is the most common type of relationship. A one-to-many relationship consists of a table with one row that relates to many rows in another table. Each order header row can consist of many order detail lines. One example of this type of relationship is an order header table and an order detail table. The order header table could consist of one row with order information such as order date and order amount. The order detail table could consist of multiple entries such as multiple products that belong to the order. The order header table in this example has a one-to-many relationship to the order detail table.

Many-to-Many Relationships

Many-to-many is the second type of relationship. A many-to-many relationship consists of many rows of one table that relate to many rows in another table. This association is achieved through the use of a junction table, which helps to relate the two tables. An example of this relationship can be found in the sample Publishers database that was referenced in yesterday's lesson.

The Titles table has a many-to-many relationship with the Authors table. A title can have multiple authors, and an author can write multiple titles. The junction table for the Titles and Authors tables is the TitleAuthor table. This table's primary key contains the primary key from the Titles table as well as the primary key from the Authors table. Figure 10.2 shows a diagram of these three tables.

FIGURE 10.2.

A many-to-many relationship.

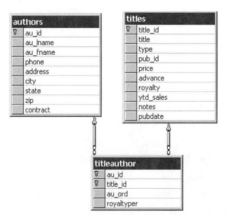

One-to-One Relationships

The third type of relationship is one-to-one. In a one-to-one relationship, a row from one table relates to a single row of another table. This type of relationship is useful when you want to put logical groupings of information in a separate table. For example, a customer table might contain customer information such as name, address, and phone number. You might also have information about a customer's employer such as employer name, address, and phone number that you would want to logically place in a separate table. Even though these two tables have a one-to-one relationship, they are separated into two logical tables.

Constraints

You'll want to enforce certain rules concerning the columns within your database. Constraints enable you to define the rules for the values of the columns in your tables. Table 10.1 displays the five types of constraints provided by MS SQL Server and their descriptions.

TABLE 10.1. MS SQL SERVER CONSTRAINTS.

Type	Description
Check	Enforces valid data values for one or more columns
Default	Provides a default value for a column
Primary Key	Avoids duplicate or null values
Foreign Key	Enforces referential integrity foreign key relationships
Unique	Ensures a unique value for a column or set of columns

Indexes

Indexes provide fast access to rows in your database. A database index is very similar to the index in this book. You use the book index to find the page for a certain topic and then turn to that page number to read about the topic. The database index works in much the same way by storing a pointer to certain data in your database. The index consists of a column or set of columns within the table. You should only establish indexes for data that the user accesses frequently. Although indexes provide fast access to data, they absorb disk space and slow the speed of inserts, changes, and deletions into the database.

Getting Started with the Database Designer

The Database Designer provides a very flexible and intuitive environment for working with your database objects. Database diagrams provide the main interface for creating and maintaining your database objects. A database diagram visually depicts the columns, tables, and the relationships of the tables within your database. I'll talk about diagrams in the next section, "Visualizing Your Database."

> **Note**
> The Database Designer supports the use of MS SQL Server 6.5 and later as well as Oracle 7.x and higher. The lesson today assumes you're using MS SQL Server as your database.

I recommend that you use Visual InterDev to create a database project for the specific purposes of administering your database. This way, you can separate the development tasks from the database administration tasks and can determine what is best for your project based on personal preference.

To create a database project, select New Project from the File menu. The New Project dialog box is displayed. Choose the New tab and select the Database Projects folder. Type a name for the new database project and click OK. You'll be prompted to add or select a database connection similar to the database connection that you added during Day 8, "Communicating with a Database." For purposes of this example, I selected the Publishers datasource that I established earlier. This data connection creates a live connection to your database that you can then use to manage your database.

> **Note**
> You can choose to add the database connection after you have created the project by choosing Add Data Connection from the shortcut menu.

Figure 10.3 shows the database project for the Publishers database.

When you have created a database project, you're ready to start. The next section provides an overview of database diagrams and their relevance to managing your database.

Visualizing Your Database

The Database Designer uses diagrams to graphically depict the objects in your database, including tables, columns, constraints, and indexes. The database diagram also shows the relationship between tables in your database. You can make modifications to these objects as well as the table relationships by using the database diagram. The Database Designer also enables you to create a diagram of possible table structures and relationships to model what-if scenarios for the database. Because your changes won't affect the database until you save them, you have the flexibility to change objects around until you decide to save the changes to the database.

FIGURE 10.3.

A sample database project.

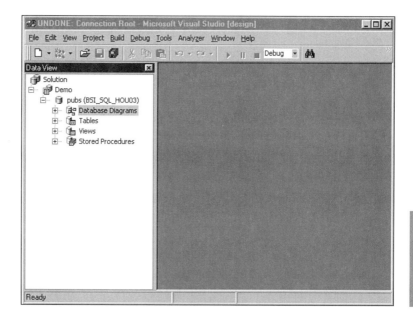

When you're finished with your modifications, you can choose to update the database, save the changes to execute later, or cancel the changes. If you choose to save the changes for later use, the modifications will be saved in a Transact-SQL script. I will provide more detail on the use of these scripts at the end of today's lesson, in the section "Utilizing SQL Scripts."

Exploring a Database Diagram

Database diagrams are saved in the Database Diagram folder within your project. You can expand this folder in the Data view to see all the database diagrams for your database. A database diagram typically contains one or more tables. Figure 10.4 displays a diagram for the Authors and TitleAuthor tables.

As you can see from the figure, the Authors table has a one-to-many relationship with the TitleAuthor table. You learned about the relationship symbols during yesterday's lesson. Each table is represented by a grid that contains its columns. A key symbol in the box next to a column designates the keys for each table. In the Authors table, there is a key beside the au_id (Author ID) column. The key for the TitleAuthor table is a combination of the au_id and the title_id columns.

Table 10.2 defines each of the columns within the database diagram grid.

FIGURE 10.4.

A database diagram.

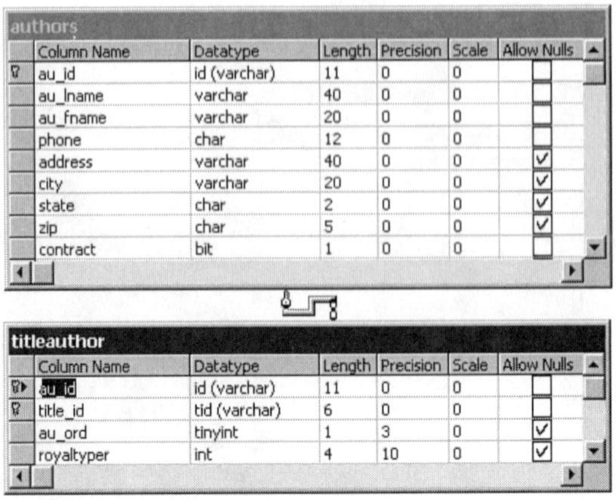

authors						
Column Name	Datatype	Length	Precision	Scale	Allow Nulls	▲
� au_id	id (varchar)	11	0	0		
au_lname	varchar	40	0	0		
au_fname	varchar	20	0	0		
phone	char	12	0	0		
address	varchar	40	0	0	✓	
city	varchar	20	0	0	✓	
state	char	2	0	0	✓	
zip	char	5	0	0	✓	
contract	bit	1	0	0		▼

titleauthor						
Column Name	Datatype	Length	Precision	Scale	Allow Nulls	▲
⟦⟧ au_id	id (varchar)	11	0	0		
⟦⟧ title_id	tid (varchar)	6	0	0		
au_ord	tinyint	1	3	0	✓	
royaltyper	int	4	10	0	✓	▼

TABLE 10.2. DATABASE COLUMN PROPERTIES.

Column Property	Description
Column Name	Name of the column
Datatype	Type of data to be stored
Length	Length of the column (determined by datatype)
Precision	Maximum number of digits used or maximum length of column for alphanumeric columns
Scale	Maximum number of digits to the right of the decimal
Allow Nulls	Specifies whether null values can be allowed
Default Value	Sets a default value for the column
Identity	Column that contains a system-generated value
Identity Seed	Initial value for the system-generated column
Identity Increment	Increment for the system-generated value

Note   The length is defined automatically when you assign a datatype for a column. You can change the length of some fields, including `binary`, `char`, `varbinary`, and `varchar`.

Understanding Database Diagram Properties

You can access and change the properties for the tables, indexes, and relationships for your diagrams by using the Properties dialog box. This window is a tabbed display dialog box that contains the properties for each of these objects. The following section explains the property fields for each of these database objects.

Table Properties

You can access the properties for your tables by selecting the table and clicking the right mouse button to display the shortcut menu. Choose Property Pages from the list of menu items. Figure 10.5 demonstrates the available properties for a sample table.

FIGURE 10.5.

Setting the table properties.

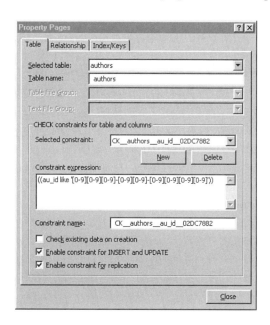

This window enables you to view and change the properties for a particular table. The Selected Table drop-down list box enables you to choose another table from the list and view its properties. This list box only displays tables that are included in the current database diagram that you are working in. The Table Name field enables you to view and change the name of the selected table. The bottom half of this window enables you to see the selected check constraints for the table and its columns. The Selected Constraint drop-down list box enables you to choose a column that contains a check constraint. See Table 10.3 for details.

TABLE 10.3. THE SELECTED CONSTRAINT DROP-DOWN LIST BOX.

Property	Description
New	Enables you to create a new check constraint for the table
Delete	Deletes the currently selected check constraint from the database
Constraint Expression field	Use it to enter the Transact-SQL syntax for the check constraint

continues

TABLE 10.3. CONTINUED

Property	Description
Constraint Name	Enables you to view and change the name of the check constraint
Check Existing Data on Creation	Applies the constraint to existing data in the database if the check box is enabled

You can select the Check Existing Data on Creation property to apply the constraint to data that already exists in the database. You can select the Enable Constraint for INSERT and UPDATE property to apply the constraint to all insertions and updates in the database. The Enable Constraint for Replication property enables you to use the constraint for replicating the table to a different database.

Relationship Properties

The Relationship Properties dialog box enables you to change the properties of the relationships of the tables contained in your database diagrams. Figure 10.6 shows the fields that are contained on this window.

FIGURE 10.6.

Setting the relationship properties.

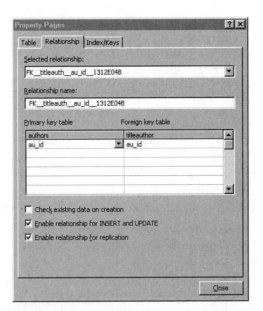

The following list explains these fields:

- The first field on this page displays the selected relationship. You can choose another relationship from the drop-down list box.

- The Relationship Name field enables you to change the name of the currently selected relationship.
- The Primary Key Table shows the name of the primary key table in the relationship and the columns that make up the primary key.
- The Foreign Key Table displays the name of the foreign key table in the relationship and the columns that make up the foreign key.

The next three check boxes are similar in meaning to the check boxes contained on the Table Properties window. These check boxes apply to the foreign key in the table relationship:

- If Check Existing Data on Creation is enabled, the constraint is applied to existing data in the database when the relationship is added to the Foreign key table.
- You can check Enable Relationship for INSERT and UPDATE to apply the constraint to all insertions and updates in the Foreign key table. Enabling this check box also prevents the deletion of a row in the Primary table if a related row in the Foreign key table exists.
- Enable Relationship for Replication enables you to use the constraint for replicating the Foreign key table to a different database.

Index/Keys Properties

You can use the Index/Keys tab to view and change the keys and indexes for the tables within your database diagrams. Figure 10.7 shows the options that are available in this dialog box.

FIGURE 10.7.

Setting the properties for the indexes and keys.

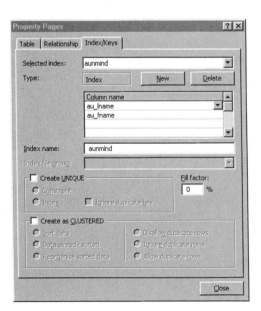

The following list explains these fields:

- The Selected Index field displays the indexes and keys for the selected table.
- The Type display box located below the Selected Index field denotes whether you're viewing a primary key, unique key, or index for the selected table.
- The Column Name grid displays the column names that are included in the index or key. You can add, change, or delete columns from the list by using the New and Delete buttons.
- Index Name enables you to establish a name for the index.
- The Create UNIQUE check box enables you to create a unique constraint or index for the table. If you create a unique index, you can choose to ignore duplicate keys.
- You can use the Fill Factor field to specify how full to make the index page within the database. This field is used by database administrators to fine-tune the performance of the database.
- The Create as CLUSTERED field enables you to create a clustered index. A clustered index provides faster access to data than a nonclustered index.

The remaining check boxes on the Index/Keys tab enable you to further specify attributes of the clustered index, and are self-explanatory.

Creating and Editing SQL Server Objects

So far, you have learned about the types of database objects that you can manipulate, as well as how database diagrams provide the main method for working with these objects. In this section, you are guided through the process of creating and saving a database diagram. The lesson also teaches you how to create and maintain the database objects within your diagrams, as well as how to maintain objects through the Data view.

Creating a Database Diagram

Creating a database diagram is an excellent way to work with database objects. You'll now create a new database diagram with the Publishers datasource that was created earlier.

1. To create a new database diagram, select the Database Diagram folder and right-click to display the shortcut menu.
2. Choose New Diagram from the list of menu items, and a blank database diagram is created.
3. Click the Tables folder to display the list of available tables for the diagram.
4. Click the Titles table, drag it to the diagram window, and drop the table into the diagram. The table and a list of columns now appear in the diagram.

5. Click the Sales table. Drag and drop it into the diagram. When you drop the Sales table into the diagram, the relationship between the Titles table and the Sales table is automatically depicted. Figure 10.8 shows a database diagram with these two tables.

FIGURE **10.8.**

A sample database diagram.

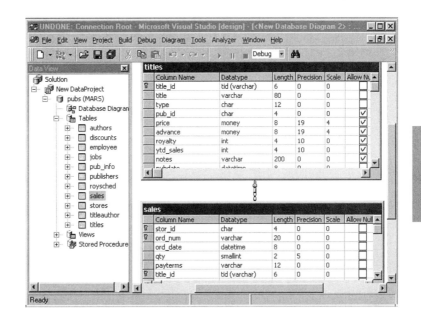

6. Choose File | Save DatabaseDiagram1. The Save New Database Diagram window appears, prompting you to enter a name for the diagram.

7. Enter SalesTitlesDiagram as the diagram name and click OK.

8. Close the diagram by choosing File | Close from the main menu.

Creating a New Database Table

You can create a new table within the database diagram. Follow these steps to create a new table:

1. Create a new database diagram as shown previously.

2. Click the New Table button on the Database Diagram toolbar (on the far left of the toolbar).

3. The Choose Name window appears, prompting you for the name of the table. The default table name is Table1. Click OK to accept this name. The table will then be ready for creation as depicted in Figure 10.9.

FIGURE **10.9.**

Creating a new table.

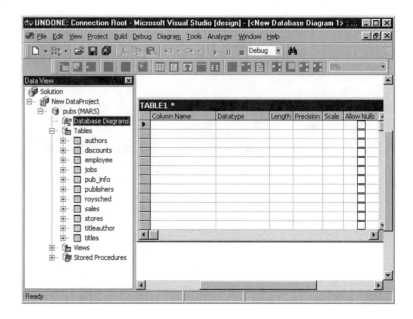

To rename the table, follow these steps:

1. Select the table and right-click to display the shortcut menu.

2. Choose Properties from the list of menu items to display the Property Pages dialog box.

3. Select the Table tab and enter Orders in the Table name field. When you change the name of the table using this field, the Selected Name drop-down list box changes to reflect the new name of the table that you enter. Figure 10.10 displays the Table Properties window with the newly created table that has been renamed.

Tip

There are several other methods for creating a new database table. First, you can right-click the mouse and choose New Table from the shortcut menu. Another method involves right-clicking the Tables folder in the Data view and choosing Add Table from the shortcut menu.

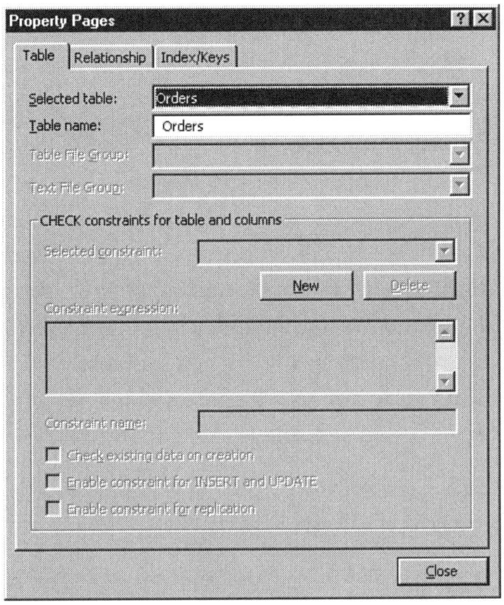

FIGURE 10.10.

Renaming the table.

10

Defining the Column Properties

When you have created the table and given it a meaningful name, you can enter the column names and properties. Follow these steps to enter column names:

1. Column name is the first property that is set for the new table. Enter OrderNumber for column name.

2. Press the Tab key to move to the next table property, which is Datatype. Select int from the datatype drop-down list.

3. The length, precision, and scale properties are automatically set after selecting the datatype.

4. Continue adding columns to the table as depicted in Figure 10.11.

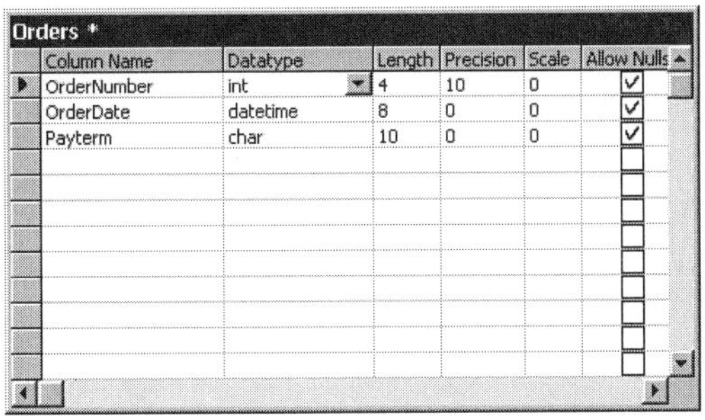

FIGURE 10.11.

Setting the datatype.

You can use the Tab and arrow keys to navigate within the fields in the grid. An arrow in the box to the left of the column name denotes the current row that you are inserting within the grid.

After you enter the columns for the table, you need to set the key values for the table. Select the row that you want to be the primary key and click the Set Primary Key button on the Database Diagram toolbar. If the primary key of the table is a combination of columns, you need to select all the columns that are a part of the key and then click the Set Primary Key button. To select multiple rows in the grid, click the mouse in the box to the left of the Column name field to highlight the first column row. Then press Shift+↓ to highlight the next column row. Repeat this step until you have highlighted all the column rows for the primary key; then click Set Primary Key on the Database Diagram toolbar. A key indicator is displayed next to the columns that you designate as the primary key.

Saving Your Database Changes

The final step to creating your new database table involves saving the changes to the database. You have learned over the last couple of days that the database connection that you establish is a live connection. In other words, the actions that you perform have an immediate effect on the database. The Database Diagram gives you the option of directly updating the database or saving the changes for later. To save a newly created table, you have several available options. First, you can choose Save New Database Diagram from the File menu. You'll be prompted to enter a name for the diagram you used to create the new tables. When you enter the name and click OK, the Database Designer inserts the new table or tables into the database.

Note   The Save All command from the File menu has the same effect as the Save New Database Diagram option. Both of these menu commands perform immediate updates against the database.

You also can choose Save Change Script from the File menu, which saves the SQL script to a text file that you can execute against the database at a later time.

Figure 10.12 shows the results of saving the Orders table against the Publishers database.

Figure 10.12.

Saving the new table.

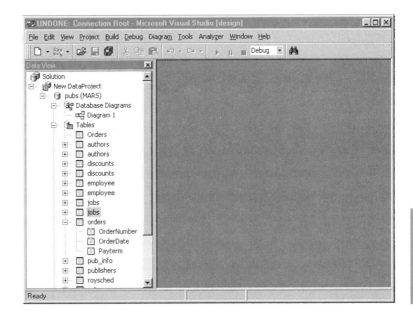

Working with Diagrams and Tables

You can use the Database Designer to view the relationships of the tables in your database. You also can use the Database Designer to modify existing table relationships and properties. To open an existing database diagram, right-click the selected diagram from within the Data view and choose Open from the list of menu items. This action opens the database diagram, enabling you to work with the tables contained in the diagram. You can make changes to the column properties as well as to the relationships between the tables. You also can add new tables to the diagram, as explained in the previous section. After you have made your modifications, you need to save your changes to the database. You can either save these changes immediately to the database or save the changes to a text file for later use.

Modifying Objects Within the Design View

In addition to the database diagram, the Design view offers an excellent way for you to work with database objects. To modify a table using the Design view, select a table from the Tables folder and click the right mouse button to display the shortcut menu. Choose Design from the list of menu items and a Design view of the table appears. Figure 10.13 shows the Design view for the Authors table in the Publishers database. From the Design view you can modify attributes of the table in the same manner that you modify tables within a database diagram.

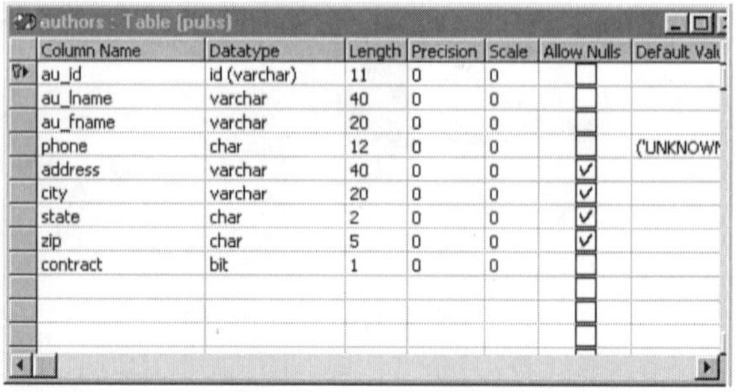

FIGURE **10.13.**

The Design view.

Column Name	Datatype	Length	Precision	Scale	Allow Nulls	Default Vali
au_id	id (varchar)	11	0	0		
au_lname	varchar	40	0	0		
au_fname	varchar	20	0	0		
phone	char	12	0	0		('UNKNOWN
address	varchar	40	0	0	✓	
city	varchar	20	0	0	✓	
state	char	2	0	0	✓	
zip	char	5	0	0	✓	
contract	bit	1	0	0		

Using SQL Scripts

In the previous section, you discovered that you can execute immediate updates against the database. You also learned that you can save these changes in a text file to be executed at a later time. These files contain Transact-SQL commands that perform administrative functions against the database.

SQL scripts can be useful, especially if you have to execute the same commands repeatedly against a database. These scripts also can be useful for creating the same databases and tables for separate development, testing, and production database environments. A good DBA learns the benefit of SQL scripts very quickly in life. It only takes having to delete a table and re-create it manually one time to see the benefit of an automated script that performs this function for you.

Saving the SQL Script

Earlier today, you learned how to create and modify tables. The last step involves saving those changes. The previous example showed you how to immediately update the database with the changes. To save the changes to a SQL script instead, follow these steps:

1. Open the Orders table in Design mode (right-click the table and select Design).
2. Change the Payterm column from a datatype of char to a datatype of int.
3. Choose Save SQL Script from the File menu. The Save Change Script dialog box displays. Figure 10.14 shows the SQL script for a change to the column datatype of the Orders table.

FIGURE 10.14.

Examining the SQL Script.

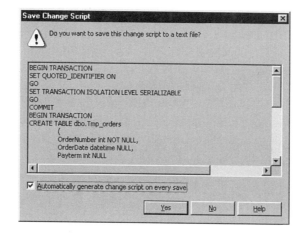

4. After you have verified that the SQL syntax is correct, you can click Yes to save the changes for the SQL script.

5. A confirmation message with a default name for the script is then displayed. The name is assigned by the Database Designer and contains the .sql extension. You can edit this file using Visual InterDev as well as any text editor. You also might want to rename the file to conform to any standards that you have established for your project.

The Save Change Script dialog box displays the actual Transact-SQL that is saved to the text file. Listing 10.1 shows the complete code sample for Figure 10.14.

LISTING 10.1. CHANGING THE DATATYPE OF A DATABASE COLUMN.

```
 1: BEGIN TRANSACTION
 2: CREATE TABLE dbo.Tmp_orders
 3: (OrderNumber int NOT NULL,OrderDate datetime NULL,
    ➥Payterm int NULL) ON "default"
 4: GO
 5: IF EXISTS(SELECT * FROM dbo.orders)
 6: EXEC('INSERT INTO dbo.Tmp_orders(OrderNumber, OrderDate, Payterm)
 7: SELECT OrderNumber, OrderDate, CONVERT(int, Payterm)
    ➥FROM dbo.orders TABLOCKX')
 8: GO
 9: DROP TABLE dbo.orders
10: GO
11: EXECUTE sp_rename 'dbo.Tmp_orders', 'orders'
12: GO
13: ALTER TABLE dbo.orders ADD CONSTRAINT
14: PK_Orders PRIMARY KEY NONCLUSTERED
15: (OrderNumber) ON "default"
16: GO
17: COMMIT
```

I'm not going to examine the entire code listing, but I do want to outline a very robust feature of the Database Designer. You can use the Database Designer to change the column datatypes of tables that contain existing data. This code listing shows the Transact-SQL that creates a temporary table named Tmp_Orders. This temporary table is used to insert any data that resides in the Orders table and convert it to the new datatype. The original Orders table with the old datatype for the Payterm column is then deleted. Finally, the Tmp_Orders table that contains the order information with the new datatype is renamed Orders. The Database Designer creates all this logic for you, which should make DBAs appreciate the robustness of the Database Designer even more.

Creating and Editing Stored Procedures

The stored procedure editor provides a very intuitive tool for creating and maintaining stored procedures for your applications. Visual InterDev supports the use of the stored procedure editor with MS SQL Server 6 and later as well as support for Oracle databases.

Creating a Stored Procedure

To create a new stored procedure, follow these steps:

1. Select the Stored Procedures folder and right-click the mouse to display the shortcut menu.

2. Choose New Stored Procedure from the list of menu items. The stored procedure editor opens and presents a template for creating your new stored procedure. Figure 10.15 displays the template that is generated for creating a new stored procedure.

3. The template includes the Transact-SQL keywords CREATE PROCEDURE, which signify all stored procedures, and follows with the name of the new stored procedure. Replace the word StoredProcedure1 with NonProfitRpt.

4. The template also provides a place for you to enter the name of the input and output parameters. This example doesn't use input or output parameters, so delete the following code from the procedure:

```
(
@parameter1 datatype = default value,
@parameter2 datatype = default OUTPUT
)
```

5. The SQL for your procedure is entered after the AS keyword. Enter the following code after the AS keyword:

```
Select * from Titles
Where price < 20
And ytd_sales < 4000
```

FIGURE 10.15.

Creating a new stored procedure.

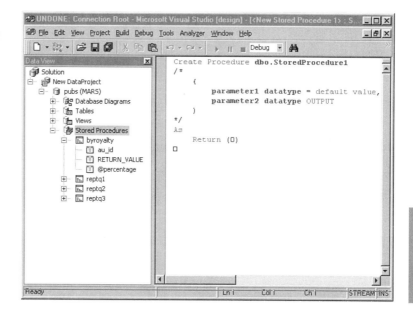

6. The stored procedure template also provides a placeholder at the end of the procedure for capturing the return code. For this example, type Return(0) for the return code.

7. Choose Save or Save As from the File menu. The Save As option enables you to save the file in a separate text file that is denoted with the .sql filename extension. Figure 10.16 shows an example of this stored procedure.

Executing a Stored Procedure

You learned during yesterday's lesson how to execute a stored procedure. After you have created and saved your stored procedure, you should test the procedure to ensure that it produces the desired results. You can execute the procedure from within the stored procedure editor by right-clicking the mouse anywhere within the stored procedure. Choose Execute from the list of menu items. If there is an error in your procedure, the stored procedure debugger displays an error message indicating the mistake, as shown in Figure 10.17.

If no errors are found, the result is displayed in the Output window at the bottom of the Visual InterDev project workspace, as depicted in Figure 10.18.

FIGURE 10.16.

A sample stored procedure.

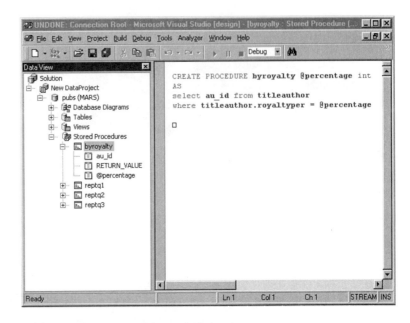

FIGURE 10.17.

An erroneous stored procedure.

FIGURE 10.18.

Executing a successful stored procedure.

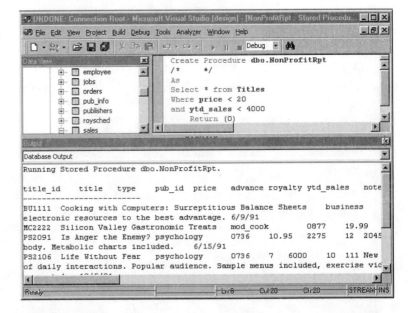

You still need to make sure that the stored procedure returned the results that you expected. A bug-free procedure doesn't mean that the stored procedure is accurate. You need to test the procedure to make sure that it meets your application requirements both now and in the future. A stored procedure is usually shared among the developers. Develop these procedures in a manner that can be universally applied across the application. This doesn't mean that you should have one stored procedure that meets everyone's needs. You should, however, create procedures that are targeted to the needs of more than a single developer.

Summary

Today's lesson concludes the last section focused solely on the database part of your application. You should be able to apply the database principles that you have learned over the last three days toward the other lessons this week and next week. You can use the Database Designer to perform routine database administration and management functions without becoming a full-fledged DBA. The Database Designer provides a visual tool that removes a lot of the mundane chores of managing your database components.

Today's lesson first provided you with an introduction to the Database Designer. You learned about the types of database objects that you can create and manipulate using the Database Designer. Next, you learned how to use database diagrams to create and maintain your database objects. You discovered the usefulness of database diagrams in providing a visual picture of your database as well as a visual tool to manage the database tables and objects.

Toward the end of the day, the lesson focused on the use of SQL scripts. You learned how the different Save options have an impact on the database and how you can use SQL scripts for database updates in the future. The final lesson for the day taught you to how to create and edit a stored procedure.

Q&A

Q Does the Database Designer replace my existing database administration tools?

A The Database Designer is meant to complement your other DBA tools. It enables you to administrate and manage database objects after you have created a database. You can use the Database Designer as yet another tool in your DBA toolbox.

Q Can I use the Database Designer to create an entity relationship diagram for my entire database?

A Yes. The Database Designer can be used to reverse-engineer your database to display an entity relationship diagram of your entire database. This is done by creating a new database diagram and dragging all the tables in your database into the diagram. The tool automatically creates the diagram with all the relationships.

Q Can I use the database administration tools to view database objects other than MS SQL Server?

A Yes. The database administration tools can be used to view database objects from any ODBC-compliant database. DBA functions such as adding tables and views can only be performed on MS SQL Server 6.5 databases as well as Oracle 7.x and later.

Workshop

The Workshop provides quiz questions and exercises to help you solidify your understanding of the material covered and to provide experience using what you've learned. You can find the answers to the quiz questions and exericises in Appendix B, "Answers."

Quiz

1. What is a foreign key?
2. What is the Default Value column property used for?
3. Name three types of column constraints.
4. What occurs if you save a database diagram?
5. What are two ways to edit the definition of a table?

Exercise

Create a database diagram for the pubs database.

DAY **11**

Fundamentals of Active Server Pages

By now you probably realize that Visual InterDev enables the construction of dynamic, Web-based applications. The primary means of creating dynamic content in Visual InterDev is through the use of Active Server Pages.

During the last few days, you learned about database integration with Visual InterDev, Visual Data Tools, and database components. For the most part, these topics deal with server-side components.

This lesson continues with that theme and introduces you to another component that resides on the server: Active Server Pages. Active Server Pages enable you to combine HTML and script code on the server to build dynamic and highly interactive Web pages. On Day 5, "Enhancing Your Web Page Through Client-Side Script," you learned about the use of scripting languages within the context of the browser on the client machine. On Day 6, "Extending Your Web Page Through Server-Side Script," you learned about the use of scripting languages within the context of the Web server. Today, you will take a look at the fundamental building blocks for using Active Server Pages to create dynamic Web content.

First, you will receive a brief introduction to making the server an active part of your Web-based application. Next, you will discover what makes Active Server Pages so dynamic and powerful. The lesson provides a closer look at the client/server picture. In exploring the conceptual architecture for a Web-based application, the lesson explains how Active Server Pages fit into the big picture, helping you understand how to use Active Server Pages within the scope of your application.

Throughout the day, I will provide examples of Active Server Pages and dissect the meaning of the code. You learned during the first week that Active Server Pages support the use of scripting languages such as VBScript and JavaScript. In today's lesson, you will use VBScript code examples. However, the principles that you will learn apply to either scripting language.

Making the Server Come Alive

The Web has been transformed into a place of interaction. Users don't just want to browse a Web page; they want to experience and interact with it. Using the server to provide this interactive experience for your users is a very important concept to master. Active Server Pages enable you to easily integrate server-side logic into your application. In the past, you may have used CGI or APIs to provide this logic. With both of these methods, you have to create an executable program on the server that involves a development process different from your Web page development.

Active Server Pages add an intriguing alternative to your choices for server-side development. You can design and develop Active Server Pages similar to the process that you use for your Web page development. Active Server Pages consist of HTML and script that reside on the server. Active Server Pages support the same popular scripting languages that you use on the client, including VBScript and JavaScript. The main benefit is that you can leverage the investment you make learning HTML and a scripting language on the client to your development for the server.

What Makes Active Server Pages So Dynamic?

Active Server Pages can be used as the main hub to control your server activity. You can code application-specific logic directly into an Active Server Page. This logic could be HTML as well as script code that changes the format of your Web pages.

Within an Active Server Page you can also include ActiveX and design-time ActiveX controls that are built specifically to execute on the server. Active Server Pages can be integrated with objects on the server to provide robust application processing. For example, you might interface with an object on the server that processes financial data and then returns the results through an Active Server Page. You also can place your database connections in Active Server Pages.

The development paradigm for Active Server Pages differs slightly from programming script on the client. If you remember the lesson on Day 5, "Enhancing Your Web Page Through Client-Side Script," the script that you develop for the client is embedded within the Web page that is sent to the browser. The browser executes the script based on system and user events. The browser must support the use of the particular scripting language to execute the code. If the browser doesn't recognize the script language, it will ignore the code.

In addition, not all Web servers support Active Server Pages. Of course, Microsoft's Internet Information Server (IIS) does support Active Server Pages. In fact, Active Server Pages were first introduced with IIS version 3. IIS contains a scripting engine that processes embedded Active Server script on the server. The results are returned to the client in a standard HTML format that is universally recognized by the browser. Because results are returned to the browser in standard HTML, any browser can read Active Server Pages. This powerful feature allows you as a developer to make applications built with Active Server Pages available to all users on the Internet or intranet, regardless of browser type.

Taking a Closer Look at the Process

This section explores how a browser interacts with an Active Server Page. First, the Web page references an Active Server Page (ASP) within the context of the application. Active Server Pages contain the filename extension of .asp. The following line of code demonstrates an example of calling an Active Server Page:

```
<FORM METHOD= "POST" ACTION="ProcessForm.asp">
```

By now, you are probably familiar with calling an Active Server Page from the lesson on Day 6, "Extending Your Web Page Through Server-Side Script." When the browser requests the ASP, the file is first processed by the server. The ASP may contain both HTML and scripting code. Any HTML code is passed directly to the browser as well as any client-side script. The server then searches for any server-side script. Similar to script on the client, server-side script is denoted by the symbols <% and %>. Upon locating the server-side code, the server processes the script and returns the results to the browser in the form of HTML. The server processes the script based on the current conditions and events. This model gives your application its unique and dynamic nature. The Web page that is formatted is based on conditions that are dynamic and changing, instead of a static HTML file that resides on the server. These conditions could be based on user input as well as information that is contained in a database.

Exploring the Client/Server Picture

Active Server Pages are an important part of your application. You can use Active Server Pages to create more intelligent server-side processing that handles the specific needs of your application. Active Server Pages are a central piece of the Web-based client/server model for your application. Figure 11.1 demonstrates the role of an Active Server Page in the overall scheme of a Web-based application.

FIGURE 11.1.

Playing an active part of the client/server picture.

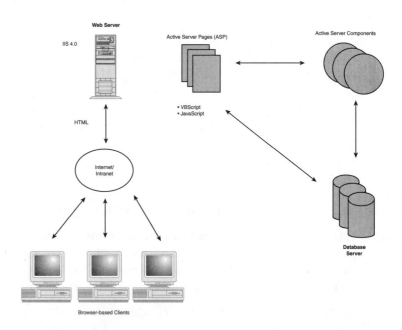

Active Server Pages reside on the Web server and play an active part in the functionality of your application. First, you can return dynamic Web pages to the client based on the preferences entered by the user. The ASP also can interface through the Component Object Model (COM) with Active Server Components. These components are applications that you develop using a more robust language such as Visual Basic, Visual C++, or Java. These components are compiled as executable (EXE) or dynamic link library (DLL) programs that handle the detailed processing of the application. You will learn more about working with and developing these components on Day 15, "Building an Integrated Solution with Components."

Also in Figure 11.1, you should notice the database component of the application. You can use Active Server Pages to directly interface with the database. The other alternative is to use an Active Server Component that is called from an ASP to handle the database processing. For database-intensive processes and transaction processing, you will probably want to use the power of a language like Visual Basic or Visual C++.

Tip

When deciding whether to access the database directly from your Active Server Pages or from a component, you may want to use the following rule of thumb. If your database access and processing logic takes up more than two pages of script code, it's probably a good idea to create a separate Active Server Component to handle the database access and processing logic.

Note

The concepts presented in this lesson are sometimes referred to as *multitier architectures*. For example, in a classic client/server application, the user interface or presentation tier accessed a relational database or data service. This access normally occurred over a local network. You could say that this type of application uses a two-tier architecture. Web applications use HTML and ASP to present information to users, multiple Active Server Components to provide processing logic, and relational databases to provide data services. Usually, the public Internet or private intranet is used to connect the various tiers involved with the application.

11

Understanding Active Server Pages

Active Server Pages can contain both script and HTML. Visual InterDev includes scripting engines for both VBScript and JavaScript.

To select the default scripting language for your Active Server Pages, first bring up the property pages for your script page by selecting the Property Pages menu option from the View menu. You should see a dialog box like the one in Figure 11.2.

In the dialog box, you should see a Default Scripting Language section with two drop-down list boxes. The list box labeled Server represents the default language for your server-side scripts. The list box labeled Client represents the default language for your client-side scripts. Select the drop-down list box for the Server and you should see two choices in the list—VBScript and JavaScript (ECMAScript). At this point, you can select the scripting language that you are most comfortable with.

Figure 11.2.

Choosing a default scripting language.

Visual InterDev formats a line of your ASP to denote the type of scripting language that is being used. This is similar to the way that client-side script is recognized in an HTML file. The following code example demonstrates an ASP that uses VBScript for the ASP scripting language:

```
<%@LANGUAGE="VBSCRIPT"%>
```

You can include both client- and server-side script in an Active Server Page. The client-side script is passed to the client along with the HTML and executes within the context of the browser. The HTML may also contain references to client-side objects such as ActiveX controls or intrinsic HTML controls.

Working with Transactions

You may be familiar with the concept of a transaction from working with other development tools or applications. A transaction is usually defined as a logical unit of work. When creating business applications, a transaction can be made up of several different and distinct processes. However, in order for the transaction to be successful, each process must complete correctly. If one piece of the transaction should fail, the actions performed by the other processes in the transaction should be undone. This process of undoing is referred to as *rolling back* a transaction.

Visual InterDev makes it easy to add transactional capabilities to your Web-based applications. Refer again to Figure 11.2. You should see a section of the Property Pages dialog box labeled ASP Settings. The first check box in the section is labeled Enable Transactions. Selecting this check box causes Visual InterDev to add the following piece of code to your Active Server Page:

```
<%@ transaction=required LANGUAGE=VBScript %>
```

That's all there is to adding transactional capabilities to your Active Server Pages. The Web server and associated scripting engine performs the rest of the work. Later on Day 13, "Unleashing the Power of the Visual InterDev Programming Model," you'll learn more about working with transactions in your applications.

Working with the Scripting Object Model

In working with the Property Pages dialog box in Figure 11.2, you may have also noticed a check box labeled Enable Scripting Object Model in the ASP Settings section. In Visual InterDev 6, Microsoft introduces the concept of the Scripting Object Model. The Scripting Object Model makes developing Web applications with script similar to developing traditional client/server applications with object-oriented programming concepts.

Using the Scripting Object Model provides many benefits to developing Active Server Pages. For example, in the Scripting Object Model, Web pages are considered objects themselves. You can reference a page as an object from other pages and from within the script code in Active Server Pages. This also facilitates the concept of remote scripting. Remote scripting allows you to call server-side script functions in an Active Server Page from within a client-side script without leaving the client-side page. In other words, you can execute script-based functions on the Web server without leaving the client Web page. This allows you as a developer to provide more powerful processing within your Web applications. You'll learn more about these features on Day 13.

To enable the Scripting Object Model, simply select the check box labeled Enable Scripting Object Model in the Property Pages dialog box (refer to Figure 11.2).

11

The Active Server Page Object Model

Active Server Pages use a robust object model that enables you to develop the correct logic to handle your application needs. This object model resembles object models that are used in Visual Basic. The following list outlines the basic objects that are available in an ASP:

- The Request object
- The Response object

- The Session object
- The Application object
- The Server object

Each of these objects is covered in detail in the following sections.

The Request Object

The Request object enables you to obtain information from a user. This object is useful when you're trying to discover preferences specified by the user. Also, you can use this object to retrieve information that is entered on a form. A User Registration Form is a good example where the user enters information into an initial form that is then later used by the application.

The Request object consists of five collections. A *collection* is a set of related objects that are accessed using the same method. An object uses a collection to access variables that define certain attributes and characteristics about the object. Table 11.1 lists the types of Request collections and their purposes.

TABLE 11.1. THE Request COLLECTIONS.

Collection	Purpose
ClientCertificate	Retrieves certification fields from the browser request
Cookies	Retrieves the value of cookies in the request
Form	Retrieves the values of a form using POST command
QueryString	Retrieves the values of a query string
ServerVariables	Retrieves the value of environment variables

You can access the information contained in a collection using the following syntax:

Request.*CollectionName*("*variable name*")

CollectionName is the name of the collection and *variable name* is the name of the collection variable containing the desired information. You can use the following method as an alternative:

Request.("*variable name*")

Note

If you use the alternative method, you must ensure that different collections contain unique variable names. You should explicitly use the collection name method to access a variable if you have collection variables with the same name.

Using the Cookies Collection

You may have used cookies while developing previous Web-based applications. At the least, you have probably heard about cookies and their use in Web applications. A cookie represents information about the user session that is stored on a client machine. You can use cookies to maintain information about the user across the scope of your application. The browser can send a cookie to the server, or the server can send a cookie to the client machine. You can use Active Server Pages to both populate and retrieve values from cookies. The syntax for the Cookies collection is as follows:

```
Request.Cookies(cookie)[(key)].attribute]
```

cookie specifies the value of the cookie to be retrieved, *key* indicates an optional parameter that is used to retrieve subkey values of the cookie, and *attribute* contains information about the cookie. For example, the *attribute* parameter can be used to determine if a cookie contains multiple key values as in the following code example:

```
<%Request.Cookies("MyCookie").HasKeys%>
```

If MyCookie contains multiple key values, the preceding code statement returns a value of True. A value of False is returned if the cookie only contains a single value.

The following code sample shows how to retrieve the value of a cookie named User that contains only one value of Male:

```
<%Request.Cookies("User")%>
```

If the HTTP request from the browser contains multiple key values for the User cookie, as in

```
Gender=Male&Age=30
```

then the code to return the value of this cookie is

```
<%Request.Cookies("User")("Age")%>
```

This code statement returns the value of the Age key value—30. As you can see from the examples, key values are used to contain type and subtype information about the user.

The Cookies collection can be used as an alternative method of storing information about the user. The use of cookies in Web applications and sites has caused some controversy. This controversy stems from the fact that information about the user is being stored on the local machine and distributed to the server without the user's knowledge. You should be careful not to store sensitive information within a cookie to ensure the security of your application and your users.

11

Using the Form Collection

The Form collection contains the values of a form that are submitted via the POST method. The syntax for using the Form collection is

```
Request.Form(parameter)[(index)].Count]
```

where *parameter* is the name of the form element that contains a value. The optional *index* attribute enables you to access the specific value of a parameter that can contain multiple values. The *Count* attribute denotes the number of possible values for a parameter in the form. The value of the index can be an integer between one and the value of the *Count* attribute.

The following examples show how you can use the Form collection in an ASP file to retrieve information from the user. Both examples use HTML forms as the basic user interface. It isn't important to understand the development of the form for purposes of these examples. For now, focus on the logic contained in the ASP and how the ASP is used to process the needs of the application.

The first example involves a basic HTML form that retrieves the username and favorite baseball team. Figure 11.3 illustrates the layout of this form.

FIGURE 11.3.

Retrieving the user preferences.

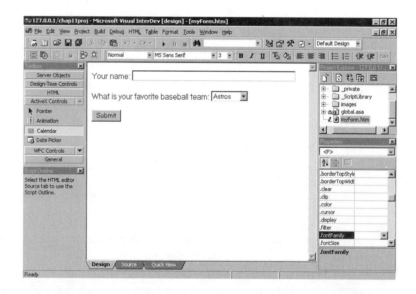

The HTML form in this example contains a text field for the username, along with a drop-down list box that contains a list of choices of different baseball teams (sorry, not all major league team are represented in the example). The form also contains a Submit button for the user to save the preferences that have been entered. When the users enter their preferences and click the Submit button, the form is submitted to the Active Server Page. Listing 11.1 displays the code for the HTML file that contains the layout of the form.

LISTING 11.1. USER PREFERENCES FORM.

```
 1: <HTML>
 2: <HEAD>
 3: <TITLE>User Preferences Form</TITLE>
 4: <H2>Please enter your preferences in the form below: </H2>
 5: </HEAD>
 6: <BODY>
 7: <form action="/chapter11Proj/scripts/submit.asp" method="post">
 8: <p>Your name: <input name="name" size=48>
 9: <p>What is your favorite baseball team: <select name="team">
10: <option>Astros <option>Braves <option>Yankees <option>Cubs
11: </select>
12: <p><input type=submit>
13: </form>
14: </BODY>
15: </HTML>
```

11

As you can see from Listing 11.1, an ASP file is referenced in the form action line. The Submit.asp file retrieves the information that is entered and displays the preferences in a new page to the user with a welcome message. Listing 11.2 shows the code for the Submit ASP.

LISTING 11.2. PROCESSING THE USER'S PREFERENCE.

```
1: Welcome, <%= Request.Form("name")%>.
2: Your favorite baseball team is the <%= Request.Form("team")%>!
```

This ASP shows how you can combine HTML with script code to construct a dynamic Web page. If you will recall the earlier discussion on the topic of collections, here the Form collection is used to obtain the name and the team parameter. Figure 11.4 demonstrates this sample in action.

Based on the user preference entered above, Figure 11.5 demonstrates how the new page will be formatted by the Submit ASP.

In this example, the ASP used the Form collection to process the user preference and create a new Web page based on these values. You may have a need to send results back to the same form that submitted the user preference. For example, you may need to perform some sort of validation on entered fields before their values are processed. If the form parameter value is incorrect, the server needs to send the message to the user within the context of the user form so that the user can correct the mistake on that form.

FIGURE 11.4.

Entering the user preference.

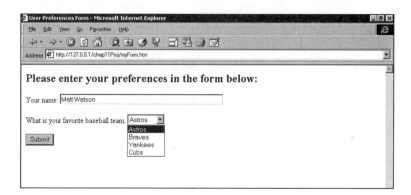

FIGURE 11.5.

Displaying the user's preference.

The other alternative is to send a message to the user on a new page indicating that a field was incorrect on the form. This method is not great for the user, however, because it requires the user to navigate to the form and correct the field. The better alternative is to develop an ASP that both creates and processes a form to handle this case and present the message within the proper context of your application.

The following sample illustrates the use of an ASP to create this dynamic form. Figure 11.6 shows a sample form within an ASP to obtain a username and email address.

This form is constructed using the ASP file that is shown in Listing 11.3.

LISTING 11.3. CREATING A DYNAMIC WEB PAGE.

```
1: <HTML>
2: <!-- This is userPref.asp -->
3: <%
```

```
 4: If IsEmpty(Request("Email")) Then
 5: Msg = "Please enter your email address."
 6: ElseIf InStr(Request("Email"), "@") = 0 Then
 7: Msg = "Please enter an email address" & _
 8: " in the form username@domainname."
 9: Else
10: Msg = "This script could process the " & _
11: "valid Email address now."
12: End If
13: %><FORM METHOD="POST" ACTION="userPref.asp">
14: <PRE>
15: <p>Name: <input name="firstname" size=48 VALUE= "<%=Request("firstname")
16: %>">
17: <p>Email: <INPUT TYPE="TEXT" NAME="Email" SIZE=30 VALUE= "<%=
➥Request("Email")
18: %>">
19: <%= Msg %><P>
20: <INPUT TYPE="SUBMIT" VALUE="Submit">
21: </PRE>
22: </FORM>
23: </HTML>
```

FIGURE 11.6.

Entering an email address.

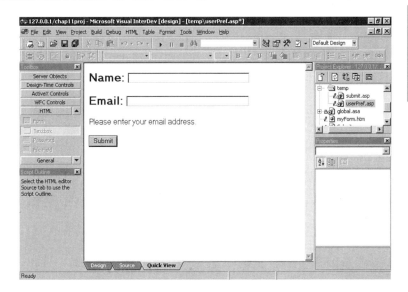

11

This code listing demonstrates the effective combination of HTML and script to construct a dynamic Web page. Also, this example shows how you can properly handle the needs of your application. From a processing standpoint, you learned earlier today that HTML contained in an ASP file is initially sent to the browser. Therefore, the HTML form contained in the userPref.asp file is created first. After the user submits the information, the ASP script processes the form using the Request object and Form collection. The email field is validated to ensure that an @ sign was included in the email address. If this character isn't in the email address, the ASP sends an error message and the original form to the browser so that the user can correct the mistake. As you can see, this method provides an effective way to process user input. The Form collection is an invaluable tool for handling the values of an HTML form.

Using the ServerVariables Collection

You can use the ServerVariables collection to retrieve environment variables that pertain to the browser request. The syntax for this collection is

```
Request.ServerVariables(variable)
```

where variable references the name of the server environment variable to retrieve.

Note

It is beyond the scope of this lesson to exhaustively cover each of the many ServerVariables that you can access. Refer to the Visual InterDev documentation for a comprehensive list and description of each of the possible variables for the ServerVariables collection.

Instead, I will cover two of the more useful variables for the ServerVariables collection in the following section. These examples should provide you with a good idea of how to use other ServerVariables for your application needs.

Two of the more useful server variables that you can access with this collection include REQUEST_METHOD and SERVER_NAME. The REQUEST_METHOD variable indicates the method with which a page has been requested. The following example demonstrates how to capture the value of the REQUEST_METHOD server variable:

```
RequestMethod = Request.ServerVariables("REQUEST_METHOD")
```

The value of this variable will be POST when the page has been referenced by another form and GET when the user has specifically requested the form.

In the previous section, you learned how to use Active Server Pages to process HTML forms. The ACTION parameter was formatted with a value of POST when the user submitted the form. If the page is called by any other method, the REQUEST_METHOD value is equal to GET. You can use this variable to provide validation for the page based on the access method. From the previous form example, you may have wondered about the results if a user accessed the ASP directly without first going through the HTML form.

A similar situation would be if the user refreshed the ASP. If a user refreshes an Active Server Page or enters the URL directly without completing the user preferences form, the page may not contain the proper values to dynamically format the page. For both of these requests, the REQUEST_METHOD is equal to the value of GET. You can add validation logic to confirm the access method for the page and then process the page based on this value. Listing 11.4 displays sample validation logic for the user preferences form.

LISTING 11.4. VERIFYING THE REQUEST METHOD FOR A PAGE.

```
 1: <HTML>
 2: <HEAD>
 3: <TITLE>Your Personal Preferences </TITLE>
 4: </HEAD>
 5: <BODY>
 6: <%
 7: DIM RequestMethod
 8: ' Captures the request method for the page
 9: RequestMethod = Request.ServerVariables("REQUEST_METHOD")
10: ' Validates the value of the request method
11: If RequestMethod = "GET" then
12: ' The user has refreshed the ASP - Display error message
13: %>
14: <P>You have chosen to refresh this page. If you want to change the
15: value of your preferences to display on this page, go back to the User
16: Preferences form and enter your choices. After you change your
17: preferences and click Submit, this page will display the results of
18: your new preferences.
19: <%
20: Else
21: %>
22: Welcome, <%= Request.Form("name")%>.
23: Your favorite baseball team is the <%= Request.Form("team")%>
24: <%
25: End If
26: %>
27: </BODY>
28: </HTML>
```

11

In Listing 11.4, the script uses an If...Then...Else statement to determine the value of REQUEST_METHOD. Based on the value of this variable, the appropriate code block is executed.

Note

As stated earlier, within an ASP, you will see a combination of HTML and script. Many times, the HTML and script will be intermingled, as shown in Listing 11.4. This coding standard is different from the method that you learned concerning client-side script. With client-side script, the recommendation is to use a strict split between the HTML and script code. Because Active Server Pages are dynamic by definition, it makes sense that script and HTML are intermingled within an ASP.

SERVER_NAME is another server variable that can be used to provide valuable information to your application. The SERVER_NAME variable contains the server's host name, DNS alias, or IP address that is used in self-referencing URL addresses. This variable can be used to format a URL link to another page in your application. The following code sample demonstrates the use of this variable:

```
<A HREF = "http://<%= Request.ServerVariables("SERVER_NAME") %>
/ASProject/scripts/MyPage.asp">Link to MyPage.asp</A>
```

In this example, the ServerVariables collection is used to retrieve the value of the host server name. This value is used to format the prefix of the URL link to an Active Server Page.

Using the QueryString Collection

The QueryString collection enables you to access the values of the variables in an HTTP query string. These values are located after the question mark in an HTTP request. The QueryString collection provides an easy method to access the value of these variables because you can reference the variables by name. The syntax for the QueryString collection is as follows:

```
Request.QueryString(variable)[(index)].Count
```

variable is the name of the desired variable in the HTTP query string, and *index* is an optional parameter that enables you to retrieve the value of a variable containing multiple values. The index can contain an integer between one and the value of the *Count* attribute.

Take a look at the User Preferences form again. You can use an ASP that contains the QueryString collection to process the user input. Listing 11.5 demonstrates an example of using the QueryString to display the name and baseball team preference for a particular user.

LISTING 11.5. USING THE `QueryString` COLLECTION TO PROCESS THE USER'S PREFERENCE.

```
1: Welcome, <%= Request.QueryString("name")%>.
2: Your favorite baseball team is the <%= Request.QueryString("team")%>
```

For variables that contain multiple values, the `QueryString` collection creates a new collection instance with the number of values that are passed to the ASP. For example, if the User Preferences form is changed to allow multiple names to be passed to the server, the `QueryString` creates a new collection instance called `name`. If three names are passed to the ASP, `name` contains three values. The `index` attribute can be used to reference each value within the `name` variable. The following example illustrates how the `name` values would be accessed by the `QueryString`. Suppose that the following values are passed to the ASP from a client request:

```
/submit.asp?name=Taylor&name=Chris&name=Travis
```

The following `QueryString` statements

```
Request.QueryString("name")(1)
Request.QueryString("name")(2)
Request.QueryString("name")(3)
```

would produce the values of

```
Taylor
Chris
Travis
```

respectively. The `Count` attribute would be three for the `name` collection instance. You also could reference the `name` collection using the following statement:

```
Request.QueryString("name")
```

This statement would produce a comma-delimited value of

```
Taylor,Chris,Travis
```

The `QueryString` can be used with forms that use both the `GET` and `POST` action commands. If you use the `QueryString` collection with a form that uses `GET`, the collection will contain all the information contained on the form. If the ASP is requested using the `POST` statement, the `QueryString` collection will contain all the information that is passed as a parameter to the ASP.

The Response Object

You can use the `Response` object to send information to the user. You can format HTML to be sent to the client as well as manipulate state and session information. Real-world examples of using the `Response` object include redirecting the user to another URL

11

address and formatting the value of a cookie on the server. The Response object supplies several properties and methods needed to accomplish these tasks. From the lesson on Day 7, "Integrating Objects into Your Applications," you probably recall the terms *properties* and *methods*. To refresh your memory, a property defines characteristics about the object that it represents, and a method indicates an action that the object can execute. The Cookies collection is the only collection of the Response object. Remember that a collection is a set of related objects that are accessed using the same method. Just as you used the Request object to retrieve information from cookies, you use the Response object to set the values of cookies. Table 11.2 defines the properties that are available for the Response object.

TABLE 11.2. THE Response PROPERTIES.

Property	Description
Buffer	Indicates whether the page is buffered
ContentType	Defines the content type for the response
Expires	Indicates the length of time before the expiration of a page that has been cached by the browser
ExpiresAbsolute	Indicates date and time of the expiration of a page that has been cached by the browser
Status	Indicates the status line value returned by the server

These properties can be used with the Response object methods to send the proper information to the user. Table 11.3 lists the methods that are available for the Response object.

TABLE 11.3. THE Response METHODS.

Method	Description
AddHeader	Defines a name for the HTML header
AppendToLog	Adds a string of text to the Web server log
BinaryWrite	Writes the output to the HTTP response without converting the characters
Clear	Erases all HTML output that has been buffered
End	Terminates ASP processing and returns the result
Flush	Sends buffered output immediately to the client
Redirect	Redirects the user to another URL address
Write	Writes the output to the HTTP response as a string

The next few sections explore some of the more powerful properties and methods of the Response object that you can use to enhance the functionality of your Active Server Pages.

Exploring the Cookies Collection

The Cookies collection for the Response object provides a way to set the value of a cookie on the server. You can create new cookies as well as change the value of existing cookies. The syntax for using the Cookies collection for the Response object is similar to the format that you used for the Request object. To use the Cookies collection for the Response object, type the following:

```
Response.Cookies(cookie)[(key).attribute] = value
```

cookie is the name of the cookie. key is an optional parameter used to define a cookie that contains multiple key values. The attribute parameter describes information about the cookie. The value parameter can be used to set the values of the key and attribute parameters. You also can use the HasKeys attribute to determine if the cookie contains key values. Table 11.4 provides a complete listing of the attributes for the Cookies collection.

TABLE 11.4. THE COOKIES COLLECTION ATTRIBUTES.

Attribute	Description
HasKeys	Determines if the cookie contains key values
Expires	Indicates expiration date for the cookie
Domain	Defines the domain for which cookies are distributed
Path	Defines the path for which cookies are distributed
Secure	Indicates whether the cookie is secure

You can update the value for all of the attributes of the Cookies collection except HasKeys, which is read-only. The HasKeys attribute evaluates to a value of True to indicate that the cookie contains key values or False to specify that the cookie does not contain key values.

Listing 11.6 demonstrates several methods for populating the value of cookies.

LISTING 11.6. SETTING THE VALUE OF COOKIES.

```
1: <%
2: 'Sets the value of cookie (example 1)
3: Response.Cookies("Name") = "Travis"
```

continues

LISTING 11.6. CONTINUED

```
 4: 'Sets the value of cookie with key values (example 2)
 5: Response.Cookies("MyCookie")("FirstName") = "Travis"
 6: Response.Cookies("MyCookie")("LastName") = "Watson"
 7: 'Changes the cookie to a non-key value cookie and sets the new value
➥(example 3)
 8: Response.Cookies("MyCookie") = "Travis"
 9: 'Sets the value of a cookie and its attributes (example 4)
10: Response.Cookies("StdCookie") = "User"
11: Response.Cookies("StdCookie").Expires = "December 31, 1999"
12: Response.Cookies("StdCookie").Domain = "mydomain.com"
13: Response.Cookies("StdCookie").Path = "/www/home/"
14: Response.Cookies("StdCookie").Secure = "TRUE"
15:   %>
```

The first sets the value of the Name cookie to Travis. The next example creates a cookie
called MyCookie and sets the key values of FirstName and LastName. The third code
example demonstrates how you can change the type for the cookie as well as its value.
This example changes MyCookie to a non-key value cookie. The values that were previously stored in this cookie are discarded, and the new value of Travis is assigned to
MyCookie. The final code example shows how to set both the value of the cookie as well
as its attributes.

Using the `Buffer` Property to Process Your Script

Earlier, you were introduced to the properties of the Response object. The properties help
describe the characteristics for an object. The basic syntax to reference a Response object
property is

```
Response.PropertyName
```

where *PropertyName* is the name of the property.

The Buffer property defines whether the page results are buffered. You can use the
Buffer property to process all the script code in your ASP before the results are sent to
the client. The syntax for the Buffer property is as follows:

```
Response.Buffer = flag
```

flag contains the value of True or False to indicate whether or not to buffer the page
output. If you set the value of the flag parameter to True, the page output is buffered,
and the script code is processed before distributing the results to the browser. The default
value for the flag parameter is False.

If you want to buffer the page output, you must set the Buffer flag to true before your
ASP sends output to the client. You cannot set the value of the Buffer property if your

ASP has previously sent output to the client. The best practice is to set the value of the Buffer property in the first line of your ASP. There are two methods that can be used to halt the processing of the script code in your ASP. You can use either the `Flush` or the `End` method to stop the script processing and send the results to the client. The syntax for these two methods is

```
Response.Flush
```

and

```
Response.End
```

Tip

> You should balance the need to process your script versus the length of time that it takes to process your script. For long scripts, you may want to send intermediate results to the user while your script continues to process. To do this, make sure that the value of the `Buffer` property is `False`.

Using the `Write` Method to Send Output to the User

You can use the `Write` method to format a string of text to send to the user. The syntax for the `Write` method is

```
Response.Write variant
```

where *variant* represents the data to be written. The *variant* parameter can contain any value that is supported by the VBScript variant data type, including characters, strings, and integers.

The `Write` method is commonly used to format HTML to be sent to the client browser. For example, you could use the `Write` method to create a dynamic header for your Web page, based on the user ID that is entered. For new users, you could display an initial greeting that is different from the greeting for return visitors to your site. Listing 11.7 demonstrates the use of the `Write` method in an Active Server Page to create this type of greeting.

LISTING 11.7. CREATING A DYNAMIC GREETING.

```
1: <%
2: If NewUser Then
3: Response.Write "<H3 ALIGN=CENTER>Welcome to the Overview Page</H3>"
4: Else
5: Response.Write "<H3 ALIGN=CENTER>Welcome Back to the Overview
➥Page</H3>"
```

continues

LISTING **11.7.** CONTINUED

```
6: End If
7: %>
```

In Listing 11.7, you must assume that the NewUser variable is set to either True or False previously. The NewUser variable is used to designate whether the ID represents a new or existing user. If NewUser is True, the initial welcome message is displayed. If this user is a return visitor, the welcome back message is displayed. Notice that the text is formatted using the header HTML tags. To extend this example, you could use this code with a procedure that verifies user IDs against a set of user IDs stored in a database.

Using the Redirect Method

The Redirect method can be used to redirect the user to another URL address. The syntax for using the Redirect method is as follows:

```
Response.Redirect URL
```

URL is the URL address location to redirect the browser.

Note   Similar to buffering output, you cannot use this method from an ASP if results have already been distributed to the client.

This method is helpful for ensuring that users follow a specific path when using your application. For example, an order entry application may require that a user enter basic order header information like name and address before selecting the items that will be ordered. If a user attempts to access the order detail page to order an item, you can use the following code sample in Listing 11.8 to redirect them to the name and address page of your application.

LISTING 11.8. GUIDING THE USER'S PATH.

```
1: <%
2: If NOT Session("OrderHeaderPage") Then
3: Response.Redirect "OrderHeader.asp"
4: End If
5: %>
```

This code example uses the Session object that you will learn about in a later section. You can use this object to store variables for a user session. In this example, a variable stored in the Session object is used to verify that the user has entered the Web application from the Order Header page. If this variable is False, the browser will be redirected to the Order Header page.

Specifying the Type of Content

You can use the ContentType property to designate the type of content that is located in the response for the page. The syntax for this property is

```
Response.ContentType = content type
```

This value is a string that conforms to the MIME standards for a Web page. The content type defines the type and subtype of information that's contained in the response that is sent to the client. The type describes the general category of the information, while the subtype specifically defines the content type. The default value for the ContentType property is "text/HTML". Other contents are typically represented in the same way. This particular example defines the content type for a response as text and the content subtype as HTML. The following code samples demonstrate other examples of using content type:

```
Response.ContentType = "text/HTML"
Response.ContentType = "image/GIF"
Response.ContentType = "text/plain"
```

The Session Object

Earlier today, you were introduced to the Session object. Let's take a closer look at this part of the ASP object model. You can use the Session object to store and retrieve information during a specific session for a user. The information contained in the Session object persists for the entire time that the user interacts with your application. You can use and access this information across the Web pages in your application.

The Web server automatically creates a Session object when a user accesses a Web page in your application. The user session persists until the user leaves the application, the session times out, or the session is explicitly abandoned. To access the Session properties, the syntax for referencing the Session object is

```
Session.property
```

To access Session methods, use the following syntax:

```
Session.method
```

The Session object consists of two defined properties and one defined method.

The SessionID property returns the Session ID for a user. The Web server creates a unique identifier as it creates each user session. The value of this identifier is a LONG data type. The syntax to reference the SessionID property is

```
Session.SessionID
```

11

Note

> The Session ID that is generated is stored as a `Session` cookie. If the user's browser doesn't support the use of cookies, the Active Server engine examines the URL references on the page. The Active Server engine determines which URL links reference another page in your application and append the Session ID to each of these references. In this way, the Session ID remains available within the user session scope of the application.

The other property of the `Session` object is the `Timeout` property. You can use the `Timeout` property to identify the maximum length of time before the session will end, or time out, for a user. This property is measured in minutes. If there is no user activity such as refreshing or requesting a page before the `timeout` period, the session terminates. The syntax for using this property is

```
Session.Timeout = nMinutes
```

`nMinutes` indicates the number of minutes for the `timeout` period. The default value for the `timeout` period is `20` minutes.

The `Abandon` method is the sole method for the `Session` object. You can use the `Abandon` method to explicitly terminate a session and destroy all the information stored in the `Session` object. The syntax for calling the `Abandon` method is

```
Session.Abandon
```

After you call the `Abandon` method, the page processes any remaining script and then terminates the session.

Working with the `Session` Object

You can create additional properties and variables for the `Session` object to store information about a user session. Think of `Session` object properties as global variables. Examples include user preferences as well as global information to be shared between the pages for a particular user session. Another example would involve storing data to be used to calculate the grand total for an order. The following example shows how to store variables in the `Session` object:

```
Session("UserName") = "Taylor Watson"
Session("Email") = "TWatson@wnf.com"
Session("ChoiceBeverage") = "Apple Juice"
Session("Age") = 4
```

These examples show how you can store various types of information using the `Session` object. The information contained in these variables can then be accessed and referenced throughout the scope of this user's session.

You also can use the predefined properties and methods of the `Session` object. For example, if you want to change the `timeout` period for a user session, you can alter the value in the `Timeout` property. The following code sample changes the `timeout` period from the default of 20 minutes to 30 minutes:

```
Session.Timeout = 30
```

Listing 11.9 demonstrates how to use a `Session` object variable to dynamically format a page based on the user preferences that were entered on an initial User Preferences form.

LISTING 11.9. USING A NEW VARIABLE IN THE `Session` OBJECT.

```
1: <HTML>
2: <% If Session("team") = "Astros" Then %>
3: <IMG SRC="/chap11proj/images/astros.GIF" WIDTH="85"
4: <% Else %>
5: <IMG SRC="/chap11proj/images/yankees.GIF" WIDTH="85"
6: <%End If%>
7: </HTML>
```

In this code example, the ASP checks the value of the user's baseball team preference, which is stored in the `Session` object. If the preference is the Astros, the page is formatted with an image of the Houston Astros logo. If the user specified something other than the Astros, the page is formatted with an image of the New York Yankees logo. This code again demonstrates the dynamic nature of Active Server Pages.

Working with the Session Events

The `Session` object is related to two events that are unique to an Active Server Page. The `Session_OnStart` and `Session_OnEnd` events can be used to execute script when a session is initially created and when the session is terminated. These events are contained in the `global.asa` file. You were first introduced to `global.asa` and these events during Day 2, "Creating Your First Visual InterDev Project."

The `Session_OnStart` event is triggered when the server creates the new session. The `Session_OnStart` script is the initial code that is processed for a new user session. In other words, the script that you place in the procedure for this event is processed before the request for the page is executed. You can access all the objects for an ASP, including the `Application`, `Session`, `Server`, `Request`, and `Response` objects, during this event. Conversely, the `Session_OnEnd` event occurs when the user session is abandoned or times out. The only ASP objects available during the `Session_OnEnd` event include the `Application`, `Server`, and `Session` objects.

11

An example of using the Session_OnStart event is initializing global variables for your Web application. In addition, you can use the Session_OnStart event to ensure that the user accesses the proper page first in the Web application. The following example does just that and is an extension of the Redirect method for the Response object that you learned earlier today.

LISTING **11.10.** STARTING THE USER OFF RIGHT.

```
 1: <SCRIPT RUNAT=Server Language=VBScript>
 2: Sub Session_OnStart
 3: ' Sets the value of the Order Header start page
 4: OrderHeaderPage = "/chap11proj/OrderHeader.asp"
 5: ' Sets the value of the current user page
 6: CurrentPage = Request.ServerVariables("SCRIPT_NAME")
 7: ' Do a case-insensitive compare on the pages with the strcomp()
➡function.
 8: ' If they don't match, send the user to the Order Header page.
 9: If strcomp(currentPage,OrderHeaderPage,1) then
10: Response.Redirect(OrderHeaderPage)
11: End If
12: End Sub
13: </SCRIPT>
```

This code example combines several of the concepts that you have learned today to demonstrate their value within the context of an application.

The Application Object

The Application object enables you to share information across all users of the ASP-based application. Common data that all users need to work with the application can be, for example, visual information such as date and time or can be internal to the workings of the Web application. While the Session object is limited to a single user, this information is globally available for all users of the application. The Application object is created when the application is initiated. Upon initial creation, the Application object is then available to each additional user who accesses your application. The syntax for accessing the Application object is as follows:

Application.*method*

where *method* is the name of the method for the Application object. The Application object supports two defined methods. The Lock and Unlock methods provide a way to prevent contention between multiple users. The Lock method enables you to prevent other users from modifying an Application object that has been accessed by a user. The Unlock method enables you to then unlock the Application object once the user has released it. When you use the Unlock method, other users are able to modify the Application object's properties and variable information.

A great example of using the Application object involves calculating the number of visits to your Web site. Almost all Web sites track this information. For commercial sites, the number of people who visit a Web site continues to be a very important number. This number is used to justify the existence of the Web site as well as to determine how much to charge advertisers that place a banner on the Web page. The code in Listing 11.11 demonstrates how to use the Application object to determine the number of hits for a Web site.

LISTING 11.11. DETERMINING THE NUMBER OF WEB SITE VISITORS.

```
 1: <%
 2: ' Locks the Application object
 3: Application.Lock
 4: ' Increments the number of visits by one
 5: Application("NumVisits") = Application("NumVisits") + 1
 6: ' Unlocks the Application object
 7: Application.Unlock
 8: %>
 9: ' Displays the number of visitors for the application
10: This application page has been visited
11: <%= Application("NumVisits") %>  times!
```

11

In this code example, the NumVisits variable is created the first time the code is executed. You can also initialize the variable to zero in the Application_OnStart event, which you learn about in the next section. The variable is initialized to zero. NumVisits is then incremented each additional time the code is executed, and the value is stored in the Application object.

The values that are stored in the Application object are contained in persistent storage. For this reason, you can access the values of these variables even if you have to stop and restart your server. You can, therefore, create and use variables for your application that need to be consistently maintained. You want to use good judgment about the kind of values that you store in the Application object. You should store simple rather than complex information.

Working with the Application Events

The Application object has two associated events that are contained in global.asa. You were first introduced to global.asa and these Application events during Day 2.

The Application_OnStart event is triggered when the first user accesses a Web page within the application. This event occurs before the Session_OnStart event. The Application_OnEnd event is activated when the application terminates. Application_OnEnd occurs after the Session_OnEnd event. The Server and the Application objects are the only objects that are available during both the Application_OnStart and the Application_OnEnd events.

The Object

The Server object enables you to interface with Active Server Components. These components provide robust application processing on the server. Active Server Pages include the following five Active Server Components:

- Database Access Component
- AdRotator Component
- Browser Capabilities Component
- File Access Component
- Content Linking Component

These components are included with Visual InterDev and IIS. They enable you to accomplish certain tasks within the context of an ASP. You also can create custom Active Server Components for your Active Server Pages. You learn how to create and interact with these components on Day 15.

The syntax for referencing the Server object is as follows:

Server.*method*

method is the name of the method for the Server object. The methods for the Server object are outlined in Table 11.5.

TABLE 11.5. THE Server OBJECT METHODS.

Method	Description
CreateObject	Creates an instance of an object
HTMLEncode	Applies HTML encoding to a string
MapPath	Maps the virtual path to a physical path
URLEncode	Applies URL encoding to a string

The `Server` object also contains one property that can be accessed. The `ScriptTimeout` property defines the length of time for a script to be able to run. The syntax for this property is as follows:

```
Server.ScriptTimeout = NumofSeconds
```

`NumofSeconds` represents the number of seconds before the script times out and terminates its processing. The default value for this property is `90` seconds. The `ScriptTimeout` property only applies to the processing of the script code. A script won't time out based on this property while a server component is processing. You set the value of this property as well as retrieve its value to store in a variable within your application. For example, if you wanted to find out the `timeout` period for the server script, you could execute the following code:

```
<% TimeoutForScript = Server.ScriptTimeout %>
```

This code sample would retrieve the value of the `timeout` period for the server script and store the value in the variable `TimeoutForScript`.

You will typically interact with the `Server` object by using the predefined server components for Active Server Pages as well as your own custom ActiveX Server Components. The following sections explain how to create and work with an instance of an object.

Creating a `Server` Object Instance

The `CreateObject` method is the most widely used method for the `Server` object. You can use this method to create an instance of a particular object that can then be used by your application. The syntax for calling this method is as follows:

```
Server.CreateObject progID
```

`progID` indicates the type of object to create. The syntax for the `progID` parameter is

```
Vendor.Component.Version
```

`Vendor` is the author of the component, `Component` is the name of the component, and `Version` is the version number of the component.

When you use this method to create an instance of an object, the scope of the object exists for the lifetime of the ASP. For example, if you execute this method in a typical ASP within your application, the component only persists while your ASP script is processed. The object is destroyed when the ASP completes its processing. Listing 11.12 demonstrates how to create an instance of an object in an ASP.

11

LISTING 11.12. AN OBJECT WITHIN AN ASP.

```
 1: <%
 2: ' Creates an instance of the Browser Capabilities object
 3: Set bc = Server.CreateObject("MSWC.BrowserType")
 4: ' Check to see whether the browser supports VBScript
 5: If bc.vbscript = "True" Then %>
 6: ' Format a friendly confirmation message
 7: Your Browser supports VBScript!
 8: <%Else %>
 9: ' Format another message
10: Your Browser does not support VBScript!
```

In this code example, the object that is created can only be referenced for the lifetime of the ASP. After the script executes the last line of code to format a message to display on the browser page, the object is destroyed. Any references to the object after the ASP has completed result in a runtime error.

However, you can create an object in a way that enables it to persist beyond the ASP. You can extend the life of your objects by calling the CreateObject method and storing its value in a Session or Application object variable. For example, you could execute the following line of code to store an object in an Application object variable:

```
<% Set Application("BrowserCapabilities") =
➥Server.CreateObject("MSWC.BrowserType") %>
```

In this example, an instance of the BrowserType object is created and stored in an Application object variable named BrowserCapabilities. The BrowserType object, also referred to as the Browser Capabilities component, enables you to determine the capabilities of the current browser. Because an Application object variable is used to store this object, the object and its methods and properties can be referenced for the lifetime of the application.

 Note

> In the previous code example, notice the Set statement used to store the component in the Application object variable. The use of this word differs from the normal convention that you learned earlier. You must use the Set keyword to store object variables.

If you would like to destroy an instance of an object yourself, you can do this with the Nothing keyword. To destroy an object, set the object variable equal to Nothing. For example, use the following line of code to destroy the bc object instance you created earlier:

```
<%Set bc = Nothing %>
```

This code will destroy the instance of the BrowserType object that has been stored in the variable bc.

You have now learned two methods for storing an instance of an object. When naming a variable to store an instance of the object, you cannot choose the name of a predefined object. For example, the following line of code would result in an error:

```
<% Set Application = Server.CreateObject("Application") %>
```

You also can use the <OBJECT> declaration to create an instance of an object in the global.asa file. You must declare these objects to contain either Application or Session scope. The syntax for using the <OBJECT> tag is as follows:

```
<OBJECT RUNAT=Server SCOPE=Scope ID=Identifier
{PROGID=ProgID¦CLASSID=ClassID}>
```

Scope indicates the scope of the object. This value of the Scope parameter will be either Session or Application. The Identifier parameter designates a name for the object. The ProgID parameter was discussed previously. The ClassID parameter represents a unique class identifier for an OLE class object. You must enter either the ProgID or the ClassID parameter. Listing 11.13 demonstrates a global.asa file that declares an object with Session scope.

LISTING 11.13. USING <OBJECT> WITH AN OBJECT.

```
 1: <SCRIPT LANGUAGE="VBScript" RUNAT="Server">
 2: <%
 3: If ProgramID Then
 4: ' Declare an object with Session scope using the PROGID
 5: <OBJECT RUNAT=Server SCOPE=Session ID=MyConnection
 6: PROGID="ADODB.Connection">
 7: Else
 8: ' Declare an object with Session scope using the CLASSID
 9: <OBJECT RUNAT=Server SCOPE=Session ID=MyConnection
10: CLASSID="Clsid:8AD3067A-B3FC-11CF-A560-00A0C9081C21">
11: </OBJECT>
```

Both the PROGID and CLASSID formats are used in this code example for the purpose of illustration. You will typically use either one format or the other, depending on the object that is being declared. This code listing shows an example of a database connection that is declared in a global.asa file. You could then reference characteristics about this connection object throughout the lifetime of a user session.

Summary

Active Server Pages provide an excellent method for constructing interactive applications. Today's lesson has provided you with a walkthrough of the fundamental features of Active Server Pages. Visual InterDev enables you to easily implement Active Server Pages within your Web-based application.

During today's lesson, you saw how Active Server Pages fit in the client/server model. You learned how Active Server Pages are processed on the Web server. In addition, you learned how the scripting languages used to create Active Server Pages are intermingled with HTML code to create dynamic and compelling Web content. You learned about the types of scripting languages that are used within an Active Server Page and saw detailed examples of VBScript code. In addition, you learned how Visual InterDev assigns the scripting language for an ASP and how you can change the default language for your Active Server Pages. You were introduced to working with transactions in Visual InterDev and the Scripting Object Model.

A majority of the lesson covers the various objects that can be used with Active Server Pages. You learned about the five types of ASP objects. You also learned in detail about the collections, methods, and properties of these ASP objects. The lesson provides detailed examples on how to access, reference, and use these objects in your applications. Today's lesson provides examples of working with each of the five ASP objects.

Finally, throughout the day, you received several tips and techniques that will make your ASP development experience rewarding and enjoyable.

Q&A

Q Can my ASP files contain the same types of content as HTML pages?

A All the logic included within an HTML file is executed on the user's browser. An ASP can include the same items as an HTML file as well as robust server-side script. This server-side script executes on the server and can interact with Active Server Components that are also on the server. An ASP can dynamically generate formatted HTML back to the client, based on both client and server conditions.

Q Would I want to create all my Web pages as Active Server Pages?

A You certainly can create all your Web content in Active Server Pages. Many interactive sites on the Web today do just that. However, keep in mind that not all Web servers support Active Server Pages. Make sure that your development and production environments support Active Server Pages.

Workshop

The Workshop provides quiz questions to help you solidify your understanding of the material covered and exercises to provide you with experience in using what you've learned. You can find the answers to the quiz questions and exercises in Appendix B, "Answers."

Quiz

1. Name the five types of ASP objects.

2. What is a collection?

3. Which object contains a collection that enables you to access the object values on a form?

4. If you create a variable in the Session object, what is its scope?

5. Name the Active Server Components that are included with Visual InterDev and IIS.

Exercise

In today's lesson, I covered the fundamentals of Active Server Page development. In creating your Active Server Page for this exercise, choose some of your favorite objects and examples from today's lesson. Experiment with these examples when creating your application. Use properties and methods that I discussed but did not show by example in today's lesson. Use the concepts you learned today to extend the functionality of your application beyond the simple user preferences functions that I discussed today. For example, you can use the baseball example from today's lesson and add functionality related to stadiums, players, games, and so on.

11

DAY 12

Extending Web Pages Through Design-Time Controls

If you are a developer, you recognize the importance of an application's design. Throughout this book, I have tried to emphasize the design as the crux of your application. A design can make or break an application. You also probably realize the importance of the design stage of a development project. It is imperative that you spend the proper time contemplating the aspects of the application design so that the system will execute successfully when the user runs the application.

These design aspects can be applied to the use of design-time controls. Microsoft has introduced a new kind of control to enable you to design specific functionality into your application that will execute when the system is run. In the same way that your application exhibits its characteristics and design concepts when it is run, design-time controls reveal their behavior at runtime.

These controls enable you to focus on designing robust functionality into your application.

Today's lesson focuses on the use of design-time controls within your Web-based applications. Upon completion of this lesson, you will be able to

- Explain the concept of a design-time control.
- Articulate how design-time controls improve your Web development.
- Explain the difference between design-time controls and ActiveX controls.
- Implement design-time controls including the Recordset control and other data-bound controls into your Web-based applications.
- Build database-driven Web pages using design-time controls.
- Use the Form Manager design-time control to build robust database-driven forms for your application.

Defining Design-Time Controls

During the first week, you learned about ActiveX controls. You realize that you can use these controls to build the interface for your application. You also know that ActiveX controls exhibit their presence and functionality when the user initiates the application. But what is a design-time control? Does this mean that you can use this control when you design the application, but not when you run it? This section answers these questions and more and provides a basic definition for a design-time control.

A *design-time control* is an important new control, developed specifically for the Web, that enables you to place rich functionality in your application without additional overhead. Design-time controls are the Diet Coke of the computer interface—same great taste with half the calories!

Design-time controls enable you to take advantage of the same benefits as ActiveX controls during the time of application design. This means that you can visually set the properties and characteristics of the control, similar to ActiveX controls.

The distinguishing factor is that design-time controls don't incur the overhead cost at runtime. When you insert a design-time control into your Web page, you establish the characteristics of the control. These property attributes are saved as text within the context of the document. The text contains special instructions based on properties that you have designed for the control.

When the user runs the application, the actual control that you used to develop these instructions exhibits itself as runtime text—runtime instructions to execute the designed functionality. In other words, you receive the same powerful functionality with a lower overhead cost, hence the Diet Coke analogy.

Design-Time Controls Versus ActiveX Controls

A design-time control is a special type of ActiveX control that enables you to integrate specific properties and behavior characteristics when designing your applications. These controls insert instructions into your documents instead of an actual control, thereby reducing the amount of processing overhead in your application.

Whereas the ActiveX control is typically a graphical object that is used to construct a user interface for your application, the design-time control provides a visual helper at the time of design. This visual aid then works behind the scenes to execute the desired functionality.

With a few exceptions, ActiveX controls are usually visible to you when you're designing your application. You have learned about several controls that enable you to build a graphical user interface. These ActiveX controls include the command button, the radio button, the check box, the list box, the marquee, and so on. You have used some of these controls during the first two weeks. After you insert the controls on your Web page, you establish the property values for the controls to affect their appearance and behavior. At runtime, these controls appear in your Web page and provide specific functionality. Runtime refers to the period of time that the user is running the application and executing the code. ActiveX controls contain a binary runtime component that provides additional functionality when the application runs. You incur the overhead of the control being alive during application runtime to receive the additional functionality.

Design-time controls, on the other hand, don't contain a runtime component. They aren't visible when the user runs the application. You can use these controls while designing your Web pages to provide powerful functionality to your application. These controls are like wizards that facilitate the construction of your application during the design phase of your development effort. When the user executes the application, the functionality is exhibited in the application without the appearance of the design-time control. Its control might not be visible at runtime, but its effects are evident to the user.

Design-Time Controls Make Effective Parents

A design-time control has a similar relationship and responsibility to the application as a parent has to a child. A parent is charged with raising children. This task includes

12

providing the proper guidance and instruction so that the child can thrive when he or she becomes an adult. The parent serves as a counselor and coach who visually provides an example in his or her actions and speech. When the child becomes an adult, he or she will exhibit behaviors, values, and characteristics that have been taught by the parents. As a parent, I can already see the effects of this relationship in my three children.

A design-time control provides a similar guide to the Web pages and application. The design-time control affects your application by the properties and characteristics that are set for the control. This information is stored in the context of the Web page documents. In a sense, the Web page is affected by the instruction, or "teaching," of the design-time control. The control tells the Web page what behaviors to exhibit.

You can think of the runtime environment as adulthood for the Web page that includes the code produced by the design-time control. During runtime, the control is no longer around to help. This is analogous to the parent who is no longer around to instruct the child, now an adult, what to do. The newly independent adult must live his or her own life, using the characteristics and values that the parents taught him or her as a child. Similarly, the runtime text code that was created in the Web page must execute independently of the design-time control when the application is executed. Although the design-time control parent is no longer visibly around, this code exhibits the properties and characteristics that were instilled during design time. Figure 12.1 illustrates both the parent/child and the design-time control/runtime code relationship.

FIGURE 12.1.

The design-time control—an effective parent.

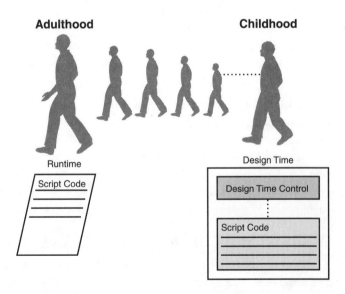

The Origin of Design-Time Controls

Visual InterDev is one of the first tools to use design-time controls as a part of the development environment. Design-time controls, like regular ActiveX controls, are based on Microsoft's Component Object Model (COM). This model provides a standard definition and structure for all design-time controls. Because a design-time control is constructed based on COM, applications can access its functionality through a standard method. You can build a design-time control with hard-core languages such as C and C++, as well as more intuitive languages such as Visual Basic. You can basically build your own design-time controls with any tool that supports COM.

> **Note** You must use Visual Basic version 5 or later to build a design-time or ActiveX control.

After you become familiar with using design-time controls, I think you will want to rush out and build your controls. You will realize their benefit and structure and recognize the importance of their reusability across your development team. You might even begin by developing reusable design-time controls across your development team.

I think you will see how easy it is to use and develop design-time controls. You will also appreciate their power and capability.

Visual InterDev provides many design-time controls that you can integrate into your application. The controls generate both HTML and scripting code that can be used in a variety of ways, including the creation of the following items:

- HTML content
- Client-side scripting
- ActiveX controls
- Java applets
- Server-side scripting
- Active Server Components

Within your Visual InterDev application, you can integrate design-time controls in your client- and server-side components. Some of the more powerful Visual InterDev design-time controls enable you to integrate rich and robust database functionality into your application. The next few sections explain and explore these exciting new controls.

12

Understanding Design-Time Controls

This section is for those intrigued minds who wonder how a design-time control can achieve its purpose without visibly appearing in the application at runtime. This part of the lesson explains how to insert a design-time control into your application. After you understand the process, I will review the inner workings of the design-time control and then explain how these controls accomplish their tasks.

Inserting a Design-Time Control

Design-time controls are typically placed within a Web page or an Active Server Page. The design-time control must be installed and registered on the machine where it is used. This requirement is the same as regular ActiveX controls. Once registered, the design-time control can be used within the context of your application.

Visual InterDev provides several standard design-time controls (DTCs) that include basic user-interface elements. These DTCs can be found on the Toolbox underneath the Design-Time Controls section. Table 12.1 defines each of the standard Visual InterDev design-time controls.

TABLE 12.1. VISUAL INTERDEV DESIGN-TIME CONTROLS.

Control	Description
Recordset	Creates a Recordset control that enables you to access data from a page
Label	Enables you to create read-only label text for your page and controls that can be read from a database
Textbox	Creates a data-bound text box or text area
Listbox	Creates a data-bound list box
Checkbox	Creates a data-bound check box
OptionGroup	Creates a group of data-bound options, or radio buttons
Button	Creates a pushbutton
Grid	Creates a data-bound grid, or table
RecordsetNavBar	Creates a set of VCR-like buttons to navigate through a recordset
FormManager	Creates a set of event-driven forms that provide browse and update capabilities for your data
PageNavBar	Enables you to provide controls to navigate through your Web pages based on the navigation structure implemented in the Site Designer
Timelines	Enables you to set a timeline and sequence for calling or executing methods, properties, and events of page objects

Control	Description
Page Transitions	Enables you to add transition effects as the user moves from one page to another in your application, similar to slide transitions in Microsoft PowerPoint
PageObject	Enables you to treat an ASP page as an object, thereby accessing methods and properties of the page

Note

All the design-time controls listed in Table 12.1 create some type of scripting object that can be used to generate a combination of HTML, script, and text. Some of the controls will also produce a visual HTML element at runtime.

You will learn more about script objects and the Scripting Object Model during tomorrow's lesson, "Unleashing the Power of the Visual InterDev Programming Model."

To insert a design-time control into your page, you simply drag the control and drop it into the desired location on the page. The following example will guide you through the process of inserting a text box design-time control into an ASP page:

1. Create a project called `DTCTest`.
2. Add an ASP page to the project and name it `DTCTextbox.asp`.
3. Drag and drop a Textbox control from the list of design-time controls on the Toolbox.
4. A message box appears, prompting you to enable the Scripting Object Model for the page. Click Yes. Figure 12.2 depicts the current display of this page as seen through the eyes of the Source editor.

From Figure 12.2, you again see the visual nature of Visual InterDev. The ability to drag and drop controls as well as see these controls visually on the page enables Visual InterDev to provide robust, RAD-like features. After you have inserted the design-time control, you can then begin to manipulate its properties and add additional functionality to the page.

Working with Design-Time Controls

Just exactly what does a design-time control look like? What magic is going on behind the scenes to enable such elaborate behavior? How does a design-time control affect my application? This section answers these questions, walks you through a review of the code of a design-time control, and explains the basic structure for all design-time controls as seen within an HTML or ASP document.

12

FIGURE **12.2.**

A Textbox design-time control.

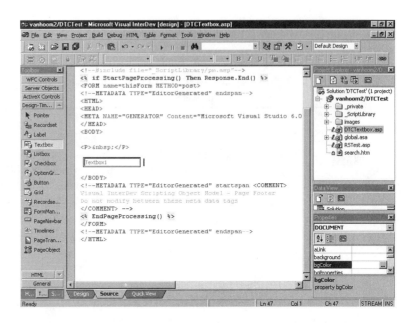

In Figure 12.2, you see the graphical view of the design-time control. You can change to the text view to see the inner workings of the control by selecting the control and choosing Text View from the shortcut menu. Figure 12.3 displays the text view for the Textbox design-time control.

FIGURE **12.3.**

Viewing the inner workings of the design-time control.

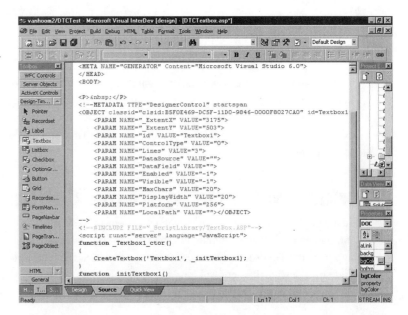

As you can see from Figure 12.3, the design-time control somewhat resembles an ActiveX control. The control is denoted by the <OBJECT> tag and contains an ID, CLASSID, and some parameters similar to an ActiveX control. The design-time control differs from an ActiveX control in that it is initially denoted with the METADATA comment. The runtime text for the control displays below the ending <OBJECT> tag. The next few sections examine the appearance and structure of a design-time control.

Examining the Structure of a Design-Time Control

The METADATA comment is used to denote the start of the design-time control. The TYPE attribute is equal to the value of Designer Control, which is true of all design-time controls. The startspan attribute indicates the beginning of the METADATA comment and causes this line of the comment to be passed over. Another reason for using the METADATA comments to surround a design-time control is to prevent instantiation of the object.

As noted earlier in this lesson, one of the key points and benefits about design-time controls is that these controls don't incur the overhead of regular ActiveX controls. Because the object is surrounded by comments, it won't be instantiated. Only the runtime text will persist, thereby reducing the overhead incurred by the application.

The <OBJECT> tag enables you to work with the control and visually sets the properties of the control. In a sense, the <OBJECT> tag informs Visual InterDev that the control is an object. This information enables you to easily edit the properties of the design-time control.

The attributes and parameters contained within the <OBJECT> tags for the design-time control help to generally define the runtime code for the control. The code in this example is displayed as script and explicitly defines the behavior of the control. This scripting code is what the application and browser execute at runtime. The object declaration is passed over, and the runtime text is the only thing that is noticed and processed. The ending METADATA comment contains the endspan attribute, which signifies to the browser the end of the runtime text for the design-time control.

In this example, a file from the Script Library called TextBox.asp is included. This file provides the basic functions to create the text box. Notice also that the runtime text for the text box is JavaScript. Visual InterDev generates JavaScript for all its design-time controls because it's the superior object model found in JavaScript. The script is set to run on the server as designated by <script runat="server". The runtime text calls the CreateTextbox function from the TextBox.asp file and uses the _initTextbox1 function to set the initial parameters for the control, such as its display length and maximum number of characters.

12

Now that you understand how the Textbox control is created, switch back to the graphical view of the control. To do this, place your cursor between the METADATA comment tags for the control and choose Graphical View from the shortcut menu. The graphical view is the default view and the one that you will use most often for interacting with controls and objects on your page. You can display just the runtime text for the control by selecting Show Runtime Text from shortcut menu.

Figure 12.4 reveals the results of this action.

FIGURE 12.4.

Viewing the runtime text for the design-time control.

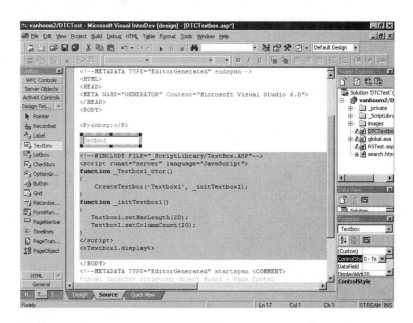

This view enables you to see the control visually on the page while also observing its designated runtime behavior.

Editing the Script for a Design-Time Control

In the previous example, the runtime script that was displayed was automatically generated based on properties defined in the Object Editor. You may be wondering whether Visual InterDev enables you to extend and customize this scripting logic. The answer is yes. There might be cases in which you need to customize the generated logic for the control.

The only thing you need to be aware of concerns the METADATA comment tags. When these comment tags are present, opening the control after you have made changes to the script replaces your customized code with the generated scripting logic defined by the control's properties. To avoid this situation, you can remove the METADATA comment tags and edit the script directly.

 Note This procedure is recommended only if you are not going to switch back to the visual method of setting the properties for the control.

Creating Database-Driven Forms with Design-Time Controls

Now that you understand the basic structure of a design-time control, you will learn how to practically apply this knowledge. Specifically, you will learn how to build dynamic, database-driven forms using a combination of design-time controls. As you learned in the earlier section "Inserting a Design-Time Control," Visual InterDev includes several design-time controls that provide rich database functionality for your application.

Selecting the Target Scripting Platform

One of the key decisions for designing, building, and deploying a database-driven Web application is where the logic, specifically the database logic, will reside. There are many factors that determine how to architect your solution. One key question is how much logic you should place in the pages that are sent to the browser. If you need to support a broad reach of browsers, you are probably going to architect for the least common denominator and place most of the logic on the server. Conversely, if you know the target browser platform supports "smart client" applications that use Dynamic HTML (DHTML), you may want to distribute more of the logic to the client browser. To select the target DTC scripting platform for the project, use the following steps:

1. Right-click the project root in the Project Explorer and select Properties from the shortcut menu.
2. Click on the Editor Defaults tab.
3. Select Server (ASP) for the DTC scripting platform.

This dialog window allows you to choose between Server (ASP) and client-side DHTML based on the type of browser you are using. When you set this at the project level, all the DTCs that you use will default to the platform that you choose.

12

Adding the Database Connection

At the beginning of the second week, you learned how to connect to a database from within your project. This section guides you through this process within the context of creating database-driven Web pages. I have provided two sets of instructions for accomplishing this task—a short version and a long version. The short version is provided first for those who feel up to the task. The long version is provided next to make sure that you remember how to accomplish this task.

Note

You will need to download the Fitch database (`Fitch_Mather.mdb`) from the Macmillan Web site at `http://www.mcp.com/info`.

Connecting to the Fitch Database—The Short Version

To add the database connection to the project, using the project created earlier in the day, add a machine database connection to your project. The ODBC driver that you choose will be contingent on which version you chose to download.

Connecting to the Fitch Database—The Long Version

Here is the long version for adding the database connection to your project:

1. Using the project created earlier in the day, select the `global.asa` file and choose Add Data Connection from the shortcut menu.

2. Click the Machine Data Sources tab and click New.

3. Select the System Data Source option and click Next.

4. Choose the Microsoft Access driver for the data source and click Next.

5. Click Finish.

6. From the ODBC Setup window, click the Select pushbutton to choose the database.

7. Using the Select Database window, choose the `Fitch_Mather.mdb` file from the location that you copied it to during the Download step, and click OK.

8. After you return to the ODBC Setup window, enter `Fitch` for the data source name and click OK.

9. Select the newly created Fitch DSN from the list and click OK.

Using Design-Time Controls to Create the Page

This section will guide you through the process of integrating design-time controls with an Active Server Page. Before you begin, make sure that the DTC scripting platform for the project is set to Server. As a reminder, you can set this option by selecting the project root in the Project Explorer and choosing Properties from the shortcut menu. From the Property Pages window, choose the Editor Defaults tab. From this tab, you can choose Server for the DTC scripting platform. After this option has been set, complete the following steps to see the practical application of design-time controls:

1. Add an ASP page to the project you created earlier in the day and name it RSForm.asp.

2. From the Design-Time Controls section of the Toolbox, drag and drop the Recordset control onto the Web page just beneath the first <BODY> tag. The Recordset control will automatically assign the Fitch data source to the Connection field, as shown in Figure 12.5.

FIGURE 12.5.

Adding the Recordset control to a page.

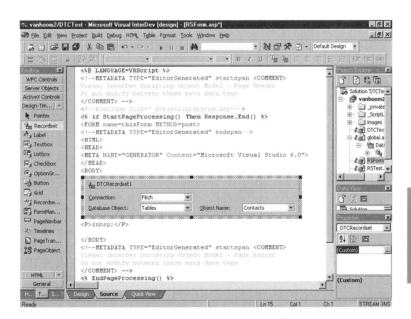

3. Make sure that Tables is selected for the Database Object. If it is not, choose Tables from the Database Object drop-down list.

4. Click the Object Name drop-down list and choose Employees from the list. This action selects the Employees table as the Recordset object.

5. With the Recordset control selected, click the right mouse button and choose Properties from the list of menu items.

6. Change the name of the control to DTCRSFitch and click the Close pushbutton.

7. Add three Textbox controls to the page.

12

Tip

To provide breaks between these fields, add the controls using the Design Editor. After you add each Textbox control, press Enter. This will provide paragraph breaks between each field, thereby placing the fields vertically on the page.

8. Change the properties for the controls using the property table depicted in Table 12.2.

TABLE 12.2. PROPERTY TABLE FOR THE TEXTBOX CONTROLS.

Control	Name	Style	Recordset	Field
Textbox1	txtFName	Textbox	DTCRSFitch	Emp_Fname
Textbox2	txtLName	Textbox	DTCRSFitch	Emp_Lname
Textbox3	txtEmail	Textbox	DTCRSFitch	Emp_Email

9. Add two paragraph breaks after the last text box on the page by pressing the Enter key twice.

10. Drag and drop a RecordsetNavBar control to the bottom of the page as shown in Figure 12.6.

FIGURE 12.6.

Adding the RecordsetNavBar control to the page.

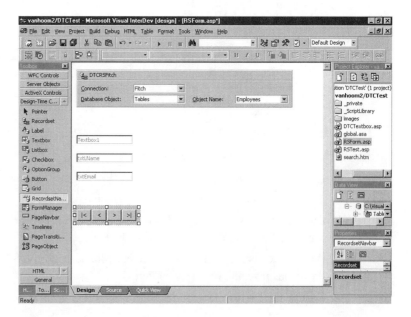

11. With the RecordsetNavBar selected, choose Properties from the shortcut menu.

12. Change the Name field to `RSNavBarFitch` and select DTCRSFitch for the Recordset.

13. Click OK.

14. Save the page and view it in your browser.

You should now be viewing a Web page similar to the one shown in Figure 12.7.

FIGURE 12.7.

Viewing a Web page that contains design-time controls.

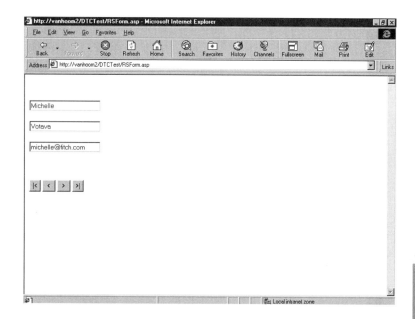

You can use the VCR buttons at the bottom to scroll through the records one at a time. The buttons at either end of the Recordset navigation bar enable you to move to the beginning or the end of the recordset. As you scroll through records, you will notice a slight refresh on the page. This refresh shows that the browser is sending the request back up to the server to retrieve the data and display it in the page. This action occurs because you chose Server for your DTC scripting platform. On Day 21, "Making a Difference with Dynamic HTML," you will learn how to use Dynamic HTML to send data down to the browser so that a round trip to the server is eliminated.

12

Analyzing the Results

In the previous example, you built a database-driven Web page using design-time controls. You learned how quickly and easily you can construct this page using the RAD-like features of Visual InterDev. Just a few drag-and-drop sequences and you are done. Let's examine some of the tasks that you accomplished along the way.

The Recordset Control

First, you set the properties for the Recordset control. In the example, you established a connection to the Fitch database, and you also set the Database Object to a value of `Tables`. This action caused the Recordset to be connected directly to a table in the database. You might have noticed the other options of Stored Procedures and Views in the list. This list basically displays all the types of objects in your database. You then selected the Employees table as the Object Name. The Object Name drop-down list is dynamically created based on which object you choose for the Database Object.

Next, you used the property page for the Recordset control to customize its property values, including the name of the control.

When you added this control to the page, you were prompted to enable the scripting object model for the page. This action, among other things, created a form for you at the top of the page as shown in the following code sample:

```
<FORM name=thisForm METHOD=post>
```

This line allowed you to associate all the other controls with the form, thereby simplifying the creation of the page and reducing the task of adding the HTML <FORM> tag.

The Textbox Controls

After you established the database object to access, you added and customized three Textbox controls to represent different fields in the Employees table. For this example, you used the first name, last name, and email address fields. You learned how to tie each of the design-time controls to the recordset and the field within the table.

The RecordsetNavBar Control

The final step was adding a set of controls to navigate through the records. You learned about the purpose of the RecordsetNavBar control and how to connect its properties to those of the Recordset.

Analyzing the Runtime Script

Now that you have retraced your steps, you may be wondering how these simple steps created a database-driven form. Let's take a look at some of the script code that Visual InterDev created based on your choices.

Most of the logic was embedded as runtime text for the Recordset control. You can look at this code by right-clicking the Recordset control and choosing Show Runtime Text from the shortcut menu. Listing 12.1 displays the runtime text for the Recordset control in this example.

LISTING 12.1. ANALYZING THE RUNTIME TEXT FOR THE RECORDSET CONTROL.

```
 1: <!--#INCLUDE FILE="_ScriptLibrary/Recordset.ASP"-->
 2: <script language="JavaScript" runat="server">
 3: function _initDTCRSFitch()
 4: {
 5:     var DBConn = Server.CreateObject('ADODB.Connection');
 6:     DBConn.ConnectionTimeout = Application('Fitch_ConnectionTimeout');
 7:     DBConn.CommandTimeout = Application('Fitch_CommandTimeout');
 8:     DBConn.CursorLocation = Application('Fitch_CursorLocation');
 9:     DBConn.Open(Application('Fitch_ConnectionString'),
        ➥Application('Fitch_RuntimeUserName'),
        ➥Application('Fitch_RuntimePassword'));
10:     var cmdTmp = Server.CreateObject('ADODB.Command');
11:     var rsTmp = Server.CreateObject('ADODB.Recordset');
12:     cmdTmp.ActiveConnection = DBConn;
13:     rsTmp.Source = cmdTmp;
14:     cmdTmp.CommandType = 2;
15:     cmdTmp.CommandTimeout = 10;
16:     cmdTmp.CommandText = '`Employees`';
17:     rsTmp.CacheSize = 10;
18:     rsTmp.CursorType = 3;
19:     rsTmp.CursorLocation = 3;
20:     rsTmp.LockType = 3;
21:     DTCRSFitch.setRecordSource(rsTmp);
22:     DTCRSFitch.open();
23:     if (thisPage.getState('pb_DTCRSFitch') != '')
24:         DTCRSFitch.setBookmark(thisPage.getState('pb_DTCRSFitch'));
25: }
26: function _DTCRSFitch_ctor()
27: {
28:     CreateRecordset('DTCRSFitch', _initDTCRSFitch);
29: }
30: function _DTCRSFitch_dtor()
31: {
32:     DTCRSFitch._preserveState();
33:     thisPage.setState('pb_DTCRSFitch', DTCRSFitch.getBookmark());
34: }
35: </script>
```

In this listing, the first line of the runtime text creates a database connection object and stores the instance of this object in the DBConn variable. The next line exhibits how the `global.asa` file and the ASP file that contains the database control work together to connect to the database. Using the `DBConn` object that was created in the first line of this runtime text, the `ConnectionTimeout` and `CommandTimeout` properties are established based on the database connection that was created for the project. The connection information can be found in the `Application_OnStart` procedure within the `global.asa` file. The information in the `global.asa` file stores general property information about the database connection. This information is used to help the ASP create the connection dynamically when it's needed. The `ConnectionTimeout` property defines the maximum length of time for the connection, whereas the `CommandTimeout` property specifies the maximum duration for execution of the SQL command.

Next, the username and password are used to connect to the database. The `cmdTemp` variable is used to create a `Command` object. This object is used later in the code to capture the SQL command to execute against the database. The `DTCRSFitch` variable is used to create the `Recordset` object. After this object is created, the `Recordset` object is opened, using the Employees table as a parameter. As a refresher, the `Recordset` object represents all the records in a specified table. You can use the `Recordset` object to retrieve the individual rows within a designated table. The remaining lines of code check the session state of the page and set a bookmark for the page. You will learn more about managing session state in tomorrow's lesson.

Now that you understand how the recordset is created and opened, you may be wondering how the navigation through the recordset is accomplished. Basically, the RecordsetNavBar control uses several functions within the `RSNavBar.asp` file located in the Script Library to accomplish the task of navigating the recordset. If you view the runtime text for the control, you will see the inclusion of the `RSNavBar.asp` file. This ASP file obtains the object data source and interprets and processes the click events for the VCR buttons, thereby allowing you to navigate the recordset.

Summary

Today's lesson has introduced you to the exciting new world of design-time controls. These new controls combine raw power with ease of use to become a developer's friend. Design-time controls can truly augment your productivity. You can use design-time controls to provide rich and robust functionality in your application while reducing the overhead costs of your application. Through the use of design-time controls, Visual InterDev takes care of the routine programming. The time that you save can be spent enhancing the design of the Web page and fine-tuning the programming logic.

In today's lesson you first learned the definition of a design-time control. You should now be able to describe the basic concept of a design-time control and to distinguish between a design-time ActiveX control and a regular ActiveX control.

The lesson provided you with an overview of the origins of design-time controls and described some common functions of these controls. The lesson then guided you through the process of using design-time controls in your Web pages. You learned about several specific design-time controls that are included with Visual InterDev, including the Recordset and the RecordsetNavBar controls. You learned how to implement these controls along with basic user interface controls to build a database-driven Web page.

You should now possess a solid foundation with which to build robust applications with Visual InterDev. Tomorrow you will learn more about the Visual InterDev programming model. The final lesson for the week enables you to build a robust database-driven application.

Q&A

Q Can I build my own custom design-time controls?

A Yes. You can build your own custom design-time controls with any tool that supports the Microsoft Component Object Model (COM) including Visual Basic, Visual C++, and Delphi.

Q How does the design-time control hide its object instantiation at runtime?

A A design-time control is created at the time of design, using `<OBJECT>` tags. These tags primarily exist to enable you to edit the properties for the control. The `<OBJECT>` tags are enclosed in comments, however, which prevents the browser from viewing or recognizing the object. For this reason, the object is never instantiated at runtime.

Q If the object is never instantiated, how does the design-time control accomplish its functionality?

A The properties that you define for the design-time control generate runtime code, which persists when the application is run. This code can be a combination of both HTML and scripting code and represents all the logic for the design-time control. When the user runs the application, this code is recognized and executed, thereby providing the functionality of the design-time control.

12

Workshop

The Workshop provides quiz questions to help you solidify your understanding of the material covered. The exercises provide you with experience in using what you've learned. For answers, see Appendix B, "Answers."

Quiz

1. What is the difference between design-time and regular ActiveX controls?
2. What is the name of the control that enables you to connect to a database from within your Web page?
3. Which control enables you to navigate through the Recordset?
4. What is the default scripting language that is generated for the standard Visual InterDev design-time controls?

Exercise

For today's exercise, change the RSTest.asp page that you created today to be updatable. Also, add another ASP to your project that includes other controls besides the Textbox controls. Experiment with these controls against other tables in the Fitch database. This will give you good practice in preparation for the lessons covered the next two days.

WEEK 2

DAY 13

Unleashing the Power of the Visual InterDev Programming Model

So far you have learned, among other things, how to present information on a Web page by using HTML tags, and you have added Java applets and ActiveX controls to provide a richer experience for the user. Now you will learn how to write client-side and server-side scripts that call and control client-side and server-side objects to create powerful Web applications. The topics covered today include

- An overview of the Document Object Model and Dynamic HTML (DHTML)
- An introduction to DHTML and server scriptlets
- Working with the Scripting Object Model
- Using the Data Environment Object Model

On the client side, you will want to use objects to validate data entry, as you did on Day 7, "Integrating Objects into Your Applications." You will want to use objects to display Java applets and ActiveX controls. With DHTML, you will also want to add special effects to your pages, such as moving text, resizable objects, and expanding text. Of course, you will have many other opportunities to use client-side objects in your Web applications.

On the server side, you will want to, among other things, use objects to connect to a database and to check the specific capabilities of the browser that is requesting your page.

You will begin today by looking at client-side objects. Then you will examine some server-side objects and finish with some tips on improving the performance of your Web applications.

The Document Object Model

On the client side, the Visual InterDev object model is the Dynamic HTML Document Object Model. It also includes any Java applets and ActiveX controls that you might have added to your page. This means that every tag on your page is an object. Every tag can have an ID, methods, and properties.

DHTML and Client-Side Scripting Overview

DHTML is covered in more detail on Day 5, "Enhancing Your Web Page Through Client-Side Script." Figure 13.1 shows a hierarchy of DHTML objects for a Web page.

In Figure 13.1, the top-level node is the document object that represents the page as a whole. Within the document object is the body element that contains various HTML tags, such as table and center. You can write script that manipulates all these objects. That means that all these objects' properties can be set and read, and their events can be executed.

One interesting use of DHTML is to produce a report from a database and then allow the client to rearrange the fields or sort order without making a return trip to the server. Table 13.1 explains some other things you can do with client-side objects.

FIGURE 13.1.

The Document Object Model object hierarchy.

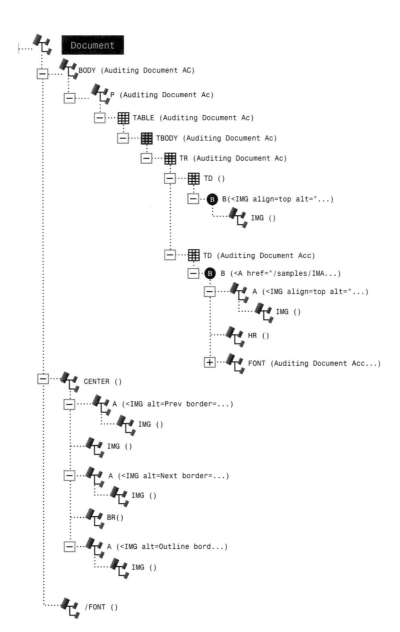

TABLE 13.1. CLIENT-SIDE OBJECTS AND SAMPLE USES.

Object	Event or Property Use
window	You can use the window object's onload event to process script, include files conditionally, open message boxes, and so on, as the page is being loaded into the client's browser. See Listing 13.1 for an example.
document	You can use the document object's various properties to change the background color of the page. You can also use the write method to write text to the HTML page. See Listing 13.2 for an example.
Other elements	You can use other elements as well, such as command buttons, images, text boxes, and so on, in your client-side scripts. You can make these objects visible or invisible. You can move them around the screen and change their fonts or their image sources. The possibilities are endless.

LISTING 13.1. CODING window EVENTS.

```
1: <SCRIPT LANGUAGE=vbscript>
2:    <!--
3:    sub window_onload()
4:            alert("Welcome to my page")
5:    end sub
6:    //-->
7:    </SCRIPT>
```

Listing 13.1 opens a message box welcoming the user to the page after it has loaded in the user's browser.

LISTING 13.2. CODING document EVENTS.

```
1: <SCRIPT LANGUAGE=vbscript>
2:    <!--
3:    document.write("This was written by client-side script")
4:    //-->
5: </SCRIPT>
```

Listing 13.2 demonstrates how to use the document object's write method.

You have had a brief look at client-side objects, scripting, and DHTML. For more information on these topics, you can refer to Day 5 and Day 7. Many other books deal specifically with these topics, including *Sams Teach Yourself JavaScript 1.1 in a Week, Second Edition, Sams Teach Yourself VBScript in 21 Days*, and *Sams Teach Yourself Dynamic HTML in a Week*. Next, I will talk about a new type of object called *scriptlets*.

An Overview of Scriptlets

Microsoft Scripting Components (scriptlets) are yet another way to create ActiveX controls and COM components. Table 13.2 describes the types of scriptlets. As you learned on Day 7, you can create ActiveX controls with tools such as Visual Basic and Visual C++. Now you can create reusable client-side ActiveX controls by using a scripting language such as JavaScript, VBScript, or ECMAScript. As you will learn on Day 15, "Building an Integrated Solution with Components," you can create reusable server-side COM components with the same tools: Visual Basic and Visual C++. Now you can create the same powerful, scalable COM component solutions with VBScript, ECMAScript, or JavaScript.

TABLE 13.2. TYPES OF SCRIPTLETS.

Object	Event or Property Use
DHTML	A DHTML scriptlet is a Web page, including HTML and script, that you package as a control. You can then add this control to your Web applications and also to your Visual Basic applications, as well as any application that supports ActiveX controls.
Server	A Server scriptlet contains only script—no HTML or any other user-interface elements. You can use Server scriptlets like any other COM components: in your ASP applications, your Visual Basic applications, or any other applications that support the use of COM objects.

 Note

This chapter doesn't cover how to build Server scriptlets. The best way is with the Scriptlet Wizard. You can download this from the Microsoft Scripting Web site.

Now I will define DHTML scriptlets, and you will create a scriptlet.

DHTML Scriptlets

There are two elements to DHTML scriptlets: the user interface and the control interface. The user-interface element is just the DHTML that you might write for a Web page. The control-interface element is composed of the properties, methods, and events that make this set of DHTML a control.

To create a DHTML scriptlet, copy Listing 13.3 into a new HTML page. You will have a page with a text box and three check boxes. When you copy this code into your HTML page, you will have finished creating the user-interface element of your DHTML scriptlet. Now let's create the control interface.

13

LISTING **13.3.** CREATING THE USER INTERFACE FOR YOUR DHTML SCRIPTLET.

```
 1: <HTML>
 2: <HEAD>
 3: <META NAME="GENERATOR" Content="Microsoft Visual Studio 6.0">
 4: <TITLE>A DHTML Scriptlet</TITLE>
 5: </HEAD>
 6: <BODY>
 7: <P>
 8: <INPUT id=text1 name=text1 style="HEIGHT: 22px; WIDTH: 196px"
    ➥value="I'm an ActiveX component Now!">
 9: <BR><BR>
10: <FONT face=Arial size=2>You can use and re-use me in:
11: <BR>
12: <INPUT CHECKED id=checkbox1 name=checkbox1 type=checkbox>.ASP
    ➥applications
13: <BR>
14: <INPUT CHECKED id=checkbox2 name=checkbox2 style="LEFT: 31px; TOP:
    ➥58px" type=checkbox>Visual Basic applications
15:<BR>
16:<INPUT CHECKED id=checkbox3 name=checkbox3 style="LEFT: 51px; TOP:
    ➥58px" type=checkbox>Any other type of application that supports ActiveX
    ➥controls
17:</FONT>
18:</P>
19:</BODY>
20:</HTML>
```

When you create methods, properties, and events for your scriptlets, you are really just exposing the methods, properties, and events of the individual elements in your scriptlet. In the sample scriptlet, you will expose the methods, properties, and events of the text box and the three check boxes.

There are two ways to expose these properties, events, and methods. You can create a JavaScript `public_description` object or use the default interface descriptions.

Note   If you choose to use the `public_description` object, the object *must* be written in JavaScript.

There are many advantages to using a `public_description` object. You can name your variables and functions (that is, your properties and methods) whatever you like. You're not limited to the default interface name. The `public_description` object also offers a convenient way to summarize and document the properties, methods, and events exposed by your scriptlet. For these reasons, you will focus on using a `public_description` object. For more information on the default interface-descriptions method for creating control interfaces for your scriptlets, refer to your Visual InterDev help, and search for Defining Properties and Methods in DHTML Scriptlets.

You will now write a `public_description` object in JavaScript to expose and manipulate the text property of the text box and the checked property of the Visual Basic check box. Copy the code from Listing 13.4 into your HTML page. Paste the code somewhere above the `</HEAD>` tag.

LISTING **13.4.** CREATING THE CONTROL INTERFACE FOR YOUR DHTML SCRIPTLET.

```
 1:  <SCRIPT LANGUAGE="JavaScript">
 2:  // public_description object used to declare scriplet
 3:  var public_description = new scriptletobject();
 4:  // general object description (MUST BE WRITTEN IN JavaScript)
 5:  function scriptletobject(){
 6:      this.get_text  = readtext;     //property (read the text box's
                                        ➥text)
 7:      this.put_text  = writetext;    //property (write the text
 8:                                     //to the text box)
 9:      this.check_vb  = checkvb;      //method that checks/unchecks the
10:                                     //vb check box
11:      }
12:
13:  function readtext(){
14:      if (text1.innerText  == ""){
15:          return "No text";}
16:      else{
17:          return text1.innerText;}
18:      }
19:
20:  function writetext(newtext){
21:      if (newtext != ""){
22:          text1.innerText = newtext;}
23:      }
24:  </SCRIPT>
25:
26:  <SCRIPT LANGUAGE="VBScript">
27:      sub check_vb()
28:              if checkbox2.checked = true then
29:                     checkbox2.checked = false
30:              else
31:                     checkbox2.checked = true
32:              end if
33:      end sub
34:  </SCRIPT>
```

13

As you can see, the `public_description` object in the example, called
`scriptletobject`, must be written in JavaScript. However, the actual properties, methods, and events can be written in any scripting language. To show this, I wrote the function that exposes the checked property of the Visual Basic check box as a VBScript sub-
routine. See line 26 of Listing 13.4.

Now that you have created the user-interface element and the control-interface element,
you have finished creating your DHTML scriptlet. Now you want to use it just as you
would any other ActiveX control on another Web page. To do that, you must specify that
this HTML page that you've created is in fact a scriptlet. Figure 13.2 demonstrates how
to do this.

FIGURE 13.2.

*Marking an HTML
page as a scriptlet.*

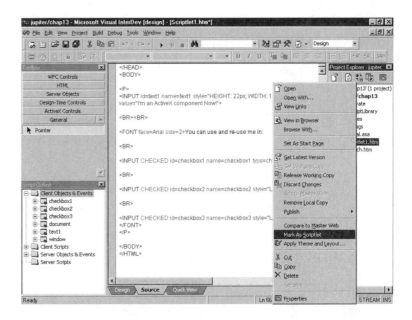

By right-clicking on the HTML page that you want to be a scriptlet, you can choose
Mark as Scriptlet from the pop-up menu to finish creating a DHTML scriptlet. When you
select Mark as Scriptlet, you will notice a change in your toolbox. A reference to your
HTML page, your scriptlet, is present under the Scriptlets tab of your toolbox, as in
Figure 13.3.

Now that your scriptlet is in the toolbox, you can use it on another Web page. Drag your
scriptlet onto an HTML page, just as you would any other ActiveX control. Refer to Day
7 if you would like a review of how to use ActiveX controls. Listing 13.5 shows some
lines of code that you could use to access the properties and methods of your scriptlet.

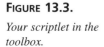

FIGURE 13.3.

Your scriptlet in the toolbox.

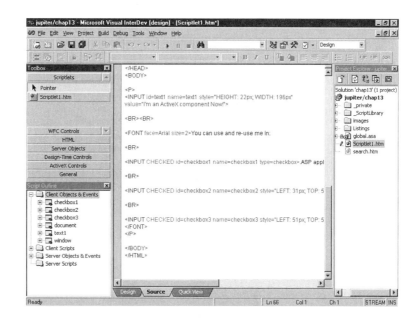

LISTING 13.5. USING SCRIPTLETS IN AN HTML PAGE.

```
1: <script language="vbscript">
2:    alert(scriptlet1.get_text) 'display the text in the text box
3:    scriptlet1.put_text("This is the new text")
4:                              'change the text in the text box
5:    scriptlet1.check_vb        'either check or uncheck the vb check
   ➥box
6: </script>
```

Line 2 in Listing 13.5 displays the text in the text box in your scriptlet. Line 3 changes that text to This is the new text. Line 4 checks or unchecks the Visual Basic check box, depending on whether it's already checked.

13

The Scripting Object Model

The Visual InterDev Scripting Object Model defines a set of objects with events, properties, and methods that you can use to make scripting your ASP applications easier and faster. The Scripting Object Model abstracts events so that you can code either client-side or server-side script in an object-oriented manner instead of the standard HTML fashion.

For example, with standard HTML, form processing generally works like this. First there is a button on the form called a Submit button. When this button is chosen, an ASP page on the server examines the form and state data sent by the form. Using the Scripting Object Model, you can place a button on a form and code for the onclick event of the button. You can put code in this event to process the form. This code can be client-side or server-side script.

This model is different from the DHTML Document Object Model. The DHTML model works only on browsers that support DHTML. The Scripting Object Model works on any browser because it can use server-side script. Some advantages of using the Scripting Object Model include the following:

- A familiar object-oriented programming model, similar to Visual Basic
- Browser and platform independence
- Logic can be easily stored in discrete, isolated procedures rather than mixed with user-interface HTML code.
- The model provides a means of maintaining state rather than using hidden fields or the session variable.
- Scripting objects can be bound to the database so that you can easily develop data-entry and editing forms.
- The model provides a simplified means of navigating between pages. Now you can navigate to a page by name instead of URL.
- The model also provides a way of remotely executing server script. This means that you can access code on another page without navigating off the page you're on.

I will begin the discussion of the Scripting Object Model by looking at design-time controls (DTCs) and the page object fit into this model. Then I will show how the model is used in your applications.

Design-Time Controls and Script Objects

You were introduced to DTCs earlier in this book (see Day 12, "Extending Web Pages Through Design-Time Controls"). You know that they are basically controls that help you generate HTML and script to solve your programming problems. When a DTC is executed at runtime, it dynamically creates a script object.

The script object is like any other object. It has properties, methods, and events. You can code for the properties, methods, and events of the script object. Figure 13.4 shows some DTCs that are included out of the box with Visual InterDev.

FIGURE 13.4.

*Design-time controls
in the toolbox.*

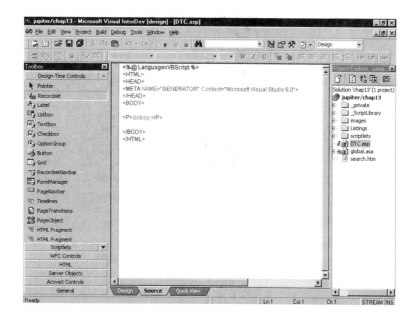

The Page Object

The page object is an ASP or HTML page that you designate as an object. If you organize your server-side script on the page into subs and functions, you can call those subs
and functions as methods of the page object. Page objects offer the following advantages,
among others:

- An easy way to execute specific script on another page without having to pass hidden variables or querystrings to the other page.

- Another way of maintaining state information. Page objects have properties (variables). You can define those properties' lifetimes.

- A way to execute script on the server from a page loaded in a browser.

To specify a page as a page object, drag the `PageObject` DTC from the toolbox onto the
ASP page that you want to be a page object, as shown in Figure 13.5.

Note
  If your scripting platform is server, the Scripting Object Model must be
  enabled to create a page object. Scripting platforms and enabling the
  Scripting object model are discussed next. In this example, when you drag at
  the `PageObject` onto your ASP page, a message box opens, asking whether
  you want to enable the Scripting Object Model. Click Yes.

13

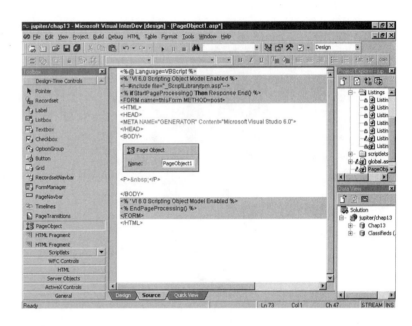

Figure 13.5.

Creating a page object.

As you can see in Figure 13.5, you can give your page object a name. This is the name you will reference in your script. After you give the object a name, you need to add some methods.

There are two types of page object methods: navigate and execute.

Note

A method can be defined as both a navigate method and an execute method, but you must add the code inside the method to accommodate both types of calls.

When a navigate method is called from a client, the application jumps to the ASP page and executes the requested code. The application can then jump to another page; the application does not have to return to the client or the page that called the method. When an execute method is called, the method is treated like a function. The application executes the requested script remotely, and when it's finished, control is returned to the client or the page that called the method.

To create a method for a page object, write your procedures or functions in a script block with the RUNAT = "Server" attribute. In Listing 13.6, I have created a method in VBScript for the page object created in Figure 13.5.

Note

Page object methods can accept any number of parameters passed to them. However, these parameters are always passed as strings. You must add the appropriate conversion code to your scripts if you need variable types other than strings.

LISTING 13.6. CREATING A PAGE OBJECT METHOD.

```
1: <script language="vbscript" runat="server">
2: sub add_five(strNumber)
3:    dim I as integer
4:    I = cint(strNumber) + 5
5: end sub
6: </script>
```

Before you can use this procedure from another page, you must first expose it as a method and define it as a navigate method or an execute method. Figure 13.6 shows the page object's property page and how to define a method as a navigate method.

Note

You can call execute methods only from a client-side script.

FIGURE 13.6.

Defining a navigate method.

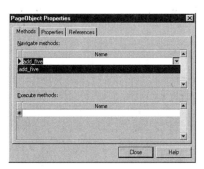

13

Right-click the page object and select Properties from the pop-up menu. Click the Methods tab. The drop-downs display all the available procedures and functions. Select the add_five() procedure from the Navigate Methods drop-down and click Close. Now you have exposed a method for your page object and defined it as a navigate method.

To execute this method from the current page, the page where it is defined, you can use the default page object name thisPage. The syntax would be `thisPage.methodName(parameters)`. To call a method from another page, you must make that page a page object and add a reference on it to the page that you want to call. To do this, follow these steps:

- Create the new ASP page.
- Drag a PageObject DTC onto the page and enable the Scripting Object Model.
- Right-click the page object and select Properties from the pop-up menu.
- Click the References tab.
- Click the browse button, the button with the three dots (...).
- Select the page that is the page object you want to reference and click OK.
- Select the Client check box if you want client-side script on this page to access the page object. Select the Server check box if you want server-side script on this page to access the page object.
- Click Close.
- Add your scripting logic.

To call the method, use the syntax
`PageObjectName.Navigate.NavigateMethodName(Parameters)` or
`PageObjectName.Execute.ExecuteMethodName(Parameters)`, depending on whether you defined the methods as execute or navigate methods.

IntelliSense displays the available methods and properties (which I will discuss in a moment) as you type the page object's name. You will notice a `show()` method. All page objects have a default `show()` method that displays the contents of the page.

Like all other objects, page objects have properties. A page object's properties are basically global variables. These properties can have one of three levels of scope: page, session, and application. Page-scope properties are available anywhere on the page until you navigate to another page. Session-scope properties are available on any page in your project. These values are stored in the same manner as ASP Session variables.

Tip

> You were introduced to ASP session variables on Day 11, "Fundamentals of Active Server Pages."

Application-scope properties are available to all users of your application on any page in your project. These values are stored in the same manner as ASP Application variables.

Note

You were introduced to ASP Application variables on Day 11.

You can also specify whether the property will be available to client-side script. If you make the property available to client-side script, you can also specify that it be either read/write or read-only. Server properties are always read/write.

To create a property for your page object, right-click the PageObject DTC and select Properties from the pop-up menu. On the Properties page, you can type the name of the property, its lifetime (scope), client-side script access, and server-side script access. Figure 13.7 shows the Properties tab of the page object.

FIGURE 13.7.

Defining a page object property.

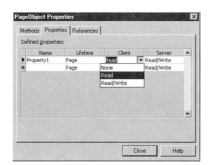

To make properties available to scripts, page objects implement get() and set() navigate methods for each property. In this example, your property is named Property1. If you want to set that property, you call the setProperty1() method. If you want to get the value of that property, you use the getProperty1() method. The syntax to get a property value is VariableName = PageObjectName.Navigate.getPropertyName. The syntax to set a property value is PageObjectName.Navigate.setPropertyName.

Now that you've examined how DTCs and page objects fit into the Scripting Object Model, you will look at how to use the Scripting Object Model in your applications.

How Does the Scripting Object Model Work?

The Scripting Object Model is implemented by script stored in the script library. If you expand the _ScriptLibrary folder in your Project Explorer window, as in Figure 13.8, you can view the script library.

13

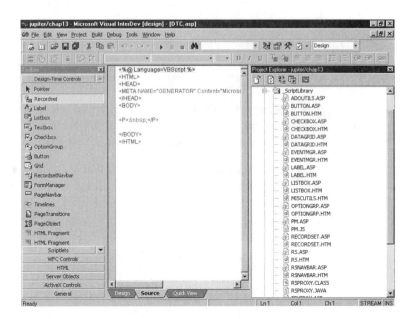

The files in the script library contain all the necessary code for abstracting the events, methods, and properties of their corresponding DTCs. The files with the `.htm` extension contain code necessary to run on the client side. The files with the `.asp` extension contain the code necessary to run on the server side. To determine where your scripting objects will run and which file from the scripting library will be used, you can set a property of your ASP page containing the DTC. Figure 13.9 shows how.

Right-click anywhere within the HTML code of your ASP page and select Properties from the pop-up menu. Figure 13.9 shows the resulting property page. In the lower-right corner, you see that you can choose Server (ASP), which will give you the broadest reach and platform/browser independence, or you can choose Client (IE 4 DHTML), which will give you a richer user interface, but the code will not run on all browsers. It might run only on Internet Explorer 4.

You can set the DTC Scripting Platform on an individual DTC basis, also. By right-clicking a DTC and selecting Properties from the pop-up menu, you can change the value of the Scripting Platform drop-down list box on the General tab. See Figure 13.10 for an example of this.

FIGURE 13.10.

Setting the DTC Scripting Platform on an individual DTC.

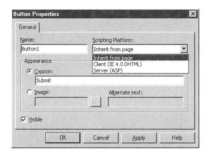

In Figure 13.10, you are telling Visual InterDev where you want the code for a DTC command button to run.

Enabling the Scripting Object Model

Before you can use the Scripting Object Model, you must enable it. There are two ways to enable the Scripting Object Model. You can set a property of your ASP page, as seen in Figure 13.11.

FIGURE 13.11.

Enabling the Scripting Object Model.

13

By right-clicking anywhere in the HTML code of your ASP page and selecting Properties from the pop-up menu, you can set the Enable Scripting Object Model property to True.

Another way to enable the model is to drag a DTC that requires the model to be enabled onto your ASP page from the toolbox. Figure 13.12 shows a recordset DTC being dragged onto a page and the resulting message box that allows you to enable the Scripting Object Model.

FIGURE 13.12.

Enabling the Scripting Object Model, take two.

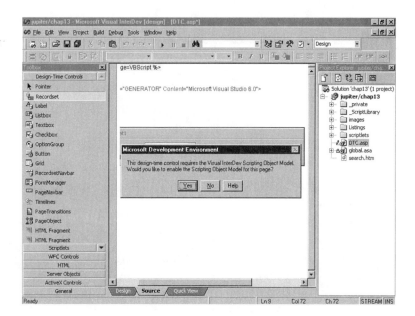

If you click the Yes button, the Scripting Object Model is enabled and some code is added to your ASP pages. As you can see in Figure 13.13, the code highlighted in gray has been added to the page that will enable you to use the Scripting Object Model.

Now that you've enabled the Scripting Object Model, you will develop a data-binding and Data Environment example by using the Scripting Object Model.

Using the Scripting Object Model

Now you're ready to do some programming. You will build a page that accesses data from a database one record at a time and lets you step through the recordset. You were shown how to connect to a database on Day 8, "Communicating with a Database," so in this chapter I will quickly go through the steps.

FIGURE 13.13.

Code added to your ASP after enabling the Scripting Object Model.

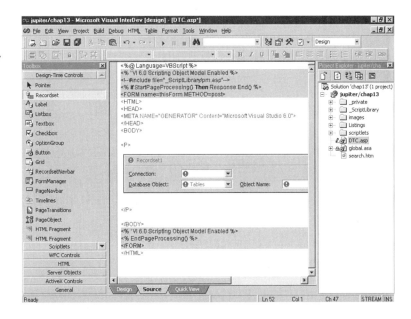

In Figure 13.14, I've added a database connection, a DTC recordset object, three DTC Databound labels, and a DTC recordset navigation bar. Answer yes to the message box that asks you whether to enable the Scripting Object Model. The recordset has been associated with a table in the database, and the labels have been associated with fields in the recordset. The navigation bar also has been associated with the recordset object.

You have now written an application that uses the Scripting Object Model. You could write script that calls the `recordset.movenext` method, or you could write script that opens a message box when you've reached the last record in the recordset, when `recordset.eof` is `true`. Now that the objects are on your page and the object model has been enabled, you can access all the methods and properties associated with these DTCs' scripting objects.

> **Note**   You can view the available methods, properties, and events for an object by using the IntelliSense feature of Visual InterDev, introduced on Day 7.

13

Next you will look at an alternative way of accessing data. The Data Environment Object Model—along with the Data Environment object—provides a means of accessing data in an object-oriented way.

FIGURE 13.14.

*Developing your
Scripting Object Model
application.*

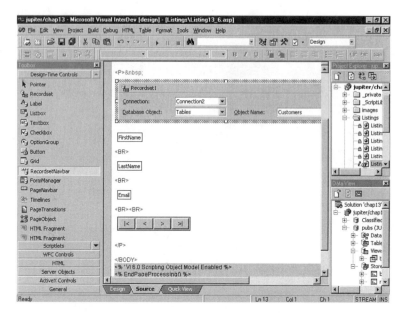

The Data Environment Object Model

In this chapter you will concentrate on the Data Environment Object Model. The Data
Environment Object Model abstracts the ADO object model and its objects—
Connection, Command, Recordset, Field, and Parameter—into an easier form. The Data
Environment Object Model exposes commands as methods. You can call these methods,
which execute the commands, and return the resulting recordset.

To use the Data Environment object, first you create a data connection by right-clicking
on the project in the Project Explorer window and selecting Add Data Connection from
the pop-up menu. After you go through the steps of specifying a DSN and have successfully connected to a database, you add a data command. This command is what you execute from script to access the database from your ASP application. If the preceding step
was successful, you will see a Data Environment object under the global.asa file in the
Project Explorer, as in Figure 13.15.

You can add a data command by right-clicking the Data Environment object in the
Project Explorer and selecting Add Data Command from the pop-up menu. Figure 13.16
shows the resulting data command Property page.

FIGURE 13.15.

Adding the Data Environment object to your project.

FIGURE 13.16.

Adding a data command to your project.

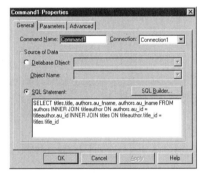

In this case, your data command is going to return the result of a query selecting all the authors' names and the titles of their books.

Now that you've created a data command, you've created a method for the Data Environment object that you can call from script and that will return a recordset to you. Listing 13.7 shows how to initialize the Data Environment object, execute the command, and finally access the recordset.

13

LISTING 13.7. USING THE DATA ENVIRONMENT OBJECT MODEL.

```
 1:   <%
 2:     thisPage.createDE()
 3:     DE.Command1
 4:     set rs = DE.rsCommand1
 5:     first_name = rs("first")
 6:     last_name = rs("last")
 7:     do while not rs.eof
 8:            Response.Write(first_name)   
 9:            Response.Write(last_name) %>
10:            <br>
11: <%
12:            DE.MoveNext
13:     loop
14: %>
```

After you create the Data Environment variable and some data commands, you can use them again and again on various pages. Code reusability is a strong advantage of using the Data Environment object.

Summary

Today you examined how to program Web applications by using the various object models available to Visual InterDev applications. Those object models include the Document Object Model, the Scripting Object Model, and the Data Environment Object Model. You also learned how to create and use both DHTML and Server scriptlets.

Q&A

Q Describe the difference between DHTML scriptlets and Server scriptlets.

A DHTML scriptlets include HTML and/or other user-interface elements. Server scriptlets include only script. They do not contain any user-interface elements. DHTML scriptlets are treated like ActiveX controls. Server scriptlets are treated like COM components.

Q Name three advantages of using page objects.

A Three advantages are

• Page objects provide a way to execute specific script on another page without passing hidden variables or querystrings.

• Page objects provide another way to keep session information with session-scope properties.

- Page objects also provide a way for your pages to call and execute script on the server without navigating from the client's browser.

Workshop

The Workshop provides quiz questions to help you solidify your understanding of the material covered. The exercises provide you with experience in using what you've learned. The answers can be found in Appendix B, "Answers."

Quiz

1. What is the difference between the page object's navigate method and execute method?

2. Why might using the Data Environment Object Model be important to a developer?

3. What are the three types of scope for a page object's properties? Describe how they're implemented.

4. Describe the two interfaces that make up a DHTML scriptlet.

Exercise

In today's exercise, you will create a small application that uses a DHTML scriptlet and a page object. The DHTML scriptlet should provide the user with a form interface including a DTC text box and a DTC command button. Use client-side script to code the on_click event for the command button. The event should call a remote page object navigate method. The method should accept the text box's value, add `Hello` to the string, and print *Hello* on the page. Place your scriptlet on a page and test your application.

13

DAY **14**

Building a Database-Driven Web Application

Now that you have learned the basics of Visual InterDev, it's time to stretch your wings and try building your own application. The best way to reinforce what you've learned is to apply it, which you'll have a chance to do in this lesson. Your two weeks of training ends with a case study of an application you will build. You'll create an Internet application for the hypothetical Northwind Foods, a large wholesale foods company that sells food products to retail businesses. This application gives you a chance to apply all the knowledge you've gained in the past two weeks to build a Web-based application. You should also get a feel for how the components fit together to meet user's needs. The following is a short list of some of the things you will be covering in today's lesson:

- Create a home page that will contain links to all functional areas of the application.
- Use an HTML form to enter search criteria and retrieve information from a database.
- Retrieve data from one page and pass that data to subsequent pages.

- Retrieve data from a database and display it in HTML tables.
- Combine a set of ASP and HTML pages together to form a working Internet application.

The first part of the lesson describes the application and its purpose and explains the different components you will be working with to build the application. Next, you jump right into development by creating the home page. You then build the Order Search page, which is an Active Server Page that allows you to enter criteria to search for an order. Next, you will build pages to retrieve records from the database based on the search criteria you entered in the search page. Finally, you will build an Active Server Page that will display detailed information about a particular order. I bet you can't wait to start!

During this lesson, you get to apply your knowledge and determine how much you have learned. If you discover that you need to brush up on a concept, feel free to refer to the lesson on that topic. This final examination is an open book test.

The Northwind Foods Case Study at a Glance

This case study involves developing an Internet application for the Northwind Foods company. As mentioned earlier, Northwind Wholesale is a large wholesaler of several different types of food products. This case study is a hypothetical situation, but it is meant to demonstrate the possibilities for Web-based applications.

The application you will build focuses on searching the Northwind database for a particular order and displaying the detailed information about that particular order. This is accomplished through an HTML home page with static information and several Active Server Pages with access to the database. The HTML and ASP pages that are used are depicted in Table 14.1.

TABLE 14.1. THE WEB PAGES.

Web Page	Description
Default.htm	Main introduction page for the application
OrderSearch.asp	Enables the user to search for a particular order or orders containing the search criteria
OrderListing.asp	Displays a list of orders based on the criteria entered from the Order Search page
OrderDetail.asp	Displays detailed information about an order chosen from the Order Listing page

The Northwind Foods Internet application uses both client and server components, including HTML Web pages, ASP scripting code, client scripting code, HTML forms, and data passing techniques. You will be using all these components to construct this application. Some pieces are given to you as part of the lesson, and others you create from scratch. Again, the goal is to reinforce your learning over the past two weeks.

 Note

For this lesson, you will use the Northwind database that is provided as a sample database in Microsoft Access. In the samples accompanying Microsoft Access, the default directory for the Northwind database is `Program Files/Microsoft Office/Office/Samples/Northwind.mdb`. If you don't have the Northwind database, you can download it from the Web site at `www.mcp.com`.

This lesson walks you through the development of the order inquiry portion of the application. You can later expand the application to include more functionality including order entry and maintenance, product entry and maintenance, and shipping inquiry and maintenance.

Getting Started

The first step in getting started with the Northwind Foods application is creating the Visual InterDev project. You will begin by setting up the project information. Follow these steps to create a new project:

1. Create a new Web project named `NorthwindFoods`.

2. Use the same defaults on the Project Wizard as in previous days and create the new Web application with the name `NorthwindFoods`.

Database Setup

The next step in setting up the application is to connect to the database. For this example, you will connect to the Northwind database. Follow these steps to connect to the Northwind database:

1. Add a new database connection to your project by right-clicking the `global.asa` file in your project and select Add Data Connection.

2. Follow the Connection Wizard by creating a new Machine Datasource for the Northwind database. Refer to previous chapters to set up a new datasource.

3. The connection properties will display with a connection name of Connection1. Change the connection name from Connection1 to Northwind and click OK.

These steps will set up a new database connection to the Northwind database and allow you to use the tables and views in your Web pages. Now it's time to start building those Web pages.

14

The Home Page

The home page is the main menu for the Northwind Foods application. It serves as an introduction to the application as well as links to each function of the application. The completed home page will look like Figure 14.1. Follow these steps to create the home page:

1. Create a new HTML page in your project and name it Default.htm.

2. Default.htm will automatically open in the HTML design editor. Place the title, Northwind Foods, at the top of the page.

3. Update Default.htm in the design editor so that the text appears the same as in Figure 14.1.

4. Save Default.htm and close the window.

FIGURE 14.1.

The home page.

As you can see, the home page has links to multiple functions in the application. During this lesson, you will be focusing on the order inquiry part of the application. You will come back to this page later in the chapter to add a link from this page to the Order Search page.

The Order Search Page

The Order Search page will enable the site visitor to search all orders in the database to find a particular order. This page consists of an order number field and a search button. The final page will look like Figure 14.2. You will now create the Order Search page:

1. Create a new Active Server Page in your project and name the page OrderSearch.asp.

2. The ASP page will automatically open in Source view. Select the Design View tab to open the page in Design mode.

> **Note**
>
> To create this page, open the following windows to assist you: Toolbox, Project Explorer, and the Design window.

3. Create a heading on the page similar to that of the home page except this heading will be named Order Search.

4. Click the HTML bar in the Toolbox to display the HTML objects. Select the Form HTML object, drag it to the workspace, and drop it just after the Order Search heading. Although it isn't visible in the Design View, this creates a form that will be used to place the HTML search items.

5. The next step is to insert a table for the search criteria. Select Insert Table from the Table menu item on the main menu.

6. Select 3 rows and 2 columns for the new table. Keep all other table defaults.

7. Click the first column of the first row in the table and type in Order ID:.

8. Click the Textbox object in the Toolbox window. Drag the Textbox from the Toolbox to the second column of the first row of the table.

9. Right-click the newly created text box and click Properties. Change the ID property and the Name property from Text1 to OrderID.

10. Click the Submit Button object in the Toolbox window and drag it to the second column of the third row in the table.

11. Select the properties of the table as in previous chapters. Change the border size from 1 pixel to 0 pixels. This will turn the borders of the table off.

14

FIGURE **14.2.**

The Order Search page.

You have completed the graphical portion of developing the Order Search page. Next, you'll change the source code so that the order selection criteria can be passed to the next page, which is the Order Listing page:

1. Click the Source tab to view the HTML source.

2. Scroll to the `<FORM>` tag in the HTML. Move the `</FORM>` tag from its current location to right before the `</BODY>` tag near the bottom of the text. This can be done by either deleting the `</FORM>` and re-entering it or by cutting the tag and pasting it near the `</BODY>` tag.

3. Change the `Action` property of the `<FORM>` tag to be `OrderListing.asp`. The `<FORM>` tag should now look like the following:

   `<FORM action="OrderListing.asp" id=FORM1 method=post name=FORM1>`

4. Save the Order Search page. Listing 14.1 displays the completed code.

LISTING **14.1.** THE ORDER SEARCH PAGE.

```
1: <%@ LANGUAGE=VBScript %>
2: <HTML>
3: <HEAD>
4: <META NAME="GENERATOR" Content="Microsoft Visual Studio 6.0">
5: </HEAD>
6: <BODY>
7: <H2 align=center><FONT color=#ff0000>Order Search</FONT></H2>
8: <P align=center>
```

```
 9: <FORM action=" " id=FORM1 method=post name=FORM1>
10: <TABLE border=0 cellPadding=1 cellSpacing=1 width=75%>
11:
12:     <TR>
13:         <TD>
14:             <DIV align=right>Order ID:</DIV>
15:         <TD>
16:             <INPUT id=orderID name=OrderID>
17:     <TR>
18:         <TD>
19:         <TD>
20:     <TR>
21:         <TD>
22:         <TD><INPUT id=submit1 name=submit1 type=submit value=Submit>
➡</TR></TABLE></P>
23:
24: </FORM>
25: </BODY>
26: </HTML>
```

The Order Listing Page

The Order Listing page will display a listing of all orders that match the criteria entered in the Order Search page. The Order Listing page contains order header information with a link on each order that will enable the user to view details about a particular order. The completed page will look like Figure 14.3.

FIGURE 14.3.

The Order Listing design.

You will first create the graphical and database components of the page. Let's get started:

1. Create a new Active Server Page in your project and name the page `OrderListing.asp`.

2. The ASP page will automatically open in Source view. Select the Design View tab to open the page in Design mode.

3. Create a heading on the page similar to that of the heading from the home page, except this heading will be named Order Listing.

4. Click the Design-Time Control bar in the Toolbox to display the Design-Time Controls. Select the Recordset control, drag it to the workspace, and drop it just after the Order Listing heading.

5. Right-click the Recordset control and click Properties. Change the Name from `DTCRecordset1` to `OrderListRecordset`.

6. Change the source of the recordset to be a SQL Statement by clicking the SQL Statement radio button. Enter the following SQL Statement:

```
SELECT Orders.OrderID, Customers.CompanyName, Orders.ShippedDate
➥FROM Orders, Customers
➥WHERE Orders.CustomerID = Customers.CustomerID and
➥Orders.OrderID = [OrderID]
```

> **Note**
>
> This SQL statement can be built through the SQL builder instead of typed in.

7. The next step is to insert a table to display the order information. Select Insert a Table Which Has 2 Rows and 3 Columns. Keep all other table defaults.

8. Click the first column of the first row in the table and type in `Order ID`.

9. Click the second column of the first row in the table and type in `Customer`.

10. Click the fourth column of the first row in the table and type in `Shipped Date`.

11. Click the `Label` control in the Toolbox window. Drag the control from the Toolbox to the first column of the second row of the table.

12. Right-click the label control and click Properties. Change the `Name` property to `OrderID`. Change the `Recorset` property to `OrderListRecordset`. Change the `Field` property to `OrderID`.

13. Repeat steps 10 and 11 again so that there are two labels in the first column of the second row for OrderID. Name this control OrderID2.

14. Create a label control in the second column of the second row in the table. Change the Name property to Customer. Change the Recorset property to OrderListRecordset. Change the Field property to CompanyName.

15. Place a label control in the third column of the second row in the table. Change the Name property to ShippedDate. Change the Recorset property to OrderListRecordset. Change the Field property to ShippedDate.

The result should look similar to Figure 14.3. As you can see, the table will contain all the order information from the criteria on the previous page. There are two things left to do to this page:

- Place the code in the page that will allow you to use the order number that is passed from the search page.
- Modify the table so that the order ID is a link to the Order Details page.

See Figure 14.4 as a reference for the code modifications.

FIGURE 14.4.

The order listing code modifications.

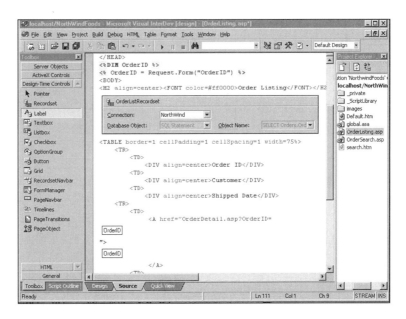

Let's jump right into modifying the code:

1. Open the page in Source view and place the cursor before the <BODY> tag. Insert the following code into the page:

```
<% DIM OrderID %>
<% OrderID = Request.Form("OrderID") %>
```

This code will retrieve the OrderID from the search page.

14

2. Next you will create a link on the OrderID from the order listing. Place the cursor before the first OrderID label.

3. Type the following before the OrderID label:

```
<A href="OrderDetail.asp?OrderID=
```

This will create a querystring tag for the Order ID that is passed to the Order Detail page when it is clicked.

4. Complete the querystring by placing the following code after the first OrderID label:

```
">
```

5. Place an </A> tag after the second OrderID label. This will complete the query-string and make the order ID label a link to the Order Details page.

You have now created the Order Listing page. When you view this page in the browser, you will see that the order ID is now a link that will pass the order ID to the Order Details page as shown in Figure 14.5. You will build the Order Details page next.

FIGURE 14.5.

The Order Listing page.

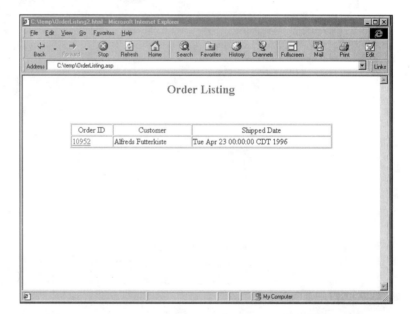

The Order Details Page

The next page in the application will display details about a particular order that has been selected from the Order Listing page. The Order Details page will contain detailed information about an order including all the products for that order. This page retrieves the order number passed to it from the Order Listing page and uses it to retrieve order details. Follow these steps to create this page:

1. Create a new Active Server Page in your project and name the page OrderDetails.asp.

2. Create a heading on the page similar to that of the heading from the home page except this heading will be called Order Details.

3. Insert the Recordset Design-Time control onto the page. Rename this Recordset from DTCRecordset1 to OrdersRecordset.

4. Change the Database Object to a SQL statement by clicking the SQL Statement radio button.

5. Type in the following SQL into the SQL Statement box:
   ```
   SELECT Orders.OrderID, Customers.CompanyName, Orders.ShippedDate
   ➥FROM Customers, Orders WHERE Orders.OrderID = [OrderID] and
   ➥Customers.CustomerID = Orders.CustomerID
   ```

   This creates the recordset that will be needed to display the information from the orders table. The next section will display the information in a table format.

6. Insert a table into the page with three rows and two columns. Insert this table immediately after OrdersRecordset.

7. Enter Order ID: in the first column of the first row. Center this heading in the field.

8. Enter Customer: in the first column of the second row. Center this heading in the field.

9. Enter Shipped Date: in the first column of the third row. Center this heading in this field.

10. Place a label from the Design-Time Control Toolbox into the second column of the first row and bind it to the OrderID field of the OrdersRecordset.

11. Place a label control into the second column of the second row and bind it to the CompanyName field of OrdersRecordset.

12. Place a label control into the second column of the third row and bind it to the ShippedDate field of OrdersRecordset.

13. After you have completed filling out the table, right-click the table and click Properties. Change the border property from 1 to 0. This will enhance the look of the order information section by removing the table outlines from the table.

You have completed the order information portion of the Order Details page. Now it is time to create the product information section of the page. The product section contains

14

all the products that are associated with a selected order. Follow these steps to create the product listing:

1. Insert a Recordset Design-Time Control onto the page immediately following the table you just created and change the name to ProductsRecordset. This Recordset will contain a SQL statement to select product information from the Products table.

2. Change the ProductsRecordset object to a SQL statement and enter the following SQL into the SQL statement box:

    ```
    SELECT Products.ProductName, `Order Details`.UnitPrice,
    ➥`Order Details`.Quantity, `Order Details`.Discount, Orders.OrderID
    ➥FROM `Order Details`, Products, Orders
    ➥WHERE `Order Details`.ProductID = Products.ProductID AND
    ➥`Order Details`.OrderID = Orders.OrderID
    ➥AND Orders.OrderID = [OrderID]
    ```

3. Insert a horizontal rule from the HTML Toolbox following the Recordset. This will separate the order header information from the products on the order.

4. Insert a table below the Products Recordset with two rows and four columns.

5. Click the first column of the first row in the table and type in Product Name.

6. Click the second column of the first row in the table and type in Unit Price.

7. Click the third column of the first row in the table and type in Quantity.

8. Click the first column of the first row in the table and type in Discount.

9. Place a label control into the first column of the second row and bind it to the ProductName field of ProductsRecordset.

10. Place a label control into the second column of the second row and bind it to the UnitPrice field of ProductsRecordset.

11. Place a label control into the third column of the second row and bind it to the Quantity field of ProductsRecordset.

12. Place a label control into the fourth column of the second row and bind it to the Discount field of ProductsRecordset.

You have completed the graphical portion of the page. The design of the page should appear as shown in Figure 14.6. The next step is to update the code on the page to retrieve the order number from the Order Listing page and loop through the products for the chosen order:

FIGURE 14.6.

The Order Details design.

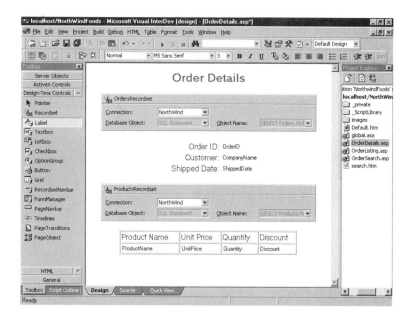

1. Open the Order Details page in the Source view.

2. Place the cursor between the `</HEAD>` tag and the `<BODY>` tag. Insert the following code between these two tags:

```
<% Dim OrderID %>
<% OrderID = Request.Querystring("OrderID") %>
```

This code will retrieve the order ID from the Order Listing page and place it into a variable called `OrderID`. The `OrderID` variable is passed to the select statement in the `OrdersRecordset` and the `ProductsRecordset`.

3. Place the cursor immediately before the second `<TR>` tag in the products table. Type in the following before the `<TR>` tag:

```
<% Do While Not ProductsRecordset.EOF %>
```

4. Place the cursor immediately after the last `</TR>` tag in the products table. Type in the following code after the `</TR>` tag:

```
<% ProductsRecordset.MoveNext()   %>
<% Loop %>
```

The code you have entered here will loop through and display all the products that are associated with the chosen order. The completed code is depicted in Figure 14.7. Figure 14.8 shows the completed Order Details page.

14

FIGURE 14.7.

*The Order Details
listing.*

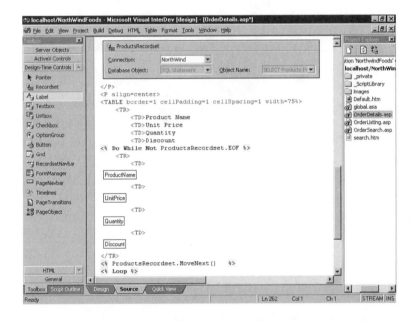

FIGURE 14.8.

*The Order Details
page.*

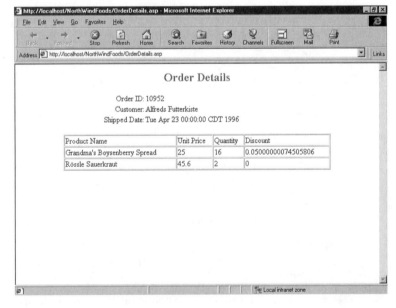

Now that you have completed building all the pages in the application, you need to go back and create a link from the home page to the first page in the application. Follow these steps to create that link:

1. Open the `Default.htm` page in Design view.

2. Highlight the text Order Inquiry and click HTML Link. The hyperlink window will display. Click the Browse button.

3. Select the `OrderSearch.asp` page from the Create URL window. This will create a link to the Order Search page.

That's it, you've done it! You just completed your first database-driven Internet application. As you can see, Visual InterDev provides you with a very powerful tool to quickly build a database-driven Web application.

Summary

Today's lesson demonstrates how the different components of a Visual InterDev project combine to form a Web-based application. The lesson should have given you the opportunity to apply the knowledge you gained over the past two weeks. How did you do? Were you able to recall the previous lessons you learned? Although the new and powerful technologies of the Web are technically cool, they have a more important mission as the critical tool to create the businesses of the future, as you learned in today's lesson.

The first part of the lesson gives you an overview of the Northwind Foods application. Next, you built the Home Page, which is the entry point of the application. You then built the Order Search page to allow the user to search for any order number in the database. Next, you built the Order Listing page, which displayed the results of the criteria entered in the Order Search page. In the final part of today's lesson, you built a page to display detailed order information from a selected order. The lesson ends with linking the home page to the first page of the application.

It will be interesting to see which technologies come out on top. Will it be ActiveX or Java applets? HTML or ASP? Whatever the outcome, you can count on Visual InterDev to support the winners!

Q&A

Q Are ASPs the wave of the future?

A Yes, jump on the ASP bandwagon now! Seriously, ASP offers a robust alternative to strict HTML. ASPs are HTML and more because they can generate both client- and server-side script. As you would expect, Microsoft's Web site includes a heavy

14

dose of ASPs. In the future, you will see more and more sites and Web-based applications using the power of ASPs.

Q Can I mix ASPs and HTML Web pages in my application?

A Yes. Today's lesson demonstrated how HTML and ASP Web pages can coexist in a Web-based application. The HTML was used for static Web pages, and the ASPs were used for creating dynamic Web pages that contained database integration.

Workshop

The Workshop provides quiz questions to help you solidify your understanding of the material covered. The exercises provide you with experience in using what you've learned. You can find the answers to the quiz questions and exercises in Appendix B, "Answers."

Quiz

1. What design-time control is used to access the database?
2. What are the main differences between HTML and ASP files?
3. What is used to pass information from one Web page to another?

Exercise

For the final exercise of the second week, you will develop more Web pages for the Northwind Foods application. You can use any of the tables in the Northwind database to support these pages. Try focusing on the concepts you might not understand as well as others. For example, you might want to create more images for the Web pages, using the Image Composer to understand its capabilities. You also should practice using ASPs to deliver dynamic content from database tables. You can examine the tables and create added functions and features for the application, based on the information in the database.

WEEK 2

In Review

You have now completed the second week of your pursuit to learn Visual InterDev. During the first week, you learned how you can use Visual InterDev to build the client portion of your application. The second week provides you with the knowledge to perfect the server side of the application equation. Week 2's lessons teach you how to integrate both the client and the server to build a better Web-based application. You now have a good handle on all the components that you can use to create the killer application. You also understand how Visual InterDev provides the tools for completing the client and the server side of the application equation.

Where You Have Been

Much of this second week has focused on database integration. At the beginning of the week, you learned how to use Visual InterDev to communicate with a database. Next, you discovered the Visual Data Tools included with Visual InterDev. Day 9 focuses on how to develop a closer relationship with your database through the use of these tools. You learned how each of the Visual Data Tools combines pure power with ease of use. Day 10 covers the topic of managing your database components; you learned how to use the Database Designer to manage and create components within your database.

After spending several lessons covering database integration, the second week switches gears to focus on other advanced topics. You received an in-depth lesson on how to integrate

8

9

10

11

12

13

14

Active Server Pages within your application. You also learned how to utilize the power of design-time controls to meet the needs of your application. You discovered how these exciting new controls can definitely make your development life easier. On the final day of the second week, you built a database-driven Web application.

WEEK 3

At a Glance

During the first two weeks, you gained a better understanding of how Visual InterDev enables you to build Web-based applications. The third and final week presents some advanced topics and considerations concerning your applications. This week provides the knowledge that you need to put the finishing touches on your applications.

Where You Are Going

The first day of Week 3 teaches you how to build components for your applications and truly integrate them into your application. On Day 16, you will receive an overview of how to use Visual InterDev to manage your Web site files. On Day 17, you will learn how to debug your Web-based application. Toward the middle of the week, you will gain an understanding of how to handle team application development issues. Visual InterDev can be integrated with source code control products such as Visual SourceSafe to facilitate effective team development. Toward the end of the week, you will learn how to use the Visual InterDev Site Designer to design and prototype the layout and structure of your Web site. The final day of this week (and of this book) covers how to use the features of Dynamic HTML for your application.

15

16

17

18

19

20

21

DAY **15**

Building an Integrated Solution with Components

During the first two weeks, you discovered how to use Visual InterDev to build Web-based applications. The first lesson of this, the third and final, week covers some of the more advanced topics and features of Visual InterDev.

As you know, the Internet provides a distributed computing platform that offers exciting and new application possibilities. These new possibilities also bring with them certain challenges. One of the key challenges is how and where to place the logic and functionality of your application across this distributed platform. Today's lesson gives some insight into how to use components within your Web application to provide an integrated solution for your end users. On completing this lesson, you will be able to

- Explain the concepts of COM and DCOM.
- Integrate components within your application architecture.
- Build a custom component by using Visual Basic 6.
- Access the component from a Web-based application.

Introduction to COM and DCOM

Microsoft developed the Component Object Model (COM) to supply a common method for communication between objects. COM's roots can be traced back to OLE technology, also developed by Microsoft. COM enables objects to communicate with each other through effective dialogue, thereby forming a synergistic relationship. With true dialogue, each object can understand the other object's interfaces, methods, and services so that they can work together for the good of the end user. Two terms concerning COM technology are used throughout this part of the lesson: *producer* and *consumer*.

The *producer* represents the object that provides the basic interfaces, methods, and services to another object; the *consumer* is the object or application that uses, or consumes, the services of the producer object. Some objects alternate being the producer and consumer, based on their capabilities and the relationship established between the two objects. An example of this kind of relationship is a project team of many members with unique skills. Each team member knows the strengths and roles of the other people on the team. Also, standard communication methods—email, meetings, and telephone conversations—have been established to facilitate sharing knowledge. The team members communicate and share their abilities and services to create an application.

Other communication is strictly one-way in nature, such as communication in a relationship between a coffee shop and its customers. The coffee shop communicates its message by advertising itself as the place to buy superb coffee drinks. Customers, including myself, realize the service it provides and consume drinks such as café mochas in large quantities. This kind of communication is similar to a COM object that advertises or publishes its unique services, whereas the client application consumes or uses these services. In summary, a producer is an object that implements and provides certain methods and services through standard interfaces. COM makes these services available to other objects. A consumer is an object that uses the services of a producer object. This type of object can also be referred to as a *client* or *container object*.

Objects use COM on the same machine. However, Microsoft has extended COM's reach by creating the Distributed Component Object Model, or DCOM, which enables you to communicate with a COM object on another machine. The following sections explain COM and DCOM in more depth and cover the benefits of each technology.

> **Note** This discussion on COM and DCOM is meant to briefly introduce these exciting and robust technologies. It only begins to scratch the surface of these topics. This section gives you a foundation for the rest of today's lesson, which focuses on Active Server Components. For more information on ActiveX, COM, and DCOM, I highly recommend *COM/DCOM Unleashed* by Jesus Chahin (Sams Publishing). Another good reference is *Understanding ActiveX and OLE* by David Chappell.

15

Examining COM and DCOM

This section explores and examines the theory and underpinnings of COM and DCOM. Also, you will develop a feel for the benefits of using COM for your components.

Understanding COM

You might not realize it yet, but you're already using COM-based components in your ASP applications. As a matter of fact, Active Server Pages is built on COM. Because of this, it can only benefit you as a Web developer to learn a little about the Component Object Model (COM) and the Distributed Component Object Model (DCOM).

What exactly is COM? COM is a specification and a set of services that enable you to create reusable objects for your applications. Using COM, you can create objects that are modular and can be leveraged across your application development projects. COM defines a standard set of interfaces for accessing and manipulating objects. This standard enables developers to use other developers' components without having to understand anything about the implementation of the object. COM also provides a set of standards, or guidelines, for creating these interoperable components.

You can build components by using COM and implement these components as either dynamic link libraries (DLLs) or executable programs (EXEs). COM provides the plumbing, including the communication methods for these components to talk to each other, as well as your application code.

DLLs are considered in-process objects because they run within the same address space as the consumer that called the component. This implementation is logically represented in Figure 15.1.

One advantage of using DLLs, or in-process components, is that you can increase the performance of your application by sharing the same address (that is, processor) space on the machine. In other words, a separate process isn't created each time the component is called or accessed. The disadvantage is that an in-process component can bring down the application if it fails.

FIGURE 15.1.

A logical view of an in-process DLL.

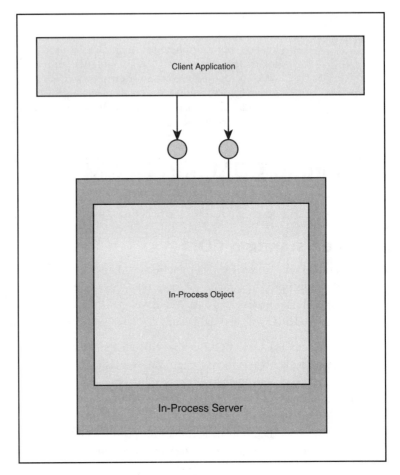

Client Process

You can also create executable programs based on COM. For example, you can create a COM component as a local server that resides as a separate process running on the same machine as the consumer or client application. You can also create an executable program that runs on a remote machine. EXEs are considered out-of-process programs because they execute in their own address space, using a shared communication protocol with the calling application.

An advantage of using EXEs is that they typically don't cause the calling program to fail because they execute within their own address space. A disadvantage of using EXEs is that they consume more processing power each time the program is called by an application. Figure 15.2 demonstrates an example of an out-of-process EXE.

FIGURE 15.2.

A logical view of an out-of-process EXE.

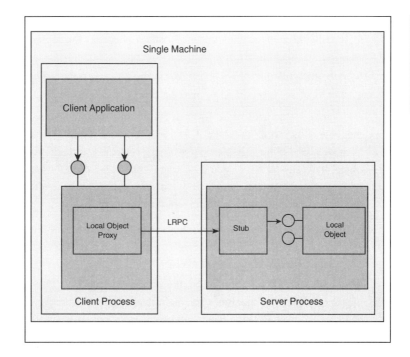

As you can see, the COM objects communicate through a special type of remote procedure call: local/lightweight remote procedure call (LRPC). LRPCs offers a way for COM objects executing in separate address spaces in memory to communicate with each other. The LRPC communication mechanism indicates that the communication is local to the machine.

Tip

When building COM components, you should typically implement them as DLLs or in-process programs.

Benefits of COM

COM offers several benefits to a developer. First, COM enables you to create reusable components for your application. You can use COM's power to create separate software components that your application can access when necessary, thereby avoiding redundancy and duplication in individual code modules. In this way, the processing logic in the COM component is isolated from the application code, so you can change the component without affecting the application. This process has two main implications. First, you can separate the true business and database logic from your presentation logic, which takes advantage of a three-tier application model. Second, you don't have to recompile and redistribute your application whenever the logic in the component changes. In other words, the component centralizes the process for software updates, giving you a simpler approach to version control.

Another benefit of COM is that it offers a consistent method for objects to converse with each other. Using a standard form of communication means that you know an object's message is received, understood, and incorporated into the life of the other object. Also, because COM objects implement a binary runtime interface, you can develop a COM object with one language and consume its services with an object or application created with another language. This benefit shows you that COM is a language-independent model for application and component development.

In the next section, you learn another name for communication across multiple machines.

Understanding DCOM

Microsoft's DCOM is founded on the same principles as COM but extends these principles across multiple machines; its main design goal is to make use of the same powerful characteristics of COM across machines in your network. DCOM enables objects on different machines to communicate, thereby integrating COM's communications strengths and the network.

DCOM also opens new possibilities for robust application processing. OLE and COM were first used to embed a spreadsheet into a word processing document. When users got over the novelty of this feature, they wanted the technology to deliver more functionality. DCOM capitalizes on the strengths of COM so that you can offer the robust functionality your users have been clamoring for. You can integrate DCOM objects and components on a server machine to give your applications powerful server programs. Later in today's lesson, you learn how to integrate DCOM components into an application.

DCOM components are considered remote servers because they're implemented remotely on a machine different from the client consumer machine. You can implement a DCOM object as a DLL or a separate executable process.

DCOM uses Object Remote Procedure Calls (ORPCs) as the communication vehicle for different machine objects, as shown in Figure 15.3.

By using ORPCs, you can make communication between objects easier and make the producer object seem local to the consumer. This process is like virtual shopping in which you electronically move through a store, picking out the items you want to buy. DCOM provides tight security to ensure that only authorized users can activate a specified DCOM component.

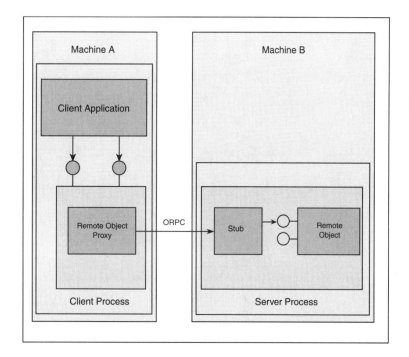

FIGURE 15.3.

The art of DCOM.

Benefits of DCOM

The same COM benefits apply to DCOM because DCOM is just COM implemented as a distributed model. You can use DCOM's strengths to integrate your Web-based applications with existing client/server and legacy systems. In addition to the benefits previously listed for COM, DCOM provides the following:

- Decoupling of application layers
- Support for n-tiered architectures
- Distributed team development

Decoupling of Application Layers

Microsoft has created a framework for building integrated solutions: Windows Distributed interNet Applications Architecture (Windows DNA). No, this acronym has nothing to do with Biology 101. Windows DNA provides a framework for building robust and integrated Web-based solutions. Figure 15.4 depicts the basic framework for Windows DNA.

FIGURE 15.4.

The Windows DNA framework.

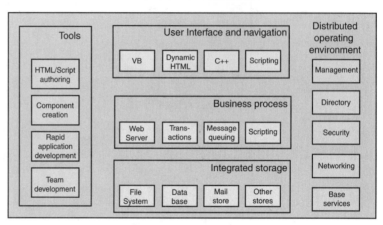

Windows DNA Framework

Using this framework, you can focus on the tools and technologies that support the different layers of your application. Windows DNA enables you to build applications that separate the presentation, business, and database logic. For example, you need tools that support HTML authoring and scripting. You also need tools such as Visual Basic and Visual J++ for creating middle-tier business components. These components usually reside on a Web server or separate application server and provide the robust business application and database access logic. The lesson today is about taking advantage of this middle tier to provide a more robust and scalable solution for your users.

DCOM provides an object model that enables you to abstract the business logic layer from the presentation layer. The presentation layer provides the user interface and navigation to the user. The business logic layer is composed of components that work behind the scenes to make the application useful.

 Tip

When designing an integrated Web-based solution, make sure that you abstract and separate your presentation, business, and database logic into logical layers. In this way, you can take advantage of the different tools, technologies, and platforms that support these layers.

Support for N-Tiered Architectures

DCOM provides an object model that supports the creation of n-tiered architectures. You might be familiar with the concept of a three-tiered application architecture used for some client/server applications. Figure 15.5 represents this model.

FIGURE 15.5.   Three-Tier Web Architecture

The three-tiered model.

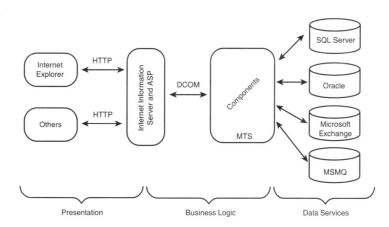

In this model, you see that the presentation, business logic, and database services reside on three logical layers. An n-tiered architecture extends this concept by not limiting you to three tiers. For example, in the business logic layer, you can provide multiple application server machines to spread the load of client machines requests. In this way, your application can scale to support more users.

Distributed Team Development

DCOM supports distributed team development by enabling you to build components that are outside your Web application. This means that you can separate the roles of a component developer and a Web application developer. In some cases, this might be the same person, but the different roles still exist. You need to be able to develop components by using robust tools such as Visual Basic, Visual C++, and Visual J++. After you build these components, you need a way to distribute and integrate them into your application. DCOM provides the plumbing and glue to integrate your components and application.

Developing Components

Now that you understand the object model for components, let's take a look at the Microsoft tools that enable you to build components. The following list outlines the main component-creation tools available within Visual Studio:

- Visual C++
- Visual J++
- Visual Basic

Visual C++

For components in which speed is the major concern, nothing beats using Visual C++ along with the Active Template Library. Components built using Visual C++ run very fast and provide scalability for your application. Many developers, however, don't have time to learn or use the C/C++ language. They must weigh the advantages of speed and scalability versus development time.

Visual J++

Java is quickly becoming the language of choice for component development. The relatively poor performance issues that have plagued Java development are now disappearing. This language is finding more and more followers. Visual J++ enables developers to create components quickly. However, Java is still a poor choice when component execution time is critical, and accessing certain system calls can be difficult.

Visual Basic

Visual Basic has come a long way. The ability to create a natively compiled executable or DLL, along with ease of use, provides a compelling argument for using Visual Basic to create your components.

Integrating Components into Your ASP Code

You can and should use Active Server Pages as the central hub within your Web-based application. In other words, you can use ASPs to direct traffic and communicate with both the client browser that requests a page as well as components that provide more robust database and business logic. COM enables you to instantiate and use components from within your ASP page.

COM objects expose a set of publicly available methods and properties. Some properties can be read-only some or all of the time. Generally, a COM object's properties are accessed like this:

```
MyVariable = myObject.someProperty
```

Methods are invoked in a similar fashion:

```
MyObject.someMethod()
```

Sets of similar objects are often grouped together in a *collection*. A collection is also considered an object, with an Item method and Count property. Collections can be iterated through with the For Each...Next construct:

```
For Each item in someCollection
...do something...
next item
```

The following code is an example of the syntax for using a component within your ASP code:

```
Dim myConn
Set myConn = Server.CreateObject("ADODB.Connection")
myConn.open
```

This example demonstrates how to use the ADO object. First, you `Dim` a variable: `myConn`. Next, you use the `Set` keyword to set this variable to the result of your `Server.CreateObject` call. You're then able to use the instantiated object. The preceding example executes the `Open` method that is supported by the object.

Creating a Component with Visual Basic 6

So far, you have learned about the Component Object Model and how you can leverage this model to build components for your application. You have also learned about the benefits of using components in your Web-based applications. The preceding section discusses some of the languages within Visual Studio that you can use to build components.

This section guides you through the process of building a component, using Visual Basic 6. After you build the component, you will create a Web-based application that leverages this component as a middle-tier business object.

Note
> If you don't have Visual Basic 6, you can download a compiled version of the component from the Web site for this book at www.mcp.com. The section "Integrating the Component into Your Application" instructs you on how to integrate this component with your Web application. You can gain some valuable insight by following along with the example in this section.

Step One: Creating the Project

First, you need to create a Visual Basic project for the component. The following steps guide you through this process:

1. Open Visual Basic 6.

2. With the New tab selected, choose ActiveX DLL and click Open, as shown in Figure 15.6.

   By default, a project named `Project1` is created that contains a class named `Class1` (see Figure 15.7).

FIGURE 15.6.

Creating a Visual Basic project.

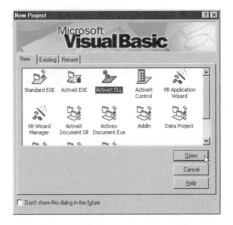

FIGURE 15.7.

Examining a Visual Basic project.

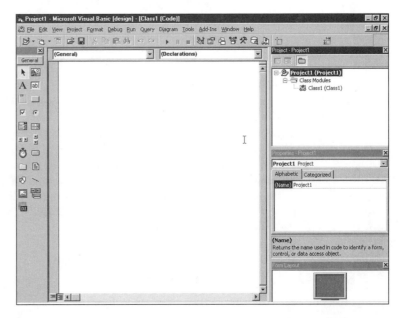

3. Select Project1 in the Project Explorer and then change its name in the Properties window to Orders. The project name represents the name of the DLL after the component has been compiled. The name of the DLL file in this case will be Orders.dll.

4. Select Class1 in the Project Explorer and then change its name in the Properties window to ProcessOrders. The class represents the interface that enables an application to access the component's methods.

5. In the Code window, enter the following logic:

```
Public Function CalculateTotal (UnitPrice as Double,
                        ➥Qty as Double) As String
 ' Calculates the total price of the order
        Dim Total As Double
        Total = UnitPrice * Qty
        CalculateTotal = CStr(Total)
End Function
```

Make sure that you enter the first line of code that declares the Function and its parameters. Visual Basic will automatically create the End Function line for you.

6. Save the project by choosing File | Save Project.

You have now created a function that accepts two parameters—UnitPrice and Qty. The function multiplies these numbers to calculate a total price, which is sent back as a string to any calling program or application.

Step Two: Compiling Your Component

Now your component is ready to be compiled and deployed on the server. The following steps guide you through this process:

1. Select File|Make Orders.dll.

2. From the Make Component dialog, click OK to compile the component. This action will build the Orders.dll file.

Tip

> By default, DLLs are compiled to native code instead of interpreted code. You can check the compile parameters by clicking the Options button and then choosing the Compile tab. This tab enables you to customize the compilation of the component to your needs.
>
> You should always compile middle-tier business objects to native code.

When compiled, Visual Basic will create and register the DLL on your machine. You're now ready to use this component from within an application.

Building a Web-Based Application

This section guides you through the process of creating an application that retrieves detailed information about sales orders. You will have an opportunity to build the Web-based part of the application as well as integrate the Orders component into the application.

Constructing the Web Application

Complete the following steps to create the Web application:

1. Create a Visual InterDev project named `Calculation`. Make sure to choose the `Redside` theme for the project.

2. Add an Active Server Page called `OrdDetails.asp` to the project.

3. Add the `Northwind` data source, which you created during yesterday's lesson (Day 14, "Building a Database-Driven Web Application"), to your project.

4. Open the `OrdDetails.asp` page.

5. Using Design view, add a title for the page, `Order Details`.

6. With the title highlighted, center the text and assign it a paragraph format of `Heading1`.

7. Drag and drop a recordset design-time control to the page. As you learned during the second week, the Recordset DTC will notice the DSN that you added to your project and provide default settings, based on the data source.

8. Choose `Tables` for the Database Object and `Order Details` for the Object Name.

9. Drag and drop five Textbox design-time controls onto the page. Make sure that each Textbox appears on a separate line.

10. Using the Property table in Table 15.1, change the properties for the first four Textbox controls.

TABLE 15.1. THE PROPERTY TABLE FOR THE TEXTBOX CONTROLS.

Control	Name	Style	Recordset	Field
Textbox1	txtOrdID	Textbox	Recordset1	OrderID
Textbox2	txtProdID	Textbox	Recordset1	ProductID
Textbox3	txtUnitPrice	Textbox	Recordset1	UnitPrice
Textbox4	txtQty	Textbox	Recordset1	Quantity

11. Change the Name of the fifth Textbox control to `txtTotal`. Do not set any other properties of this control. The component will calculate the total price for the order and store its results in this field; therefore, you don't need to assign it a database field.

12. Drag and drop five label controls onto the page. These labels should be placed to the left of each Textbox control with the text shown in Figure 15.8.

FIGURE 15.8.

Assigning labels for the Textbox controls.

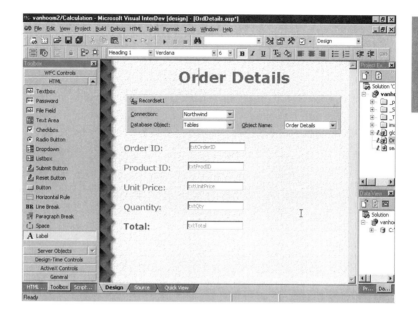

15

13. Save your changes and preview the results in your browser. You will see a page similar to the one in Figure 15.9, displaying order detail information but no total price for the ordered item.

FIGURE 15.9.

Previewing the results without a total price.

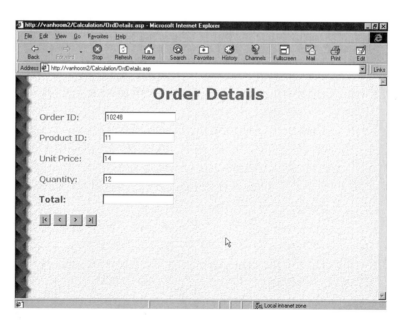

Integrating the Component into Your Application

Now that you have constructed a basic Web application, you need to integrate the component that you built earlier today. This component will calculate the total price for the order detail line, based on the unit price and quantity of items. The following steps guide you through this process:

1. Follow this step only if you didn't build the Visual Basic component earlier today and instead downloaded the `Orders.dll` file from the Web site. From the Project Explorer, drag and drop the `Orders.dll` file into your Visual InterDev project. This action will publish and register the control onto the machine, enabling you to use it within your application.

 Note

> If you built the component by using Visual Basic, you don't need to register the component or drag and drop it into your Visual InterDev project. When you compile a component with Visual Basic, it takes care of the proper registration of the control for you.

2. Open the `OrdDetails.asp` in Source view.

3. Drag and drop the Page Object DTC, which you learned about on Day 13, "Unleashing the Power of the Visual InterDev Programming Model," onto the page, right below the Total field.

4. Click the Script Outline for the page. If the Script Outline doesn't currently appear within the Visual InterDev environment, choose View|Other Windows|Script Outline.

5. Expand the Server Objects and Events for the page by clicking the plus (+) sign next to Server Objects & Events in the Script Outline.

6. Using the same technique in step 4, expand the events for the object `thisPage`. As a reminder, this object enables you to call remote script contained in the current page from the client.

7. Double-click the `onenter` event. This action creates a server-side event handler that will be triggered when the page is first entered.

8. Enter the following code for the sub procedure `thisPage_onenter()`:

```
Dim Myobj, total
Set MyObj = Server.CreateObject ("Orders.ProcessOrders")
        total = MyObj.CalculateTotal(txtUnitPrice.value,
        ➥ txtQty.value)
        txtTotal.value = total
```

9. Save the page and preview the results in your browser. You will see a page like the one in Figure 15.10.

FIGURE 15.10.

Previewing the results with a total price.

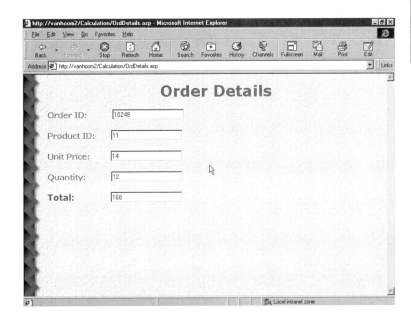

Analyzing the Results

Let's examine what you accomplished today. First you built a component using Visual Basic 6. Then you built a Web-based application to retrieve order detail information from a database. You then integrated the component into your application by writing some logic to instantiate and use the logic within the component.

Let's take a look at some of the key statements within your ASP code. First, you used the `Server.CreateObject` statement to instantiate, or create, the object within the context of your application. The following is the full statement:

```
Set MyObj = Server.CreateObject ("Orders.ProcessOrders")
```

In this statement, you used the parameter of `Orders.ProcessOrders` to create the object instance. This parameter represents the public interface for the object, which you created using Visual Basic. The public interface provides the mechanism that enables other applications and programs to access the object's methods and properties. Next you entered the following code:

```
total = MyObj.CalculateTotal(txtUnitPrice.value, txtQty.value)
```

This line of code executes the object's `CalculateTotal` method. When you typed `MyObj.`, you might have noticed that the `Calculate` method appeared in a drop-down list box. This example demonstrates that the statement completion feature also works for custom components that you build. The component's method accepted the two parameters—unit price and quantity—and calculated a total, which was passed backed to the ASP logic and displayed on the page.

This example demonstrates how you can use components for your business logic. It also shows how to take advantage of the Scripting Object Model to call remote server-side script from the client.

The great thing about this component is that it can be used in places besides ASP pages. You can write a Visual Basic client/server application that uses this same ActiveX DLL. The main lesson for today is the importance of separating your business and critical database logic into components, which can be leveraged across both Web-based and client/server applications.

Summary

Today's lesson opens your eyes to the world of components. The server side of your Web-based application needs all the help it can get, and components can do the job. In the future, you will see companies such as Microsoft integrating more robust features into their servers to meet the needs of organizations' applications. Server components are only one part of the server equation. Middleware and transaction-processing software will become increasingly important for your Web-based applications, as they have for client/server technology.

To review what you learned in today's lesson, you received an overview of Microsoft's COM and DCOM technologies. The lesson explains each of these models, their benefits, and how they can be used. Next, you examined components and examples of how they can be applied within the architecture of your application. The lesson outlines some of the languages within Microsoft Visual Studio that enable you to build components.

You then built a component, using Visual Basic 6. You saw how easy it is to create a reusable business object with Visual Basic. After building the component, you constructed a Web-based application and integrated the component into the application.

Q&A

Q What's the difference between Active Server Pages and components?

A Active Server Pages combine HTML with client-side and server-side script to create dynamic Web pages for your application. An ASP can be created with a text editor. Components, on the other hand, are executable programs or dynamic link libraries that can be called from your ASP. Components are constructed by using a robust development tool, such as Visual Basic or Visual C++.

Q When I try to make the DLL, I receive an error saying that VB can't write the file. What do I do?

A Generally, this occurs because the Web service is still running and has the DLL loaded into memory. First, exit InterDev if you have that open; then stop the Web services from inside the IIS Management Console. After you have done this, go ahead and make the DLL. Now it should work. (Occasionally, I have found that the only way to get write abilities to an Active Server Component DLL I am writing is to reboot the server. Ideally, you won't have to cope with that, but it's always an option.) Make sure you restart the Web service before you test the component.

Q Where can I learn more about Microsoft COM?

A I highly recommend *COM/DCOM Unleashed* (Sams Publishing) by Jesus Chahin.

Q I've created a component but now find that my ASP page takes even longer to run. What's wrong?

A An overhead is incurred each time a call is made to a component. If you find the page is slower, you might have too many calls to the component. Try to redesign the component so that fewer calls need to be made.

Workshop

The quiz questions and exercises are provided to help further your understanding. You can find the answers to the quiz questions and exercises in Appendix B, "Answers."

Quiz

1. What are some reasons for creating components?
2. What is the basic difference between COM and DCOM?
3. Name three languages you can use to create a component.
4. What statement do you use to instantiate an object within your ASP code?

Exercises

1. Install the Island Hopper C sample application from the Visual Studio CD-ROMs. This application is used for tomorrow's lesson to demonstrate the role of components within your application.

2. Choose one of the tools or languages mentioned today. If you are already familiar with the tool but have never considered building middle-tier business objects, do so immediately! If you're not familiar with any of the tools, pick Visual Basic—a powerful tool that is easy to learn. Apply the knowledge from today's lesson to build custom components and integrate these into your own applications.

DAY 16

Managing Your Web Site with Visual InterDev

During the last three weeks, you have absorbed a lot of information about the creation of Web pages and components to include in your Web-based application. You should now possess the knowledge to create a variety of essential items to build the killer app. Given this newfound ability, how in the world are you going to manage the plethora of files that you develop for your application?

Today's lesson answers that question by presenting the robust site management tools that are included with Visual InterDev. These tools contain some highly integrated features that can help you organize your site and create order out of chaos. Some of the topics that you will be covering today include

- How to use the Link View to manage the files contained in your Web site and their relationships.
- How to copy part of or all your Web site files to other directories or Web servers.
- How to maintain and repair broken links within your Web site.

Getting a Handle with the Link View

The Link View presents a new way to look at your Web site. This exciting and powerful feature enables you to truly get a handle on all the files that are contained in your Web-based application. The Link View provides a graphical tool that enables you to visually examine the files within your Web site and their relationships. You have the ability to expand or contract the view to explore different aspects of your site. For example, you may want to focus solely on a certain section or group of Web pages or objects. The Link View gives you the power to pick the right view for your needs. In addition to viewing the relationships, you also can use the Link View to identify the file types for each of the items in your application. This feature covers everything from HTML Web pages to Java applets. In short, the Link View provides a rich, graphical tool to help you conceptualize the design of your Web site.

Exploring the Link View Features

The Link View not only presents a comprehensive picture of your Web site; it also enables you to interact with your Web site objects from within the same view. Figure 16.1 illustrates the power of the Link View as it graphically displays a sample Web site.

FIGURE 16.1.

Getting a clearer picture with the Link View.

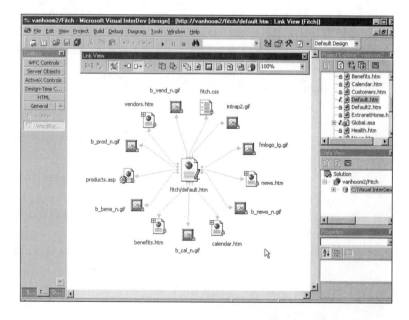

This illustration depicts a robust Web site that includes just about every type of file imaginable for a Web-based application. You can see that graphical icons depict the file type for each item in the view, and lines and arrows indicate the relationship between the files. The arrows and circles located at the ends of the lines serve as visual indicators that describe the nature of the relationship. A circle next to an object indicates that it is the parent, and the arrow next to an object signifies that it is the child.

From Figure 16.1, you can determine that the HTML Web page in the middle of the diagram is the parent of all the surrounding files. You can describe the relationship another way by stating that the products.asp file is the child of the default.htm Web page. In other words, the ASP file is a part of or related to the Web page. As with every relationship, you will have times when the communication link is broken. The Link View graphically displays broken links in red, which you will discover a little later in the lesson, indicating that there is a problem. You can use the Link View to see both links to objects within your Web site and links to external sites such as a news server or a Web site.

The Link View enables you to see a multitude of files, including HTML Web pages, images and sound files, ActiveX controls, Java applets, and HTML layout files. You can basically examine any file that is a part of your Web site using the Link View. From the Link View, you can then select and edit an object using its default editor. You can also choose to browse a Web page from within this view and filter the Link View to see only the files of a certain type. This filter enables you to work with a discrete number of files contained in your Web site, thereby simplifying the site management process.

The object contained in the middle of Figure 16.1 appears with a large icon, while all the surrounding items display with smaller icons. The large icon signifies that the developer opened a Link View for this object.

Opening a Link View

You can view a Web site object using the Link View by selecting the file in the Visual InterDev project workspace and clicking the right mouse button to display the shortcut menu, as shown in Figure 16.2.

You can then select View Links from the shortcut menu to display a Link View for the file. Figure 16.3 depicts the Link View for the default Web page used in the Fitch and Mather sample application.

As you can see, the Default.htm consists of several GIF images and several additional HTML files. The link to the b_news_n.gif file appears in red and is broken, indicating that the link to this file is broken. When you open a file to view its links, the Link View initiates a verification process that gathers information on all the object's associated files, including their file type and the nature of their relationship to the selected object. Figure 16.4 demonstrates the state and appearance of the associated files as they progress through the verification process.

FIGURE 16.2.

*Opening a file with
Link View.*

FIGURE 16.3.

Viewing the links.

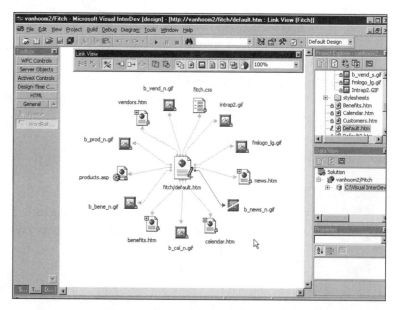

The file located at the top of Figure 16.4 represents a file whose relationship link hasn't been determined. Notice that it looks grayed out. After the Link View verifies the relationship, the icon is either displayed in its natural color, indicating that the link has been verified and established, or the icon appears red and broken, signifying that the link relationship has been broken.

FIGURE **16.4.**

The visual progression of an object.

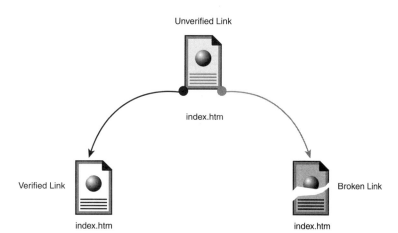

Link View Verification Process

You can open a Link View on any object that appears within the Link View diagram. This feature enables you to drill down to obtain a picture of your Web site's hierarchy. To accomplish this task, select the desired object within the Link View diagram and right-click the mouse button. The shortcut menu will be displayed for the object, enabling you to select View Links, as shown in Figure 16.5.

FIGURE **16.5.**

Drilling down on your Web site.

When you select the View Links menu item, a Link View diagram is created, enabling you to view the selected object and its related files (see Figure 16.6).

This view presents both the inbound and outbound links. For example, in Figure 16.6, the links coming from the Default pages represent the inbound links to the News page. The outbound links are represented by the two image files that appear on the page.

You also can view the links for any URL address by choosing the Tools menu and selecting View Links on WWW. You are then prompted to enter a URL address for the Web page that you want to see in Link View. This feature is helpful when you want to examine the structure of a Web site without having to open the project within Visual InterDev.

You can use this feature for your own internal intranet addresses as well as for external Internet URL addresses. Figure 16.7 depicts a Link View diagram for the BSI Consulting Web site.

FIGURE 16.6.

Viewing another object's links.

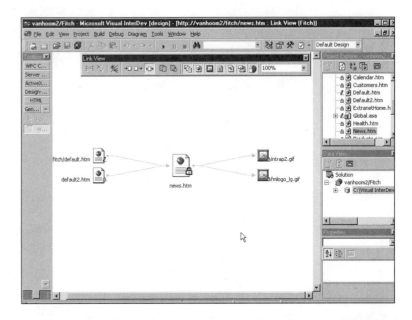

FIGURE 16.7.

Viewing the links for a URL on the Web.

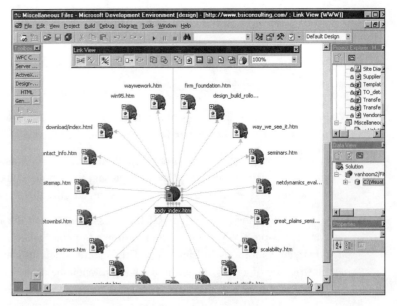

Tip

When a Link View diagram has been created, you can choose the appropriate display size for the diagram by using the Zoom Link View icon on the View Link toolbar. This tool enables you to choose different percentages for the diagram display, which means that you can zoom in and zoom out on the objects. You can select a default value or enter a custom value for the zoom percentage. You also can select Fit from the drop-down list box, which fits the Link View diagram into the Link View display area.

16

Using the Link View to Manage Your Site

Now that you have seen some examples of Link View features, let's apply these concepts to the site that you created on Day 15, "Building an Integrated Solution with Components."

Opening the Link View Diagram for Your Application

The following steps will guide you through the process of using Link View with your application:

1. Open the Island Hopper application that you installed during yesterday's exercise.
2. Right-click the `Headlines.asp` file in the Project Explorer and choose View Links from the shortcut menu. Figure 16.8 displays the Link View diagram for the site.

FIGURE 16.8.

Viewing the links for the Headlines page.

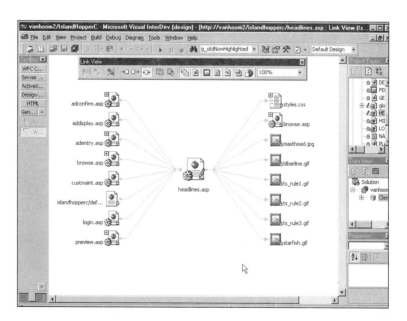

Now that you are looking at a basic Link View diagram for the site, the next few sections will walk you through the process of interacting with a diagram to obtain a more granular view of the site.

Filtering Your Link View

The Link View enables you to filter the amount and type of information displayed in your diagram, so you can more easily decipher and understand your Web site structure. You can choose the Diagram menu to display a menu list of available filter choices as depicted in Figure 16.9.

FIGURE 16.9.

Selecting a filter for your Link View.

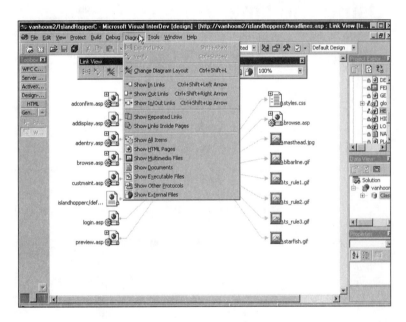

Tip

All these options are also available from the Link View toolbar.

As you can see, Visual InterDev provides many choices to filter the objects that are displayed within your Link View diagram. Table 16.1 provides an explanation for each available filter option.

TABLE 16.1. FILTER CATEGORIES.

Icon	Category	Description
	Show In Links	Displays the inbound links; in other words, the pages that refer to this page
	Show Out Links	Displays the outbound links; in other words, the items and pages that the page refers to
	Show In/Out links	Displays both the inbound and outbound links for the page
	Show Repeated Links	Displays any repeated links for the page
	Show Links Inside Pages	Displays the links inside the individual pages in the diagram
	Show All Items	Displays all objects
	Show HTML Pages	Displays HTML Web pages
	Show Multimedia Files	Displays images and multimedia files
	Show Documents	Displays document files (MS Word, PowerPoint, and so on)
	Show Executable Files	Displays program files such as EXEs and DLLs
	Show Other Protocols	Displays links to non-HTTP objects, such as news servers, Mail, and Telnet
	Show External Files	Displays objects external to the project

You can use any of these filters to limit the types of files that are displayed in your Link View diagram. Initially, all the available items will be enabled. Selecting a filter option from the list toggles the choice on and off. In order to show only images and multimedia files in your diagram, you would need to turn off all the other filter choices by selecting them.

For example, the default behavior of the Link View diagram chooses to display all items. To filter the diagram to show only the images and multimedia files, complete the following steps:

1. Using the Link View diagram for the Headlines page, click the Show All Items icon on the Link View toolbar. This action should deselect the option and hide all the related items for the page.

2. Click the Show Multimedia files icon on the toolbar. This action will display only the images and multimedia files related to the page as shown in Figure 16.10.

Working with Objects

The purpose of opening a Link View for your objects is to examine and understand the structure and relationships that exist within the Web site. Upon further review of your site, you may want to interact with the objects contained in the diagram. The Link View enables you to directly access the object and activate the default editor for one or more objects. When the object is selected, you can click the right mouse button to display the shortcut menu. For example, Figure 16.11 depicts the shortcut menu for an Active Server Page.

FIGURE 16.10.

Viewing the images for the Headlines page.

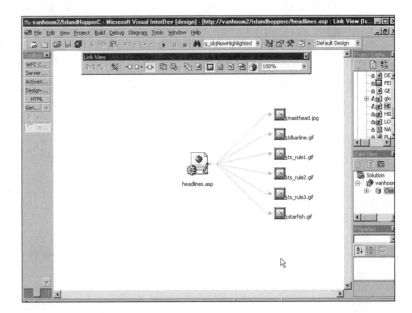

FIGURE 16.11.

Opening the object from within the Link View.

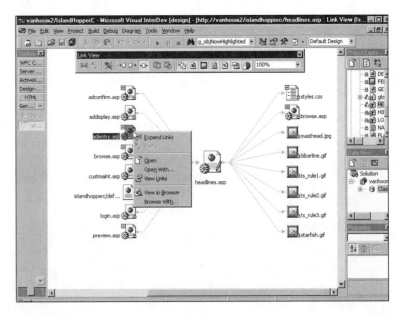

Figure 16.11 displays the menu options that are available for all Link View objects. Table 16.2 lists and describes each of these options.

TABLE 16.2. OBJECT SHORTCUT MENU OPTIONS.

Menu Item	Description
Expand Links	Expands the diagram to include the links of the selected object
Verify	Verifies a broken link
Open	Opens the object using its default editor
Open With	Enables you to choose an editor to open the selected file
View Links	Creates a new Link View diagram for the object
View in Browser	Enables you to preview the Web page using the default browser
Browse With	Enables you to choose a browser to browse the selected page

Tip

A + (plus) sign in the top right corner of an item icon indicates that the item contains links to the other items. You can expand the links for one of these items by clicking the + (plus) sign.

To open the ADENTRY.asp file, right-click the file and choose Open from the shortcut menu. Figure 16.12 demonstrates the results of choosing to open the Ad Entry ASP file from the shortcut menu in the Link View.

As you can see from the illustration, the selected .asp file is opened using the Source view, enabling you to make changes to the page.

You have just learned how to select and edit a single object. You can also select multiple objects in the Link View diagram by holding down the Ctrl key and clicking the left mouse button on each object that you want to select. After you have made your selections, you can click the right mouse button to choose an action. For example, you may want to open and work with an image and a Web page at the same time. You can select both the image and the HTML Web page file from within the Link View and choose Open. Both objects are opened with their respective default editors, enabling you to make any necessary changes.

Another example involves expanding the links for your objects. You may want to expand the links for a portion of or all your Web site to gain a comprehensive look at its structure. In this case, you could individually select the objects using the previously described method, or you can choose Select All from the Edit menu to select all the items in the diagram. Then you can select Expand Links from the shortcut menu to display the links for all the selected objects.

FIGURE 16.12.

Editing an ASP page.

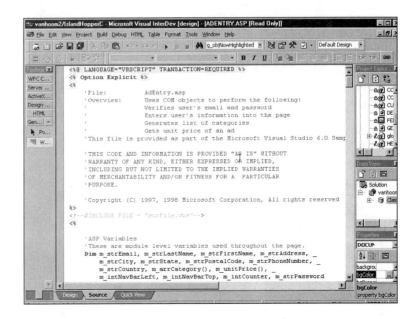

Note

The order in which the files are opened is determined by the order in which they are selected.

Tip

You also can select multiple files by dragging the mouse cursor over the objects that you want to select in the diagram. To accomplish this task, click the mouse in the diagram and drag it across the objects that you want to select. A rectangle will display as you drag the mouse to guide you through the selection. When the rectangle encloses all the desired objects, release the mouse button. All the objects contained in the rectangle will then be selected.

The ability to interact instantly with your objects from within the Link View provides a significant time-saver to your development effort. Whether you want to preview the design of a Web page or directly modify an image file, Visual InterDev truly promotes the idea of an integrated development environment through the implementation of this feature.

Leveraging Your Web Site for the Future

One of the biggest challenges that business users and IT departments face is how to leverage their current investment. Executives want to capitalize on the investments that are made in people, knowledge, or technology. A project isn't worth investing in if there's no return on the investment (ROI).

Visual InterDev helps you leverage your technology investment in two significant ways. First, you can use the power of Visual InterDev to augment your productivity for a single Web-based application development effort. Second, you can leverage the functionality of your applications across multiple Web-based projects. Both of these methods involve the capability within Visual InterDev to copy an entire Web site. The lesson describes the two methods and then demonstrates how to use this powerful feature.

Reaping the Benefits Within a Project

Visual InterDev contains a powerful feature that enables you to copy an entire Web site to another location. This section describes how you can capitalize on this feature to facilitate and streamline your application development process. With any project, you will usually have a development, testing, and production environment. These three environments can be used to contain the different stages of your application. These concepts apply whether your development team consists of the three-person team of me, myself, and I, or a team of 50 people.

First, you need to create a development environment that supports the initial design and development of your Web-based application. Next, you need to create a testing area that reflects individually tested modules. This testing environment supports the integration testing of all the components within your application.

The testing, or staging, area is the final checkpoint before the application is released to the users. By having a separate testing environment, you can separate modules that are still being worked on versus those that have been adequately tested. In this way, you can ensure that individual developers don't hinder the work of their cohorts. The production environment represents the third stage. This environment supports the use of your Web site by its constituents. This environment contains your fully tested Web-based application and separates the work of the developers from the users. Modules that are still being developed won't cause the user's version of the application to crash because they operate in separate worlds. Figure 16.13 illustrates the concept of these three environments.

FIGURE 16.13.

The three phases of development.

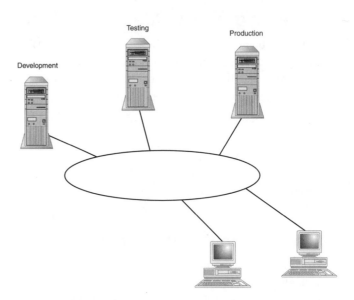

Visual InterDev supports the use of these environments by enabling you to copy your entire Web site across the different environments. Given that you have established a unique directory structure for each site, you can use Visual InterDev to promote your site between each stage of development. You also could copy the Web site to a different machine. In this way, you can ensure that all the components in your Web site are migrated properly without your having to identify and copy the individual files contained in your site. You will learn how to take advantage of this feature in the later section "Copying a Web Site."

Reaping the Benefits Across Multiple Projects

You also can use the copying feature across multiple projects. Invariably, you will want to use prior Web sites as a starting point for future development efforts. By so doing, you don't have to reinvent the wheel every time you develop a Web-based application. You can use the Copy Web feature to copy the Web site to a new location and then begin tailoring the components to meet the needs of your new application. Again, Visual InterDev enables you to leverage your prior investment in technology for the future by providing a starting point for new projects.

Copying a Web Site

Now that you understand the context of this feature, you can learn how to actually execute it. The Copy Web feature enables you to copy an entire Web site to another server or to the same server with a new name. One of the new capabilities of Visual InterDev 6 involves the copying of components as well. In Visual InterDev 1, the Copy Web function only pertained to Web site content such as HTML and ASP pages, as well as images and so on. Visual InterDev 6 now supports copying components as well. This feature includes not only the physical copying of business objects and components to another machine or area on a Web server, but also the proper registration of these components on the machine.

Note

> You must have administrator privileges on the destination server to execute the Copy Web command. This security restriction is a function of the server operating system, not Visual InterDev. Visual InterDev attempts to execute the command on the destination server using your user ID and password. If you have the correct administrator privileges, the Web site will be copied.

To copy a Web site select Project, Web Project, Copy Web Application to display the Copy Project dialog box. Figure 16.14 illustrates the options that are available on this window.

FIGURE 16.14.

Copying a Web site.

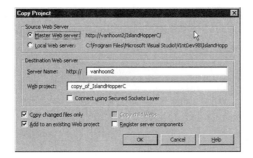

The first two options on this dialog box enable you to choose the project that you are copying. These options support copying a Local or Master Web project. The next section of the dialog box enables you to specify the Destination Web server. You can enter or change the name of the destination server machine. You can also enter a new name for the destination Web project. You can enable a Secure Sockets Layer (SSL) connection by clicking the check box next to this option.

The options at the bottom of this box enable you to customize what is being copied. First, you can choose to copy only the changed files. This option is useful when you have initially copied a Web site to the destination and you are copying an updated version to the destination. This option can be applied to the three stages of application development, when you are constantly migrating updated versions of your application from development to testing and from testing to production. You save a lot of time during the application promotion process by selecting this option because only the files that have changed are copied to the destination location.

The Add to an Existing Web Project option is similar to the one that you have used to create new projects. You can choose to add this Web to an existing site or create a new Web for this site.

 Note

Remember from the lesson on Day 2, "Creating Your First Visual InterDev Project," if you don't select the Add to an Existing Web option, the name of the project is combined with the name of the Web server to form the virtual root name for the Web site.

The Copy Child Webs option is enabled only if you are copying the root Web. In this case, you can check this option to copy all the child Webs that exist within the root Web.

The Register Server option is new in Visual InterDev 6 and allows you to register any components within your project on the destination server.

To make a copy of this Web, accept the defaults for the destination Web server and destination Web project name After you confirm your entries and click OK, the Web is copied to the new destination, and you receive a friendly confirmation notice like the one shown in Figure 16.15.

FIGURE 16.15.

A successful copy.

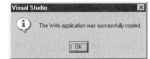

The newly copied Web site assumes the security settings of the root Web on the destination server machine.

You must create a Visual InterDev project to access the copied Web site. To do this, complete the following steps:

1. Select New Project from the File menu.

2. Enter `TestIslandHopper` for the name of the new project and click Open.

3. Choose the Web server where you copied the Web in the previous section. For this example, it may be the same machine and Web server where the original Web project exists.

4. After you have chosen the server, click the Next button to proceed to the second step in the process. You will see the name of the project that you are creating as well as an option to connect to an existing server. Click this radio button and choose the name of the Web that you entered during the Copy Web Project phase of this process. Because you accepted the default name, you should pick `copy_of_IslandHopperC` as demonstrated in Figure 16.16.

FIGURE 16.16.

Connecting to a newly copied Web site.

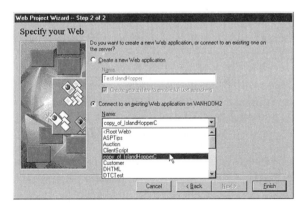

You can then click Finish to complete the process and create a new Visual InterDev project for the copied Web as shown in Figure 16.17.

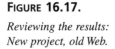

Figure 16.17.

Reviewing the results: New project, old Web.

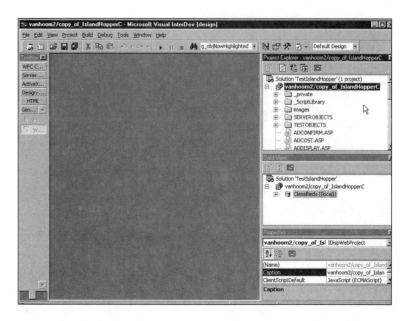

This process is very intuitive and straightforward. In a nutshell, it involves two major steps—copying the Web site, and creating a new project for the newly copied Web site. This feature definitely removes the headache of migrating your Web-based applications.

Repairing the Links

The final lesson for the day teaches you how to resolve broken relationships within your diagram. Visual InterDev consists of an automatic tracking system that monitors the links between the objects and files in your project. The Automatic Link Repair option is enabled from within the Properties window for the project. You can access this window by right-clicking the project root from within the Project Explorer and choosing Properties. The window opens with the General tab displayed as shown in Figure 16.18.

This option is enabled by default. When you have set this option, Visual InterDev will track the files and make you aware of the impact when you change, delete, or move a file. For example, when you rename a file in your project, you receive a warning message similar to the one displayed in Figure 16.19.

This dialog box enables you to update the links in files that refer to this object so that a conflict won't arise when you try to run your application. This proactive approach to conflict resolution ensures a happy home for your project. There will be occasions when conflicts do arise, however, as with the image file in the Fitch and Mather application shown earlier in the day. The next section takes a closer look at the broken link and searches for a resolution.

FIGURE 16.18.

Enabling automatic Link Repair.

16

FIGURE 16.19.

Resolving a conflict: the proactive approach.

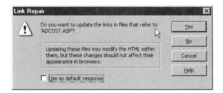

You can use the ToolTips help for an object that contains a broken link to identify the conflict. For example, Figure 16.20 displays a ToolTips message for a file that is crying out for help.

You can access error message information for an item with a broken link by placing the mouse cursor over the item in the Link View diagram. The file location information is displayed along with an error message for this object, which describes the conflict in the link relationship. The image file has been moved and cannot be found. Based on this information, you can repair the damage by copying the image file back to the images folder.

You can also create a Broken Links Report by choosing View, Broken Links Report. This action will create a list of tasks in the Task List enabling you to address each of the issues with the structure of your site.

This example demonstrates the process to follow on those rare occasions when you have a conflict in your application. Because Visual InterDev takes a proactive approach to managing these conflicts, you can feel confident that your objects will remain in constant communication about their whereabouts, so conflicts will be minimal.

FIGURE **16.20.**

*Identifying the
problem.*

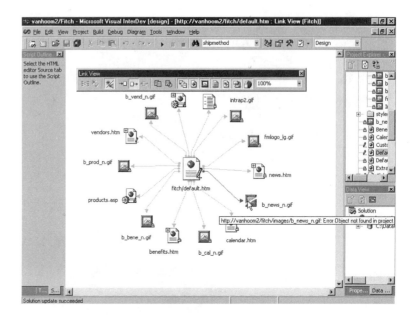

FIGURE **16.20.**

*Identifying the
problem.*

Summary

Today's lesson demonstrates how you can take control of your projects and manage them
effectively. Web-based application development can quickly get out of hand if you don't
have the proper tools and methods in place to manage your projects. You have now discovered the tools that Visual InterDev includes to address the issue of site management.
You also have learned about some effective methods surrounding the use of these tools. It
is up to you to use them for efficient and effective management of your Web sites.

The first part of today's lesson demonstrates how to get a handle on your projects by
using the Link View. This powerful feature offers robust functionality for viewing and
interacting with your application objects. This part of the lesson takes you on a guided
tour of the features of the Link View and shows you how to properly use these features to
your advantage. You learned how to view the links between your objects and how to filter
the information that appears in the diagram.

The lesson next explains how to leverage your current development investments for
future applications. You learned how to copy your Web sites and how to use this feature
within the context of a single development project and across multiple projects. The
Copy Web Project feature provides excellent support through the three key stages of your
project—development, testing, and production. The lesson then shifts gears and outlines
the inherent file management features of Visual InterDev.

The final lesson explains how Visual InterDev proactively manages and resolves conflicts within your application. You also learned how to use the Link View to debug conflicts that arise between objects in your application.

Q&A

Q Does the Copy Web Project feature provide source code control for my application?

A The Copy Web Project feature enables you to copy entire Web sites to different locations on the same server as well as to directories on different servers. This feature really has nothing to do with source code control. Visual InterDev does support tight integration with Visual SourceSafe to provide robust source code control features for your application projects. You will learn about this integration during tomorrow's lesson.

Q What is the main purpose of the Link View?

A The Link View provides a robust site visualization tool that enables you to oversee and manage the structure of your Web site. One of the main strengths of this tool is that you can view and interact with your application objects, all within the confines of one integrated development environment.

Workshop

The Workshop provides quiz questions to help you solidify your understanding of the material covered and exercises to provide you with experience in using what you've learned. You can find the answers to the quiz questions and exercises in Appendix B, "Answers."

Quiz

1. What is the difference between an inbound link and an outbound link?
2. What is the name of the feature that enables you to view your Web site structure?
3. Name the feature that enables you to copy an entire Web site to another location.

Exercises

1. Today's exercise involves a research project. I want you to research Web site management and site visualization tools on the Internet. This field is expanding at a rapid pace as the issues surrounding the proper management of a Web site continue to gain importance. You should make a list of these tools and search for their

purpose, features, strengths, and weaknesses. Then compare the purpose and qualities of these tools with the site visualization and management tools contained in Visual InterDev. In what ways are the other products weaker? In what ways are they stronger? Document answers to these questions and others that you have regarding this topic so that you can refer to them in the future.

2. Develop a promotion and deployment strategy for your Web applications. This may entail mapping out the creation of development, testing, and production environments that effectively support the design, build, testing, and rollout of your applications. Be sure to note how the features of both Visual InterDev and Visual Studio can support your efforts.

DAY **17**

Debugging Your Applications with Visual InterDev

The true test of any application development tool is its debugging capabilities. This has been true in any age of computing, from the traditional mainframe style of programming to the more recent client/server model. Ask any application developer, and he will more than likely tell you that strong debugging capabilities are a major factor in selecting a development tool. Back in the mainframe era, the debugging process was fairly straightforward because everything, from presentation logic to business logic to database logic, ran on a central machine. Things got a bit more complicated with the advent of client/server. All of a sudden, programming logic was divided between two platforms. It took awhile, but the client/server application development tools eventually caught up and added strong debugging capabilities to their toolsets.

Web application development tools are at a similar point. Many first iteration tools have been released for true Web application development. The majority of these tools lack true integrated development capabilities. This is not surprising because Web-based applications have many challenges that past computing platforms didn't have to face. Typical Web application environments consist of a Web browser for presenting information to the user, a Web server to manage the delivery of the information, an application server to process business rules, and finally, a database server that contains the actual data.

Each of these areas is referred to as a *tier*. Tiers are often used to describe an application. Client/server applications are usually referred to as 2-tiered applications. Web applications are usually described as n-tier applications because of the multiple computing environments involved in the delivery of the application logic to the user.

Today, next generation Web application development tools are offering strong, integrated debugging capabilities. Visual InterDev is no exception. Today's lesson will focus on

- The integrated debugging capabilities of Visual InterDev
- Using these capabilities during application development
- Types of errors to expect when developing Web applications
- Other common considerations related to code debugging

Let's get started.

Types of Errors

Before you get started with specific Web application errors, take a step back and review programming errors in a generic sense. Regardless of the technology used to develop your applications, you will be faced with several different types of errors. This holds true for traditional client/server development and Web application development. The types of errors are

- Syntax errors
- Runtime errors
- Logic errors

Syntax errors occur when you mistype a reserved word in the scripting language or make some other type of mistake related to the correct construction of a piece of script code. Runtime errors occur when your script code attempts to perform an invalid action. The code syntax is fine, but the developer's use of the code is wrong. The third category of programming errors is the logic error. Logic errors occur when your code doesn't execute as you intended. Typically, developers spend the majority of their debugging time on logic errors. A good debugger can go a long way in helping you solve all these types of errors.

Because Visual InterDev supports the use of many different technologies, you will face these types of errors at some point. Fortunately, many of the advanced objects that you will use in your projects can be debugged with their own debugger. For example, if you create and use an Active Server Component built with Visual Basic, you can use Visual Basic's powerful debugger to analyze problems with your component.

You will encounter several types of errors that are unique to the environment of Web application development. These errors are as follows:

- HTML errors
- Component errors
- Database errors
- Script errors

Let's take a look at the different types of technology-related errors you will face while developing Web-based applications.

HTML Errors

HTML serves as the foundation language for constructing pages on the Web. For this reason, you will implement a large amount of HTML within your Visual InterDev project, leaving room for errors.

One type of HTML error you may encounter involves invalid hyperlinks. This error is sometimes the result of a URL address that has been deleted or changed in some way. Another cause of a bad hyperlink involves a URL address where content has been changed. In this scenario, the user accesses the hyperlink expecting to go to one page and ends up viewing another one. You also may encounter errors that involve forms, tables, and overall document structure. For example, your code could contain unclosed tags that will cause an error in your code. Also, your HTML could be completely valid for some browsers, but not for others.

Although Visual InterDev's debugging capabilities don't specifically relate to solving HTML errors, other features can help you as a developer to avoid many of the HTML-related pitfalls. Examples of these features are Visual InterDev's site management and editing capabilities. These types of features, coupled with experience and practice, can help you eliminate HTML errors from your Web application development efforts.

Component Errors

This category involves those errors that occur while using a component such as a Java applet, an ActiveX control, or an Active Server Component program. You will invariably incorporate these objects into your application. If you encounter a problem with one of

17

these components, you need to use the software tool that was used to create the object to debug the error. For example, if you encounter a problem with a Visual Basic Active Server Component, you can use the robust debugger included with Visual Basic 6 to resolve the problem. If you don't locate the problem within the Visual Basic environment, the other option is to verify that you're setting the right properties and using the object correctly within your Visual InterDev project.

Database Errors

Database errors involve problems that you encounter while trying to access your database. These errors include SQL syntax errors, logic errors, connection problems, and access errors. To resolve database errors, you must tackle them in the correct order. First, you need to make sure that you can connect to the database and access the desired tables and information. Next, you need to make sure that your syntax is correct for SQL statements. Then, you need to test your logic to ensure that the SQL produces accurate results. The Visual Data Tools provided in Visual InterDev and covered on Day 9, "Using the Visual Data Tools for Maximum Productivity," enable you to address all these possible problem situations.

Script Errors

The use of scripting languages like VBScript and JavaScript is increasing due to the growing number of dynamic applications that are being created. Because this increases the complexity of Web applications, this development greatly increases the chance for programming errors in your Visual InterDev projects. In addition, the fact that the scripting languages are accessible to everyone, including less experienced developers, increases the chance for coding errors. The types of script errors that you can expect to find include syntax, runtime, and logic errors. Earlier today, I discussed each of these categories of errors. The majority of today's lesson covers using Visual InterDev's debugger to solve these errors in your script code.

Presenting the New Visual InterDev Debugger

Visual InterDev contains a full-featured source level debugger that enables you to solve even the most complex problems with script code in your Web applications. Visual InterDev's debugger works for both VBScript and JavaScript. In this part of today's lesson, you will get an overview of the debugger's features. If you have worked with the debugger in Visual Basic 5, the debugger in Visual InterDev should look familiar to you.

> **Note** During today's lesson, I will focus primarily on the features of the Visual InterDev debugger and how you can use them to debug and test your application. Although I will cover some generalized debugging techniques, this section in no way covers all the ways and means of debugging a Web-based application.

The quickest way to get a feel for the features of the debugger is to work with Visual InterDev itself. To view the Debug menu from within Visual InterDev, pull up a page within your project and select Source view in the Visual InterDev editor. Then select the Debug menu option. You should see a menu selection like the one in Figure 17.1.

FIGURE 17.1.

The Debug menu.

You can also view the various debugging windows available in Visual InterDev by selecting View | Debug Windows. You should see a selection of windows like those displayed in Figure 17.2.

> **Note** You can only work with the Visual InterDev debugger in Source view for both HTML and ASP documents.

At its most basic, the Visual InterDev debugger enables you to perform three key functions:

- Control the execution of your script code.
- View and modify variable and property values during script execution.
- Debug scripts that are executed on remote computing resources.

FIGURE 17.2.

Debug windows.

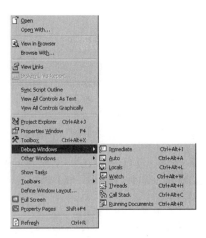

In today's lesson, you'll take a look at how the Visual InterDev debugger enables these functions and how you can use the debugger to enhance your development process.

Starting the Debugging Process

To enable script debugging in Visual InterDev, you must first set up your project for client- and server-side debugging. To do this, right-click in the Visual InterDev Project Explorer and select Properties. From here, select the Launch tab. The dialog box in Figure 17.3 appears.

FIGURE 17.3.

Setting up your project for debugging.

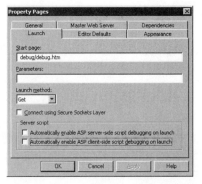

In the Launch tab, you'll see two check boxes labeled Automatically Enable ASP Server-Side Script Debugging and Automatically Enable ASP Client-Side Script Debugging. Check both boxes to set up your project for both client and server-side script debugging.

Setting Breakpoints

A key element of script debugging involves controlling the execution of the script code. Visual InterDev's debugger enables you to stop the execution of script code through the use of breakpoints. A breakpoint causes your script code to pause its execution at a point that you specify. A set breakpoint stops the execution of the script before executing the line of code containing the breakpoint. To set a breakpoint, open your HTML or ASP file within Visual InterDev using Source view. Place your cursor on the line of script where you want to set a breakpoint. From the Debug menu, select the Insert | Breakpoint menu option. You should see a red octagon next to the line of script where you set the breakpoint. You can also double-click next to the specified line to set a breakpoint. Figure 17.4 displays the Source view with breakpoints set.

FIGURE 17.4.

Setting breakpoints.

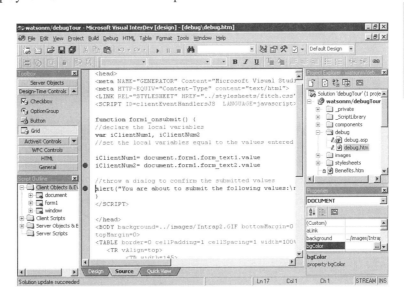

17

Launching the Visual InterDev Debugger

To launch the Visual InterDev debugger, select the start page for your project. To do this, right-click the HTML or ASP file in the Project Explorer and choose Set As Start Page. Next, choose the Start menu option from the Debug menu. From here, Visual InterDev loads the selected page into your default browser and executes the HTML and script code until the first breakpoint is reached. In addition, Visual InterDev launches several debugging windows, as shown in Figure 17.5.

FIGURE 17.5.

Visual InterDev's debugging environment.

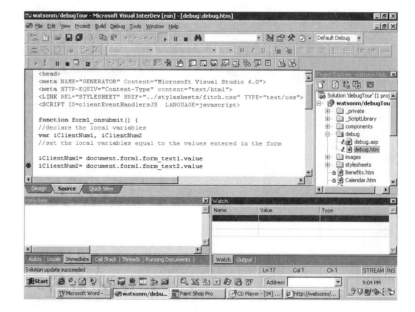

You should also notice the Debug toolbar that appears as part of the debugging environment. During this lesson, I will refer to both the Debug menu items and the Debug Windows menu option under the View menu to demonstrate the features of the Visual InterDev debugger. The Debug Windows menu option under the View menu displays the various windows used during the debugging process. The Debug menu items are used to access the primary features of the Visual InterDev debugger. You can also access the primary debugger features via the Debug toolbar. The Debug toolbar appears automatically when you start the debugger. Next, I'll take a look at the powerful features of Visual InterDev's debugging environment.

Debugging Your Script on the Client and Server

At the beginning of today's lesson, I discussed why debugging a Web-based application is difficult. In a typical scenario, HTML or script code is executed on both clients and servers. Visual InterDev's debugger supports the debugging of HTML pages and script code on the client and server-side ASP code. Because your Web server is typically located on another machine and ASP code executes on the Web server, the debugging of server-side script is referred to as remote debugging. This is a key concept for true enterprisewide application development with script code executed on both browser clients and Web servers.

> You must use Microsoft's Internet Information Server version 4 or later in order to work with the remote debugging features of Visual InterDev.

Regardless of whether you are debugging client-side script, sever-side script, or both at the same time, Visual InterDev offers several powerful debugging features. Let's take a closer look at these debugging features.

Working with Variables

When a breakpoint is reached, you can work with and analyze the values of variables in your script code. You can quickly see the value of a variable or expression in Source view by placing the cursor over the variable or expression. A Value Tip is displayed with the current value of the variable or expression. Figure 17.6 shows this feature in action.

FIGURE 17.6.

Displaying the current value of a variable.

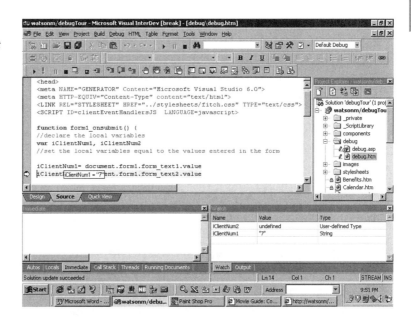

Using the Locals and Auto Windows

You can also use the Locals and Auto debug windows to view and modify the values of variables within your script code. To display the Locals and Auto debug windows, choose the windows for display from the Debug Windows menu option under the View menu. The Locals window displays the current values of all variables that are in the scope of the current procedure or thread. The Auto window displays the current values of all variables that are within scope of all currently executing procedures or threads. Figure 17.7 displays the Locals window in action.

FIGURE 17.7.

The Locals debug window.

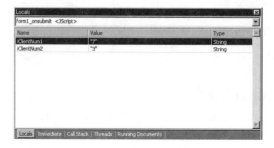

To modify the value of a variable in the Locals or Auto window, select the value in the window that you want to change. Next, simply type in the new value that you want to assign to the variable or expression. As your script code continues to execute, the new value assigned to the variable will be used.

Tip

> You can change the scope of the Locals window by using the drop-down list box at the top of the Locals window. This drop-down box displays the current active procedures.

Note

> As your code continues to execute while in debug mode, the content of the Locals window changes to reflect the variables that are part of the current procedure.

Watching Variable Values with the Watch Window

You can use the Watch window to view and modify the values of selected variables and expressions. To display the Watch window, choose View|Debug Windows | Watch Window. The Watch window works the same way as the Locals and Auto windows. To add a variable or expression to the Watch window, right-click the variable. Choose the Add Watch menu option to add the variable to the Watch window. Figure 17.8 displays this menu option with the Watch window.

To delete a variable from the Watch window, select the variable in the Watch window and then press the Delete key on the keyboard or right-click the variable and choose Delete Watch.

FIGURE 17.8.

The Watch window.

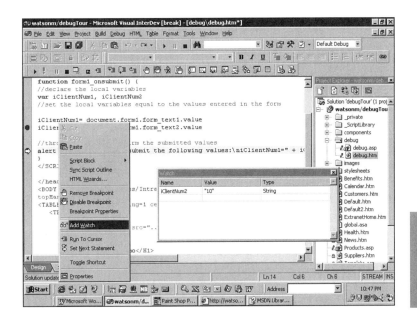

Using the Immediate Window

You can use the Immediate Window to set and change the values of variables and expressions in the currently executing script using script commands. The Immediate window gives you full interaction with your application while it is in debugging mode. A great way to use the Immediate window is for testing logic points of your script code. For example, your application may take some sort of action based on the value of a variable. You can use the Immediate window to test the behavior of your application for different variable values. Figure 17.9 shows the variable iClientNum1 being changed in the Immediate window.

Note

Now that I have talked about interacting with your application via the Immediate window, you may be wondering about modifying your script code while debugging your application. Although it sounds like a great idea, you cannot edit your code while debugging your application with Visual InterDev. You must make note of any code changes that are needed and make them outside of your debugging sessions. When your changes are made, simply restart your debugging session with Visual InterDev.

FIGURE 17.9.

Changing values in the Immediate window.

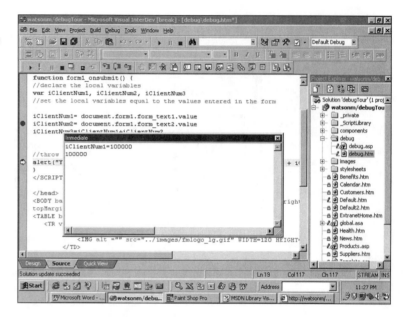

Controlling the Execution of Your Script

Another key element of the debugging process involves controlling the execution of your script code. When a breakpoint is reached, you, as a developer, need to have the ability to step through your code line by line. In addition, the ability to step over and around sections of code is equally important. Visual InterDev's powerful debugger enables you to have complete control of your script code execution during the debugging process. Next, I will take a look at the specific features within the Visual InterDev debugger related to script code execution.

Stepping In, Out, and Over Your Code

After a breakpoint is reached in the Visual InterDev debugger, you have the ability to control the execution of the remaining lines of code. Keep in mind that a breakpoint stops the execution of your script before executing the line of code containing the breakpoint. Usually, you use breakpoints as a way to analyze certain aspects of your application. For example, earlier you saw how you can use the debugger to analyze the values of variables and expressions. To execute the line of code containing the breakpoint and subsequent lines, use the Step Into, Step Over, or Step Out menu options from the Debug menu. As you use these menu options to advance the debugger through your script code, you will notice an arrow pointing to the current line of code in Source view. The arrow indicates the statement that will be executed next by the debugger. Figure 17.10 displays the Source view with the current statement arrow present.

FIGURE 17.10.

Current statement in Source view.

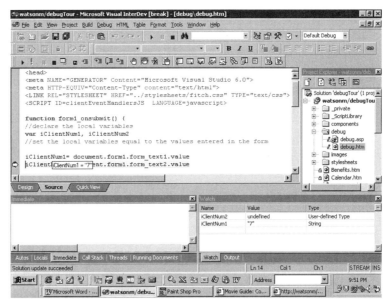

Step Into causes the debugger to execute the current statement and break at the next statement. The next statement could be in the current procedure or another procedure. The Step Into menu option will break within a called procedure.

Step Over causes the debugger to execute the current statement. However, instead of stepping into a called procedure and breaking at the next statement within the procedure, Step Over executes the called procedure and breaks at the statement following the called procedure.

Step Out executes the remaining script code in the current procedure and breaks at the statement following the statement that called the procedure.

These three Debug menu options give you great flexibility in executing procedures and statements in your debugging sessions. Previously, you worked with the Visual InterDev debugger to view and modify the values of variables and expressions.

Now would be a good time to experiment with the Step Into, Over, and Out features discussed during this section. Set breakpoints at individual statements and statements that call other procedures.

Other Script Execution Features

Visual InterDev contains other useful script execution features that enhance the development experience. You can cause the debugger to continue executing your script after a breakpoint is reached with the Continue menu option. This menu option is found under the Debug menu and is only available while you are debugging your script code.

You can also place your cursor at a certain point in your script code and cause the debugger to execute until it reaches your cursor. This is accomplished via the Run to Cursor menu option under the Debug menu. At a breakpoint, simply place the cursor where you want to stop execution and select the Run to Cursor menu option. Visual InterDev will continue executing your script until the line with the cursor is reached.

You can use the Restart menu option to start your debugging session over from the specified start page. Again, you can find the Restart menu option under the Debug menu.

The final two features of the Visual InterDev debugger that relate to script execution are the Set Next Statement and Show Next Statement menu options. Both of these options are part of the Debug menu. Set Next Statement enables you to choose the statement that is executed next by the debugger. For example, you could select a line of code that is five lines below the current statement and choose the Set Next Statement option. Once execution of the script is resumed, the debugger would skip to your specified statement as the next statement to be executed. Show Next Statement is a visual tool that places the cursor on the next line of code that will be executed by the debugger. This is a useful feature if you get lost during your debugging session. It quickly shows you the next statement that the debugger will execute in your code.

Experiment with these script execution features to get a feel for how they work. As you can see, the Visual InterDev debugger gives you, as a developer, the ultimate flexibility in executing your script code.

Working with Breakpoints

To remove breakpoints from the Source view editor during a debugging session, simply double-click the set breakpoint with the mouse. In addition, you can place the cursor on the line containing the breakpoint and access the Remove Breakpoint menu option from the Debug menu. You can disable a breakpoint and later re-enable it during your debugging session.

Let's experiment with this feature. Place your cursor on the line containing the breakpoint you want to disable. Select the Debug|Disable Breakpoint. You should see a change in the color of octagon that indicates a set breakpoint. As stated earlier, a red octagon represents a set breakpoint. A white octagon represents a disabled breakpoint. To re-enable the breakpoint, place your cursor on the line containing the disabled breakpoint. Select Debug | Enable Breakpoint. At this point, the breakpoint octagon should change its color back to red.

You can clear all breakpoints in your script code by choosing Debug | Clear All Breakpoints. Keep in mind that once you clear all breakpoints, your application will run to completion unless you use the Step Into, Over, or Out commands discussed earlier. When debugging a large application, you may set many breakpoints in your code. Keeping track of all your set breakpoints can be cumbersome. To display a list of your currently set breakpoints, select the Breakpoints menu option from the Debug menu. Figure 17.11 displays the Breakpoints dialog box with a list of breakpoints that are currently set in Source view.

FIGURE 17.11.

Displaying set breakpoints.

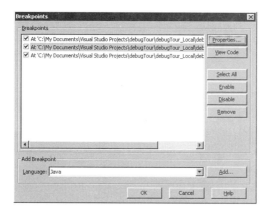

From this dialog box, you can perform many of the breakpoint features that were discussed in this section. For example, you can remove breakpoints, disable/enable breakpoints, and quickly move to the exact line of script code that contains the breakpoint. The Breakpoints dialog box shows all set breakpoints across all HTML or ASP files that make up your application.

Working with Your Processing Environment

In addition to the values of variables and expressions in your application, information about the application's processing environment provides other useful information during a debugging session. For example, you might need information about procedures that are called while your application is executing. You might also need to know which processes are currently executing and which documents are active on the Web server. Most likely, your use of this information depends on the complexity of your application. Let's take a look at how Visual InterDev's debugger provides useful information about your applications processing environment.

Displaying Call Stack and Thread Windows

The Call Stack window displays a list of called procedures that are active in your Web-based application. This is a useful feature when debugging script code that contains a series of nested procedure calls. Working with such situations while debugging script code can be difficult. The Call Stack window enables you to see a list of called procedures in the order that they were executed. To view the Call Stack window, select the View menu and select the Call Stack window from the Debug Windows menu option. The window in Figure 17.12 appears.

FIGURE 17.12.

The Call Stack window.

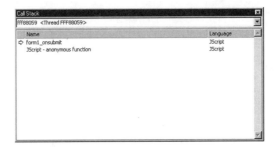

To work with the Call Stack window, set a breakpoint in your script code. Start the debugger and execute the script until your breakpoint is reached.

The Threads window works in much the same way and displays a list of active threads in your Web application. It is also viewed via the Debug Windows menu option under the View menu. The Threads window displays all active threads in your application and their processing location. Figure 17.13 depicts the Threads window.

FIGURE 17.13.

The Threads window.

Displaying Active Documents and Processes

To view running documents during a debugging session, use the Running Documents window. You can find the Running Documents window as part of the Debug Windows menu option under the View menu. You can also find this window on the Debug toolbar.

This window simply displays all active Web pages for your debugging session. Figure 17.14 displays the Running Documents window.

FIGURE 17.14.

The Running Documents window.

To view running processes on the client or server machine, use the Processes window. You can find the Processes window under the Debug menu and on the Debug toolbar. Figure 17.15 shows the Processes window.

FIGURE 17.15.

The Processes window.

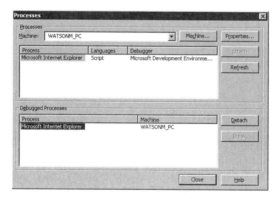

Using Error-Handling Routines

Depending on the complexity and scope of your Web-based application, you may want to consider adding code for handling different types of errors to your scripts. You can use these error-handling routines for debugging purposes, or you may find yourself defining errors and associated processes that are specific to your application. For example, a value may be in error that causes your application not to process properly. Or a piece of work flow required for a particular process may be skipped within your application. For these types of error situations, you need to add error-handling logic to your application that will allow your application to recover and continue processing or exit gracefully. Fortunately, VBScript enables you to insert error-handling routines as a part of your code. VBScript includes several methods that enable you to trap errors within your script and deal with them in the proper manner. The following sections cover two of the more popular methods.

Resolving Errors with a Statement

The first methods involve the use of the VBScript On Error statement. This statement enables you to capture an error and enables the application to continue executing. Accomplished Visual Basic programmers may be familiar with using this method in their client/server applications. The basic syntax for the On Error statement is as follows:

```
On Error Resume Next

... Block of Code ...

On Error Resume Next
```

The On Error statement tells the VBScript interpreter to ignore the error and proceed to the next statement as though nothing happened. With Visual Basic, you can both recognize the error as well as send the logic to an error-handling routine to determine the severity of the error and take the necessary actions. VBScript is limited in that you can only proceed to the next statement using this method. The next section demonstrates how to extend the effectiveness of the On Error statement to debug your code.

Resolving Errors with an Object

The On Error statement can be extended to handle your VBScript errors within your application by using the err object. This object is an inherent VBScript object and enables you to incorporate debugging and runtime logic into your application. Because the err object is an intrinsic object, it's freely available throughout your code without any extra effort on your part. All you need to do to use the object is to reference it after the On Error statement. Table 17.1 explains the available properties of the err object.

TABLE 17.1. err OBJECT PROPERTIES.

Property	Description
Number	Numeric error code
Description	Description of the error code
Source	Name of the program that caused the error
Helpfile	Name of a help file with more information on the error
HelpContext	ID of the topic index for the help file

You also can use two methods with the err object—Raise and Clear. The Raise method enables you to create an error within your script code. This is useful when you are testing and simulating errors within your application. You use the Clear method to clear the contents of the err object. This method should only be used after an error has been detected and dealt with properly. The worst thing you can do is clear out the err object before the application has processed the error. This situation results in disaster for your application because it no longer knows the error it is processing or what to do next.

Listing 17.1 demonstrates an example of using the On Error statement with the err object to properly handle the potential errors in your application.

LISTING 17.1. EFFECTIVE ERROR HANDLING.

```
 1: Sub cmdSubmit_OnClick ()
 2: On Error Resume Next
 3: Dim SalePrice
 4:
 5: SalePrice = (txtRetailPrice.Text -
    ➥(txtRetailPrice.Text*txtDiscount.Text))
 6:
 7: If err.number <> 0 Then
 8: MsgBox "Error #: " & err.number & " Description: " & err.description &
 9: "Source: " & err.Source
10: End If
11:
12: End Sub
```

This code calculates the sale price based on the retail price and discount that the user enters on the form. The err object is used to check for a number that isn't equal to zero, which indicates an error. If an error occurs, a message box is displayed to the user.

Common Consideration About Bugs

You might as well resolve yourself to the fact that errors will occur as you develop your Web-based application code. As a Web developer, you realize and understand the complexity of testing the various components of your Web-based application. However, using Visual InterDev's debugger should give you an advantage when faced with the task of conquering bugs and errors in your Web-based application code.

You're probably not going to find an integrated debugging tool that tests your application from front to back; that is, from your HTML Web page through your ActiveX controls and Java applets to your Active Server Pages and Components to your database. You need to break your application into its respective parts and test these components with the best tool or method possible. You can use Visual InterDev's debugger to work with errors in your script code and the native development environments of tools such as Visual Basic or Visual J++ to work with errors in your application's components. You can use other features of Visual InterDev, such as site management and visual data tools, to work with HTML and database errors.

Summary

Today, you looked at the features and capabilities of Visual InterDev's integrated debugger. By now, you should realize what a welcome addition Visual InterDev's debugger is to the Web-application development world. You began the day discussing the evolution of application development tools and the importance of a strong debugging environment. You also covered the basic types of errors that face a developer of Web-based applications. You learned about HTML errors, component errors, database errors, and script errors. Visual InterDev handles each of these types of errors in different ways.

However, the Visual InterDev debugger really shines when it comes to debugging script on both the browser client and Web server. Through its remote debugging capabilities, the Visual InterDev debugger can assist you with solving errors that occur on remote server machines. In the same way, it can help you fix bugs in your client-side JavaScript or VBScript.

Visual InterDev's debugger enables you to control the execution of your script code, stopping its execution at breakpoints that you specify. From here, you can examine and modify the values of variables and expressions in your script code. By using the Immediate window, you can fully interact with your application by executing script commands and examining the values of properties and variables. In addition, you can step through your code line by line in the debugger. By doing this, you can examine the effect of each line of code on your application's behavior. You can also choose how you step through procedures in your code with the Step Over and Step Out commands. The Visual InterDev debugger enables you to analyze the processing environment of your application. You can examine the application's call stack, processing threads and active Web documents.

At the end of the day, you took a look at using error-handling routines in your code to debug and process errors in your application properly at runtime. Finally, you focused on some common considerations and concepts to ponder concerning the testing of your application.

Q&A

Q What's the best way to debug errors in any Active Server components that are part of my application?

A You should use the tool used to create the Active Server component. Active Server components can be created with a variety of tools such as Visual Basic, Visual J++, and Visual C++. Most of the tools have robust and integrated debuggers built into their development environments. As with any problem solving activity, it's a good idea to break your application errors down into smaller pieces. For example, you may want to solve your component errors before moving on to solving your HTML and script errors.

Q Does the Visual InterDev debugger handle situations where my Active Server Pages contain both client and server script in the same file?

A Yes. The Visual InterDev debugger can handle both server- and client-side script in the same Active Server Page file. Visual InterDev's debugger tracks breakpoints in both client- and server-side script. It even keeps track of your set breakpoints after the Active Server Page generates HTML code for the browser. Typically, server-side script breakpoints are processed first followed by any client-side script breakpoints.

17

Workshop

The Workshop provides quiz questions to help you solidify your understanding of the material covered and exercises to provide you with experience in using what you've learned. You can find the answers to the quiz questions and exercises in Appendix B, "Answers."

Quiz

1. Name the three categories of Web-application programming errors.
2. What are the three ways to access features of the Visual InterDev debugger in the development environment?
3. Name two ways to set a breakpoint in your script code.
4. Name three ways to view the contents of a variable or expression in your script code.
5. Name three ways to control the execution of your script code.

Exercises

For today's exercise, practice what you learned about Visual InterDev's debugger. I want you to create script code that executes on the client and server. If you already have a good example in one of your applications, feel free to use it in this exercise. (If you don't have a sample application, you could go to the Microsoft Visual InterDev Web site [http://www.microsoft.com/vinterdev/download/samples/default.htm] and download the Dos Perros Chile Company example.)

Set up your application for debugging as discussed earlier in today's lesson. Set breakpoints in your script code—both client- and server-side. Then use the features of the Visual InterDev debugger that were discussed today to thoroughly test the behavior of your application. Experiment with the different ways to step through your code and examine the values of variables. Check out the call stack and threads windows as you execute client- and server-side script code. Most importantly, have fun while you experiment with the great debugging features of Visual InterDev.

DAY **18**

Exploring the Working Modes of Visual InterDev

So far, you have learned a lot about developing Web-based applications using Visual InterDev. The lessons assume that you are an individual developer working on applications and are using this book to further your knowledge about Visual InterDev. Web-based applications, however, typically involve a team of developers with diverse skill sets. Invariably, you will need to learn how to utilize the team development features of Visual InterDev to support your development team.

The next two days focus on how to use the team development features within Visual InterDev and Visual Studio. Tomorrow you'll focus on how to use Visual SourceSafe for source control; today's lesson focuses on how to isolate your developers using Visual InterDev's new project model. Specifically, at the end of this lesson you will be able to

- Explain the design and development considerations when building a Web-based application.
- Understand the Visual InterDev project model.

- Explain the difference between Master, Local, and Offline working modes that support developer isolation.
- Use the different project working modes of Visual InterDev during application development.
- Use the Copy Web function to deploy your Web content.
- Explain how the Visual Component Manager can be used to manage and deploy your custom components.

Choosing a Development and Deployment Platform

Choosing a proper development architecture and platform is critical to the success of any project. This section focuses specifically on platform considerations for selecting the right development and deployment environment.

Visual InterDev can run on Windows 95, and Windows NT Workstation and Server. Each platform offers a viable alternative. You also can use a combination of these operating systems to support your efforts. In selecting a development platform, you need to consider the following factors:

- Scalability
- Development tools
- Standards
- Architecture
- Database

Scalability

You need to think about the current and future needs of your application. You may be supporting 50 users currently, but the popularity of your application may grow and with that growth will come an increase in user count and the size of your database. Scalability refers to how well a platform can scale or move to handle an increase in the growth of your application needs. You may originally size your database and plan your application based on these current needs but allow no room for growth. When planning your application, you need to choose a platform and build an application that permits growth.

Development Tools

You also need to select the proper development tools to support the user requirements of your application. Before you select these tools, you will need to perform a proper analysis of what the user needs are and how your application is going to address these needs. These requirements will help you choose what tools you need to build the most effective application.

You should select these tools before you begin the development phase of your project. Integration is much harder when you incrementally add tools along the way. One of the best ways to proceed is to establish a toolset and provide the tools in it as an integrated package to the developers. This toolbox significantly increases the productivity of the programmers. Also, the chance for having development environment problems is drastically reduced because the tools have already been selected and tested for interoperability.

Standards

Without standards, there is anarchy. Some would say that with standards, there is no room for creativity. In truth, though, you need to have standards and allow room for developer creativity. You can accomplish both.

You need to provide a set of standards that give your developers a consistent platform. If you're a project manager, you should assign a developer to set these standards. You need to get involvement from any and all members of the development team who have an interest in establishing the standards. Those members who don't help are saying that they can live with the standards that are set. You should establish these standards for all aspects of your development, including programming, testing, and documentation. Some of these standards will be how-to documents that define how to perform such operations as testing your application and promoting your application between the environments. You also should construct standard programming shells for your developers. These shells will augment the productivity of your developers and promote consistency within your application code. Style sheets for your HTML pages are an excellent example of this concept.

Standards aid in all phases of your development and help resolve conflicts when questions and issues arise.

Architecture

Establishing the right architecture is a critical step in your development effort. You need to create an architecture that supports your development both on the client and the server. If you create a standard architecture for connecting to the database and communicating with server-side programs and applications, you can be assured that every developer is performing these functions in the same manner. Also, this process enables you to build an architecture that effectively supports your application's needs.

18

Database

Choosing the right database is crucial to your application. I will talk about this process a little later in the day. For now, I'll simply mention what you need to focus on from a development perspective after you have selected a database.

First, you should logically design your database based on user requirements. These user requirements keep appearing, but they drive many aspects of your application development. Entity/Relationship (E/R) diagramming tools can definitely help with this task. Some of the more popular tools include Erwin from Logic Works and S-Designor from Sybase's Powersoft division. These tools are very robust and should handle all your database administration needs. If you're using MS SQL Server as your database, you can use the Database Designer within Visual InterDev to create and maintain your database objects. You should assign a specific person to handle the database administration functions for your project if you have the luxury. This person can work with the users and translate their functional requirements into technical requirements for the database model.

After you have logically designed the database, you will physically create the database. Most of the E/R tools on the market automatically create the physical database based on the logical model that you construct. You need to create a development, testing, and production environment for each of your databases. Each environment should support the different phases of your project.

 Note

For big projects with many development team members and users, you might need to create a fourth database environment for training the users. You can use the testing environment for training, but problems will invariably occur due to the nature of the environment. Conflicts will happen between the testing by the development team and the training of the users. I have conducted many training sessions in which the system crashed and then wished I had a separate training environment. In the long run, this can save an initial bad impression of your application on the part of users.

You should perform regular backups of your database. You also should maintain a pristine copy of the database, especially when you begin the testing phases of your project. This copy will represent the initial set of test data. As developers run their tests, their actions will insert, change, and delete this data. After they have completed their tests, you can restore the data to its initial state. This process provides a controlled environment for your testing.

Now that you have learned about some general aspects and considerations for your application architecture, it's time to talk more specifically about Visual InterDev alternatives and their implications.

Using Windows 95 as Your Client and Server

Visual InterDev can run on a Windows 95 platform. This means that you can use Visual InterDev to develop your application as well as deploy both your client and server portions on Windows 95. There are specific benefits and considerations you need to think about when developing and deploying on a Windows 95 platform. Each of these subjects is discussed within the context of the client/server model and the database model for your Windows 95 Web-based application.

Note

The considerations discussed in this section apply to both Windows 95 and Windows NT Workstation. Although Windows NT Workstation is a full 32-bit operating system and more robust than Windows 95, it is still a client platform. The ideal model for medium to large applications with high transaction volumes is a client/server platform that includes either Windows 95 or Windows NT Workstation on the client and Windows NT Server for your server.

Client/Server Model on the Windows 95 Platform

18

You can develop and deploy your Visual InterDev applications solely on the Windows 95 platform. For example, you could use Windows 95 as your client and server in low user/low volume applications. Although this is not recommended from a scalability standpoint, there are some benefits to using this client/server model for development.

The client side of this equation involves the use of a browser, such as Internet Explorer, Netscape Navigator, or another type of browser. The server involves the use of the Microsoft Personal Web Server for Windows 95. This Web server was developed to compete with products such as Netscape's Fastrack Server, which also runs on Windows 95. The primary goal of this server is to provide a local server for those people developing on Windows 95 who don't have the luxury of a network connection.

Microsoft's Personal Web Server supports all of the server-side scripting functionality of Active Server Pages as well as other server features of Visual InterDev. The very name of the product suggests its scalability limitations. The Microsoft "Personal" Web Server was designed to be a personal, individual Web server. The benefit is that you can develop your application on a single machine. The limitation is that you won't be able to support a high volume application with a large number of users.

Windows 95 is an ideal development environment for Visual InterDev. Deployment of your client-side components is also very viable on the Windows 95 operating system. But again, deployment of your application server components on a Windows 95 environment should be avoided if your application is going to be a medium to high-volume application.

Database

The robustness of your database options on a Windows 95 platform is somewhat limited. Some of the same scalability and transaction support questions arise concerning the database ingredient of the application equation on a Windows 95 platform. The robustness of your database is a function of the Windows 95 operating system and the type of products that are offered for this environment. Your choices of PC databases include Microsoft Access, Microsoft FoxPro, Sybase SQL Anywhere, and any other ODBC-compliant database for Windows 95. PC databases provide an easy-to-use environment to create the database for your applications. These databases provide an alternative for those applications that support a low number of users, have a database that is small to medium in size, and don't need the power of a traditional client/server database.

For the more robust applications, you can still use a PC database for part of your development effort. An example of this scenario involves the use of Microsoft Access. You can use a single Windows 95 machine to build a prototype of your application that uses the Personal Web Server as the server and Access as the local database.

Using this architecture, you can rapidly build your prototype application. During this development, you can conduct joint application design (JAD) sessions with your users to demo your application and record their feedback. Along the way, you construct the logical model and physical creation of your database in Microsoft Access.

After you have refined the prototype and incorporated the user recommendations, you can upsize your application to a more traditional client/server platform. Microsoft provides an upsizing wizard that enables you to transform your Access database to an MS SQL Server database. I have used this method for both client/server and Web-based development projects to greatly reduce the development time of my projects.

Combining Windows 95 and Windows NT

You can use Visual InterDev to develop and deploy Web-based applications in a mixed environment like Windows 95 and Windows NT.

> **Note**
>
> When I talk about mixed environments, I'm speaking specifically about platforms that support Visual InterDev features like ActiveX controls, Active Server Pages, and so on. You can also build applications with Visual InterDev to inter-operate in a mixed environment with legacy applications and other custom-developed programs that run on platforms such as UNIX.

This platform is probably the preferred environment both from a development and deployment standpoint. You also can substitute Windows NT Workstation for Windows 95 in this model. The client considerations are practically the same.

Client/Server Model on a Windows 95/Windows NT Mixed Environment

In this model, the client machines run on Windows 95, and the server is Windows NT. From a development standpoint, you can support team development by using this networked environment to provide central source code management on the server. Also, you can adequately test your server components to see how these components perform in a robust client/server environment. Regarding deployment, Windows NT Server and Microsoft's Internet Information Server provide a very robust, industrial strength platform to serve the needs of your application.

Database

The database options in this model are more powerful. You can use true client/server databases that have a plethora of features and support a high volume application with a large number of users. Choices include Oracle, MS SQL Server, Sybase SQL Server, and other ODBC-compliant databases.

The benefits of using a SQL database for this model include more administrative control and a more robust environment to develop your applications. You can truly take advantage of the power of a database in this class to meet the more advanced needs of your application.

Isolating Your Developers for the Best Results

Developer isolation sounds like a psychological condition that all programmers encounter as they pursue their goal of becoming the supreme guru of programming. Truly Dilbert and Wally from Scott Adams's popular comic strip have faced this at one

18

time or the other as they toil their lives away in the cubicle abyss. Although I would like to provide a resolution for this condition, I am focusing today's lesson on the type of isolation that every development team needs to be effective.

Visual InterDev 6 supports a new project model that allows you to truly isolate individual developers within a project team. What does this mean? Developer isolation in this context means that each developer can work on their individual parts of the application without overwriting or affecting the work of other team members. Using this feature, you can maintain a central version on the master Web server that is accessible to all of your developers. Visual InterDev simultaneously provides a local version of these files for individual development, testing, and debugging. Developer isolation provides the mechanism for each individual developer as well as the team as a whole to be productive.

Understanding the Visual InterDev Project Model

Visual InterDev supports developer isolation through its powerful project model. You learned about the concept of projects during the second day of this book. As a refresher, a Web application contains all of the content and functionality for your Web site including HTML files, ASPs, images, ActiveX controls and Java applets, and middle-tier components. Using Visual InterDev, you create a Web project that allows you to create and manipulate all the content and functionality within your Web application by using the Project Explorer. You have become very familiar with the integrated development environment (IDE) of Visual InterDev and its Project Explorer, which allows you to interact with and manage these files.

This section of today's lesson will now elaborate on the working modes of Visual InterDev and how these modes support a team of developers using the project model. There are three basic working modes of Visual InterDev:

- Master mode
- Local mode
- Offline mode

Each of these modes are explained in the following sections.

Master Mode

Master mode is the default working mode for Visual InterDev. You may recall that during Step 1 of the Web Project Wizard. The two options are Master mode and Local mode. The wizard defaults to the Master mode option. This means that all of your changes will be saved automatically to the master Web server. Figure 18.1 demonstrates the Master mode development process.

FIGURE 18.1.

Working in Master mode.

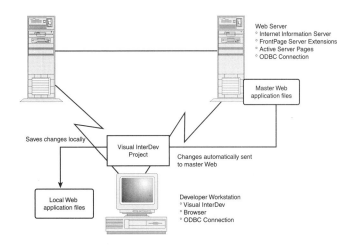

MASTER MODE

Database Server
° ODBC-Compliant
Database

Web Server
° Internet Information Server
° FrontPage Server Extensions
° Active Server Pages
° ODBC Connection

Master Web application files

Saves changes locally

Visual InterDev Project

Changes automatically sent to master Web

Local Web application files

Developer Workstation
° Visual InterDev
° Browser
° ODBC Connection

18

Any time you create a project, Visual InterDev creates two sets of files—the master set that resides on your Web server and a local set of files that resides on your developer machine.

Note

If you are developing on a standalone machine using Personal Web Server, both sets of files will physically reside on the same machine in different directories. Refer to Day 2, "Creating Your First Visual InterDev Project," for a detailed explanation of the client and server directory structure.

In the example shown in Figure 18.1, you see a development machine, a Web server, and a database server. Visual InterDev has created a local set of application files on the development machine as well as a master set of files on the Web server machine. Because the project is working under Master mode, all changes are simultaneously saved to the local version as well the master version.

Local Mode

Local mode allows you to isolate your development from the rest of the team. Changes that you make are automatically saved in the local version. You decide when to update the files in the master version. Figure 18.2 demonstrates this process.

FIGURE 18.2.

Working in Local mode.

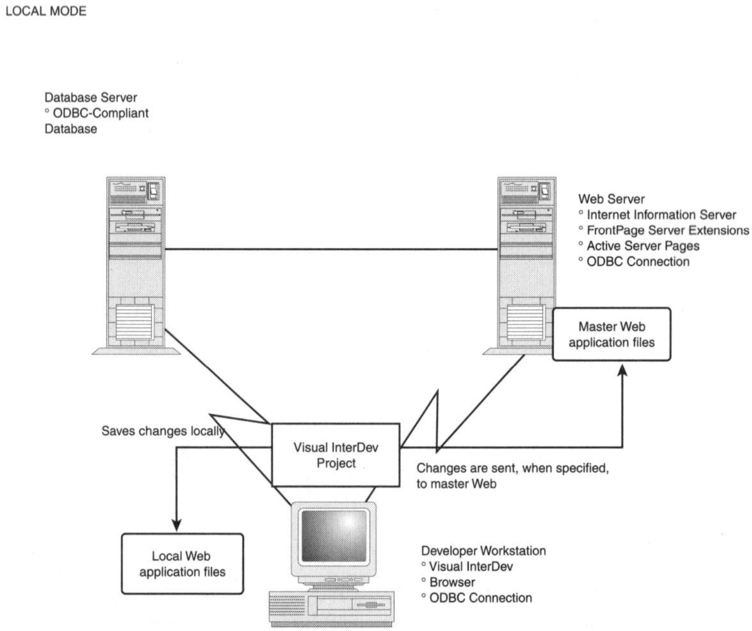

LOCAL MODE

Database Server
° ODBC-Compliant
Database

Web Server
° Internet Information Server
° FrontPage Server Extensions
° Active Server Pages
° ODBC Connection

Master Web
application files

Saves changes locally

Visual InterDev
Project

Changes are sent, when specified,
to master Web

Local Web
application files

Developer Workstation
° Visual InterDev
° Browser
° ODBC Connection

As you can see from Figure 18.2, this project is operating under Local mode. All the changes are saved locally to the development machine and then sent, when specified by the developer, to the master version on the Web server.

> **Note**
>
> Again, if you are developing on a standalone machine, two sets of files will be maintained on the same machine in different directory structures.

Local mode directly supports the methodology concept of unit testing your individual pieces of the application. You will learn more about how to apply this concept later in the day.

Offline Mode

The third working mode that Visual InterDev supports is Offline mode. This mode allows you to work offline, or disconnected, from the Web server.

Now I know most of you don't take work home, but just in case you need to, Visual InterDev provides this mode to allow you this luxury. Of course, if you are working on a standalone machine, you really don't need to worry about being offline. The most common scenario for using Offline mode is the situation where you are developing an application and need to take it on the road in a standalone mode. Offline mode allows you to continue working on the files within the project without a connection to a Web server. You are somewhat limited in that you can only execute functions that don't rely on Web server interaction. The following list provides functions that you can execute while in Offline mode:

- Open a project.
- Edit local working copies of files.
- Preview changes to HTML files using Quick View.
- Save your changes to the local working copies of the files.

Because you don't have a connection to a Web server while in Offline mode, there are some functions that you cannot carry out, including the following:

- Update the master version of files on the Web server.
- Retrieve the latest versions of files from the master Web server.
- Release the working copies of files back to the master Web server.
- Move files in the project.

Establishing the Working Mode for the Project

You basically have two methods of setting the working mode for the project. First, you can establish a working mode at the time you create the project. As mentioned earlier, the Web Project Wizard enables you to select either Master or Local mode during Step 1 of the process (see Figure 18.3).

FIGURE 18.3.

Choosing the working mode for the project.

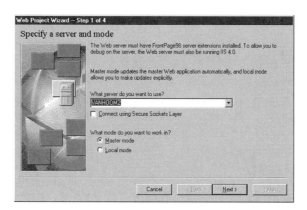

You can also change the working mode for the project after you have opened or created the project from within the Visual InterDev IDE. With the project open, select the project root and click the right mouse button to reveal the shortcut menu. From the list of menu items, choose Working Mode. This action will reveal the three working modes allowing you to select one from the list. The icon for the currently selected mode will be highlighted, as shown in Figure 18.4.

FIGURE 18.4.

Viewing the working mode for the project.

Another method for changing the working mode involves using the Project menu. After you select the Project menu, choose Web Project, Working Mode, which reveals the same list of menu items as shown in Figure 18.4.

Using the Different Project Modes Effectively

Now that you are familiar with the basic working modes that Visual InterDev supports, you will get an opportunity to walk through a basic example of using the different modes.

Working in Isolation

For most projects where you have a team of developers, Local mode should be the working mode of choice. As you have learned, Local mode allows you to isolate your part of the application from the work of other developers. You can develop, debug, and test your pages while being insulated from the changes that other developers are making to their parts of the application. They are also insulated from your changes. The benefit is that Local mode enables each individual to develop in peace and promotes the idea of fully testing your work before you check it back in to the master Web server version. In this way, you can reduce the chance of code being overwritten as well as the chance that the master version contains faulty code.

As stated previously, you can select the working mode in one of two ways. You can either set the working mode when you create the project or you can change the working mode after the project has been created. In this example, you will work with a previously created project and change the working mode after you have opened it. The following steps will guide you through this process:

1. Install the Fitch & Mather demo. You will need to download the file `tour.exe` from the Macmillan Web site and then follow the setup instructions.

2. Follow the instructions with the Guided Tour document for setting up the Fitch & Mather sample application.

3. After you have installed the demo and created a valid project, right-click the Fitch project root in the Project Explorer.

4. Select Working Mode | Local to set the project working mode to local mode.

5. Open the `Default.htm` file. Make sure that you have a working copy of the file as indicated by the pencil icon located next to the file in the Project Explorer.

6. Using the Design editor, change the title text Intranet Home Page to `Welcome to the Source!`.

7. Change the text of the First Quarter Sales Results link to `Second Quarter Sales Results`.

8. Add the text `This month we honor Macey Landrum as the Employee of the Month!` after the current sentence for the Employee of the Month section. Figure 18.5 displays the results of these changes as seen through the Design view.

9. Save your changes to this file.

10. Select the file and choose View in Browser from the shortcut menu. The page will be loaded from the local version and displayed in the browser, as shown in Figure 18.6.

Caution

If you do not have a Web server on your local development machine, the file will be loaded from a file URL (located on the file system versus a web server) and server script will not work.

18

FIGURE **18.5.**

Making changes to the local version.

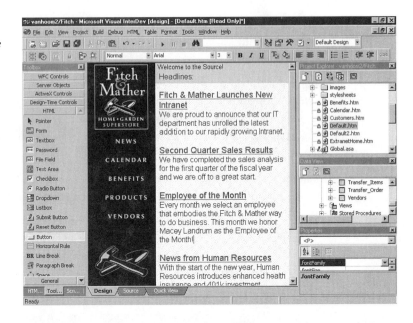

FIGURE **18.6.**

Viewing the local version through the browser.

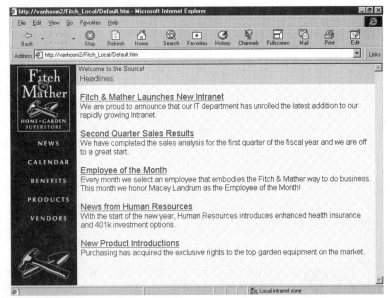

11. From within Visual InterDev, right-click the `Default.htm` file in the Project Explorer and select Compare to Master Web from the shortcut menu. This action displays the Differences dialog window that enables you to compare the differences between the local version and the master Web version.

12. Close the Differences dialog window.

13. To update the master Web server with your changes, select the file and choose Release Working Copy from the shortcut menu. This action will update the master version of the Web application with any changes that you have made to your files.

A Practical Scenario

This section focuses on the discussion of how Visual InterDev facilitates the development process. You will see the three distinct phases of application building:

- Development
- Testing
- Production

 Note

There are many Systems Development Life Cycles and methodologies surrounding application development. Most of them include planning, gathering requirements, design, development, training, testing, conversion, and production. This discussion simplifies the process and focuses on the main phases involved in the implementation of an application. This discussion assumes that you have planned the project, gathered the requirements, and designed the application.

18

Along the way, you'll learn what each phase is composed of and how you use Visual InterDev to accomplish the various tasks within each phase.

Development

This phase focuses on building the application. So far, you have seen the most common files that you will use to design and develop your application. For a typical development project, you first create your Web pages using HTML and a scripting language, possibly VBScript or JScript.

Next, you develop an Active Server Page to handle your needs from the server, such as creating a dynamic Web page or connecting to a database. You also might create an Active Server Page to control the flow of logic while interacting with an Active Server Component. You should insert a database connection into your application. For the sake of this example, the discussion is focused on using a server database such as MS SQL Server, although the basic tenets apply to desktop databases such as Microsoft Access as well.

As you create your files, save them locally on your development machine. You will use the Visual Database Tools to interact with your database through an ODBC connection to the database server. This connection is live, and enables you to create and maintain objects and manipulate the data. You also can design and test your SQL calls for inserting, selecting, updating, and deleting data in the database.

Figure 18.7 gives an overview of the development architecture and process and how Visual InterDev facilitates this process.

FIGURE 18.7.

The development process.

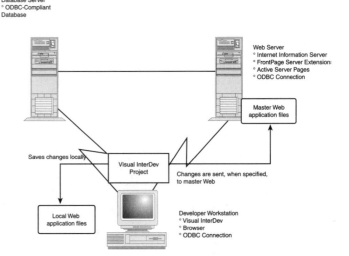

Note that you use Visual InterDev on your development client machine to design and build your application. You interface directly with the development Web server machine as well as the development database server. These interactions are distinct in nature. In other words, you maintain a network connection to the Web server and interact with files on the server. You can use the View in Browser menu option to view your Web pages and test the look and feel of the interface. The use of this command enables rapid application development by enabling you to test the Web pages within the confines of Visual InterDev.

You also can use a commercial release of a browser to view your Web pages within the eventual production environment. For database access, you're connected through an ODBC connection over the network. This architecture assumes that your network contains separate database and Web server machines and that these machines are on the same network.

Testing

After you build your application, you need to test it. This phase involves previewing the Web pages in the browser to make sure that they're visually correct. You also need to make sure that your scripting code reacts to user events properly and creates the dynamic effect for your Web pages. You need to test your database connections to make sure that your users are able to retrieve the correct information. You should use these test cycles to test specific user tasks and actions.

You can use the development client machine or your main Web server to preview the Web pages through a browser. You can use the View in Browser command during the development and testing phase to view the Web pages, but during the testing phase, you should use the browsers that will be in the production environment to test the whole application.

As you view the Web pages, you will be accessing the Web server machine. You should migrate your application from a development area to a separate test environment. By using separate and distinct development and testing areas, you can manage different releases, changes, and fixes more effectively. Your developers have an environment to test individual changes that then can be migrated and incorporated with other developer changes to create a new release. This new release then can be tested in an environment similar to the production environment. After the application has been fully tested, the Web site can be migrated to a separate production environment.

18

Note While having separate environments for development, testing, and production is recommended, don't think that all of these areas have to reside on separate machines. You can place your development Web site and testing Web site on the same machine with different directory structures. You should, however, have a separate machine for the production environment Web server for your applications and Web sites.

In the development phase, you connected directly to the database server. During the testing phase, the client/server model changes. The Web server now connects to your database server to process your database requests. While you still can connect to the database server directly from your client machine, you will want to simulate the production environment process for database connectivity using the Web server as the central hub for these requests. The Web server maintains an ODBC connection to the database server and processes database requests from the client. The Web server receives the results and returns the formatted data to the client machine browser. Figure 18.8 illustrates this process.

FIGURE **18.8.**

The testing process.

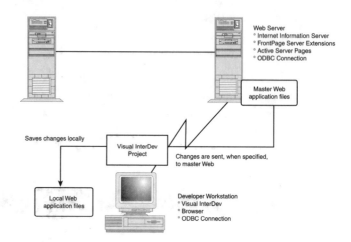

LOCAL MODE - TESTING

Database Server
° ODBC-Compliant
Database

Web Server
° Internet Information Server
° FrontPage Server Extensions
° Active Server Pages
° ODBC Connection

Master Web
application files

Saves changes locally

Visual InterDev
Project

Changes are sent, when specified,
to master Web

Local Web
application files

Developer Workstation
° Visual InterDev
° Browser
° ODBC Connection

Production

After you have thoroughly tested your application, you will deploy the Web site to a production environment. The user machine now becomes the client machine. A user requests
Web pages from the Web server, and the Web server processes the request by executing
any server-side script and interacting with the database server to send the resulting pages
back to the user's client machine browser. As the user interacts with a page, client-side
script is executed on the client machine, based on certain user events and actions.

Visual InterDev contains some good tools for supporting these phases of developing and
deploying a Web site. Many of them will be discussed in detail on Day 16, "Managing
Your Web Site with Visual InterDev."

Summary

I hope today's lesson has been helpful and piqued your thinking about the application
development process. Many of the things that were discussed today apply to both
client/server and Web-based application development. Other concepts are only pertinent
to Web-based development.

Visual InterDev provides a pretty compelling project model to support your team of
developers. Today's lesson focuses on providing you with an understanding of the project

model to enable you to be successful in your Web development efforts. First, you learned about the different alternative platforms for developing and deploying your application. In this section, the focus is on the benefits, strengths, and limitations of each alternative. You discovered how to use each alternative to enhance your productivity.

Next, you learned about the three working modes that Visual InterDev supports—Master mode, Local mode, and Offline mode. You gained an understanding of how each of these modes works together to provide the right features for your team of developers. You then walked through an example of how to use the Local mode to make isolated changes to your files. You also practiced synchronizing your files with the master Web server.

Q&A

Q Do the Developer Isolation features of Visual InterDev remove the need for source code control software such as Microsoft Visual SourceSafe?

A Not really. Although the working modes provided in Visual InterDev 6 are very robust, you still need to use source code control to provide the maximum benefits for your developers. You will learn more about how to integrate Visual SourceSafe with Visual InterDev during tomorrow's lesson.

Q When should I use Master mode?

A Master mode is typically used when you are the sole developer of an application, and there is no chance of interfering with anyone else's work.

Q Is Local mode the preferred working mode for Visual InterDev projects?

A Any time you have a team of developers, you should use Local mode for your individual development. The ideal scenario involves using the developer isolation features of Local mode with a source code control software package like Visual SourceSafe. These features combine for a very effective environment for your team to thrive.

18

Workshop

The Workshop provides quiz questions to help you solidify your understanding of the material covered and exercises to provide you with experience in using what you've learned. You can find the answers to the quiz questions and exercises in Appendix B, "Answers."

Quiz

1. What is the difference between Master mode and Local mode?

2. Define Offline mode.

3. What is the Visual Component Manager?

Exercises

For today's exercises, grab a few of your friends and test out the developer isolation features of Visual InterDev. Specifically test the following features:

1. Extend the Fitch & Mather demo by further developing some of the pages within the application. Choose Local mode and develop one portion of the Web site while another developer works on his or her portion. Have the other person save her changes to the master Web server. Synchronize your local copy with the master Web server to see the latest changes to the application.

2. Work on the same file within the Fitch & Mather application as another developer while in Local mode. Have him save his changes to the master Web server. Then, save your changes to the master version and see how the two files will be merged.

DAY 19

Effective Team Development with Visual InterDev and Visual SourceSafe

There has been much discourse in recent years about the concepts of efficiency and effectiveness within corporate America. Efficiency and effectiveness can be applied to development projects as well. You must begin with a final goal in mind and chart a course to reach this goal. The art and ability to work effectively with others is paramount to accomplishing your goal. Good interpersonal skills are a critical factor for members of any development team, but that topic is for another book. Today's lesson focuses on the technical effectiveness of a project team. How can team members on an application development team use technology to effectively reach their goal? More specifically, how does Visual InterDev integrate with other products to help you accomplish effective team development?

You will be able to answer both of these questions after completing today's lesson. Specifically, you will learn the following concepts during today's lesson:

- An overview of how Visual InterDev facilitates team development.
- How to integrate Visual SourceSafe with Visual InterDev for maximum team productivity.
- How to check-in/out your files from within the Visual InterDev development environment.
- How to leverage advance features of Visual SourceSafe including comparing and merging file differences, tracking revisions, and rolling back to previous versions of your files.

 Note   All references to Visual SourceSafe in this lesson represent version 6 of the product.

This lesson provides yet another ancillary but important advanced topic that you need to understand to develop your Web-based application effectively.

Visual InterDev Team Support Features

Effective team development tools are a pressing need for information technology managers and developers. For the past three weeks, you have learned about all the powerful bells and whistles of Visual InterDev. Today's lesson focuses on the important question of how Visual InterDev supports your team of developers.

There are two main areas where Visual InterDev can enhance the effectiveness of your development efforts. First, Visual InterDev is completely compatible with Microsoft FrontPage. The compatibility of these products provides effectiveness and improves the productivity of your team members. The second method by which Visual InterDev influences your team's effectiveness is in the area of source code control. You can integrate the power of Microsoft's Visual SourceSafe with Visual InterDev to properly manage your project's file and source code. The following sections expound on these two aspects of Visual InterDev.

FrontPage and Visual InterDev

FrontPage and Visual InterDev are complementary products that combine harmonious features to support the different skill levels of your team. Whereas Visual InterDev provides a robust set of programming tools targeted towards the needs of developers,

FrontPage provides a WYSIWYG development environment that allows you to design and build Web pages without having to know the underlying HTML. Visual InterDev and FrontPage share a common bond through the FrontPage Server Extensions. These extensions enable you to create and maintain Web projects that can be accessed by either tool. In other words, a FrontPage Web is a Visual InterDev Web and vice versa. Figure 19.1 depicts a sample Web development team and their respective tools.

FIGURE 19.1.

A complementary relationship.

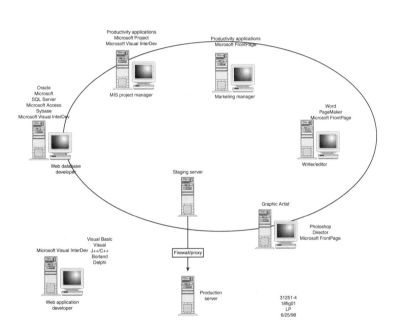

In this example, the development team consists of a marketing person as well as a Web developer/programmer. Although your team could consist of many more types of personnel, including graphics artists and database programmers, the team has been simplified to illustrate the relationship between a Web developer and a less technical person in the Marketing department. For this Web site, the marketing person assumes the role of content author and uses FrontPage to develop and construct the Web pages. By using FrontPage, the marketing person is removed from the intricacies of HTML and other Web technologies and is able to focus on the overall design, layout, and content of the Web site.

The Web developer uses the more powerful Visual InterDev to build and integrate various components as well as to code the application's logic. This more technical person is familiar with HTML, VBScript, Java, ActiveX, and database programming. After the

19

marketing team member authors the content of the Web pages using FrontPage, the developer can extend them by using Visual InterDev to further develop the application, including advanced HTML, scripting logic, and database integration.

The key point in this example is that the developer can leverage the work that is performed by the FrontPage author because the files are completely compatible. This feature enables you to assign the development tasks to the people with the right skills without having to worry about the tools that are used. The marketing person, who possesses the most knowledge on the team about the contents of the Web page, can use the more simplistic FrontPage without having to learn more technical Web topics. Meanwhile, the Web developer, who is more intimate with the underlying technologies, can concentrate on the more technical components of the application and use the power of Visual InterDev to accomplish these tasks.

Visual SourceSafe and Visual InterDev

Another complementary relationship consists of Visual SourceSafe and Visual InterDev. The combination of these two products provides a robust solution for source code control issues among your development team. You may be familiar with version control issues from past client-server projects. This issue only heightens in importance when considering a Web project because of all the various technologies that can be used in your application. Visual InterDev addresses this issue by enabling you to integrate Visual SourceSafe into the mix.

Using Visual SourceSafe, you can control the versions and changes that are made to a Visual InterDev project. Projects that include source code control protect developers from overwriting individual module changes. These controlled projects also prevent developers from organizing different releases, or versions, of the application. Given the frequency of updates to your Web site, the versioning feature can relieve many administrative nightmares. The rest of today's lesson concentrates on the integration and use of the powerful features of Visual SourceSafe and Visual InterDev to manage your Web-based applications effectively.

Integrating Visual SourceSafe with Visual InterDev

You can use the abilities of Visual SourceSafe to get a handle on the contents of your Visual InterDev project. These abilities include general library functions like check-in/check-out, version control, and differential tracking.

Visual InterDev's library functions enable you to check out a specific item in your project, like an HTML Web page or ASP file, just as you would check out a book in a library. After you have finished using the object, you can check the item back in to the Visual SourceSafe database or library.

The version control feature enables you to maintain multiple versions of your application. This feature helps you to properly manage the contents of the different versions and migrate the versions between your different environments. You also can use Visual SourceSafe to track the different versions of your files so that you can compare and contrast the changes. Based on this comparison, you can choose to merge the differences of the versions into one consolidated version, thereby resolving the conflict between the files.

The following sections explore the installation and integration of Visual SourceSafe with your Visual InterDev projects. The latter part of the day demonstrates how to use the features of Visual SourceSafe.

Note

Although you may not have the Visual SourceSafe product, you can still benefit from the topics that are covered in this lesson. Source code control is a major issue that you need to address for your application development teams. Visual SourceSafe is included with Visual Studio 98, Enterprise Edition. You also can purchase the product individually.

Installing Visual SourceSafe

This section is meant to serve as an overview of how to get up and running with Visual SourceSafe in a short amount of time so that you can place your Web projects under its control. This section doesn't present all the nuances of the installation process and configuration parameters, but it does guide you through the process of installing the server component of Visual SourceSafe, setting up the users, and using Visual SourceSafe's features within Visual InterDev.

Note

This section explains the general process of integrating the two products and is not meant to cover every detail of the Visual SourceSafe installation process. Refer to the Visual SourceSafe documentation for more detail on this process.

19

The first step is to run the setup program for Visual SourceSafe, which displays an introductory dialog window, enabling you to enter a directory location for the product. You should choose a secure but accessible directory on the server machine that supports your development project. You will then be able to install the Visual SourceSafe server.

 Note

> If you are installing SourceSafe on a Windows 95 computer with Personal Web Server, you may need to download and install the Distributed Component Object Model (DCOM), which can be found at http://www.microsoft.com/search/default.asp. When you get to this Web site, search for DCOM.

You will receive a confirmation message upon completion of this process.

Setting Up the Users

After you have installed Visual SourceSafe on the server, you need to set up access to the SourceSafe database for all the users (developers). You can configure this access by accessing the Visual SourceSafe Administrator tool from the Windows Start menu. Upon opening this tool, you will see the main window, as depicted in Figure 19.2.

FIGURE 19.2.

The Visual SourceSafe Administrator.

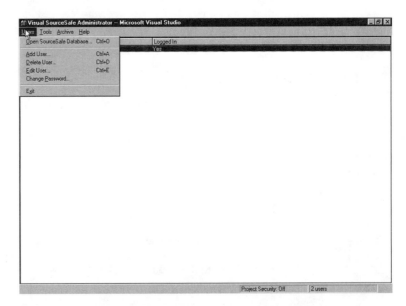

This administrator tool enables you to configure users for your SourceSafe projects as well as establish characteristics and properties for your project databases. The main window displays the users who have already been established for Visual SourceSafe access.

To provide access for your individual developers, select Add User from the Users menu. The Add User dialog window appears, as shown in Figure 19.3.

FIGURE 19.3.

Adding a new user.

From this window, you can enter a username and password as well as specify that the person has read-only access to a project database. If you don't check the Read Only box, the person will be able to read and write to the project database. After you have established the users, you are ready to use the Visual SourceSafe features from within Visual InterDev.

> **Note**
>
> For Windows NT servers, the installation process should, by default, install the anonymous user account IUSR_*computername*, where *computername* is the name of the NT server machine. You can verify the name of this account by running the User Manager For Domains application that is included with Windows NT Server. If this name doesn't appear in the user list, you will need to add the anonymous account using the method as just described. You don't need to enter a password, nor do you need to check the Read Only box.

Placing a Project Under Its Spell

After you install Visual SourceSafe and set up the developers, you can configure a Visual InterDev project to use its source code control capabilities. You can either open an existing project or create a new one to take advantage of these features. Both processes are examined in the following sections.

Enlisting Version Control on an Existing Project

To enable source code control features for an existing project:

1. Open the project within Visual InterDev.

2. From the Project Explorer, select the project name and choose the Project menu.

3. Choose Source Control | Add to Source. A dialog box containing a confirmation message appears, explaining the process that you are initiating (see Figure 19.4).

19

FIGURE 19.4.

Enabling source control for an existing project.

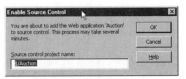

This dialog window displays the name for the source control project that you're establishing. This name will be used by Visual SourceSafe to establish a database entry for the project and to manage and maintain its files and components. The name consists of a $ (dollar) sign and a / (forward slash) along with the name of the Visual InterDev project. All source code control project names must contain the $/ prefix. It is recommended that you use the default name that is provided and click OK to place the project under the control of Visual SourceSafe. When the process is complete, you will receive a confirmation message similar to the one shown in Figure 19.5.

FIGURE 19.5.

Confirming the process.

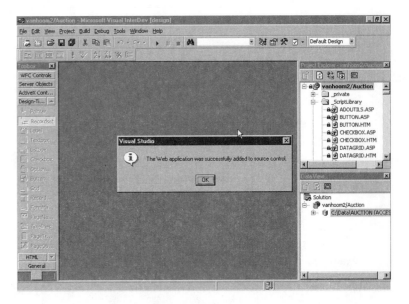

After the process is complete, the source control features will be in effect for your project. Enabling a project for source control affects all the other projects within that particular Web. For example, after a project for a specific Web has been configured for source control, all the other projects within that Web also are enabled for this feature. After the process completes for the first project, a developer for another project within that Web can open or refresh his or her project to experience the source control features.

Creating a New Project

You also can integrate source control into new Visual InterDev projects that you create. Use the Web Project Wizard to initiate the process of creating a new Web site. If you create a project for a new Web site, you will need to follow the same steps listed in the previous section after the wizard has finished to activate source control for the new project. If the project that you're creating is associated with an existing Web site that already contains source control, the newly created project will also contain source control.

Determining the Characteristics of the Project

One way to verify whether a Web project has been enabled for source control is to right-click the name of the project in the project workspace. You can then choose Properties from the list of menu items to display the Properties window for the project. Click the Master Web Server tab, shown in Figure 19.6, to view properties of the project's master Web server.

FIGURE 19.6.

A project under source control.

From this window you can see that source control has been enabled for this Web server and project. The name of the source control project also is displayed in the middle of this window.

After you have enabled source control for a project, you will notice new icons located beside the files within the Project Explorer, as shown in Figure 19.7.

FIGURE 19.7.

A new set of icons.

19

Notice in Figure 19.7 that a padlock appears next to the project name as well as a connection icon. These icons visually identify that the project is connected and enabled for source control. You will also notice that all the filenames have a lock next to them indicating that they are locked into source control.

Adding Files to a Source Controlled Project

After you enable source control for an existing or new project, every file that you add or create for the project will be added to the source control database. You must ensure that you add the files through the Visual InterDev method to assume the source control characteristics instead of copying the files using the file system. To add a file to your project within Visual InterDev, you can right-click the mouse button on the project name and select Add.

Disabling Source Control

To remove source control from a project, perform the following steps:

1. Open the project within Visual InterDev.

2. From the Project Explorer, select the project name and choose the Project menu.

3. Choose Source Control | Disconnect Web Project. A dialog box containing a confirmation message will display, explaining the process that you are initiating.

This feature turns off the source control features within Visual InterDev, but it doesn't delete the Visual SourceSafe project database. If you decide to activate source control on this same project, it is reattached to the existing Visual SourceSafe project database. Figure 19.8 displays the Property Pages dialog box for a project that is not enabled for source control.

FIGURE 19.8.

A project that is not under source control.

Notice the clear and concise message in the middle of this window, indicating that source control hasn't been enabled for this Web server or project.

Caution Because the Visual SourceSafe database entry isn't deleted when you disable source control, you need to be careful about turning source control repeatedly on and off. If you disable source control for a project, delete some files, and then turn source control back on, the files that you delete reappear within the Visual InterDev project workspace. This scenario exists because the project workspace retrieves the entries from the Visual SourceSafe project database when source control is re-enabled. To resolve this conflict, you can use Visual SourceSafe to remove the files directly from the database for this project.

Unleashing the Power of Visual SourceSafe

This section demonstrates some of the more robust features of Visual SourceSafe concerning the library functions. Visual SourceSafe and Visual InterDev combine to properly monitor and control the files contained in your project. These tools support effective team development by promoting the integration of individual components while not allowing your developers to interfere with each other's work. This uncanny ability is the measure of a tool's worth to a development team. You must be able to answer the following questions to weigh any tool's value:

- Can the tool support my team in achieving my purpose without getting in the way or hindering me along the way?
- Can the tool enhance the productivity of my team in this endeavor?

With the integration of Visual InterDev and Visual SourceSafe, you can definitely answer these questions with a resounding *yes*!

Using the Library Functions

You can access the check-in/check-out library functions from within the Visual InterDev development environment. This feature enables developers to exclusively reserve files contained within the Web project. The developer can make any changes to the file and then check the file back in to the Visual SourceSafe project database. There are two basic modes of checking out a file—Exclusive Check Out and Multiple Check Outs. Exclusive Check Out is the Visual SourceSafe default and allows only one user to check out a file. While the file is checked out, or reserved, other developers may be permitted to access a read-only copy of the file. When the developer is through making the changes and the updates are sent back to Visual SourceSafe, other developers can reserve a copy to make their updates.

The other mode, Multiple Check Outs, allows more than one person to check out the same file at a time. I will discuss this feature later in the section "Checking In Your Files."

19

Note The ability to update a file is contingent upon the access privileges that have been established for that user.

Checking Out Your Files

To check out a file within your project, right-click the file within the Visual InterDev Project Explorer and choose Check Out from the shortcut menu. The name of the file that you have selected will also appear as part of the menu item. Because source control has been enabled for the project, the Check Out Items dialog box will display, as shown in Figure 19.9.

FIGURE 19.9.

Checking out a file.

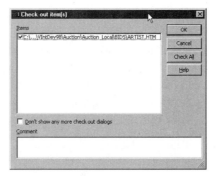

This dialog box displays the item or items that you have selected to check out. You can check out multiple files at a time. A check box in the middle of the window enables you to hide the dialog box for future check-outs. For example, if you have been assigned a module that is exclusively yours to develop, you may want to select this check box so that you won't have to see this window every time you access the file. There is also a place to add comments to explain the reason for checking out the file. After you click OK, the file will be checked out and you can proceed to make updates to it. Notice that a check mark now appears next to the name of the file in the Project Explorer, indicating that the file has been checked out (see Figure 19.10).

FIGURE 19.10.

A file that has been checked out.

Tip

Files in the Project Explorer that appear in color are write-enabled, whereas read-only copies appear gray.

Checking In Your Files

As you make changes to the file, you can perform intermittent saves to the file, which will save the file in the local and/or master Web applications depending on the working mode for your project. Remember from yesterday's lesson that while working in Master mode, saves that you make will automatically update both the local and master versions of your application. Local mode differs in that it allows you to isolate your changes from the master Web application and then synchronize your files with the master Web when you are finished making changes. One important thing to remember is that saving a file does not update your changes to the SourceSafe database.

Caution

You must check the file back in to update the source control version.

To check a file back into the SourceSafe database, complete the following:

1. Select the file from within the Project Explorer.
2. Right-click the file and choose Check In from the shortcut menu. An alternative method is to select the file in the Project Explorer, and choose Project | Source Control | Check In.

A confirmation dialog box appears, as shown in Figure 19.11.

FIGURE 19.11.

Checking in a file.

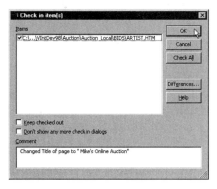

19

This dialog window enables you to check one or more items and add comments describing the changes that were made to the file. You can also indicate that you want to keep the file checked out after you check in your current updates to the SourceSafe database. If you need to see the different versions of the file that have been maintained in the source control database, you can click the Differences button. If you are checking in multiple files, you can choose to use the entered comment for all files that you edit.

Suppose that you needed to make a change to multiple files in your project. You should enter a meaningful comment for the updates in the space provided. All too many times I have seen developers who didn't take the time to document their code.

The ability to enter comments is very helpful in enabling you to document the changes in your code for future reference. There are two main benefits to tracking your changes with comments. First, if something goes wrong and the change that you made now causes the server to crash, you can use the comments to trace the problem back to the change that you made. Second, it's very helpful for other team members to understand your code, in case they end up supporting and testing it. If the changes that you make are properly documented, the team members can better understand the code's history.

Discarding the Changes

Another option that is available from the file's shortcut menu is Undo Check Out. This option enables you to ignore and discard any updates that you have made to the file. If you choose this option, the file is sent back to the server without the updates you have made. When you select this option, you are prompted with a confirmation message, as shown in Figure 19.12.

FIGURE 19.12.

Discarding the changes.

You have the option of discarding changes to this file or discarding the updates to all the files you have changed. Clicking Cancel abandons this process, enabling you to make further updates.

Using Advanced Features of Visual SourceSafe

Visual SourceSafe offers many robust and advanced features that can be used in accordance with Visual InterDev to properly manage your Web project. This section explores the Visual SourceSafe environment and provides an overview of some of the more useful features.

Note   This section of the chapter assumes that you're using Visual SourceSafe on the server as an administrator. This section covers the use of some of the more powerful features you can use for your Web project within the Visual SourceSafe environment. At the end of today's lesson you will learn about a method to further integrate these features into Visual InterDev so that you can execute them from the project workspace.

Exploring the Visual SourceSafe Environment

The Visual SourceSafe environment resembles the Windows Explorer environment and gives you easy access to the files within your Web project. Figure 19.13 depicts the Visual SourceSafe Explorer.

FIGURE 19.13.

Visual SourceSafe unveiled.

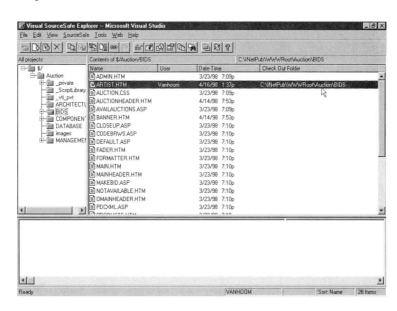

19

Your projects are listed in the pane to the left, while the contents of the currently selected project are displayed on the right side of the environment. The Visual SourceSafe Explorer operates just like the Windows Explorer in that you can access and interact with folders and files on the directory tree by clicking and double-clicking the mouse buttons.

Figure 19.13 depicts a sample Web project. The files that contain a red check mark over their icon represent files that have been checked out. The name of the user who has checked out the files as well as the folder that contains the reserved files is also displayed with these files.

From this window, you can right-click to display the shortcut menu, as shown in Figure 19.14.

FIGURE 19.14.

Displaying the options of the shortcut menu.

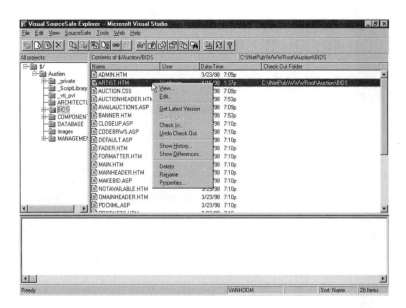

Table 19.1 describes each of the options on the shortcut menu.

TABLE 19.1. SHORTCUT MENU OPTIONS.

Item	Description
View	Enables you to view the file
Edit	Opens a copy in a working folder that you can edit
Get Latest Version	Retrieves the most up-to-date version of the file
Check Out	Reserves a copy of the file
Check In	Checks the file back into the project

Item	Description
Undo Check Out	Reverses the reservation of a file
Show History	Displays a history of updates to the file
Show Differences	Displays the differences between two or more versions of a file
Delete	Deletes the files
Rename	Renames a file
Properties	Displays the Properties window for a file

Viewing the History of a File

The Show History option is a very valuable feature that enables you to view the history of updates to a file and track the individual changes to your files and why they are made. When you select Show History for a particular file, the window in Figure 19.15 appears.

FIGURE 19.15.

Viewing the history of a file.

This window displays a list box that shows the history of changes to a particular file. The first column in the list box reveals the version number, which is automatically generated by Visual SourceSafe. The next few columns display who made the change, the date the change was made, and the action that was taken regarding the change.

From this window, you can choose to view the file as well as get a working copy of the file that you can edit. You also can see more details about a particular change that was made as well as view the differences between the different versions of the files. This window also enables you to roll back to a previous version of a file, given you have the right authority (which includes read/write access).

Seeing the Differences

Visual SourceSafe enables you to view the differences between two or more versions of a file. This feature is helpful in resolving conflicts between versions of a file and can help you roll back to a previous version of a file. To effectively use this feature, open the Show History dialog window for the desired file. Then select the versions of the file that you want to compare. You can select multiple files by using the combination of the right mouse button and the Ctrl key. Click an item in the list to select the first item. Next, press the Ctrl key and click each additional file that you want to select. After selecting all the files that you want to compare, click the Diff button. The Differences dialog window displays, as shown in Figure 19.16.

FIGURE 19.16.

Examining the differences.

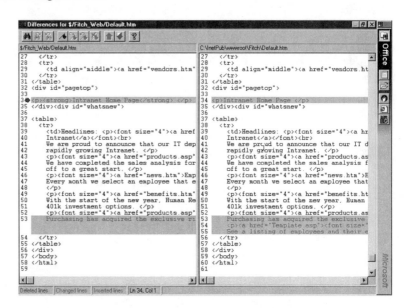

All the differences between the files will be highlighted, enabling you to compare and contrast the versions. The status bar at the bottom of the window defines the color-coded syntax contained in the files. This legend helps you discern what has been added, changed, and deleted.

Further Integrating the Features of Visual SourceSafe

Now that you have learned about the available features from within Visual SourceSafe, take a look at the tight integration of these features from within Visual InterDev.

Examining the Remnants of Visual SourceSafe

You can execute many of the Visual SourceSafe functions from within the Visual InterDev IDE (integrated development environment). To discover these options, choose the project root and select Project | Source Control. You will see the SourceSafe features available within Visual InterDev, as shown in Figure 19.17.

FIGURE 19.17.

Examining the capabilities.

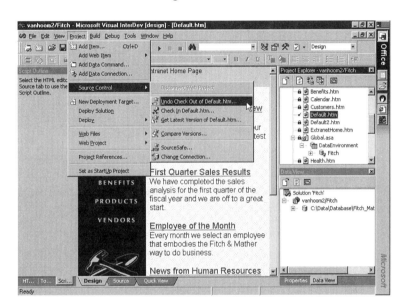

You now have the ability to execute many of the SourceSafe features from within Visual InterDev, including an option to start Visual SourceSafe. These features give your developers a lot of power and flexibility in accomplishing their tasks.

As you can see, the combination of Visual SourceSafe and Visual InterDev provides the support you need to effectively work in harmony with your other team members.

Summary

Unity in diversity is the central theme of effective team development. For an application development project to be a success, you must be able to bring together various people, processes, and technologies to work toward a common goal. You have discovered today how Visual InterDev facilitates effective team development through its integration with other tools. The harmonious relationship that exists between Visual InterDev and FrontPage brings together people of different backgrounds and skills for the good of the application. The synergy and tight integration that exists between Visual InterDev and

Visual SourceSafe enables developers to achieve maximum productivity through the proper management and control of the application's files and content.

During the first part of the day, you learned the importance of effective team development and how Visual InterDev promotes the productivity of your team members. Specifically, the lesson explains how Visual InterDev and FrontPage can be used on your project to enable different members of your team to be productive. You also learned about the tight integration that exists between Visual InterDev and Visual SourceSafe and why source code control is important.

The lesson then demonstrates how Visual SourceSafe can be integrated with Visual InterDev. You received a personal tour through the process—from installing Visual SourceSafe to enabling source control for your Visual InterDev project. Next, the lesson provides an overview of the robust features of Visual SourceSafe. You gained an understanding of these features and learned how to take advantage of them within the Visual InterDev and Visual SourceSafe environments. Throughout the day, the lesson illustrates how the marriage of Visual InterDev and Visual SourceSafe can definitely increase the productivity and effectiveness of your development team.

This lesson provides you with the knowledge you need to work effectively with others. There still may be interpersonal conflicts that arise during the course of your projects, but at least you won't have developers writing over each other's code.

Q&A

Q **Now that Visual InterDev has a Design Editor that performs WYSIWYG editing, is there still a need for FrontPage?**

A In short, yes. The two tools complement each other very nicely. FrontPage provides a non-intimidating tool that is specifically geared toward the more functional end-user. The lesson today provides insight into how you can use FrontPage with Visual InterDev. The results that are produced by FrontPage can be used within your Visual InterDev projects, enabling team members with different skill sets to work in congruence. The Design Editor within Visual InterDev provides a powerful feature within a powerful tool that is targeted toward developers.

Q **Should I use Visual SourceSafe to edit files contained in my Visual InterDev project?**

A While this capability does exist, you should not edit your Visual InterDev project files using Visual SourceSafe. As a general rule, you should use the Visual InterDev development environment and tools to make all updates to your project files. In this way, you can be assured of the results of your application. You should, however, take advantage of the integrated features that are available by integrating the two products.

Workshop

The Workshop provides quiz questions to help you solidify your understanding of the material covered. The exercises provide you with experience in using what you've learned. You can find the answers to the quiz questions and exercises in Appendix B, "Answers."

Quiz

1. What is the command that enables you to activate source control for your Visual InterDev project?

2. What happens when you disable source control for your Visual InterDev project?

3. Describe the Visual SourceSafe library functions.

Exercises

Today's exercises extend the lesson for today by enabling you to practice using the integrated features of Visual SourceSafe:

1. Create a Visual InterDev project and enable the source control for the project. You also should make several updates to one of your Web pages and then compare the differences of the versions to understand how this process works.

2. When you have accomplished this step, use Visual InterDev to create some files for your project. These files can consist of HTML pages, ASP files, images, and any other item that you want to include. As you develop these components, notice the behavior of Visual InterDev as the Visual SourceSafe features are enforced.

3. Practice merging different versions of files as well as rolling back to a different version of a file from within the Visual InterDev environment.

19

DAY 20

Designing an Effective Site with the Site Designer

The design and development of a Web-based application is a very intricate process. The application can be implemented rapidly, but you should definitely spend adequate time planning the end result. With proper planning, you can create an application that is a success both in your eyes and in the eyes of your users. Today's lesson focuses on the most important aspects to consider when designing and developing your Web-based applications.

Upon completing this lesson, you will be able to

- Apply effective user interface design for your Web-based application.
- Explain the pros and cons of using browser-specific extensions.
- Design your Web site with the Visual InterDev Site Designer.
- Add, arrange, and organize your Web site pages.

- Create the proper navigation design for your Web site.
- Apply a considerations checklist when designing your Web site.

Effective User Interface Design

User interface design is one of the most important aspects of your application. You may personally prefer talking about the intricacies of ActiveX controls or C++ programming, and you may want to spend more time developing new components and class libraries that are fast and efficient.

No matter how much you enjoy other phases of development, however, you can't overlook the most important customer of the application: the user. If users don't want to experience your application, your miraculous code will be banished by your users and the Web community and dissipate in a vast wasteland of despair.

I have been a student of user interface design since my COBOL mainframe days. Those are days that I would like to forget. We have come a long way, through advances in the Macintosh and OS/2 interfaces to all the Windows interfaces, including Windows 3.1 and Windows 95. I have truly enjoyed studying as well as writing about each of these new developments and the promises that they exhibited.

Today developers have to contend with the Web interface. From a computing model, some say that we have gone back in time to the mainframe, dumb-terminal days. I personally think we have finally figured out a way to effectively use the client/server model of computing. Whatever the case, there is a new challenge: to use the browser to exploit the advantages of the World Wide Web.

The following list outlines some basic steps to consider when designing an effective user interface for your Web-based application:

1. Define a purpose for the interface.
2. Identify the users' expectations and needs.
3. Design the user interface.
4. Conduct usability testing.
5. Incorporate the feedback into your interface.

Define a Purpose for the Interface

The first step involved in creating an effective user interface is to define the purpose of your interface and how that purpose accomplishes the mission of your application. Why are the users here? Why should someone use your application? Defining a purpose sets the context for how you will present the information and application to the user. If you can't define why your pages exist, why should users visit your application?

In defining a purpose for your interface, you should consider the following things:

- Content: What information should be included?
- Audience: Who is the target audience?
- User benefits: What benefit will the users gain from the application?

Identify the Users' Needs and Expectations

While building applications, developers often take an overbearing parent approach to programming. This method could also be called the "I-know-what's-best approach." This approach is analogous to a father or mother who takes action for their son or daughter based solely on their knowledge of the situation. The parent forms an opinion that is one-sided and then acts on that knowledge without seeking to understand the child's point of view. Likewise, developers design and build an application without consulting the end user and are distraught when the users don't appreciate the finished product. Many times this situation is due to a lack of communication between developers and end users.

This is the next step in designing an effective interface. Talk to the users. Find out their expectations for your application. Identify their specific needs. You can answer these questions by conducting user interviews or focus group sessions.

In facilitating these discussions, you need to make sure that you establish a specific agenda and that these meetings don't become gripe sessions about current applications. Keep the group focused on the issue at hand. The use of a white board can really facilitate good discussion during a meeting with your users. Using the white board, you can construct a flowchart of the Web pages and outline specific implementation objectives for each page. You also can scope out the basic design of the Web pages and application. For example, you may want to limit the amount of information that is distributed to the client to 50KB. Accomplishing these tasks can take several sessions but will save you much grief and sorrow in the long run.

20

Design the User Interface

After you have defined the purpose and have identified the users' needs and expectations, you're ready to begin designing the interface for your application. In designing the interface, you need to choose a metaphor that is easy and intuitive to use and understand. You may be thinking that you don't have many choices in the matter because the browser is the metaphor. Whereas the browser does serve as the universal client for all users, you have many choices concerning the design of your Web pages. Just as with client/server applications and tools, you have many objects, designs, and tools to choose from. You need to make sure that you use the tools in your toolbox wisely. Don't consider every-thing a nail just because you have a hammer. Proper discernment and consideration is crucial in designing your interface.

Before you begin designing individual pages, you need to consider the overall flow of the application. A roadmap is very helpful for defining the links and possible paths that your users can take. The Web presents a greater challenge than client/server applications in that the users have more flexibility in choosing the route that they take. Users may enter a certain page in your hierarchy without passing through the default home page first. Your application must be able to account for this situation and present the user with choices for navigating through your application. Figure 20.1 illustrates a roadmap for a sample Web site.

FIGURE 20.1.

Visualizing the final product.

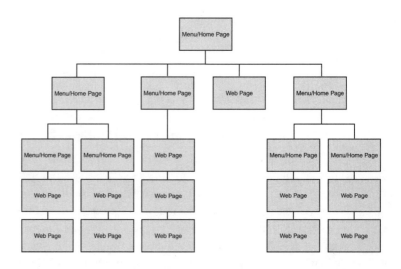

A roadmap for your Web-based application can help you visualize the final product. As shown in Figure 20.1, the menu structure is balanced and isn't too deep or shallow. Your application should provide relevant access to information within three levels of menus. If they don't receive the access to information or tasks within this range, don't expect them to become a return customer. A Web site full of menus provides very tedious navigation for the user. Likewise, a Web site that only contains a collection of pages with little or no coordination isn't very intuitive. You must be careful to design your application so that it balances logical organization with timely access to information and action. In diagram-ming your roadmap, you also need to make sure that there are no dead ends. A dead end is a Web page that doesn't provide a path to any other pages within your Web site. The only way to leave this page is to use the navigational buttons supplied by the browser.

Think about how you feel when you take a wrong turn down a dead-end street with no warning. You feel frustrated. You say to yourself that you will never come in this neighborhood again. Users react to your applications in the same way if they have no defined navigation path to other areas in your site. From every page, a user must be able to choose a course. You might be tempted to rely on browser menus or option buttons that provide back-and-forward scrolling options. Don't submit to this alluring temptation. You should take as much control of user choices as you can so that you can guide their experience. Your users should receive the full benefit of your Web site, and the best way to accomplish this is to present the user with options.

Note   Visual InterDev provides several methods for designing the appropriate navigation for your site including the Site Designer and the PageNavBar design-time control. You will learn how to use both of these features later in the day beginning with the section "Construct Your Web Site with the Site Designer."

After you have created a roadmap, the next step is to choose a metaphor for your application. This decision will drive the design of the individual pages and components that fit into your application. You can use many different designs. You can choose a basic Web page, including heading and body sections. The use of frames also can be used. You can choose to provide a very graphical experience so that users can click images and other multimedia options. You can use the Virtual Reality Modeling Language (VRML) to provide a 3D metaphor for virtual exploration of a physical site.

After you make a selection, you need to use this metaphor throughout your application to provide a consistent look and feel to the user. For example, choosing a frame-based metaphor means that you need to use frames for each of your Web pages. The overall goal is to choose the metaphor that will best suit the needs of your users.

After you select the metaphor, you can begin designing the individual pages. On any development effort, the use of style guidelines can significantly augment programmer productivity and drastically eliminate design inconsistencies. You should create common templates for each of your developers, content authors, and graphic artists so that they can complete their specific piece of the application puzzle. The use of cascading style sheets, which you learned about on Day 4, "WYSIWYG Editing with Visual InterDev," can also greatly enhance the team's productivity.

20

Other design considerations include the following:

- Aesthetics
- Page design and layout
- Semantics
- Navigation

Aesthetics

You need to design an interface that is aesthetically, or visually, pleasing to the user. The application should provide a rich and rewarding experience for the user. Most people interpret this point to mean that they need to go overboard on the use of images and graphics. Consider the hammer and nail discussion again. You must choose the tools that you use to create your interface carefully. Moderation is the best guideline to follow concerning any of the tools that you have available. Color should also be used properly. Use color to enhance, not overshadow, the content of your application.

Page Design and Layout

The design of your pages is paramount to the success of the application. Your pages should employ a common look and feel that is consistent across the application. You should present information in the same way where possible. You need to use the proper tool for presenting your information in the best way. Use color, where appropriate, to highlight useful information. Images and graphics can add a lot to your application. Be sure that you consider the placement and performance of these objects when designing your pages.

You also must logically organize the layout of your pages. Regardless of the metaphor that you choose, most pages will contain a header area, a body, and a footer area. The header area should include title and heading information for the page. The body section will contain the detailed information part of your application. The body section will be different based on the metaphor you choose. The key point is to make sure that your information is logically organized on the page. Remember that people read top to bottom and left to right. Design the layout of your application accordingly. The footer section usually includes copyright and usage information as well as the contact name and email address for the Web page.

Your Web page design should be consistent with your application's purpose. The interface should facilitate the accomplishment of the application's mission and enable users to receive a rewarding experience.

Semantics

Semantics refers to how you present meaning to your user through the design of your Web pages. You use different visual cues to convey this meaning. For example, you may use certain images to portray concepts about your application and Web pages. Make sure that the image you choose is a good representation of the concept you're communicating. The user should clearly understand what the symbol means. If you feel there could be some confusion, use another visual cue.

Navigation

A user must be able to easily and properly navigate through your application. You can use the header and footer areas of your page to provide navigational cues to guide the users in their journey. Examples include toolbars, tabs, and textual hyperlinks to other pages in your application.

You should make sure that you inform the users where they are in the application. Don't assume that they know where they are or where they're going. You need to effectively present them with options about where to travel next. Remember the example of dead-end streets? Providing navigational links is one way to avoid a dead-end Web page. You need to be cognizant of the fact that users may enter detailed pages in your Web hierarchy through another Web page. You should provide a technique for navigating to your home page so that users receive the full experience of your Web site. Search utilities also are nice for first time and experienced users. For first time users, a search engine can help overcome information overload by providing a utility to find their required information or action. For experienced users, the search utility provides a big time-saver for navigating to an exact location or service.

Conduct Usability Testing

You should continue to evaluate the usefulness and usability of your Web-based application throughout the development process. Does the application achieve its mission and purpose? Does the application enable the user to achieve his or her needs? You need to designate time in your development plan for usability testing. A team member as well as some of your end users should perform this task. Monitor their effectiveness at using the application to accomplish their tasks. Note those areas in the application where there is confusion or concern.

You also should record the strengths of the interface for future reference for other applications. During this process, you need to involve development team members, including your programmers, content authors, and graphic artists. These team members will be able to gain firsthand insight and feedback from watching the users and can incorporate this knowledge into constructing a more user-friendly interface.

The best way to conduct usability testing is to develop a script for some of the most important tasks that a typical user would want to accomplish. For example, a task for a sales order entry application may be to place an order for an item. You should group these tasks into cycles. A cycle consists of a certain number of steps to carry out a specific task. In other words, the steps would be everything the user needed to accomplish to place an order for an item using your application. Figure 20.2 demonstrates a sample form for documenting a usability test.

FIGURE 20.2.

A sample form.

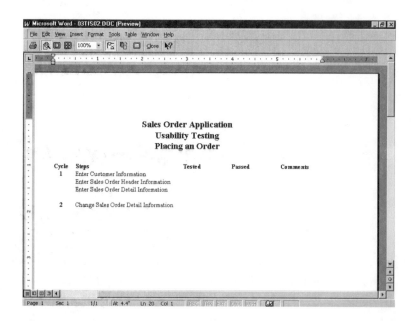

This form is for scripting the user actions. Another form can be downloaded from the Macmillan Web site for documenting the results, strengths, and opportunities for improvement. Figure 20.3 shows the layout of this form.

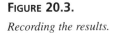

FIGURE 20.3.

Recording the results.

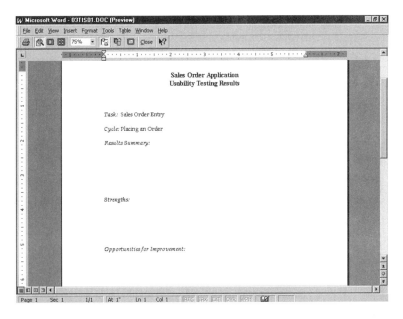

> **Note**
>
> These forms aren't rigid standards and can be adapted for a variety of purposes. Perhaps usability is a new concept to you, and you have never really considered performing these tests before you deploy your application. Whatever the case, usability is important, and you should consider the concepts that are mentioned in this section.

Usability is usually performed during the system testing stage of a development project. I overheard a conversation the other day in which a project manager was talking to one of his developers. The project manager asked the programmer if he was going to perform a system test on the application that would include a usability test. The programmer answered with a very confident response, "No, I am going to deploy the application and let the users figure it out!" Don't wait until your application is deployed to absorb feedback from users. Be proactive.

20

Incorporate the Feedback into Your Interface

After you conduct the usability test and document the results, you should evaluate the strengths and possible opportunities for improvement in your application. You need to assess what the user feels comfortable with and where the user needs further assistance. The opportunities for improvements relate directly to possible changes to the application.

You should prioritize each of these changes and analyze the time and effort needed to make each change. Does the benefit to the user outweigh the cost to make the change and delay deployment of your application? If the benefit is greater than the cost, make the change. If the cost is greater than the benefit, document the change for possible implementation later. You need to communicate to your users why the change wasn't made and that it will be considered in future releases.

Construct Your Web Site with the Site Designer

Now that you realize the importance design bears on the success of your application, it would be great to have a tool that facilitates the design process. Visual InterDev provides a tool to accomplish this task. You can rapidly design and prototype a Web site using the Visual InterDev Site Designer. You may already be familiar with this feature if you have used the Navigation View found in FrontPage 98. The Site Designer enables you to create, add, and organize pages in your Web site as well as provide the overall navigation for the site. You can also use the Site Designer to redesign existing Web sites. The Site Designer accomplishes this task by enabling you to create a site diagram. During this part of the lesson, you will learn how to use the Site Designer and apply the design principles that have been discussed so far.

Creating a Site Diagram

Using the Site Designer, you can create site diagrams that graphically portray the layout and structure of your Web site. Site diagrams accelerate the design process by enabling you to create the pages and structure for your application. You can create new pages as well as add existing pages from your Web application and other Web applications. The visual nature of the Site Designer enables you to create the right relationships and structure for your Web site as shown in Figure 20.4.

As you can see from Figure 20.4, the Site Designer provides a visual workspace for you to design the organization of your Web site. A special Site Diagram menu also appears providing you the most relevant options or commands for working with and organizing your site diagram. Table 20.1 outlines each of these menu options and their purpose.

TABLE 20.1. SITE DIAGRAM MENU OPTIONS.

Menu Option	Description
New HTML Page	Adds an HTML or ASP page to the diagram
Add Existing Page	Enables you to add an existing page from a current project or another project

Menu option	Description
Add Home Page	Adds a home page
Add to Global Navigation Bar	Adds page to the global navigation bar for the site
Reorder pages	Reorders the pages on the global navigation bar for the site
Delete	Deletes the page from the site diagram and the project
Remove	Removes the page from the site diagram
Expand	Expands the site diagram view
Rotate	Enables you to rotate the site diagram
Zoom	Enables you to zoom in on specific areas of the site diagram

FIGURE 20.4.

The Visual InterDev Site Designer.

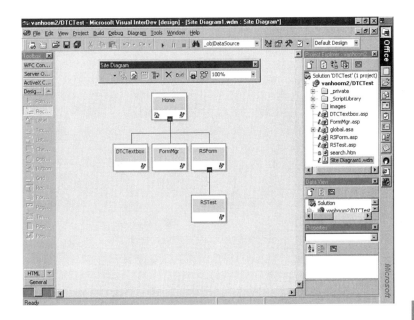

Let's walk through an example of how to utilize the Site Designer when prototyping an application. The following example will guide you through this process:

1. Create a Web project called `SiteDesign`. Make sure that you include a `search.htm` page when walking through the Web Project Wizard. For now, don't choose a layout or theme. You will apply those items later.

2. Right-click the project root in the Project Explorer and select Add, Site Diagram from the shortcut menu.

20

You can also add a site diagram by choosing Add Item from the Project menu.

3. With the New tab selected, choose Site Diagram from the list of items. Change the Name of the site diagram to SDIntranet.wdm and click Open. Figure 20.5 displays the results of your actions so far.

FIGURE 20.5.

An initial view of a site diagram.

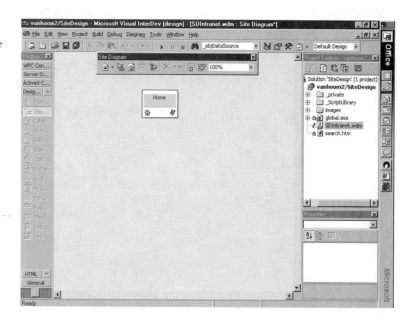

When you initially create a site diagram, the Site Designer creates a home page for your site. The Site Designer also provides a work area for you to add new or existing pages to the diagram as shown in Figure 20.5.

Creating New Pages for the Site

Because you are designing a site diagram for a new site, the next step is to add and organize the pages in the site. To accomplish this task, complete the following steps:

1. With the Home Page selected, choose New HTML Page from the Diagram menu. A new page will be added to the site diagram with a default name of Page1. Notice that the page is automatically related and linked to the home page. I will discuss the different types of relationships in a later section.

2. Click the text Page1 in the box for this page as demonstrated in Figure 20.6.

FIGURE 20.6.

Changing the name of the page.

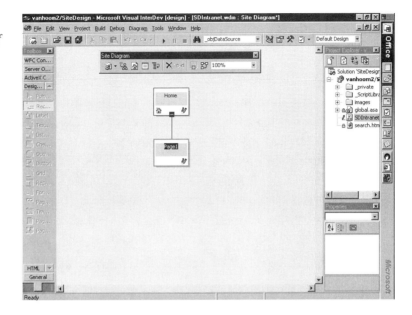

3. With the text highlighted, enter the name What's New for this page.

4. Choose Properties for the What's New page to see the URL that was created from this action. You will notice that the title of the page is What's New and the URL link to the page assumes the name of What'sNew.htm.

5. Right-click the Home Page and choose Properties to see its name and URL link. Notice that for the home page, the Site Designer created a title of Home but a URL link of default.htm. If you change the name of the Home Page using the technique described in step 3, it won't affect the actual Home Page filename. By design, the Site Designer associates the URL name of default.htm for home pages within a site diagram.

20

Note

The naming convention used for URL link names for the files will actually vary depending on the Web server that you are using. In general, if you are using Internet Information Server, the Site Designer will specify a URL link name of default.asp. When using Personal Web Server, the Site Designer will create a URL link name of default.htm.

> **Tip**
> Using the Property page, you can change the name of the title and URL link for the page.

6. From the Site Diagram view, select the Home page.

7. Click the drop-down list box next to the New HTML Page icon. This action will display two choices for adding a new page.

8. Choose New ASP Page from the list of options.

9. You should now see a page titled Page2 associated with the Home Page. Click the Page2 text and change the name of the title to Employee Listing.

10. View the Property page for this page. Notice that the title of this page is Employee Listing and the URL link is EmployeeListing.asp.

> **Tip**
> You can also use the most common commands for a site diagram such as adding HTML or ASP pages by right-clicking the mouse anywhere on the Site diagram workspace, as shown in Figure 20.7.

FIGURE 20.7.

Accessing commonly used site diagram menu options.

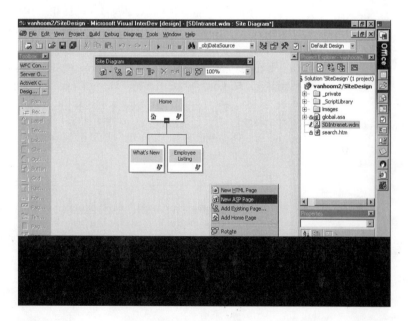

Adding Existing Pages to the Site Diagram

You may also want to add existing pages to a site diagram. These could include pages from the existing project or other projects that you have already created. For example, you may have already implemented an application and want to include some pages from that in an application that you are creating. Using the existing project, let's add some existing pages to the site diagram:

1. With no current page on the diagram selected, choose Add Existing Page from the Diagram menu. The Choose URL dialog box appears, as shown in Figure 20.8.

FIGURE 20.8.

Adding an existing page to a site diagram.

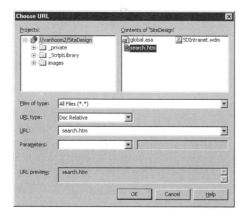

2. Choose the search.htm file from the items in the Contents section on the right side of this dialog box.

3. Drag the Search page up near the home page. When you see a visible link being established between the two pages, drop the Search page at that location on the site diagram. This method is demonstrated in Figure 20.9.

In this example, you added the Search page, which was previously created when you created the project, to the site diagram. You used the Site Diagram menu option to perform this task. You can also drag and drop files directly from the Visual InterDev Project Explorer into the site diagram. Moreover, you can add pages from other applications such as Microsoft Internet Explorer and Microsoft FrontPage. The following example walks you through the process of adding a page from Internet Explorer:

1. Make sure you are connected to the Internet and browse to one of my favorite sites:

   www.bsiconsulting.com

20

FIGURE 20.9.

FIGURE 20.9.

Establishing a relationship between the home page and the Search page.

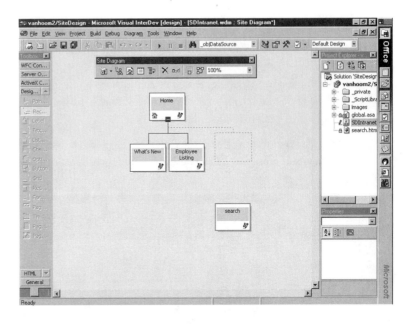

You should now be looking at the Web page shown in Figure 20.10.

FIGURE 20.10.

The BSI Consulting home page.

2. Position Internet Explorer and Visual InterDev as shown in Figure 20.11 so that you can see both the BSI Web page and the Site Diagram.

FIGURE 20.11.

Viewing both applications.

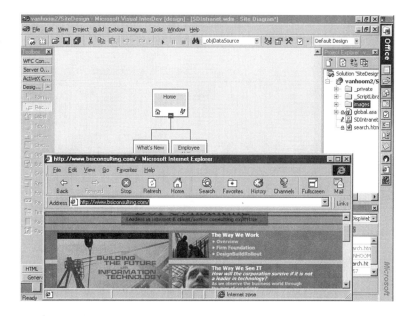

3. Highlight the URL within Internet Explorer.

4. Position the mouse over the URL near the beginning of the URL name so that the cursor becomes an arrow as demonstrated in Figure 20.12.

FIGURE 20.12.

Preparing to drag the Web page.

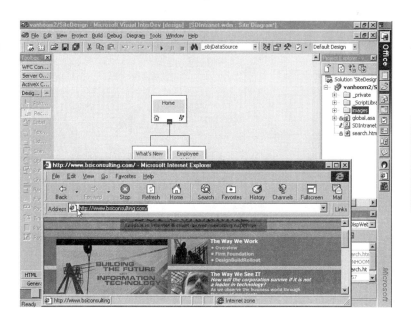

20

5. Drag the URL over to the Visual InterDev site diagram and establish a relationship between the page and the home page as shown in Figure 20.13.

FIGURE 20.13.

Adding an existing page from another application.

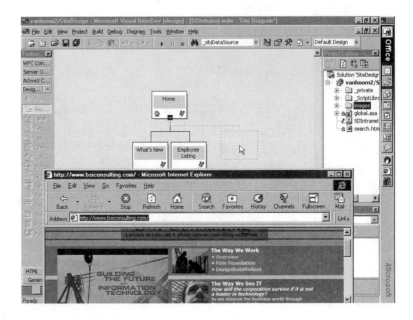

Figure 20.14 depicts how the page appears within the site diagram.

FIGURE 20.14.

Viewing an external Web page within the context of a site diagram.

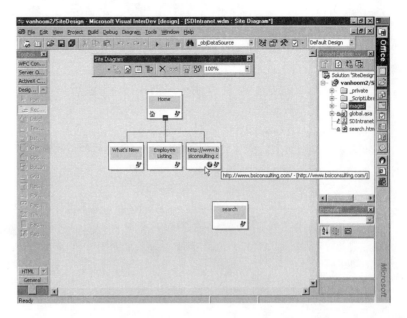

Notice that the full, external URL is shown along with a globe icon indicating that this page is an external page. Table 20.2 lists the other icons that you may encounter for a page within a site diagram.

TABLE 20.2. SITE DIAGRAM PAGE ICONS.

Icon	Meaning
🏠	Indicates the home page for a site
📝	Page and/or navigation structure has been modified but changes have not been saved
🔵	Represents a page that is external to the currently opened project
📄	Represents a page that serves as the default navigation link for all site navigation bars

Designing Effective Navigation for the User

Now that you have learned how to create and add pages to a site diagram, you will walk through the process of using the Site Designer to create effective site navigation for your users. As discussed earlier in the day, an effective user interface is essential to the success of your application. Site navigation, the manner in which a user traverses through your Web site, is a critical component of the interface.

In this section you will learn the following topics:

- The different types of relationships between pages in your site.
- How to use the Site Designer to arrange your Web pages.
- How to use the PageNavBar design-time control to provide the proper navigation bars for your users.

Establishing the Page Hierarchy

Proceeding with the lesson example, you have established a relationship with some of the Web pages in your site diagram. You have also added a page that has no relationship with any of the other pages. Before you walk through the process of how to use the Site Designer to arrange and rearrange your Web pages, let's examine the different types of relationships that can exist between your Web pages.

Within a site diagram, you create relationships between pages and groups of pages. These relationships are grouped into trees. A tree contains one or more parent pages and their associated child pages. Figure 20.15 depicts the site diagram that you have created so far.

20

FIGURE 20.15.

Understanding the relationships between Web pages.

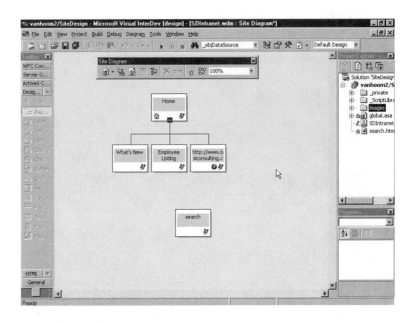

There is one tree in this diagram along with an independent page that is not associated with any other page in the diagram. The Home page serves as the sole parent in this diagram. It is called a parent because the page has child pages that are associated with it. The child pages in this diagram are the What's New page, the Employee Listing page, and the BSI Consulting Web page. These three pages share a parent-child relationship with the Home page and a sibling relationship with each other. The Search page is the loneliest page on the diagram because it has no parent and no siblings.

As you add pages to your site diagram and link the pages together, the Site Designer creates a hierarchy among the pages based on the relationships that you establish. You will learn in a later section how to provide the proper navigation links for your end users. The important thing to remember is that the URL references are established within the site diagram. All this information is maintained in a site structure file. When you use layouts or the PageNavBar design-time control, the Site Designer uses the information in the site structure file to provide the right types of links between the pages.

Let's make a few adjustments to the site diagram and then view our overall results:

1. Drag and drop the Search page so that is becomes a child of the Home page.

2. Select the Home page and click the New HTML Page icon to add a new child for the Home page.

3. Change the name of the page to Employee Page.

4. Drag and drop the Employee Listing page underneath the Employee Page so that the Employee Listing becomes a child of the Employee Page.

5. Choose File, Save to save the site diagram. When you save the site diagram, any pages that did not previously exist will be added to your project. After you save the diagram, you will see these files displayed in the Project Explorer.

After you create the proper structure for your site, you need to provide the users with the proper options for navigating through your Web site. Visual InterDev provides two options for accomplishing this task. First, you can use a special design-time control called the PageNavBar. This design-time control enables to you to provide the proper HTML for navigating your site. The second option involves applying a layout to your pages and site. Each of these options is explored in the following sections.

Using the PageNavBar Design-Time Control

The PageNavBar design-time control provides you with a navigation bar object at design time. You can use this object to visually set the properties to execute the proper HTML for generating navigation links at runtime. The PageNavBar is a very powerful design-time control (DTC) that enables you to establish navigation links to appear as buttons, regular text, or custom HTML hyperlinks. The following example will guide you through the process of using the PageNavBar DTC on the pages for this site:

1. Double-click the `Default.htm` file in the Project Explorer to open the Default page in the Design Editor.

2. Select the PageNavBar design-time control from the Design-Time Controls tab within the toolbox.

3. Drag and drop the control onto the Default page.

4. Add a paragraph break by pressing Enter.

5. Add another PageNavBar DTC to the Default page using the method in step 3. Your page should look similar to the one shown in Figure 20.16.

6. Right-click the first PageNavBar DTC and select Properties from the shortcut menu. Figure 20.17 depicts the Property Pages for the PageNavBar DTC.

   From this dialog box, you can set the properties for the PageNavBar DTC that will execute at runtime. As you can see from Figure 20.17, the first tab is called the General tab and enables you to indicate the type of navigation page. Table 20.3 outlines the different types of pages that you can provide navigation to and their meaning.

20

FIGURE 20.16.

*Adding navigation for
your pages with the
PageNavBar DTC.*

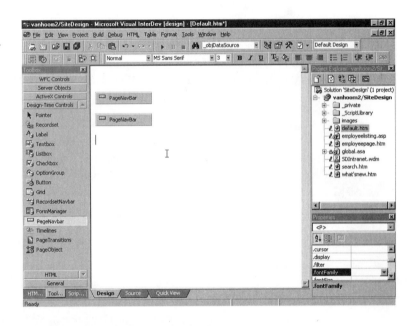

FIGURE 20.17.

*Setting the properties
for the PageNavBar
DTC.*

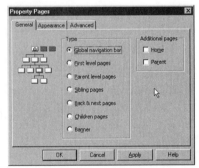

TABLE 20.3. TYPES OF NAVIGATION PAGES.

Type	Meaning
Global Navigation Bar	Provides navigation to any page included on the Global navigation bar pages in the site diagram for the project, such as a Search page
First Level Pages	Provides navigation to any first level page, or those pages one level below the Home page
Parent Level Pages	Provides links to parent level pages, or those pages one level above the currently opened page
Sibling Pages	Provides links to the siblings of a currently opened page

Type	Meaning
Back and Next Pages	Provides back and next links to the current and previous pages based on the hierarchy of the Web site
Children Pages	Provides links to child level pages, or those pages one level below the currently opened page
Banner	Provides the page label, title, or filename overlaid on an image, provided by a theme that has been applied to the page

7. Select Parent Level Pages for the Type of the first PageNavBar DTC.

8. Click the Appearance tab for the DTC. This dialog box enables you to tailor the display, or appearance, of the navigation links as well as their orientation on the page.

9. Choose Text for the Appearance option and Vertical for the Orientation.

10. Click the Advanced tab. This tab provides you with two options. First, the Frame Target enables you to set the target frame for displaying the navigation bars. The Alternate page option enables you to select the navigation structure of a different page to generate the navigation bar links for the current page.

11. Without setting any options on the Advanced tab, click OK.

12. Right-click the second PageNavBar DTC on the page and choose Properties from the shortcut menu.

13. Choose Global Navigation Bar for the Type.

14. Click the Appearance tab and choose Text for the Appearance and Vertical for the Orientation. Click OK.

15. Open the Site Diagram and make sure that the Search page is defined as a global navigation page. To accomplish this task, select the Search page and click the Add to Global Navigation Bar icon on the Site Diagram menu. This action will detach the page from the Home page and add it as a navigation link on all pages. In other words, the Search page becomes universally available to all pages in the application. You will notice in the site diagram that the Search page now displays a global navigation icon.

20

Tip

To remove a page that has been added to the global navigation bar, select the globally available page and click the same icon as indicated in step 15. You will notice that the ToolTips for the icon is now labeled Remove from Global Navigation Bar. For the purposes of this example, do not perform this action.

16. Save the Default page and view the results in your browser.

Leveraging Layouts and Themes

You can also provide navigation links to your pages by applying layout. A layout provides a template that specifies where navigation bars should be placed on the page. In addition to the layout of the page, you can apply themes to spice up the look of your pages. Themes include graphics, fonts, and special page elements that provide a consistent look and feel across your Web pages. Visual InterDev provides many default themes and layouts to choose from. The following example will guide you through the process of adding and applying a layout and theme for the site.

Applying a Layout

To apply a layout to a page, complete the following steps:

1. Open the site diagram for the project.
2. Right-click the Employee Page and select Apply Theme and Layout from the shortcut menu.
3. Click the Layout tab and choose Apply Layout and Theme.
4. Select the Top and Left 1 layout.
5. Click OK. This action creates a Layouts folder with the actual layout template and applies the layout to the current page based on information stored in the site diagram structure.
6. Save the page.
7. From within the site diagram, right-click the Employee Page and choose View in Browser from the shortcut menu to view your newly applied layout.

Applying a Theme

To apply a theme to a page, complete the following steps:

1. Open the site diagram for the project.
2. Right-click the Employee Page and select Apply Theme and Layout from the shortcut menu.
3. With the Theme tab selected, choose Apply Theme.
4. Select Redside for the theme.
5. Click OK. This action creates a Themes folder with several images and cascading style sheets and applies the theme to the current page based on information stored in the site diagram structure.

6. Save the page.

7. From within the site diagram, right-click the Employee Page and choose View in Browser from the shortcut menu to view your newly applied layout.

Notice how the theme truly accentuates the look of the layout. Remember, you can apply layouts and themes for the entire application by selecting the project root within the Project Explorer and choosing Apply Theme and Layout.

Reviewing HTML Form Design

So far, the lesson has addressed basic considerations and techniques for effective user interface design. You also walked through some pretty detailed examples of how to use the Site Designer to design and prototype your site. This section covers some of the basic design principles surrounding HTML form design.

The form's design of the user interface is crucial to your application's success. Using the house analogy, if you hired a builder to build a new house, you wouldn't want him to suddenly grab a hammer and nails one day and decide to build the house. You hope that the builder spends some time designing the house first, and you want him to follow blueprint designs and approved standards for constructing the rooms. You have asked for the rooms to be built in a particular way because you want living in the house to be a rich, rewarding experience—a place you look forward to returning to.

Form design might not be as important as providing a roof over your head, but this analogy shows you the importance of form design. You should definitely spend time contemplating your form's design. Ask yourself: "What is the user trying to do by using my application? How does this form help her perform certain tasks? Which controls should I use to make performing those tasks easier?" As a developer, the task of choosing the right control to perform the task is a vital part of constructing the user interface. Choosing the right tool is a required skill when you're designing and developing an application.

The next section outlines some design tips for HTML forms.

Designing an Effective Form

You should design your form with effectiveness in mind. In other words, you should design and develop an interface that lets the user be effective in performing the necessary tasks. Here are some tips to remember for designing an effective form:

- Group your controls in a logical, related manner on your form.
- Design forms that are consistent across your application.

20

- Use consistent fonts, colors, and backgrounds for your forms.
- Place the controls on your form in a logical order.
- Use the right control for the job.
- Supply default selections, when possible, for radio buttons, check boxes, and selection lists.

Using the Proper Name

During today's lesson, I have given you standard naming conventions for each control. These standards make it easier to distinguish each control and its type. A summary of these naming standards is given in Table 20.4.

TABLE 20.4. NAMING CONVENTIONS FOR HTML FORM CONTROLS.

Control	Prefix	Example
Button	cmd	cmdSubmit
Checkbox	chk	chkHighSchool
Password	txt	txtPassword
Radio Button	opt	optCreditCard
Selection List	lst	lstVacationSpots
Text	txt	txtName
Textarea	txa	txaMemo

Considerations Checklist

In closing the lesson for the day, I want to summarize the material that I have presented. The following list represents a considerations checklist that provides some general tips for Web-based development:

- Create a rich and rewarding experience for your users. Make them glad that they visited and provide a reason for them to return.
- Design and develop an effective user interface. The interface should enable the user to be effective in accomplishing his tasks. Effectiveness has as much to do with the interface as the efficiency of your code.
- Provide a common and consistent look and feel across your application. Your pages should reflect a consistent font, color, page background, and page layout.

- Use an appropriate metaphor for the overall structure of your application. Also, use appropriate metaphors and symbols on your Web pages that associate the correct meaning to the user.

- Give navigational cues to the user that provide the proper guidance.

- Provide the user with a path at all times. Do not create dead-end pages.

- Use graphics, multimedia, and advanced features to contribute to the overall mission and purpose of your application and Web pages. Avoid the use of too many features. Resist the temptation to use advanced features just for the sake of using them.

- Avoid having the user scroll excessively either horizontally or vertically. Provide a table of contents for long documents that provide jumps to the individual sections.

- Provide textual cues for your images. These cues will inform the user about the hyperlink when images are being loaded initially or are turned off.

- Provide search features for your site that enable a user to find information easily.

- Take advantage of the different development and deployment platform options to enhance your productivity.

- Choose the right database for the job. Proactively plan your application needs and select the proper database and tools to accomplish these requirements.

In summary, think about what you're trying to accomplish by developing your application. After you have considered the users' needs, devise a plan to design and develop the "killer app."

Summary

I hope today's lesson has been helpful and piqued your thinking about the importance of design in the success of your application. Many of the things that were discussed today apply to both client/server and Web-based application development. Other concepts are only pertinent to Web-based development.

At the beginning of the day, you learned about effective user interface design. Hopefully, your interfaces are already effective and this section served as a review. You learned about specific steps to follow when designing your application interface. Important steps to follow involve defining a purpose for your application, identifying user needs, and conducting testing to ensure the usability of your application. You learned about specific factors that affect your interface such as aesthetics, page design and layout, and navigational cues.

20

The majority of today's lesson covers the Visual InterDev Site Designer. The lesson guided you through several examples about how to use the Site Designer to design and prototype your Web application. You learned how you can use the Site Designer to quickly design and build the structure and layout of your site. You also learned how to create navigation links for your users using the PageNavBar design-time control. Toward the end of the day, you discovered how to apply layouts and themes to your Web pages.

At the close of the day, you reviewed some concepts about effective form design for Web-based applications. You also were provided with a summary of the lesson's material in the form of a considerations checklist. This checklist should help to provide some general guidelines you can use when designing and developing your applications.

Q&A

Q Should I use the Site Designer for prototyping my Web-based applications?

A Yes. The Site Designer provides a very good tool to quickly design and build a prototype of your application. The Site Designer enables you to design the hierarchy and structure of your Web site. You can then save the site diagram, thereby adding the pages to your project. This process provides a jump-start to your development efforts.

Q What is the relationship between a site diagram and the PageNavBar design-time control?

A When designing your application, you will typically use the Site Designer to design your Web pages and create the hierarchy and structure for the site. After you create the site diagram using the Site Designer, you can add navigation links between the pages using the PageNavBar design-time control. This design-time control uses the information stored in the site structure file to create the navigation links between the pages.

Workshop

The Workshop provides quiz questions to help you solidify your understanding of the material covered and exercises to provide you with experience in using what you've learned. For answers, see Appendix B, "Answers."

Quiz

1. Name the five basic steps for designing an effective user interface.
2. What are dead ends?
3. What is the difference between a theme and a layout?

Exercises

Web-based development presents a new and interesting challenge. The proper design and development of a Web-based application is essential to its acceptance. You can choose from many metaphors, features, and standards to implement your Web pages. For today's exercise, I want you to visit several of your favorite sites to determine the strengths and weaknesses of the Web pages. Note the features that you like and those features that are unnerving. You should record some of these features to be able to use in later lessons and future applications. Make sure that you note the context of the interface. In other words, think about the intended audience for the Web site. Does the metaphor support the intended purpose for users of that site? In addition to your favorite sites, take a look at these sites for additional ideas:

- ESPNET Sportszone (`espnet.sportszone.com`)
- Land's End (`www.landsend.com`)
- Virtual Vineyards (`www.virtualvin.com`)
- Microsoft (`www.microsoft.com`)
- Netscape (`www.netscape.com`)

20

DAY **21**

Making a Difference with Dynamic HTML

Today's lesson focuses on the exciting capabilities of Dynamic HTML, or DHTML. You may be familiar with the concept of DHTML. You already know that standard HTML presents static Web content to a browser. You also learned how to enhance your Web application with client-side script on Day 5, "Enhancing Your Web Page Through Client-Side Script." DHTML has become very popular with the advent of the version 4 browsers from Microsoft and Netscape. You will learn how DHTML can be used to truly make your Web pages come alive and provide the best experience for your users.

Upon completing this lesson, you will be able to

- Define DHTML.
- Explain the main technologies that are a part of DHTML.
- Dynamically alter the content of your Web pages.
- Understand the DHTML Document Object Model (DOM).
- Create client-side data bound forms that use DHTML.

Note

> This lesson serves as an initial primer into the world of DHTML. It is not meant to serve as an exhaustive chapter on all of the features, tips, and tricks of DHTML. At the end of today's lesson I will provide you with some further references that focus specifically on DHTML.
>
> For purposes of this lesson, I will focus on Microsoft's version of DHTML, which is completely compatible with the W3C (World Wide Web Consortium) specifications for HTML 4.

What Is Dynamic HTML?

Dynamic HTML means different things to different people. To me, it's a set of technologies and specifications that is continually changing in order to make the Web a more inviting and invigorating place to visit. Traditionally, HTML has been a very boring language that presents static Web pages to the user. Developers have incorporated the use of multimedia, images, and scripting languages to make these dull pages come alive. Companies like Microsoft and Netscape have been working with the W3C to enliven the very nature of HTML to include these capabilities. Hence, the introduction of DHTML.

DHTML provides a set of technologies that enables you to create dynamic content for your Web site. This dynamic content provides a very inviting experience for the user. Another key benefit from an architecture standpoint is that the content is dynamically rendered and altered on the client without having to make a round trip to the server.

DHTML can incorporate cascading style sheets (CSS) to define a common look and feel across your Web pages. Cascading style sheets enable you to define a color scheme, layout, or other strategy for defining the visual display of your Web pages. The key benefit of using style sheets is that you define the template in one place and then apply it across all the pages in your application.

DHTML also includes the use of scripting languages such as JavaScript and VBScript. These languages provide you with programming power to manipulate the objects on your Web pages.

An essential part of DHTML is the Document Object Model (DOM). The DOM provides a method for treating all the parts of your Web page as objects. This feature then lets you call methods and set properties for the objects on your Web pages, thereby manipulating their behavior and appearance.

Overall, DHTML provides some very valuable features for presenting the best experience to your users.

The Components of Dynamic HTML

Now that you have a general idea of what Dynamic HTML is, let's take a closer look at the set of technologies that make up DHTML. I mentioned a few of the components in the previous section. More specifically, DHTML can be grouped into the following areas:

- Document Object Model
- Dynamic Styles
- Dynamic Positioning
- Dynamic Content
- Data Binding

The following sections will explain each of these concepts.

Document Object Model

The Document Object Model (DOM) provides a common way to view the document and each of its elements. Without an object model for the document, there is no mechanism to manipulate the elements on the page. The DOM provides this mechanism by treating everything on the page as an object. Using this recognition, you can set and alter properties for each object on the page. You can also manipulate their behavior by activating different methods for the object.

The Document Object Model works within the context of existing HTML tags, style sheets, and scripting languages. The same tags that you know and love are the ones you work with in the DOM. The difference is that you now have access to them individually instead of one page at a time.

You will get a chance to manipulate these objects in several examples presented throughout the day.

Dynamic Styles

Dynamic Styles enables you to dynamically manipulate the style of the page as well as elements on the page. With Dynamic Styles, you can change the formatting and appearance of elements on the page programmatically without adding or removing elements. This feature provides instant feedback to your user while preserving the size of your scripts and documents. For example, you might want to change the appearance of a section of the page when the user clicks a button or drags the mouse over the section.

Using the feature of Dynamic Styles, you can change an inline style of an element as well as style definitions located within a cascading style sheet. An inline style refers to a

21

CSS style element that has been applied to an element of the page using the STYLE attribute. You can use popular scripting languages like JavaScript or VBScript to accomplish these tasks.

Dynamic Positioning

Dynamic Positioning refers to the ability to reposition elements and graphics on the Web page. After the page is downloaded to the browser, the styles and style sheets for the page are fully accessible through the object model. This access enables you to change the position of an element as well as provide animation for the elements and present this dynamic experience to the user.

Dynamic Content

As its name implies, the Dynamic Content feature enables the developer to dynamically change the content of the Web page after it has been loaded. Changes include inserting, altering, and removing the text of the page as well as changing the colors of the text.

Data Binding

Data Binding is the most practical component of Dynamic HTML. This feature enables you to bind individual elements of the page to a data source such as a text file or a database. A practical application of this feature involves binding an HTML table to a database. After the page is loaded from the server, the table displays the information contained in the database. Because the data is bound to the table, you can extend its functionality by enabling the user to sort and filter the data without making a round trip back to the server. The table is re-created on the client using the previously retrieved data. From this functionality, we get the term *smart* client. Using DHTML, the client is smart enough and has enough information to sort the data without re-communicating with the server.

Manipulating the Content of Your Web Pages

Now that you are familiar with the different types of DHTML functionality, let's walk through some examples of how to use DHTML features to dynamically alter the content of your application.

Creating the Base Content

Use the following steps to complete this task:

1. Create a Web project called DHTML. Make sure that you choose to apply the Redside theme to the project.

2. Add four HTML pages named `Default.htm`, `Dcontent.htm`, `DStyle.htm`, and `CustomerList.htm`.

3. Open the Default page in Source view.

4. Drag and drop the file `theme.css` from the Project Explorer over to the top of the Body section of the Default page. This action applies the theme to the page, inserting the proper relative link to the stylesheet.

5. Switch to Design view and add the following title to the top of the page: "Welcome to the Dynamic Home Page."

6. Highlight the text and change the font to Times New Roman and the font size to 6.

7. Center the text. Your Web page should now look like the one shown in Figure 21.1.

FIGURE 21.1.

Adding the title to the home page.

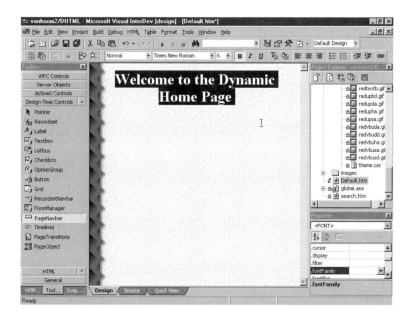

8. Add two paragraph breaks by pressing the Enter key twice.

9. Click the Align Left button to left-align the cursor position.

10. Click the Increase Indent to indent the cursor as shown in Figure 21.2.

11. Change the font size to 3.

12. Enter the following text: `Customer Listing`.

13. Press the Enter key to create another paragraph break and add the words `Dynamic Content`.

14. Press the Enter key and add the words `Dynamic Style`.

21

FIGURE **21.2.**

Indenting the text.

Indicates indent

15. Highlight the Customer Listing text and click the Link button to create a hyperlink for this text.

16. Enter the URL for the CustomerList.htm page. You may want to use the Browse button to locate the exact URL address.

17. Repeat steps 15 and 16 to create the proper links for the Dynamic Content and Dynamic Style pages.

18. Repeat steps 3 and 4 for the Customer Listing, Dynamic Content, and Dynamic Style pages.

19. Save all the project files.

You have now created the base content for the project. The next sections will build on this content to demonstrate the power of Dynamic HTML.

Unleashing the Power of Dynamic Content

For this part of the lesson, you will walk through an example to help realize the power of Dynamic Content. After you complete this example, you will be able to experience a page whose contents change when the user places the cursor over the title of the page. Complete the following steps:

1. Open the Dynamic Content page.

2. Using the Design Editor, add the words This is Dynamic Content.

3. Change the font to Times New Roman and the font size to 6.

4. Center the title text. Figure 21.3 depicts the results of your actions so far.

FIGURE 21.3.

Adding the title for the Dynamic Content page.

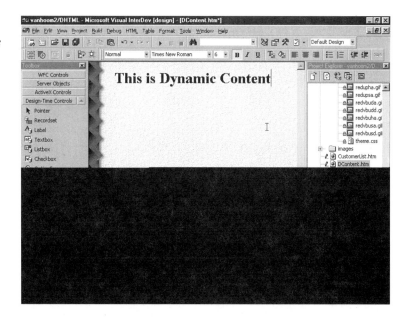

5. Change the ID for the title text to MyHeading in the Properties window for this object. This action enables you to create an intuitive name for the object that you can reference when manipulating the text.

6. Switch to Source view. Notice that the Script Outline now displays a client object called MyHeading.

7. Expand the MyHeading object to reveal the standard events for this object.

8. Double-click the onmouseover event. This action creates a function shell for the onmouseover event.

9. Add the following lines of code for the onmouseover event:

```
MyHeading.innerText = "It Changed!"
MyHeading.style.color = "green"
```

Note

Notice the helpfulness of Intellisense after you type the period immediately following the words MyHeading. Because the text is considered an object, Visual InterDev provides a visual way to reveal the methods and properties for the object.

21

10. Save your changes and preview the page within the browser. Be sure to move the mouse over the text in the page to see the content dynamically change as shown in Figure 21.4.

FIGURE 21.4.

Dynamically changing the title of the page.

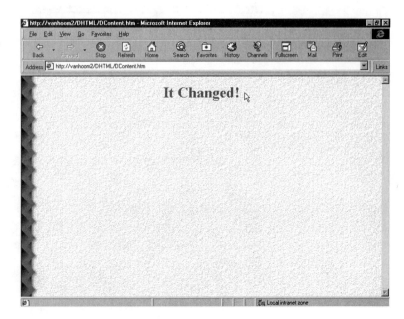

Analyzing the Results

In the previous example, you added a title for the Dynamic Content page. This text was initially loaded as the title when the page was loaded. You then added code for the onmousover event. This event occurs any time a user moves his mouse over the element in the page. Because you created the ID MyHeading for the title text of the page, you were able to address this element as an object and record the onmouseover event.

Let's take a look at the code that you added. The first line changed the actual content of the title by manipulating one of its properties. The innerText property enables you to adjust the actual text value of an element.

Additionally, you added a line of code to change the color of the text to green. You used the inline style property of the element to accomplish this task. Now when a user views the page and moves her mouse over the title of the page, the text changes its content and color. The next section will build the concepts that you have learned in this section.

Extending the Concept of Dynamic Content

Now that you understand the basics of Dynamic Content, let's extend the example to add some additional logic to the Dynamic Content page. In the previous example, the text changes when the user moves their mouse over the title text. The problem is that the text doesn't return to its original state. You need to add some logic to handle this situation and restore the text to its original state once the user has moved the mouse to another part of the page. The following steps will guide you through this process:

1. Open the Dynamic Content page in Source view.

2. Click the Script Outline for the page.

3. Expand the window client object.

4. Double-click the `onload` event. This action creates a function for the event that is fired when the window for the page is loaded.

5. Add the following logic at the top of the Script section in your page. You are adding variables that need to be referenced across all the script in your page; therefore, the declaration of these variables is outside the scope of any one function. Visually, the declaration looks like this:

```
<SCRIPT ID=clientEventHandlersJS LANGUAGE=javascript>
<!--
var strTitleText;
var strTitleColor;
function window_onload() {

}
```

6. Add the following logic for the `onload` event for the window:

```
strTitleText = MyHeading.innerText
strTitleColor = MyHeading.style.color
```

7. Expand the `MyHeading` client object.

8. Double-click the `onmouseout` event. This action creates a function for the event.

9. Add the following logic for the event:

```
MyHeading.innerText = strTitleText
MyHeading.style.color = strTitleColor
```

10. Save the page and preview the results in your browser. Figures 21.5–21.7 demonstrate the transition of the text.

Analyzing the Results

In this example, you added two variables to store the original state of the title for the Dynamic Content page when it is loaded. You declared these variables outside the scope of any one function so that their values could be accessed by all functions.

21

FIGURE 21.5.

The original title of the page.

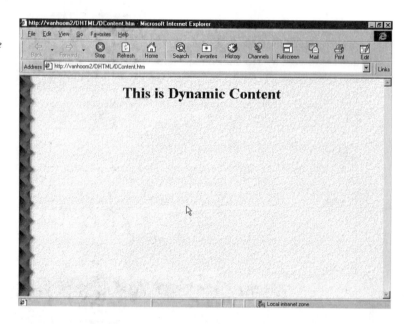

FIGURE 21.5.

The original title of the page.

FIGURE 21.6.

Moving the mouse over the title to dynamically alter it.

FIGURE 21.7.

Restoring the title to its original state when the mouse is moved to another part of the page.

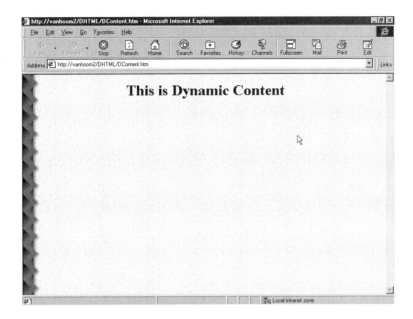

You then added some logic for the window `onload` event. This event occurs when the page and window are initially loaded. You added two lines of code to store the original values of the text and color of the title. Then, you added logic for the `onmouseout` event for the `MyHeading` object. This event occurs when the mouse is moved out of the block element. The code that you added restored the title text to its original text and color when the page was initially loaded. Listing 21.1 displays the entire code for the Dynamic Content page.

LISTING 21.1. ANALYZING THE CODE FOR THE DYNAMIC CONTENT PAGE.

```
 1: <HTML>
 2: <HEAD>
 3: <META NAME="GENERATOR" Content="Microsoft Visual Studio 6.0">
 4: <SCRIPT ID=clientEventHandlersJS LANGUAGE=javascript>
 5: <!--
 6: var strTitleText;
 7: var strTitleColor;
 8: function window_onload() {
 9: strTitleText = MyHeading.innerText
10: strTitleColor = MyHeading.style.color
11: }
12:
13: function MyHeading_onmouseout() {
14: MyHeading.innerText = strTitleText
```

21

continues

LISTING **21.1.** CONTINUED

```
15: MyHeading.style.color = strTitleColor
16: }
17:
18: function MyHeading_onmouseover() {
19: MyHeading.innerText = "It Changed!"
20: MyHeading.style.color = "green"
21: }
22:
23: //-->
24: </SCRIPT>
25: </HEAD>
26: <BODY LANGUAGE=javascript onload="return window_onload()">
27: <LINK rel=stylesheet href="_Themes/redside/theme.css">
28: <P align=center><STRONG><FONT face="Times New Roman"
29: size=6 id=MyHeading LANGUAGE=javascript onmouseover="return MyHeading_
➥onmouseover()" onmouseout="return MyHeading_onmouseout()">This is Dynamic
30: Content</FONT></STRONG></P>
31:
32: </BODY>
33: </HTML>
```

This example shows you how you can change existing text. You can now apply these principles dynamically to alter the content of your Web pages.

Unleashing the Power of Data Binding

Data Binding is a very practical feature of Dynamic HTML. In this section, I will cover the benefits of binding data to the client and guide you through some examples of how to use Data Binding.

Note   At the time this book was published, Netscape had not provided the Data Binding feature in its specification of DHTML. Microsoft, however, does include Data Binding in its version of DHTML.

You learned how to build data-bound forms with design-time controls on Day 12, "Extending Web Pages Through Design-Time Controls." The examples that you completed used server-side logic to retrieve the data from the database as well as navigate through the recordset. In this section, I will show you how to build a table that has "smart" client features—that is, it can manipulate the recordset on the client.

Adding Some Smart Content

For this example, you will need to add some content from the Macmillan Web site (http://www.mcp.com/info) that supports this book. The following steps will guide you through this process:

1. Download the 21Stuff.zip file.

2. Unzip the file and extract it to your hard drive in a place you can remember.

3. Using the Visual InterDev Project Explorer, add the content to the project that you have been using for today's lesson. The images should be placed in the images folder.

4. Add a System machine data connection to the Auction database named Auction. This database is a Microsoft Access database.

5. Open the ShowAuctionsDHTML.htm file in Source view and replace the comment Add Datafld logic here with the following code:

```
<td><span datafld="Name"></span></td>
        <td><span datafld="Description"></span></td>
        <td><span datafld="ImgURL"></span></td>
        <td>$<span datafld="MinBid"></span></td>
        <td><span datafld="LastBidTime"></span></td>
```

6. Replace the comment Add Sorting logic here with the following code:

```
if window.event.srcElement.id <> "" then
        auctionlist.Sort = window.event.srcElement.id
        auctionlist.Reset()
    end if

    window.event.returnValue = false   ' stop bubbling
```

7. Save your changes and preview the page within your browser.

Interacting with the Auction Page

You should now be looking at a page like the one in Figure 21.8.

This page displays a list of auctions that are currently in progress for an Auction House. The table displays the name of the auction along with its description, the image URL location for the auction, a minimum bid for the item, and the date the bid expires.

To see the power of DHTML, click the Name column. The data should sort in alphabetical order by name as shown in Figure 21.9.

This sort takes place without making a return trip to the server. In fact, the user can sort the data using any of the different columns. All the sorting logic executes on the client, thereby making this page a "smart" client. Let's explore how this feat was accomplished.

21

FIGURE 21.8.

The Auction page.

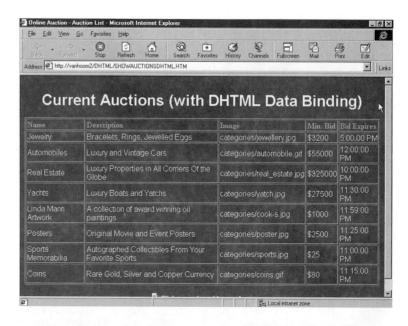

FIGURE 21.9.

Sorting the data by name.

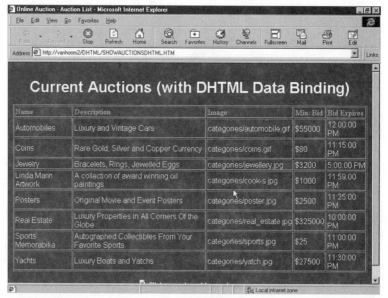

Analyzing the Code

First, let's take a look at the ShowAuctionsDHTML page and investigate its contents. Listing 21.2 displays the code for this page.

LISTING 21.2. ANALYZING THE CODE FOR THE SHOWAUCTIONSDHTML PAGE.

```
 1: <html>
 2:     <head>
 3:         <title>Online Auction - Auction List</title>
 4:         <link rel="stylesheet" href="showauctions.css" type="text/css">
 5:     </head>
 6:
 7:
 8:     <body background="images/swallows.jpg">
 9:
10:     <center>
11:
12:     <br>
13:     <h1> Current Auctions (with DHTML Data Binding)</h1>
14:
15:
16:     <object id="auctionlist" classid="clsid:333C7BC4-460F-11D0-BC04-
   ➥0080C7055A83" width="0" height="0">
17:
18:             <param name="DataURL" value="getdata.asp">
19:             <param name="UseHeader" value="True">
20:             <param name="FieldDelim" value="¦">
21:
22:     </object>
23:
24:
25:     <table border="1" id="atbl" datasrc="#auctionlist">
26:
27:     <thead>
28:         <tr id="headings">
29:             <td><div id="Name" class="heading">Name</div></td>
30:             <td><div id="Description"
   ➥class="heading">Description</div></td>
31:             <td><div id="Image" class="heading">Image</div></td>
32:             <td><div id="MinBid" class="heading">Min. Bid</div></td>
33:             <td><div id="LastBidTime" class="heading">Bid
   ➥Expires</div></td>
34:         </tr>
35:     </thead>
36:
37:     <tbody>
38:         <tr>
39:           <td><span datafld="Name"></span></td>
40:           <td><span datafld="Description"></span></td>
41:           <td><span datafld="ImgURL"></span></td>
42:           <td>$<span datafld="MinBid"></span></td>
43:           <td><span datafld="LastBidTime"></span></td>
44:         </tr>
```

continues

21

LISTING 21.2. CONTINUED

```
45:        </tbody>
46:
47:        </table>
48:
49:
50:
51:        <script language="VBSCRIPT">
52:
53:            function headings_onclick()
54:
55:                if window.event.srcElement.id <> "" then
56:                    auctionlist.Sort = window.event.srcElement.id
57:                    auctionlist.Reset()
58:                end if
59:
60:                window.event.returnValue = false   ' stop bubbling
61:
62:            end function
63:
64:        </script>
65:
66:
67:        <br>
68:
69:        <div CLASS="sub-right" style="cursor:hand" onclick="window.open
➥'codebrws.asp?source=ShowAuctionsDHTML.htm', '', 'resizable,scrollbars,
➥width=640,height=480'">
70:
71:            <img src="images/page.gif" title="Click here to see how this
➥was done" WIDTH="16" HEIGHT="16">
72:            Click to see how this was done
73:        </div>
74:
75:        </center>
76:
77:    </body>
78: </html>
```

As you look at this code, notice several distinct sections that provide the DHTML smarts for the page. First, you notice a data source object (DSO) control that is used to provide the data to the page. DSOs can be written as ActiveX controls as well as Java applets and help provide both the data access mechanism and the object model for scripting against the data. In this case, you are using the Tabular Data Control (TDC). This control enables you to read and sort data from a tabular data file. You cannot update data using the TDC, but you can sort and filter your data.

You will notice that the DataURL parameter is set to a value of getdata.asp. This ASP page actually retrieves the data from the Auction database and places it in a delimited text file format. The TDC that is used in this example requires that the data be formatted in a text-delimited file on the client for security purposes.

Next, you will notice that an ID has been assigned to the table as well as a DATASRC value. The DATASRC attribute specifies the ID of the DSO instance on the page.

Note

The ID specified in the DATASRC value must match the ID of the DSO.

The format for specifying a DATASRC value is as follows:

```
DATASRC="#IDRef
```

IDRef is the ID of the DSO instance. In this case the value is #auctionlist.

The table headings follow this section in the code listing. For each column, an ID has been assigned so that it can be referenced as objects later in the code. Notice that an ID has been assigned to the table heading section of the table.

You added the code for the table body section. This code labels each cell in the body of the table with the DATAFLD attribute. This attribute enables you to specify the name of the column to which the HTML element should be bound.

The final section of the page includes custom script that you added. In this example, you added some VBScript to handle the click event for the headings. This code executes any time one of the column headings is clicked. The element ID is passed to the procedure, and the Sort method is used to sort the data by the column that has been specified.

The last line of VBScript code turns off event bubbling. Event bubbling involves the passing of event messages up through the document hierarchy of a page. For example, if a user clicks a column in the table, two events can occur—the onclick event for the table column and the onclick event for the document. This feature is unique to DHTML and can help you when you only want to put your code in one place, thereby reducing redundancy for multiple event code procedures. Many times, you will want to make it a practice to cancel this feature in order to distinguish what event the user actually performed.

In the last line of VBScript code in this example, you stopped the event bubbling feature. In this manner, you can truly distinguish between the user clicking a column heading and the user clicking another area of the document.

21

Considerations Checklist

In closing the lesson for the day, I want to summarize the material that I have presented. The following represents a checklist that provides some general considerations and tips when developing a DHTML application:

- Know your audience and their browsers. Author for the least common denominator that you will have to support.
- Design rich end-user experiences for those times when you are sure of the browser and its capabilities.
- As with anything, use the features in DHTML in moderation. In others words, just because you make the color of text change back and forth, don't implement this feature if it doesn't support the overall effectiveness of your page and application.
- Use the W3C standard of CSS-P for positioning elements as opposed to the Netscape-only `<Layer>` tag.
- Use lowercase names for your event handlers.
- Provide intuitive names for elements that you are planning to manipulate as an object.
- Use alphanumeric characters for your element names.
- Understand the differences between the various Document Object Models from Microsoft, Netscape, and the W3C Draft.
- Use DHTML to provide a rich and rewarding experience for your users.
- Use features such as Dynamic Content and Dynamic Styles to provide the appropriate feedback to your users based on their actions.

Summary

Today has been a whirlwind tour through the world of Dynamic HTML. This lesson only touches the tip of the iceberg as far as the capabilities of DHTML. First, those additional resources I promised. I would highly recommend the following books as a follow-up to this lesson:

- *Dynamic HTML Unleashed* (Sams.net Publishing, ISBN: 1-57521-353-2, 1998)
- *Sams Teach Yourself Dynamic HTML in a Week* (Sams.net Publishing, ISBN: 1-57521-335-4, 1997)

Also, the following Web sites should serve as valuable resources:

- `www.insideDHTML.com`

- www.DHTMLZone.com

- www.microsoft.com/workshop/author/default.asp

At the beginning of the day, you discovered exactly what Dynamic HTML is. You learned how DHTML accentuates HTML and is really a set of component technologies. You then received an overview of those technologies including Dynamic Styles, Dynamic Content, Dynamic Positioning, Data Binding, and the Document Object Model.

Next, you walked through a series of examples on how to implement DHTML within the context of an application. The examples focused on how to dynamically alter the style and content of your Web pages.

Toward the end of the day, you walked through a very practical example of how to use data binding on the client. You were able to add the logic to put some intelligence into your browser to sort the data within a table. The final lesson of the day provided some general guidelines and tips on the use of DHTML.

Q&A

Q Which standard should I use?

A It depends. Both Microsoft and Netscape are working very hard with the W3C on the draft specification of DHTML. At the time this book went to publishing, a standard had not yet been finalized by the W3C. It has been my experience that Microsoft's standard for DHTML is more compatible with where the W3C specifications are going. The overriding point is that you should develop pages that will work for your users regardless of the browser that they choose. If you are absolutely sure of the target browser and its capabilities, develop an application that takes advantage of these features.

Q Is DHTML the same thing as HTML 4?

A Yes and No. There are some DHTML capabilities that have been included in HTML 4 like the ability to use cascading style sheets. Other capabilities are still being worked on to be included in future specifications of HTML. In general, DHTML represents a combination of technologies including cascading style sheets, HTML, and scripting technologies that enable you to dynamically manipulate your Web pages.

Workshop

21

The Workshop provides quiz questions to help you solidify your understanding of the material covered and exercises to provide you with experience in using what you've learned. See Appendix B, "Answers," for the answers.

Quiz

1. What is the DOM?
2. What is event bubbling?
3. Name three component technologies of DHTML.

Exercises

For today's exercise, research the Web sites mentioned in the Summary section of today's lesson. These sites, as well as the books that are mentioned, provide a wealth of knowledge on the subject of DHTML. Some of the sites provide other examples. Try out some of their examples and apply the concepts to the project that you created today.

WEEK 3

In Review

You have now completed the third and final week of your pursuit of knowledge about the exciting new version of Visual InterDev. During the first and second weeks of your journey, you learned about the client and server components that can be integrated into your Web-based applications. Week 3 covers some advanced Visual InterDev topics and teaches you how to integrate these components into your application. You also learned about some ancillary tools that can aid in your development.

Where You Have Been

The first part of the third week teaches you how to build components for your applications and integrate them into your application. On Day 16, you discovered how to properly manage your Web site files using the tools included in Visual InterDev. On Day 17, you learned about the new debugger found in Visual InterDev and how to debug your applications. Toward the middle of the week, you also learned how to integrate source code control into Visual InterDev with Microsoft Visual SourceSafe. Toward the end of the week, you learned how to use the Visual InterDev Site Designer to design and prototype the layout and structure of your Web site. The last day of this week (and of this book) teaches you how to use the features of Dynamic HTML.

My wish for you is that you use the knowledge contained in this book to develop killer applications for the Web. These are exciting times for developers, and Visual InterDev is the perfect tool to sustain your enthusiasm. I hope you have enjoyed the journey as much as I have enjoyed presenting this

15

16

17

18

19

20

21

dynamic and integrated tool for Web-based development. Armed with the lessons you have learned from this book and the power of Visual InterDev, you should now be prepared to untangle the technologies of the Web.

APPENDIX A

Additional Resources

You have learned a lot of information by completing the 21 lessons contained in this book. The topics covered have probably piqued your interest about a lot of different Web technologies. This appendix provides some additional resources that would be very good next steps for you to take in your pursuit of the killer app for the Web.

There is a wealth of information on the Web, and it's growing and changing every day. The URL addresses outlined in this appendix should provide you with additional tools and knowledge to support you in developing your Web-based applications.

MCP Home Page

`http://www.mcp.com/info`

You can use this URL to access the home page of Macmillan Computer Publishing USA. You can check out updates to the information contained in this book, as well as additional Internet book resources.

Microsoft Home Page

`http://www.microsoft.com/`

This URL address is the main home page for Microsoft. Because Visual InterDev integrates many Microsoft technologies for the Web, you can access this Web site to keep up with all the new tools and technologies from Microsoft.

Microsoft Visual InterDev Home Page

`http://www.microsoft.com/vinterdev/`

This URL address is Microsoft's home page for Visual InterDev. This site includes FAQs, white papers, demos, tutorials, and links to other information and resources concerning Visual InterDev.

Microsoft Visual Studio Home Page

`http://www.microsoft.com/vstudio/`

This URL address is Microsoft's home page for Visual Studio. This site includes FAQs, white papers, demos, tutorials, and links to other information and resources concerning the Visual Studio suite of tools including Visual Basic, Visual InterDev, Visual J++, Visual C++, and so on.

VBScript Home Page

`http://www.microsoft.com/vbscript/`

This site contains general information concerning VBScript.

Microsoft SiteBuilder Workshop

`http://www.microsoft.com/workshop/default.asp`

This site is an excellent resource for any Web developer. From this site, you can access information concerning every aspect of Web development, from designing a Web site to the site's final implementation.

Microsoft Data Access Home Page

http://www.microsoft.com/data

This URL address is Microsoft's home page for everything concerning its data access strategies.

Microsoft Usenet Newsgroups for Data Access

microsoft.public.ado

This newsgroup includes discussion about ADO.

microsoft.public.odbc

This newsgroup includes discussion about ODBC.

microsoft.public.mdac

This newsgroup includes discussion about MDAC (Microsoft Data Access) strategies.

microsoft.public.oledb

This newsgroup includes discussion about OLE DB.

microsoft.public.oledb.providers

This newsgroup includes discussion about OLE DB providers.

Gamelan EarthWeb

http://www.gamelan.com/

This site is an excellent resource for information about Java.

JavaSoft Home Page

http://www.javasoft.com

This site is another excellent resource for information on Java.

Java Boutique

http://www.j-g.com/java/

This site enables you to download over 100 Java applets that you can integrate into your applications.

World Wide Web Consortium

http://www.w3.org/pub/WWW/

You can use this site to keep up with the latest drafts on HTML specifications.

Microsoft Internet Information Server Home Page

http://www.microsoft.com/iis/

This URL address represents the home page for Internet Information Server (IIS). You can access a wealth of knowledge about IIS as well as Active Server Pages.

Microsoft Visual Basic Home Page for Web Developers

http://www.microsoft.com/vbasic/icompdown/default.htm

This Web site contains information concerning Visual Basic that is targeted at Web developers.

APPENDIX B

Answers

This appendix provides the answers to the quiz and exercise sections at the end of each chapter.

Day 1

Quiz

1. What is the main benefit of Web-based applications over typical client/server applications?

   The main benefit to Web-based applications is that code changes to the client are practically reduced, simplifying software distribution, version control, and administration. The reason for this is the use of a browser as a universal client and the use of the server as the primary location of the presentation, application, and database logic. In a client/server configuration, an executable file resides on the client. When you make changes to your application, you have to re-deploy the application to each of the client machines. In the Web-based model, you make your changes in one place on the server.

2. What is the purpose of the Design view?

   The Design view provides a powerful WYSIWYG editor that enables you to visually construct the layout of your Web pages without worrying about the underlying HTML code. You also can use the Design view to insert HTML, ActiveX, and design-time controls.

3. What is the difference between Active Server Pages and ActiveX Server Components?

   Active Server Pages are a combination of HTML and scripting code that enable you to perform dynamic actions for your applications at the server. All the script is processed on the server, and the results are sent back to the client. Active Server Components are executable programs or dynamic link libraries that execute at the server to handle tasks such as file I/O and resource-intensive processes. The difference is that an Active Server Component is a compiled program. Active Server Pages are not compiled and are typically used to call ActiveX Server Components.

4. What is the difference between an ActiveX control and a design-time control?

   ActiveX controls differ from design-time controls in that ActiveX controls include a runtime component that executes within the context of the browser. Design-time controls provide a visual guide for establishing properties that are generated into HTML and scripting code. Design-time controls don't exhibit a visual component at runtime.

Exercises

1. Install Visual InterDev 6 (if you have not already done so).

   Refer to the Visual InterDev setup notes for information on installing Visual InterDev 6.

Day 2

Quiz

1. What two components make up the virtual root?

   The virtual root is composed of the name of your Web server and your project name.

2. What is the purpose of the virtual root?

   The virtual root enables a user to logically access your Web without knowing the physical location of your files and the file directory structure. By selecting the virtual root URL, a user can have access to all the Web page files within the application.

3. What is the default editor for HTML pages?

The Design Editor.

Exercises

1. In today's exercise, you get to create your own application. Use today's lesson as a guide to create several HTML and ASP pages that relate to each other. You should practice using the various concepts that you learned about today. Start a new project and walk through the whole process. Also, use Windows Explorer to view the file structures and files as they are created. You should understand the basic building blocks by using Visual InterDev to produce your application. Practice makes perfect!

2. Using the information in Table 2.1, change the details.asp page to display a list of orders. This information is provided as static text; that is, not from a database. You will learn how to create dynamic, database-driven applications during the second week of this book.

   Follow these steps:

   1. Open details.asp using the Design Editor.

   2. Using the data in Table 2.1, enter the information in the appropriate columns in the table.

   3. Save the page and choose View in Browser to view your results in your browser.

Day 3

Quiz

1. Name the tabs that are present in the Visual InterDev Toolbox.

   HTML, ActiveX Controls, Design-Time Controls, Server Objects, and General.

2. What are the two things that you can modify in relation to an object?

   Properties and methods.

3. What does the term IDE stand for?

   Integrated development environment.

4. How do you customize the Visual InterDev development environment?

   With the Options window under the Tools menu.

5. When working with script, which folders are present in the HTML Outline pane?

   Client Objects and Events, Client Scripts, Server Objects and Events, and Server Scripts.

Exercise

Now that you are familiar with the Visual InterDev development environment, you are going to create a Web page using each of the three editor views. This exercise should give you more experience developing Web pages with Visual InterDev. You have the freedom to select the idea and content for your pages as long as they contain the following:

- Formatted text
- ActiveX controls or HTML controls
- Custom scripts that manipulate your ActiveX or HTML controls
- Tables

Follow these steps:

1. Add a new HTML page to your project by choosing Project | Add Item.
2. Use the Design view to add a table with 3 rows and 3 columns to your Web page by choosing Table | Insert Table.
3. Type some text into your table; use the Formatting toolbar to make the text bold or italic.
4. Add the ActiveX calendar control to your Web page by dragging the control from the Toolbox to the Web page in Design view.
5. Add the script code presented earlier today to modify the behavior of the ActiveX calendar control.
6. Add other ActiveX or HTML controls and experiment with their properties.

Day 4

Quiz

1. What are two ways that you can format text in Design view?

   The HTML format toolbar and the Format menu option.
2. Name the menu items under the HTML menu option.

   Link, Bookmark, Image, Marquee, and Div.
3. How can you control the order of images and objects on your Web pages?

   With the Z order menu item under the Format menu.
4. How do you turn on the absolute positioning mode in Design view?

   Use the Format menu.
5. Name three elements that you can format with the cascading style sheet editor.

   Font, background, borders, layout, position, and lists.

Exercise

Now that you are familiar with the Visual InterDev's Design view, you are going to create a Web page using the WYSIWYG editing capabilities that you learned today. First, create a new Web page with text and images. Use the formatting techniques described today to add some excitement to your text. Next, add a link to another page in your project with the HTML menu. Add other elements such as a scrolling marquee or dividing lines. Finally, create a new cascading style sheet in Visual InterDev and apply it to your page.

B

1. To create a new Web page, select Add Item from the Project menu. Select HTML Page from the New tab. Name the page `Page1.htm`.

2. Type `This is the exercise for Chapter 4 of Teach Yourself Visual InterDev 6.0 in 21 Days` on the Web page in Design view.

3. To add an image to your page, select HTML | Add Image. Use the dialog box to select an image file on your PC to insert on the Web page.

4. Create another new Web page in your project using the Add Web Item from the Project menu. Name the page `Page2.htm`.

5. Type the text `Page2` in Design view for `Page1.htm`. Select the text with the right mouse button. Add a link from Page1 to Page2 using the Link menu item under the HTML menu. You can also simply drag the file you want to link with from the Project Explorer and drop it in Design view.

6. Add other HTML items such as the Marquee, dividing lines, and so on, to Page1 using the HTML menu.

7. Create a cascading style sheet named `Style1.css` by choosing Project | Add Web Item. Using the Cascading Style Sheet editor, change the default font to Comica Sans MS and the default font color to Maroon. Use the Font tab in the Cascading Style Sheet editor to accomplish this.

8. Apply the Style1 stylesheet to the `Page1.htm` file by typing the following between the `<HEAD>` and `</HEAD>` tags in Source view: `<LINK REL="stylesheet" TYPE="text/css" HREF="Style1.CSS">`.

Day 5

Quiz

1. What is the difference between Java and JavaScript?

   Java is a programming language designed to create applications and applets, or "mini" applications. Java is a compiled language. JavaScript, on the other hand, is an interpreted language that resides within HTML on a Web page. JavaScript is designed to provide scripting functionality to your Web pages.

2. What is the difference between a function and a sub procedure?

   A subprocedure is a group of related code statements that work together to complete a task. A function is different from a subprocedure in its ability to actually return a value back to the program that called the function. A subprocedure cannot return a value back to the calling program. A subprocedure and a function are two types of procedures.

3. What is the difference between `Null` and `Empty`?

   `Null` indicates that the variable has been intentionally set to equal nothing. `Empty` represents a variable whose contents have not been assigned a value.

4. What does the `ByVal` statement do?

   The `ByVal` statement enables you to pass a variable by value to a procedure. Passing a variable by value makes a copy of the variable for the procedure to access and modify within the scope of that procedure. Any changes made to the variable within the procedure aren't reflected back to the calling program.

5. Given the following code segment, how many times will the code within the loop execute before the loop terminates?

```
Sub cmdCalculate_OnClick()
Dim A, B, C
A = 10
B = 20
Do While A > B
C = A - B
A = A - B
Loop
End Sub
```

   The answer is zero. The `Do...While` loop executes a block of code as long as a condition is true. The `Do...While` loop checks the condition first before executing the code. If the condition is false, as in this case, the code within the loop won't be executed.

Exercise

Create a Web page that includes several HTML text box controls including name, address, city, and state. Provide a Submit button for the user. Add client-side validation logic that verifies each of the fields have been filled in when the user clicks on the Submit button.

1. Create a Web project and add an HTML page to the project.

2. Using the Design Editor, drag and drop four HTML text box controls onto the page. Make sure to align them vertically on the page, providing a line break between each control.

3. Change the name and ID of the controls to `txtName`, `txtAddress`, `txtCity`, and `txtState`, respectively.

4. Drag and drop a Submit HTML button to the page after the last text box control.

5. Change the name and ID of this control to `cmdSubmit`.

6. Switch to the Source view. Make sure that the client-side script property for your page is set to `VBScript`.

7. Double-click the `onclick` event for the Submit button and enter the following code:

```
Sub cmdSubmit_onclick()
    If txtName.value = "" or txtAddress.value = "" or
    ➡txtCity.value = "" or txtState.value = "" Then
    MsgBox "You need to enter values for all of the fields"
    Else
    MsgBox "Your transaction was submitted successfully"
    End If
End Sub
```

Day 6

Quiz

1. What is the difference between client- and server-side script?

   Client-side script executes on the client machine and is typically used for validation and client event handling. Server-side script executes on the server and is not sent to the browser. Server-side script is cross compatible among different browsers and is typically used for forms processing and accessing a database or business component.

2. What are some advantages of Active Server Pages?

   Active Server Pages enable you to combine HTML, ActiveX objects, Java applets, and client- and server-side script to create dynamic Web pages. A big advantage to ASPs is that you can dynamically manipulate content on the server and then distribute the results in pure HTML.

3. What is the default editor for Active Server Pages?

   The Source Editor.

4. What is the name of the Visual InterDev feature that helps you build the script for your objects and events?

   The Script Outline.

Exercise

Change the input form application so that the message displays not only the user preferences but also the date and time.

Follow these steps:

1. Add the following code to the end of the ProcessForm.asp file:

```
<BR>
<%Response.Write Date
%>
<BR>
<%
Response.Write Time
 %>
```

2. Save your changes.

3. View the input form in your browser.

4. Enter a name, select a team, and click Submit to see the new results. You will see a welcome notice with your selections as well as the date and time.

Day 7

Quiz

1. What is a method?

   A method is a predefined procedure associated with a control that performs a specific action to affect its behavior. You can use a control's method to further change its behavior and characteristics in your application.

2. What method do you use to add items to a combo box?

   AddItem.

3. What property enables you to define the text for the label control?

   Caption.

4. What exciting Visual InterDev feature automatically generates script code based on your input?

   The Script Wizard enables you to visually choose controls, actions, and events to automatically generate script code for your application.

Exercise

Write a timesheet-type application. The timesheet should include a calendar control, a text box, a combo box, and two command buttons. All these controls should be ActiveX controls. Code the calendar control to make sure that the user can't pick a date that is in the future or that is more than two weeks old. Make one of the command buttons a Submit button. Code the timesheet so that the user must select a project from the combo box and enter the number of hours worked (less than 24) in the text box. If the preceding criteria is met, a message box should pop up confirming the entered data. Make the other button a Cancel button that resets the other controls to their original state. Populate the combo box with the names of several projects when the page is loaded into the browser.

B

The following code is one solution:

```
<HTML>
<HEAD>
<META NAME="GENERATOR" Content="Microsoft Visual Studio 6.0">
<TITLE></TITLE>
<SCRIPT ID=clientEventHandlersJS LANGUAGE=vbscript>
<!--

sub Calendar1_Click()
    if date() -- window.Calendar1.Value > 14 then
        alert("too long ago")
    elseif window.Calendar1.Value > date() then
        alert("that's the future")
    end if

end sub

Sub window_onload()
    window.MdcCombo1.AddItem("DMD Project")
    window.MdcCombo1.AddItem("EH&P Project")
    window.MdcCombo1.AddItem("JBS Project")

End Sub


Sub CommandButton1_Click()
if window.MdcCombo1.Value = "" then
        alert("Pick a project from the drop down")
        exit sub
    end if

    if window.MdcText1.Value = "" or window.MdcText1.Value > 24 then
        alert("Enter your number of hours in the text box")
        exit sub
    end if

    alert("Confirmed Entry: You worked " & window.MdcText1.Value &
" hours on " & window.MdcCombo1.Value & " on " &
window.Calendar1.Value)
End Sub
```

```
Sub CommandButton2_Click()
    window.Calendar1.Value = Date()
    window.MdcCombo1.Value = ""
    window.MdcText1.Value = ""
End Sub

//-->
</SCRIPT>
<SCRIPT LANGUAGE=javascript FOR=CommandButton1 EVENT=Click>
<!--
'return CommandButton1_Click()
//-->
</SCRIPT>
<SCRIPT LANGUAGE=javascript FOR=CommandButton2 EVENT=Click>
<!--
return CommandButton2_Click()
//-->
</SCRIPT>
</HEAD>
<BODY>

<P>
<TABLE border=1 cellPadding=1 cellSpacing=1 width=75%>

    <TR>
        <TD><FONT color=navy
            face=Arial><STRONG>TimeSheet
            Application</STRONG></FONT></TD></TR>
    <TR>
        <TD>
            <OBJECT classid=clsid:8E27C92B--1264--101C--8A2F--040224009C02
            id=Calendar1 style="LEFT: 0px; TOP: 0px">
<PARAM NAME="_Version" VALUE="524288">
<PARAM NAME="_ExtentX" VALUE="7620">
<PARAM NAME="_ExtentY" VALUE="5080">
<PARAM NAME="_StockProps" VALUE="1">
<PARAM NAME="BackColor" VALUE="--2147483633">
<PARAM NAME="Year" VALUE="1998">
<PARAM NAME="Month" VALUE="6">
<PARAM NAME="Day" VALUE="26">
<PARAM NAME="DayLength" VALUE="1">
<PARAM NAME="MonthLength" VALUE="2">
<PARAM NAME="DayFontColor" VALUE="0">
<PARAM NAME="FirstDay" VALUE="1">
<PARAM NAME="GridCellEffect" VALUE="1">
<PARAM NAME="GridFontColor" VALUE="10485760">
<PARAM NAME="GridLinesColor" VALUE="--2147483632">
<PARAM NAME="ShowDateSelectors" VALUE="--1">
<PARAM NAME="ShowDays" VALUE="--1">
<PARAM NAME="ShowHorizontalGrid" VALUE="--1">
<PARAM NAME="ShowTitle" VALUE="--1">
```

```
    <PARAM NAME="ShowVerticalGrid" VALUE="--1">
    <PARAM NAME="TitleFontColor" VALUE="10485760">
    <PARAM NAME="ValueIsNull" VALUE="0">
            </OBJECT>
</TD></TR>
    <TR>
        <TD>
            <OBJECT classid=clsid:978C9E23--D4B0--11CE--BF2D--00AA003F40D0
➡height=26
            id=LabelControl2
            style="HEIGHT: 26px; LEFT: 0px; TOP: 0px; WIDTH: 61px"
width=61>
    <PARAM NAME="ForeColor" VALUE="0">
    <PARAM NAME="BackColor" VALUE="16777215">
    <PARAM NAME="VariousPropertyBits" VALUE="8388635">
    <PARAM NAME="Caption" VALUE="Project">
    <PARAM NAME="PicturePosition" VALUE="458753">
    <PARAM NAME="Size" VALUE="1614;688">
    <PARAM NAME="MousePointer" VALUE="0">
    <PARAM NAME="BorderColor" VALUE="2147483654">
    <PARAM NAME="BorderStyle" VALUE="0">
    <PARAM NAME="SpecialEffect" VALUE="0">
    <PARAM NAME="Accelerator" VALUE="0">
    <PARAM NAME="FontName" VALUE="Arial">
    <PARAM NAME="FontEffects" VALUE="1073741824">
    <PARAM NAME="FontHeight" VALUE="240">
    <PARAM NAME="FontOffset" VALUE="0">
    <PARAM NAME="FontCharSet" VALUE="1">
    <PARAM NAME="FontPitchAndFamily" VALUE="2">
    <PARAM NAME="ParagraphAlign" VALUE="1">
    <PARAM NAME="FontWeight" VALUE="400">
            </OBJECT>

            <OBJECT classid=clsid:8BD21D30--EC42--11CE--9E0D--00AA006002F3
➡height=24
            id=MdcCombo1 style="HEIGHT: 24px; WIDTH: 129px" width=129>
    <PARAM NAME="VariousPropertyBits" VALUE="746604571">
    <PARAM NAME="BackColor" VALUE="2147483653">
    <PARAM NAME="ForeColor" VALUE="2147483656">
    <PARAM NAME="MaxLength" VALUE="0">
    <PARAM NAME="BorderStyle" VALUE="0">
    <PARAM NAME="ScrollBars" VALUE="0">
    <PARAM NAME="DisplayStyle" VALUE="3">
    <PARAM NAME="MousePointer" VALUE="0">
    <PARAM NAME="Size" VALUE="3413;635">
    <PARAM NAME="PasswordChar" VALUE="0">
    <PARAM NAME="ListWidth" VALUE="0">
    <PARAM NAME="BoundColumn" VALUE="1">
    <PARAM NAME="TextColumn" VALUE="65535">
    <PARAM NAME="ColumnCount" VALUE="1">
    <PARAM NAME="ListRows" VALUE="8">
```

B

```
        <PARAM NAME="cColumnInfo" VALUE="0">
        <PARAM NAME="MatchEntry" VALUE="1">
        <PARAM NAME="ListStyle" VALUE="0">
        <PARAM NAME="ShowDropButtonWhen" VALUE="2">
        <PARAM NAME="ShowListWhen" VALUE="1">
        <PARAM NAME="DropButtonStyle" VALUE="1">
        <PARAM NAME="MultiSelect" VALUE="0">
        <PARAM NAME="Value" VALUE="">
        <PARAM NAME="Caption" VALUE="">
        <PARAM NAME="PicturePosition" VALUE="458753">
        <PARAM NAME="BorderColor" VALUE="2147483654">
        <PARAM NAME="SpecialEffect" VALUE="2">
        <PARAM NAME="Accelerator" VALUE="0">
        <PARAM NAME="GroupName" VALUE="">
        <PARAM NAME="FontName" VALUE="Arial">
        <PARAM NAME="FontEffects" VALUE="1073741824">
        <PARAM NAME="FontHeight" VALUE="240">
        <PARAM NAME="FontOffset" VALUE="0">
        <PARAM NAME="FontCharSet" VALUE="1">
        <PARAM NAME="FontPitchAndFamily" VALUE="2">
        <PARAM NAME="ParagraphAlign" VALUE="1">
        <PARAM NAME="FontWeight" VALUE="400">
            </OBJECT>
    <TR>
        <TD>
            <OBJECT classid=clsid:978C9E23--D4B0--11CE--BF2D--00AA003F40D0
➥height=25
            id=LabelControl1
            style="HEIGHT: 25px; LEFT: 0px; TOP: 0px; WIDTH: 62px"
➥width=62>
        <PARAM NAME="ForeColor" VALUE="0">
        <PARAM NAME="BackColor" VALUE="16777215">
        <PARAM NAME="VariousPropertyBits" VALUE="8388635">
        <PARAM NAME="Caption" VALUE="Hours">
        <PARAM NAME="PicturePosition" VALUE="458753">
        <PARAM NAME="Size" VALUE="1640;661">
        <PARAM NAME="MousePointer" VALUE="0">
        <PARAM NAME="BorderColor" VALUE="2147483654">
        <PARAM NAME="BorderStyle" VALUE="0">
        <PARAM NAME="SpecialEffect" VALUE="0">
        <PARAM NAME="Accelerator" VALUE="0">
        <PARAM NAME="FontName" VALUE="Arial">
        <PARAM NAME="FontEffects" VALUE="1073741824">
        <PARAM NAME="FontHeight" VALUE="240">
        <PARAM NAME="FontOffset" VALUE="0">
        <PARAM NAME="FontCharSet" VALUE="1">
        <PARAM NAME="FontPitchAndFamily" VALUE="2">
        <PARAM NAME="ParagraphAlign" VALUE="1">
        <PARAM NAME="FontWeight" VALUE="400">
            </OBJECT>
```

```
          <OBJECT classid=clsid:8BD21D10--EC42--11CE--9E0D--00AA006002F3
➥height=24
          id=MdcText1 style="HEIGHT: 24px; WIDTH: 128px" width=128>
    <PARAM NAME="VariousPropertyBits" VALUE="746604571">
    <PARAM NAME="BackColor" VALUE="2147483653">
    <PARAM NAME="ForeColor" VALUE="2147483656">
    <PARAM NAME="MaxLength" VALUE="0">
    <PARAM NAME="BorderStyle" VALUE="0">
    <PARAM NAME="ScrollBars" VALUE="0">
    <PARAM NAME="DisplayStyle" VALUE="1">
    <PARAM NAME="MousePointer" VALUE="0">
    <PARAM NAME="Size" VALUE="3387;635">
    <PARAM NAME="PasswordChar" VALUE="0">
    <PARAM NAME="ListWidth" VALUE="0">
    <PARAM NAME="BoundColumn" VALUE="1">
    <PARAM NAME="TextColumn" VALUE="65535">
    <PARAM NAME="ColumnCount" VALUE="1">
    <PARAM NAME="ListRows" VALUE="8">
    <PARAM NAME="cColumnInfo" VALUE="0">
    <PARAM NAME="MatchEntry" VALUE="2">
    <PARAM NAME="ListStyle" VALUE="0">
    <PARAM NAME="ShowDropButtonWhen" VALUE="0">
    <PARAM NAME="ShowListWhen" VALUE="1">
    <PARAM NAME="DropButtonStyle" VALUE="1">
    <PARAM NAME="MultiSelect" VALUE="0">
    <PARAM NAME="Value" VALUE="">
    <PARAM NAME="Caption" VALUE="">
    <PARAM NAME="PicturePosition" VALUE="458753">
    <PARAM NAME="BorderColor" VALUE="2147483654">
    <PARAM NAME="SpecialEffect" VALUE="2">
    <PARAM NAME="Accelerator" VALUE="0">
    <PARAM NAME="GroupName" VALUE="">
    <PARAM NAME="FontName" VALUE="Times New Roman">
    <PARAM NAME="FontEffects" VALUE="1073741824">
    <PARAM NAME="FontHeight" VALUE="240">
    <PARAM NAME="FontOffset" VALUE="0">
    <PARAM NAME="FontCharSet" VALUE="0">
    <PARAM NAME="FontPitchAndFamily" VALUE="2">
    <PARAM NAME="ParagraphAlign" VALUE="1">
    <PARAM NAME="FontWeight" VALUE="400">
          </OBJECT>
    <TR>
       <TD>
          <TABLE border=1 cellPadding=1 cellSpacing=1 width=100%>

             <TR>
                <TD>
                   <OBJECT
                   classid=clsid:D7053240--CE69--11CD--A777--
➥00DD01143C57
                   id=CommandButton1><PARAM NAME="ForeColor" VALUE=
➥"2147483666"><PARAM NAME="BackColor" VALUE="2147483663">
```

B

```
➡<PARAM NAME="VariousPropertyBits" VALUE="27"><PARAM NAME=
➡"Caption" VALUE="Submit"><PARAM NAME="PicturePosition" VALUE=
➡"458753"><PARAM NAME="Size" VALUE="2540;847"><PARAM NAME=
➡"MousePointer" VALUE="0"><PARAM NAME="Accelerator" VALUE="0">
➡<PARAM NAME="TakeFocusOnClick" VALUE="--1"><PARAM NAME="FontName"
➡VALUE="Arial"><PARAM NAME="FontEffects" VALUE="1073741824">
➡<PARAM NAME="FontHeight" VALUE="240"><PARAM NAME="FontOffset" VALUE=
➡"0"><PARAM NAME="FontCharSet" VALUE="1"><PARAM NAME=
➡"FontPitchAndFamily" VALUE="2"><PARAM NAME="ParagraphAlign"
➡VALUE="3"><PARAM NAME="FontWeight" VALUE="400"></OBJECT>

</TD>
                                <TD>
                                    <OBJECT
                                    classid=clsid:D7053240--CE69--11CD--A777--
➡00DD01143C57
                                    id=CommandButton2 name=btnCancel>
        <PARAM NAME="ForeColor" VALUE="2147483666">
        <PARAM NAME="BackColor" VALUE="2147483663">
        <PARAM NAME="VariousPropertyBits" VALUE="27">
        <PARAM NAME="Caption" VALUE="Cancel">
        <PARAM NAME="PicturePosition" VALUE="458753">
        <PARAM NAME="Size" VALUE="2540;847">
        <PARAM NAME="MousePointer" VALUE="0">
        <PARAM NAME="Accelerator" VALUE="0">
        <PARAM NAME="TakeFocusOnClick" VALUE="--1">
        <PARAM NAME="FontName" VALUE="Arial">
        <PARAM NAME="FontEffects" VALUE="1073741824">
        <PARAM NAME="FontHeight" VALUE="240">
        <PARAM NAME="FontOffset" VALUE="0">
        <PARAM NAME="FontCharSet" VALUE="1">
        <PARAM NAME="FontPitchAndFamily" VALUE="2">
        <PARAM NAME="ParagraphAlign" VALUE="3">
        <PARAM NAME="FontWeight" VALUE="400">
                                    </OBJECT>
</TD></TR></TABLE></TD></TR></TABLE>


</P>

</BODY>
</HTML>
```

Day 8

Quiz

1. What are the four panes of the Query Designer?

   The four panes of the Query Designer are the Diagram pane, Grid pane, SQL pane, and Results pane.

2. What is the difference between a file data source and a machine data source?

A file data source enables you to capture database connection information within a DSN file. Visual InterDev inserts the information contained in this file into an Active Server Page, thereby creating a DSN-less connection. A file DSN is preferred because you don't have to establish the data source name on every user's machine.

A machine data source creates a data source connection that's specific to a machine. If you move the application to another machine, you also have to re-create the DSN for the new machine.

B

3. Name the two types of machine data sources.

The two types of machine data sources are a user DSN and a system DSN. The user DSN is tied to a specific user, whereas a system DSN can be shared among all users.

4. In the ADO model, what is the `Recordset` object?

The `Recordset` object enables you to access the properties and values of a result set that is returned from your database. An example is accessing the properties of a table and modifying the contents of the table or rows that are returned from a specific SQL call.

Exercise

Create the data source that was presented in the lesson. If you're using a database other than SQL Server, create a data source connection to your particular database. After you have established the connection, practice using the Data View and the Query Designer so that you will be familiar with these tools when you put them to the test during tomorrow's lesson. Practice using all four of the Query Designer panes to produce the desired results from your SQL statements. Some things to practice include the following:

1. Selecting two (or more) related tables to perform a query.

Given that you have set up a proper data source to your database, drag and drop two related tables to the Diagram pane.

2. Selecting the fields to perform the query on.

Within the Diagram pane, click the fields from the table that you want to display in the Results pane.

3. Entering parameters to further qualify the results.

Using the Criteria column of the Grid pane, enter a qualifier for one of the fields. For example, Figure B.1 shows an example of selecting the orders that have a unit price greater than $15.00.

FIGURE B.1.

Using the Criteria column.

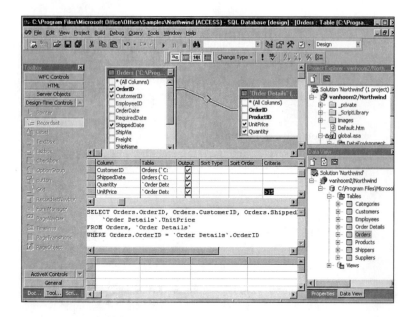

4. Executing the query and displaying the results.

   Click the Run Query icon on the Query Designer toolbar to execute the query and display the results in the Results pane.

Day 9

Quiz

1. What is an update query?

   An update query enables you to update columns within a single row or multiple rows of data. The update query creates an UPDATE SQL statement to execute the command. The update query provides a very effective method for updating multiple rows of data rather than manually updating each row.

2. What is a stored procedure?

   A stored procedure is a precompiled procedure that executes SQL statements on the server database. Stored procedures are more efficient and take fewer steps to execute than dynamic SQL, which is passed to a database to be processed.

3. What is a computed column?

   A computed column is a virtual column that is created based on another column's values. A computed column isn't stored in the database, but is calculated and displayed in the query results as if it were a database column.

Exercises

1. Use the Publishers database to create a query that displays the royalties and year-to-date sales for authors sorted by author last name.

   Drag the Titles, TitleAuthor, and Authors table onto the Diagram pane. Select the first name and last name columns from the Authors table and the title, royalty, and ytd sales column from the Titles table. Choose Ascending for the Sort Type for the last name column in the Grid pane.

2. Customize the query in exercise 1 to list just those authors that have royalties greater than 10 percent.

   Change the Criteria for the royalty column to > 10.

Day 10

Quiz

1. What is a foreign key?

   A foreign key is a column or set of columns whose value matches the primary key value of another table.

2. What is the Default Value column property used for?

   The Default Value property enables you to specify a default value for a column. This property can be used in situations when you want to populate the value of the column if the user doesn't enter a value for the field within the context of your application.

3. Name three types of column constraints.

   Possible answers include

   - Check
   - Default
   - Primary Key
   - Foreign Key
   - Unique

4. What occurs if you save a database diagram?

   Saving a database diagram causes all changes in the diagram to be applied to the database. The database diagram is an effective tool for making database modifications and applying them to the database.

B

5. What are two ways to edit the definition of a table?

   Table definitions can be edited in a database diagram and can also be edited in Design mode.

Exercise

Create a database diagram for the pubs database.

Figure B.2 depicts a database diagram of the pubs database.

FIGURE B.2.

The pubs database.

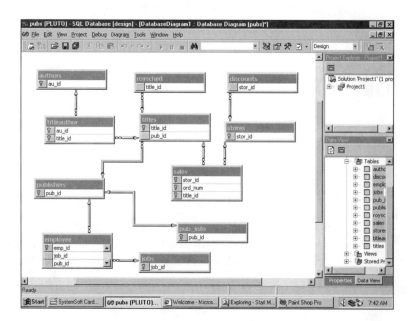

Day 11

Quiz

1. Name the five types of ASP objects.

   `Request`, `Response`, `Session`, `Application`, and `Server`.

2. What is a collection?

   A set of related objects that are accessed using the same method. An object uses a collection to access variables that define certain attributes and characteristics about the object.

3. Which object contains a collection that enables you to access the object values on a form?

   `Request`.

4. If you create a variable in the `Session` object, what is its scope?

   The `Session` object pertains to an individual user's session with the application. The scope of a variable created in the `Session` object extends for the lifetime of a user session, and information stored in a `Session` variable is only available to the specified user. As long as the user interacts with the application, the variable is available to the user.

5. Name the Active Server Components that are included with Visual InterDev and IIS.

   - Database Access Component
   - AdRotator Component
   - Browser Capabilities Component
   - File Access Component
   - Content Linking Component

Exercise

In today's lesson, I covered the fundamentals of Active Server Page development. In creating your Active Server Page for this exercise, choose some of your favorite objects and examples from today's lesson. Experiment with these examples when creating your application. Use properties and methods that I discussed but did not show by example in today's lesson. Use the concepts you learned today to extend the functionality of your application beyond the simple user preferences functions that I discussed today. For example, you could use the baseball example from today's lesson and add functionality related to stadiums, players, games, and so on.

Listings B.1 through B.3 demonstrate working with the concepts covered on Day 11. Feel free to work with these and your own examples to practice working with Active Server Pages.

LISTING B.1. USER PREFERENCE FORM FOR BASEBALL STADIUMS.

```
 1: <HTML>
 2: <HEAD>
 3: <TITLE>Favorite Ball Parks</TITLE>
 4: <H2>Please enter your favorite ball park: </H2>
 5: </HEAD>
 6: <BODY>
 7: <form action="/chapter11Proj/scripts/submit.asp" method="post">
 8: <p>Your name: <input name="name" size=48>
 9: <p>What is your favorite baseball stadium: <select name="park">
10: <option>Astrodome <option>Wrigley <option>The BOB <option>Ballpark at
    ➥Union Station
```

continues

LISTING B.1. CONTINUED

```
11: </select>
12: <p><input type=submit>
13: </form>
14: </BODY>
15: </HTML>
16: Welcome, <%= Request.Form("park")%>.
17: Your favorite baseball park is <%= Request.Form("park")%>!
```

LISTING B.2. WORKING WITH THE Application OBJECT.

```
1: <%
2: ' Locks the Application object
3: Application.Lock
4: If Application("FavoriteTeam") = "Astros" Then
5: Application("AstrosHits") = Application("AstrosHits") + 1
6: Else
7: If Application("FavoriteTeam") = "Rangers" Then
8:  Application("RangersHits") = Application("AstrosHits") + 1
9: ' Unlocks the Application object
10: Application.Unlock
11: %>
```

LISTING B.3. WORKING WITH THE Session OBJECT.

```
1: <HTML>
2: <% If Session("team") = "Astros" Then %>
3: <H1>Let's head to the Astrodome</H1>
4: <% Else If Session("team") = "Rangers" %>
5: <H1>Let's head to the Ballpark at Arlington</H1>
6: <%End If%>
7: </HTML>
```

Day 12

Quiz

1. What is the difference between design-time and regular ActiveX controls?

   A design-time control is a special type of ActiveX control that provides code that persists and executes at runtime without incurring the overhead of a control object. Regular ActiveX controls exist both at design time and runtime. ActiveX controls are typically used to construct a user interface for your application. An ActiveX control object is instantiated at runtime.

2. What is the name of the control that enables you to connect to a database from within your Web page?

   The Recordset control.

3. Which control enables you to navigate through the Recordset?

   The RecordsetNavBar control.

4. What is the default scripting language that is generated for the standard Visual InterDev design-time controls?

   JavaScript.

Exercise

For today's exercise, change the RSTest.asp page that you created today to be update-able. Also, add another ASP to your project that includes other controls besides the Textbox controls. Experiment with these controls against other tables in the Fitch database. This will give you good practice in preparation for the lessons covered the next two days.

Although today's exercise is more of a practice session for you, refer back to the tips and techniques shared in this lesson and apply these to your practice session today.

Day 13

Quiz

1. What is the difference between the page object's navigate method and execute method?

   When a navigate method is called, control of the application jumps to the page object, the requested code is executed, and control of the application can jump to another page. After the method executes, control of the program does not have to return to the calling page. When an execute method is called, the method executes, and when it is finished, control of the program returns to the calling program. This is similar to how method calls work in Visual Basic, for example.

2. Why might using the Data Environment Object Model be important to a developer?

   Using the Data Environment Object Model can be useful if you need database access from many different pages. By using this model, you can reuse database connection code. Rather than connect to a database, construct and run a query, and return a resultset, you can call a method on the Data Environment object and return a resultset.

3. What are the three types of scope for a page object's properties? Describe how they're implemented.

The three levels of scope available to a page object's properties are page, session, and application. Page-scope properties are available on the page until the page is exited. Session-scope properties are available to all the pages in your project. Session-scope properties' values are store in the same manner as ASP session variables. Application-scope properties are available to all users of your application across all pages in your project. Application-scope properties' values are stored in the same manner as ASP application variables.

4. Describe the two interfaces that make up a DHTML scriptlet.

The first interface is the visual, or user, interface. This interface is the DHTML interface that the user would see even if this were a Web page and not a scriptlet. The second interface is the control interface. The control interface includes all the properties, methods, and events that you will make available to other users in your scriptlet.

Exercise

In today's exercise, you will create a small application that uses a DHTML scriptlet and a page object. The DHTML scriptlet should provide the user with a form interface including a DTC text box and a DTC command button. Use client-side script to code the `on_click` event for the command button. The event should call a remote page object navigate method. The method should accept the text box's value, add `Hello` to the string, and print *Hello* on the page. Place your scriptlet on a page and test your application.

The solution to this exercise is provided on the book's information site at `www.mcp.com`. Look for the files `ExerciseClient.htm`, `ExercisePageObject.asp`, and `ExerciseScriptlet.htm`.

Day 14

Quiz

1. What design-time control is used to access the database?

The Recordset control.

2. What are the main differences between HTML and ASP files?

ASP files can generate HTML as well as scripting code for the client- and server-side portions of your application.

3. What is used to pass information from one Web page to another?

A querystring.

Exercise

For the final exercise of the second week, you will develop more Web pages for the Northwind Foods application. You can use any of the tables in the Northwind database to support these pages. Try focusing on the concepts you might not understand as well as others. For example, you might want to create more images for the Web pages, using the Image Composer to understand its capabilities. You also should practice using ASPs to deliver dynamic content from database tables. You can examine the tables and create added functions and features for the application, based on the information in the database.

As this is mainly a practice session, there is no pat "answer." You can refer to earlier chapters for more guidance and tips. For further information on content issues, refer to Days 3 and 4. For database, ASP, and DTC information, refer to Days 10–12.

B

Day 15

Quiz

1. What are some reasons for creating components?

   Reusability, maintainability, scalability, and performance.

2. What is the basic difference between COM and DCOM?

   DCOM facilitates the communication of objects located on different machines. COM is used for objects and components residing on the same machine.

3. Name three languages you can use to create a component.

   Visual C++, Java, Visual J++, Visual Basic, Delphi.

4. What statement do you use to instantiate an object within your ASP code?

   `Server.CreateObject`.

Exercises

1. Install the Island Hopper C sample application from the Visual Studio CD-ROMs. This application is used for tomorrow's lesson to demonstrate the role of components within your application.

   Refer to the Visual Studio help and perform a search on Island Hopper. The help files will provide installation instructions for the sample application.

2. You're on your own for this one. Experiment!

Day 16

Quiz

1. What is the difference between an inbound link and an outbound link?

   An inbound link defines a direct relationship between an object that has been expanded and one of its associated objects. An outbound link differs in that it represents a relationship between two or more of the associated objects.

2. What is the name of the feature that enables you to view your Web site structure?

   Link View.

3. Name the feature that enables you to copy an entire Web site to another location.

   Copy Web Project.

Exercises

1. Today's exercise involves a research project. I want you to research Web site management and site visualization tools on the Internet. This field is expanding at a rapid pace as the issues surrounding the proper management of a Web site continue to gain importance. You should make a list of these tools and search for their purpose, features, strengths, and weaknesses. Then compare the purpose and qualities of these tools with the site visualization and management tools contained in Visual InterDev. In what ways are the other products weaker? In what ways are they stronger? Document answers to these questions and others that you have regarding this topic so that you can refer to them in the future.

2. Develop a promotion and deployment strategy for your Web applications. This may entail mapping out the creation of development, testing, and production environments that effectively support the design, build, testing, and rollout of your applications. Be sure to note how the features of both Visual InterDev and Visual Studio can support your efforts.

Although today's exercises involve self-reflection, you should think about these important questions and issues when maintaining and managing your site.

Day 17

Quiz

1. Name the three categories of Web-application programming errors.

   Syntax errors, runtime errors, and logic errors.

2. What are the three ways to access features of the Visual InterDev debugger in the development environment?

   You can access the debugger via the Debug Windows menu option (under the View menu), the Debug menu, and the Debug toolbar.

3. Name two ways to set a breakpoint in your script code.

   You can set a breakpoint in your script code by double-clicking next to the line of code in Source view. The other way is to place the cursor on the line of code in Source view and select Insert Breakpoint from the Debug menu.

4. Name three ways to view the contents of a variable or expression in your script code.

   You can view the contents of a variable or expression by using the Watch window, the Locals window, or the Immediate window.

5. Name three ways to control the execution of your script code.

   You can use Step Into, Step Over, Step Out, Run to Cursor, Continue, Restart, and Set Next Statement to control the execution of your script code.

Exercise

For today's exercise, practice what you learned about Visual InterDev's debugger. I want you to create script code that executes on the client and server. If you already have a good example in one of your applications, feel free to use it in this exercise. (If you don't have a sample application, you could go to the Microsoft Visual InterDev Web site [http://www.microsoft.com/vinterdev/download/samples/default.htm] and download the Dos Perros Chile Company example.)

Set up your application for debugging as discussed earlier in today's lesson. Set breakpoints in your script code—both client- and server-side. Then use the features of the Visual InterDev debugger that were discussed today to thoroughly test the behavior of your application. Experiment with the different ways to step through your code and examine the values of variables. Check out the call stack and threads windows as you execute client- and server-side script code. Most importantly, have fun while you experiment with the great debugging features of Visual InterDev.

To perform this exercise, use the sample Web applications available from this book's Web site at http://www.mcp.com/info. The sample Web application contains script code that will test your abilities as well as the features of the Visual InterDev debugger.

B

Day 18

Quiz

1. What is the difference between Master mode and Local mode?

   Local mode allows you to isolate your development from the rest of the team. Changes are saved to a local version of your files and synchronized with your master Web server only when you specify to do so. When in Master mode, all changes are automatically saved to both the local version and master version.

2. Define Offline mode.

   Offline mode allows you to work on files in your application while disconnected from the Web server.

3. What is the Visual Component Manager?

   The Visual Component Manager allows you to publish and provide COM-based components to a team of developers.

Exercises

Day 18's exercises require multiple people and multiple machines to be effective. These are practice sessions, so there aren't real "answers."

Day 19

Quiz

1. What is the command that enables you to activate source control for your Visual InterDev project?

   Add to Source Control, found under the Project menu in Visual InterDev.

2. What happens when you disable source control for your Visual InterDev project?

   Source control is deactivated, and your files are no longer governed by the Visual SourceSafe rules of versioning and source code control. The Visual SourceSafe database entry that contains your Visual InterDev project, however, isn't deleted.

3. Describe the Visual SourceSafe library functions.

   The Visual SourceSafe library functions include check-in and check-out, which enable you to reserve working copies of your project files. The check-out function enables you to reserve an exclusive copy of a file that can be either read-only or read- and write-enabled. The check-in function enables you to send your file changes back to the Visual SourceSafe database where others are then free to reserve their working copy of the file. Both functions are available from within the Visual InterDev environment.

Exercises

Today's exercises extend the lesson for today by enabling you to practice using the integrated features of Visual SourceSafe:

1. Create a Visual InterDev project and enable the source control for the project. You also should make several updates to one of your Web pages and then compare the differences of the versions to understand how this process works.

2. When you have accomplished this step, use Visual InterDev to create some files for your project. These files can consist of HTML pages, ASP files, images, and any other item that you want to include. As you develop these components, notice the behavior of Visual InterDev as the Visual SourceSafe features are enforced.

3. Practice merging different versions of files as well as rolling back to a different version of a file from within the Visual InterDev environment.

Although Day 19's exercises are more of a practice session for you and your team, here are some general points to remember across each of the exercises:

- To enable source control, right-click the project root within the Visual InterDev Project Explorer and select Project | Source Control | Add to Source Control.

- To check out a file, right-click on the file and select Check Out from the shortcut menu.

- To check in a file, right-click on the file and select Check In from the shortcut menu.

Day 20

Quiz

1. Name the five basic steps for designing an effective user interface.

   The following steps outline the five basic steps to designing an effective interface:

   1. Define a purpose for the interface.

   2. Identify the users' expectations and needs.

   3. Design the user interface.

   4. Conduct usability testing.

   5. Incorporate the feedback into your interface.

2. What are dead ends?

   Dead ends are like dead-end streets—they leave you with no place to go. A dead-end page is a Web page that provides no navigational path within the context of the application. The only way for a user to navigate out of a dead end is to use the browser navigational buttons of Back and Forward.

3. What is the difference between a theme and a layout?

A theme includes graphics, fonts, and special page elements that provide a consistent look and feel for your Web site. Themes use cascading style sheets for their implementation. A layout provides a template that indicates where navigation bars are placed on the page.

Exercises

Compare the sites you visit. What strengths and weaknesses do you notice?

Day 21

Quiz

1. What is the DOM?

DOM stands for Document Object Model and represents a way to define page elements as objects. By using this object model, you can alter the properties and methods of the element objects, thereby manipulating their appearance and behavior.

2. What is event bubbling?

Event bubbling is a feature of DHTML that allows for the passing of event messages up through the document hierarchy object model.

3. Name three component technologies of DHTML.

Possible answers include

> Dynamic Styles
>
> Dynamic Content
>
> Dynamic Positioning
>
> Data Binding
>
> Document Object Model

Exercise

For today's exercise, research the Web sites mentioned in the Summary section of today's lesson. These sites, as well as the books that are mentioned, provide a wealth of knowledge on the subject of DHTML. Some of the sites provide other examples. Try out some of their examples and apply the concepts to the project that you created today.

Try out the Web sites mentioned as well as extend your knowledge of DHTML by reading one of the aforementioned books.

INDEX

Symbols

+ (plus sign), Link View icons, 391

A

Abandon method, 286
absolute positioning, 96-97
Absolute Positioning command (Format menu), 96
accessing
  Application object, 288
  collections, 270
  files, 41
Active Server Components, 290
Active Server Page command (Add menu), 143
Active Server Pages, *see* **ASPs**
ActiveX controls, 25, 160
  adding, 166-168
  advantages, 164
  aligning, 162
  class IDs, 161

  defining, 163
  HTML markup, 160-163
  limitations, 164-165
  methods, 169-171
  naming conventions, 492
  parameters, 163
  properties, 168-169
  security, 176
  sizing, 162
  Toolbox, 69-70, 100
  see also design-time controls
Add Existing Page command (Site Diagram menu), 476, 481
Add Home Page command (Site Diagram menu), 477
Add HTML Page command (Project menu), 85
Add HTML Page dialog box, 85
Add Item command (Project menu), 94
Add menu commands, Active Server Page, 143
Add to Global Navigation Bar command (Site Diagram menu), 477

Add User command (Users menu), 451
Add User dialog box, 451
AddHeader method, 280
ADO (ActiveX Data Objects), 34
  ASP integration, 370-371
  collections, 207
  Command object, 205
  Connection object, 205
  Data Environment Object Model, 336-338
  DTC, 207-208
  Error object, 207
  Field object, 206
  model, 204-205
  OLE DB, 209
  overview, 34, 201-204
  Parameter object, 206
  properties, 207
  Property object, 207
  RDO, 209
  Recordset object, 206
aggregate functions, 230-232
aliases (columns), 225-226
ALIGN attribute
  APPLET tag, 159
  OBJECT tag, 162

aligning
ActiveX controls, 162
Java applets, 159
ALT attribute (APPLET tag), 159
analysis, projects
clients, 50-51
directories, 52-53
servers, 49
AppendToLog method, 280
<APPLET> tag (HTML)
ALIGN attribute, 159
ALT attribute, 159
CODE attribute, 159
CODEBASE attribute, 158
HEIGHT attribute, 159
HSPACE attribute, 160
NAME attribute, 159
VSPACE attribute, 160
WIDTH attribute, 159
applets (Java), 25, 156-157
advantages, 165-166
aligning, 159
alternative text, 159
controls (Toolbox), 100
HTML markup, 158-160
limitations, 166
parameters, 160
running, 158
security, 176
sizing, 159
Application object
events, 289
methods, 288
applications
abstracting layers
(DCOM), 367-368
debugging errors
component, 405-406
database, 406
HTML, 405
logic, 404
overview, 403-404
runtime, 404
script, 406
syntax, 404
development, 393,
439-440
EXEs (executable pro-
grams), 363-364
FrontPage Web develop-
ment, 446-448

holistic applications, 185
Northwind case study
creating project, 343
database, 343
home page, 344
Order Details page,
350-355
Order Listing page,
347-350
Order Search page,
345-347
overview, 342-343
Web pages, 342
production, 393, 442
Scripting Object Model,
334-335
testing, 393, 441
Timesheet
combo box, 171
confirming input, 174
Hours Worked field,
174
methods, 169-170
properties, 168-169
validating input, 175
Web
creating, 373-375
integrating compo-
nents, 376-378
see also projects
applying
layouts, 490
themes, 490-491
architecture
developing, 427
multitier architecture, 141,
267
n-tiered (DCOM),
368-369
**arguments (VBScript proce-
dures), 114-115**
**ASPs (Active Server Pages),
138, 263, 309**
Active Server
Components, 290
advantages, 264
Application object
events, 289
methods, 288
browser interaction,
265-266
capabilities, 139

client/server model,
140-141, 266
components comparison,
379
cookies
defined, 271
querying, 271
retrieving values, 271
setting values, 281-282
creating, 56-57, 142-144
database connections,
Data view, 51
DCOM object integration,
370-371
defined, 26
design-time controls,
308-311
development paradigm,
139, 265
forms, 272
dynamic forms,
274-276
processing, 273
user preferences form,
273
HTML pages
connecting, 41-48
interaction, 356
HTTP request processing,
278-279
objects, 12
output
buffering, 282-283
content type, 285
sending to user,
283-284
Request object, 270
Cookies collection, 271
Form collection,
272-276
QueryString collection,
278-279
ServerVariables collec-
tion, 276-278
Response object, 279
AddHeader method,
280
AppendToLog method,
280
BinaryWrite method,
280
Buffer property,
280-283

Clear method, 280
ContentType property, 280, 285
Cookies collection, 281-282
End method, 280
Expires property, 280
ExpiresAbsolute property, 280
Flush method, 280
methods, 281
Redirect method, 280, 284-285
Status property, 280
Write method, 280, 283-284
script
  debugging, 408-410
  form-processing example, 149-150
  Hello, World example, 144-146
scripting languages, 141-142, 267-268
Scripting Object Model, 269
Server object
  instantiating, 291-293
  methods, 290
  properties, 291
  referencing, 290
servers
  support, 140, 265
  variables, 276-278
Session object
  Abandon method, 286
  events, 287-288
  SessionID property, 285
  storing variables in, 286-287
  Timeout property, 286
sessions
  ending, 286
  starting, 287-288
Source view, 53
transactions, 268-269
users
  counting, 289
  redirecting, 284-285
viewing, 152

attributes
defined, 205
HTML
  ALIGN, 159, 162
  ALT, 159
  CLASSID, 161-162
  CODE, 159
  CODEBASE, 158
  HEIGHT, 159, 162
  HSPACE, 160, 163
  ID, 162
  NAME, 159
  VSPACE, 160, 163
  WIDTH, 159, 162
Authors table (Pubs database), 214
Auto window (debugger), 411-412
AVG function, 230-232

B

backup databases, 428
Banner pages (Site Designer), 489
BinaryWrite method, 280
binding data
defined, 500
example, 508-513
<BODY> tag (HTML), 106
bold text, 90
Bookmark command (HTML menu), 94
bookmarks (HTML), 94
breakpoints
debugging, 416-417
setting, 409
Breakpoints command (Debug menu), 417
Breakpoints dialog box, 417
broken links
displaying, 383
repairing, 398-399
Broken Links Report command (View menu), 399
Browse With function, 21
Browser With command (Link View shortcut menu), 391

browsers
ASPs, 152
Internet Explorer 4.0, 20-21
selecting, 21
browsing Web pages, 58
Buffer property (Response object), 280-283
buffering page output, 282-283
bugs, *see* **debugging**
Button control, 302
buttons
JavaScript, 112
JScript, 110
VBScript, 110

C

Call keyword (VBScript), 115-116
Call Stack window (debugger), 418
calling
functions (VBScript procedures), 118
methods, 169
sub procedures (VBScript procedures), 115
cascading style sheets, (CSSs), 97-99
Case statements (VBScript procedures), 128-129
Change Type button (Query Designer toolbar), 217
changing mode, 436-439
character set translation (ODBC), 195
Check constraint, 243
Check In dialog box, 457
Check Out Items dialog box, 456
Checkbox control, 302
checking Visual SourceSafe files
in, 457-458
out, 456-457
Children pages (Site Designer), 489

**Choose URL dialog box,
481**
choosing, *see* **selecting**
**class IDs (ActiveX controls),
161**
**CLASSID attribute
(<OBJECT> tag), 161-162**
clauses
    HAVING, 232
    WHERE, 232
**Clear All Breakpoints com-
mand (Debug menu), 417**
Clear method, 280, 421
**Client Object and Events
folder (ScriptBuilder),
27-28**
**Client Scripts folder
(ScriptBuilder), 28**
**Client Server and Events
folder (ScriptBuilder), 30**
client/server model
    ASPs, 266
    mixed environments, 431
    Windows 95 platform,
      429-430
    see also ASPs
client-side scripting
    advantages, 104
    debugging, 408-410
    DHTML DOM, 318-320
    documents, 320
    HTML pages, 105-106
    limitations, 104
    server-side script integra-
      tion, 150-152
    Web pages, 108-112
    windows, 320
clients
    COM consumers/
      containers, 362
    project analysis, 50-51
code
    breakpoints, 409
    color-coding, 23-24
    customizing, 73-75
    debugging
      breakpoints, 416-417
      execution, 414-417
      server-side, 14
      syntax errors, 404
    editing (Outline windows),
      76-77
    scraps, 75-76

source code, 449
    see also HTML;
      scripting languages/
      scripts
**CODE attribute (APPLET
tag), 159**
**CODEBASE attribute
(APPLET tag), 158**
collections
    accessing, 270
    ADO, 207
    COM/ASP integration,
      370-371
    Cookies, 271, 281-282
    defined, 270
    Form, 272-276
    QueryString, 278-279
    ServerVariables, 276-278
color
    script, 23-24
    text (HTML), 91
columns, 221-223
    adding to queries, 224
    delete query column, 222
    deleting from queries, 224
    insert query column, 222
    keys, 241
    naming, 225-226
    order, 225
    properties (diagrams), 246
    rows
      grouping query results,
        228-232
      searching, 226-228
    symbols, 223
    update query column, 222
**COM (Component Object
Model)**
    consumers, 362
    DCOM, 362
      developer roles, 369
      n-tiered architectures,
        368-369
      objects, ASP integra-
        tion, 370-371
      ORPCs, 366
      overview, 366
      remote servers, 366
      Visual Basic, 370
      Visual C++, 370
      Visual J++, 370
      Windows DNA
        (abstracting applica-
        tion layers), 367-368
    DLLs, 363-365

EXEs, 363-364
    LRPCs, 365
    objects, ASP integration,
      370-371
    overview, 362-366
    producers, 362
    see also components
**Command object (ADO),
205**
commands
    Add menu, Active Server
      Page, 143
    ADO, 205
    Debug menu
      Breakpoints, 417
      Clear All Breakpoints,
        417
      Continue, 415
      Disable Breakpoint,
        416
      Enable Breakpoint, 416
      Insert, 409
      Remove Breakpoint,
        416
      Restart, 416
      Run to Cursor, 416
      Set Next Statement,
        416
      Show Next Statement,
        416
      Start, 409
      Step Into, 415
      Step Out, 415
      Step Over, 415
    File menu
      Make Orders.dll, 373
      New Project, 43
    Format menu
      Absolute Positioning,
        96
      Lock, 96
      Z Order, 95
    HTML menu
      Bookmark, 94
      Div, 95
      Image, 94
      Link, 93
      Marquee, 95
    Link (View object shortcut
      menu), 391
    Project menu
      Add HTML Page, 85
      Add Item, 94

Site Diagram menu
  Add Existing Page,
    476, 481
  Add Home Page, 477
  Add to Global
    Navigation Bar, 477
  Delete, 477
  Expand, 477
  New HTML Page,
    476-478
  Remove, 477
  Reorder Pages, 477
  Rotate, 477
  Zoom, 477
Table menu, Insert Table,
  22, 67
Tools menu
  Customize Toolbox,
    100
  Options, 78
  Snap to Grid, 97
  View Links on WWW,
    385
Users menu, Add User,
  451
View menu
  Broken Links Report,
    399
  Debug Windows, 407
  Other Windows, 76
  Toolbox, 69
Web Project menu, Copy
  Web, 395
Working Mode menu,
  Local, 437
comment tags (HTML), 106
compiling DLLs, 373
Component Object Model,
  see **COM**
components
  ASP
    comparison, 379
    DCOM integration,
      370-371
  debugging errors, 405-406
  Visual Basic, 371-373
  Visual SourceSafe, 455
  Web applications, 376-378
  see also COM
configuring
  file DSNs, 190-191
  system DSNs, 191-192

user DSNs, 191-192
Visual SourceSafe access,
  450-451
Connection object (ADO),
  205
connections
  data, 190
  databases, 190-198
  DSN-less connections,
    191
  file DSNs, 190-191
  system DSNs, 191-192
  user DSNs, 191-192
constraints, 243
consumers, *see* **clients**
containers, *see* **clients**
ContentType property
  (Response object), 280,
  285
Continue command (Debug
  menu), 415
control structures
  (VBScript), 125-127
controls
  ActiveX, 25
    adding, 166-168
    advantages, 164
    aligning, 162
    class IDs, 161
    defining, 163
    HTML markup,
      160-163
    limitations, 164-165
    methods, 169-171
    naming conventions,
      492
    parameters, 163
    properties, 168-169
    security, 176
    sizing, 162
    Toolbox, 69-70, 100
  customizing, 73-75
  DSO, 512
  DTC (design-time
    control), 35, 111,
    297-301
    ActiveX controls com-
      parison, 299
    ADO, 207-208
    database-driven forms,
      307-314
    defined, 25-26,
      298-299

PageObject, 327
Scripting Object Model
  (SOM), 13, 326-327
scripts, 306-307, 333
standard controls,
  302-303, 312,
  487-490
structure, 305-306
text view, 304-305
Toolbox, 72-73, 100
Web pages, 303
HTML controls
  Horizontal Rule, 71
  Toolbox, 71-72
interfaces (DHTML
  scriptlets), 322-324
methods, 74
properties, 74
TDC, 512
Toolbox, 68-69, 100
cookies
  attributes, 281
  defined, 271
  querying, 271
  values
    retrieving, 271
    setting, 281-282
Cookies collection, 271,
  281-282
Copy Project dialog box,
  395-396
Copy Web Application com-
  mand (Web Project
  menu), 395
copying
  files, 51
  Web sites, 395-398
    benefits, 394
    child Webs, 396
    destination Web server,
      396
    security, 395
    source code control,
      401
COUNT function, 232
counting Web site visitors,
  289
Create New Data Source
  dialog box, 192
CreateObject method, 290
CSSs (cascading style
  sheets), 97-99

Customize Toolbox command (Tools menu), 100
Customize Toolbox dialog box, 100
customizing
    code, 73-75
    IDE, 78
    queries, 224-232
        output, specifying, 226
        results, grouping, 228-232
        rows, searching, 226-228
    Toolbox, 99-100

D

DAO (Data Access Objects), 202
data
    binding
        defined, 500
        example, 508-513
    connecting, 190
Data Environment Object Model, 336-338
Data Form Wizard, 35
data source object (DSO) controls, 512
data sources
    character set translation, 195
    creating, 192-194, 197
    default databases, 194
    DSNs (data source names), 190
        DSN-less connections, 191
        file DSNs, 190-191
        system DSNs, 191-192
        user DSNs, 191-192
    listing, 197-198
    logging in, 196
    security, 194
    selecting drivers, 192-193
    testing, 195
data types (VBScript variables), 121-125
Data view, 51, 188-189

Database Connection Wizard, 190-198
Database Designer, 243-244
    database projects, 244
    diagrams, 244-250
    overview, 34
    tables, relationships, 255
database diagrams, 244-250
    creating, 250-251
    properties
        column properties, 246
        index/keys properties, 249-250
        relationship properties, 248-249
        table properties, 247-248
    tables
        column properties, 253
        creating, 251-255
        database changes, 254-255
database-driven forms
    database connections, 308
    design-time controls, 308-311
        Recordset, 312
        RecordsetNavBar, 312
        Textbox, 312
    runtime scripts, 312-314
    scripting platforms, 307
databases
    ASP connections, 51
    backups, 428
    choosing, 428
    connecting, 190-198
    connectivity
        leveraging, 184
        options, 185-186
    data, editing, 235-236
    designing, 428
    errors (debugging), 406
    integration, 185
    log in, 196
    mixed environments, 431
    Northwind case study, 343
    objects
        constraints, 243
        indexes, 243
        relationships, 240-242
        tables, 240
        viewing, 188-189

    ODBC, 194-196
    projects
        creating, 244
        Visual Data Tools, 43
    Pubs
        Authors table, 214
        connecting to (Query Designer), 212-214
    SQL, 34
    Windows 95 platform, 430
    wizards, 35
DCOM (Distributed Component Object Model), 362
    developer roles, 369
    n-tiered architectures, 368-369
    objects, ASP integration, 370-371
    ORPCs, 366
    overview, 366
    remote servers, 366
    Visual Basic, 370
    Visual C++, 370
    Visual J++, 370
    Windows DNA (abstracting application layers), 367-368
    see also COM
Debug menu
    commands
        Breakpoints, 417
        Clear All Breakpoints, 417
        Continue, 415
        Disable Breakpoint, 416
        Enable Breakpoint, 416
        Insert, 409
        Remove Breakpoint, 416
        Restart, 416
        Run to Cursor, 416
        Set Next Statement, 416
        Show Next Statement, 416
        Start, 409
        Step Into, 415
        Step Out, 415
        Step Over, 415
    viewing, 407

Debug toolbar, 410
**Debug Windows command
(View menu), 407**
debugger
ASPs, 407
HTML, 407
launching, 409-410
overview, 406-408
windows
Auto, 411-412
Call Stack, 418
Immediate, 413
Locals, 411-412
Processes, 419
Running Documents,
418
Threads, 418
Watch, 412
debugging
applications, 403-404
code
breakpoints, 409,
416-417
execution, 414-417
server-side, 14, 410
errors
component errors,
405-406
database errors, 406
error-handling routines,
419-421
HTML errors, 405
logic errors, 404
runtime errors, 404
script errors, 406
syntax errors, 404
files, 418
procedures, 418
processes, 419
remote debugging, 410
setup, 408-410
stored procedures, 260
threads, 418
variables
editing values, 412
locally, 411-412
logic, 413
Default constraint, 243
defining
ActiveX controls, 163
relationships, 241

scope of variables, 125
table column properties,
253
**Delete command (Site
Diagram menu), 477**
Delete query, 217
delete query column, 222
deleting
database data, 236
scraps, 75-76
**Design view (Visual
InterDev editor), 66**
HTML
adding, 85-86
bookmarks, 94
color, 91
dividers, 95
drag and drop HTML,
22
fonts, 89-90
Format menu, 87
formatting, 86-91
hotspots, 94
HTML toolbar, 87
images, 94-95
linking pages, 93
lists, 91
marquees, 95
paragraphs, 88-89
properties, 86
starting in, 86
tables, 91-93
objects
absolute positioning,
96-97
modifying, 255
snap-to positioning, 97
overview, 84-85
tables, 67-68
text, 66
Web page layout, 55-56
**design-time controls
(DTCs), 35, 111, 297-301**
ActiveX controls compari-
son, 299
ADO, 207-208
database-driven forms,
307
ASPs, 308-311
database connections,
308

runtime scripts,
312-314
scripting platforms,
307
defined, 25-26, 298-299
PageObject, 327
scripts
editing, 306-307
platforms, 333
Scripting Object Model
(SOM), 13, 326-327
standard controls, 302-303
PageNavBar, 487-490
Recordset, 312
RecordsetNavBar, 312
Textbox, 312
structure, 305-306
text view, 304-305
Toolbox, 72-73, 100
Web pages, 303
designing
CSS, 97-99
databases, 428
forms, 491-492
Site Designer, 15
adding pages, 481-484
creating pages,
478-480
icons, 485
layouts, 490
navigation bars,
487-490
organizing pages,
485-487
site diagrams, 476-478
themes, 490-491
user interfaces, 468-470
aesthetics, 472
design checklist,
492-493
goals, 468-469
layout, 472
metaphors, 471
navigation, 473
semantics, 473
usability testing,
473-475
user needs/expecta-
tions, 469
development, 393, 439-440
developers
DCOM, 369
developer isolation,
431-432

development teams, 14-15
Visual SourceSafe, 450-451
DHTML pages, 514
environment (IDE), 64
  benefits, 186-188
  customizing, 78
  editors, 64, 78
  Internet Explorer 4, 20-21
  Microsoft Development Environment, 17-19, 50, 190
  properties, 10
  robustness, 188
  speed, 187
  SQL, 187
  Visual SourceSafe, 463
FrontPage Webs, 446-448
platforms
  architecture, 427
  choosing, 426
  development tools, 426
  mixed environments, 430-431
  scalability, 426
  standards, 427
  Windows 95, 429-430
DHTML (Dynamic HTML), 497-498
  data binding, 500, 508-513
  DOM, 318-325, 499
  dynamic content
    base content, 500-502
    defined, 500
    text changes, 504-507
    titles, 502-504
  dynamic positioning, 500
  dynamic styles, 499
  HTML 4 comparison, 515
  online resources, 514
  scriptlets
    control interface, 322-324
    marking, 324
    user interface, 321-322
  standards, 515
  support, 15
  Web page sample
    base content, 500
    developing, 514

Dynamic Content page, 507-508
ShowAuctionsDHTML page, 511-513
diagrams, 244
  creating, 250-251
  properties
    column properties, 246
    index/keys properties, 249-250
    relationship properties, 248-249
    table properties, 247-248
  Site Designer
    adding pages, 481-484
    creating, 476-478
    creating pages, 478-480
    deleting pages, 477
    icons, 485
    organizing pages, 485-487
    rotating, 477
    zooming in/out, 477
  tables
    column properties, 253
    creating, 251-255
    database changes, saving, 254-255
dialog boxes
  Add HTML Page, 85
  Add User, 451
  Breakpoints, 417
  Check In, 457
  Check Out Items, 456
  Choose URL, 481
  Copy Project, 395-396
  Create New Data Source, 192
  Customize Toolbox, 100
  Insert Table, 67, 92-93
  Make Component, 373
  New Project, 43
  Open Project, 18
  Options, 78
  Property Pages, 86, 454
  Select Data Source, 190
differences (Visual SourceSafe files), 461-462
directories
  domain names, 40
  file management, 31-32

projects
  analysis, 52-53
  default, 44
  file organization, 40
  local, 53
  servers, 49
  working directories, 45
subdirectories, 40
URLs, 41
virtual root directories, 40
  see also folders
Disable Breakpoint command (Debug menu), 416
displaying links, 383-386
  broken links, 383
  filters, 388-389
  zoom percentage, 387
Distributed Component Object Model, *see* DCOM
Div command (HTML menu), 95
dividers (HTML), 95
DLLs (dynamic link libraries), 363-365
  COM, 363-365
  compiling, 373
  troubleshooting, 379
Do loops (VBScript procedures), 130
Document Outline window, 76-77
documents, client-side scripting, 320
DOM (Document Object Model), 318-325, 499
domain names, 40
Domain property (Cookies collection), 281
domains, *see* servers
drag and drop, 11, 22
drivers, data sources, 192-193
DSNs (data source names), 190
  DSN-less connections, 191
  file DSNs, 190-191
  system DSNs, 191-192
  user DSNs, 191-192
DSO (data source object) control, 512
DTCs, *see* design-time controls

dynamic content
defined, 500
example, 504-508
Dynamic HTML, *see*
DHTML
dynamic link libraries, *see*
DLLs
dynamic positioning, 500
dynamic styles, 499

E

ECMAScript, 142, 268
editing
ActiveX control proper-
ties, 168-169
code (Outline windows),
76-77
files, 51
HTML code, 73
objects (Link View), 391
script, 73-75
scripts (DTC), 306-307
WYSIWYG, 12
editors
comparison, 78
external, 78-79
IDE, 64
Script Editor, 172-173
Stored Procedure Editor,
34
creating stored proce-
dures, 258-260
running stored proce-
dures, 259-261
Trigger Editor, 34
Visual InterDev editor, *see*
views
Enable Breakpoint com-
mand (Debug menu), 416
enabling Scripting Object
Model, 269, 333-334
End Function keyword
(VBScript), 116
End method, 280
End Sub keyword
(VBScript), 114
environment
development (IDE), 64
benefits, 186-188
customizing, 78

editors, 64, 78
Internet Explorer 4,
20-21
Microsoft Development
Environment, 17-19,
50, 190
properties, 10
robustness, 188
speed, 187
SQL, 187
Visual SourceSafe, 463
Visual SourceSafe,
459-463
err object (VBScript),
420-421
Error object (ADO), 207
errors
component errors,
405-406
database errors, 406
error-handling routines,
419-421
HTML errors, 405
logic errors, 404
runtime errors, 404
script errors, 406
syntax errors, 404
event procedures (VBScript
procedures), 119-120
events
Application object, 289
Client Object and Events
folder, 27-28
Client Scripts folder, 28
Client Server and Events
folder, 30
onload (window object),
320
Session object, 287-288
write (document object),
320
execute method (page
object), 328-330
executing
Java applets, 158
queries, 223
stored procedures,
259-261
EXEs (executable pro-
grams), 363-364
Expand command (Site
Diagram menu), 477

Expand Links command
(Link View shortcut
menu), 391
expanding links, 391-392
Expires property
Cookies collection, 281
Response object, 280
ExpiresAbsolute property
(Response object), 280

F

Field object (ADO), 206
fields (ADO), 207
File menu commands
Make Orders.dll, 373
New Project, 43
files
accessing (URLs), 41
copying, 51
debugging, 418
editing, 51
file management, 31-32
global files, 41
opening, 51
projects
Project Explorer, 50
subdirectories, 40
root directories, 40
saving, 51
search files, 41
Visual SourceSafe
checking in, 457-458
checking out, 456-457
history, 461
versions, 461-462
see also projects
filtering (Link View),
388-389
First Level pages (Site
Designer), 488
Flush method, 280
folders
file management, 31-32
projects (servers), 49
Script Outline, 26-30
Client Object and
Events, 27-28
Client Scripts, 28
Client Server and
Events, 30

Web Projects, 43
see also directories
fonts (HTML)
 color, 91
 formatting, 89
 size, 89
 style, 90
For...Next loops (VBScript procedures), 130
Foreign Key constraint, 243
foreign keys, 241
Form collection, 272-276
Format menu commands, 87
 Absolute Positioning, 96
 Lock, 96
 Z Order, 95
formatting
 Design view, 86-91
 Format menu, 87
 HTML
  bookmarks, 94
  dividers, 95
  fonts, 89-90
  hotspots, 94
  images, 94-95
  linking pages, 93
  lists, 91
  marquees, 95
  paragraphs, 88-89
  tables, 91-93
  text color, 91
 HTML toolbar, 87
 objects
  absolute positioning, 96-97
  snap-to positioning, 97
FormManager control, 302
forms
 controls, naming conventions, 492
 database-driven forms
  database connections, 308
  design-time controls, 308-312
  runtime scripts, 312-314
  scripting platforms, 307
 designing, 491-492
 dynamic forms, 274-276

processing
 ASPs, 273
 server-side script, 146-150
 user preferences form, 273
FrontPage Web development, 446-448
Function keyword (VBScript), 116
functions
 aggregate functions, 230-232
 AVG, 230-232
 Browse With, 21
 COUNT, 232
 get(), 331
 MAX, 232
 MIN, 232
 set(), 331
 show(), 330
 SUM, 232
 VarType (VBScript), 122-123
 VBScript procedures, 116-119
  calling functions, 118
  subtype conversion functions, 124
 Visual SourceSafe library functions, 455-456
  checking in files, 457-458
  checking out files, 456-457
  undoing changes, 458
 see also methods

G

Gamelan EarthWeb Web site, 521
get() method, 331
global files, 41
Global Navigation Bar pages, 488
Grid control, 302
GROUP BY statement, 228
grouping query results, 228-232
 aggregate functions, 230-232

calculation method, choosing, 231
GUIs (graphical user interfaces)
 designing, 468-470
  aesthetics, 472
  design checklist, 492-493
  goals, 468-469
  layout, 472
  metaphors, 471
  navigation, 473
  semantics, 473
  user needs/expectations, 469
 DHTML scriptlets, 321-324
 usability testing, 473-475

H

HasKeys property (Cookies collection), 281
HAVING clause, 232
<HEAD> tag (HTML), 106
HEIGHT attribute
 <APPLET> tag, 159
 <OBJECT> tag, 162
Hello, World server-side script, 144-146
history (Visual SourceSafe files), 461
holistic applications, 185
Horizontal Rule (HTML controls), 71
hotspots, 94
HSPACE attribute
 <APPLET> tag, 160
 <OBJECT> tag, 163
HTML
 ASP interaction, 356
 attributes
  ALIGN, 159, 162
  ALT, 159
  CLASSID, 161-162
  CODE, 159
  CODEBASE, 158
  HEIGHT, 159, 162
  HSPACE, 160, 163
  ID, 162

NAME, 159
VSPACE, 160, 163
WIDTH, 159, 162
bookmarks, 94
code, editing, 73
DHTML, 497-498
    base content, 500-502
    data binding, 500,
        508-513
    development guide-
        lines, 514
    DOM, 318-325, 499
    dynamic content, 500,
        507-508
    dynamic positioning,
        500
    dynamic styles, 499
    dynamic text changes,
        504-508
    HTML 4 comparison,
        515
    online resources, 514
    page titles, 502-504
    scriptlets, 321-324
    ShowAuctionsDHTML
        page, 511-513
    standards, 515
    support, 15
dividers, 95
drag and drop, 22
errors, debugging, 405
fonts, 89-91
forms, 491-492
hotspots, 94
images, 94-95
lists, 91
marquees, 95
pages
    adding (Design view),
        85-86
    ASP connection, 41-48
    client-side scripting,
        104-106
    creating, 53-58
    creating with client-
        side scripting,
        108-113
    enhancing Web pages,
        131
    formatting, 86-91
    linking, 93
    procedures (VBScript),
        120

properties (Design
    view), 86
selecting views, 86
paragraphs, 88-89
tables, 91-93
tags
    <APPLET>, 158-160
    <BODY>, 106
    comment, 106
    <HEAD>, 106
    <OBJECT>, 160-163
    <SCRIPT> tags,
        105-106
    see also code; scripting
        languages/scripts
HTML controls
    Horizontal Rule, 71
    Toolbox, 71-72
HTML menu commands
    Bookmark, 94
    Div, 95
    Image, 94
    Link, 93
    Marquee, 95
HTML Outline window,
    76-77
HTML toolbar, 87
HTMLEncode method, 290
HTTP
    requests, 278-279
    SSL, 46
hyperlinks
    broken links
        displaying, 383
        repairing, 398-399
    expanding, 391-392
    HTML pages, 93
    verifying, 383
    viewing, 383-386
        filters, 388-389
        zoom percentage, 387
    Web pages, 55

I

icons (Site Designer), 485
ID attribute (OBJECT tag),
    162
IDE (integrated develop-
    ment environment), 64
    benefits, 186-188
    customizing, 78

editors, 64, 78
Internet Explorer 4,
    20-21
Microsoft Development
    Environment, 17-19, 50,
    190
properties, 10
robustness, 188
speed, 187
SQL, 187
Visual SourceSafe, 463
If...Then...Else control
    structure (VBScript),
    126-127
IIS Web site, 522
Image command (HTML
    menu), 94
images, HTML, 94-95
Immediate window (debug-
    ger), 413
index/keys properties (dia-
    grams), 249-250
indexes, 243
inner joins, 219-220
InputForm application,
    146-148
Insert command (Debug
    menu), 409
Insert query, 216
insert query column, 222
Insert Table command
    (Table menu), 22, 67
Insert Table dialog box, 67,
    92-93
Insert Values query, 216
inserting design-time con-
    trols, 303
installing Visual SourceSafe,
    449-451
instantiating Server objects,
    291-293
integrated development
    environment, see IDE
integrating client-side and
    server-side script, 150-152
Intellisense (statement com-
    pletion), 11, 74, 173
interfaces (user interfaces)
    designing, 468-470
        aesthetics, 472
        design checklist,
            492-493
        goals, 468-469

layout, 472
metaphors, 471
navigation, 473
semantics, 473
user needs/expecta-
tions, 469
DHTML scriptlets,
321-324
usability testing, 473-475
**Internet Explorer 4, 15,
20-21**
isolated mode, 46
**isolating developers,
431-432**
italicized text, 90

J

Java
applet controls (Toolbox),
100
applets, 25, 156-157
advantages, 165-166
aligning, 159
alternative text, 159
HTML markup,
158-160
limitations, 166
parameters, 160
running, 158
security, 176
sizing, 159
Web sites
Gamelan EarthWeb,
521
Java Boutique, 522
JavaSoft home page,
521
Java Boutique Web site, 522
JavaScript
code example, 107-108
ECMAScript standard,
142, 268
Hello World program
code, 112-113
public description objects
(DHTML scriptlets),
322-324
**JavaScript button proce-
dure, 112**

JavaSoft Home Page, 521
joins
inner joins, 219-220
outer joins, 220-221
relationships, 219
types, 218
JScript, 107, 142, 268
JScript button, 110

K

keys, 241
keywords (VBScript)
Call keyword, 115-116
End Function, 116
End Sub, 114
Function, 116
Sub, 114
While, 130

L

Label control, 302
**launching debugger,
409-410**
layout
CSSs, 97-99
themes, 48
Web pages
Design view, 55-56
designing, 472
Site Designer layouts,
490
**leveraging database connec-
tivity, 184**
libraries
DLLs (dynamic link
libraries)
COM, 363-365
compiling, 373
troubleshooting, 379
Visual SourceSafe func-
tions, 455-456
checking in files,
457-458
checking out files,
456-457
undoing changes, 458

**Link command (HTML
menu), 93**
Link View, 382
advantages, 401
features, 382-383
filters
applying, 389
categories, 388-389
object shortcut menu,
389-393
opening, 383-388
zooming in/out, 387
links
broken links
displaying, 383
repairing, 398-399
expanding, 391-392
HTML pages, 93
verifying, 383
viewing, 383-386
filters, 388-389
zoom percentage, 387
Web pages, 55
Listbox control, 302
listings
ASPs, 292
cookies, 281-282
Data Environment Object
Model, 338
database columns,
datatypes, 257
debugging (error-handling
routines), 421
DHTML
Dynamic Content page,
507-508
scriptlets, 322-325
ShowAuctions page,
511-512
document events, 320
dynamic greeting, 283
dynamic Web page,
274-275
function variables, formatting, 117
If...Then...Else statement,
127
ODBC data sources,
197-198
Order Search page, 346
page objects, methods,
329

Providing right organization for scripts, 120
QueryString collection, 279
Recordset control runtime text, 313
request methods, verifying, 277
returning a value, 117
Select Case statement, 128
scripts
    JavaScript code example, 108, 112
    separating, 120
    server-side script, 145-146
VBScript code example, 105, 112
sessions
    object variables, 287
    starting, 288
Timesheet application
    combo box, 171
    confirming data, 174
    Hours Worked field, 174
    validating data, 175
users
    preferences form, 273
    redirecting, 284
    validating input, 131
variants
    data types, 129
    subtypes, 122
Web site visitors, counting, 289
window events, 320
lists (HTML), 91
Local commmand (Working Mode menu), 437
local directories, 53
Local mode, 434, 443
local procedure calls, see LRPCs
Locals window (debugger), 411-412
Lock command (Format menu), 96
Lock method, 288
log in (ODBC databases), 196
logic errors, debugging, 404

logical database design, 428
loops (VBScript), 130
LRPCs (local/lightweight remote procedure calls), 365

M

Macmillan Computer Publishing Web site, 212, 519
Make Component dialog box, 373
Make Orders.dll command (File menu), 373
Make Table query, 217
many-to-many relationships, 242
MapPath method, 290
marking DHTML scriptlets, 324
Marquee command (HTML menu), 95
marquees (HTML), 95
Master mode, 14, 432-433, 443
MAX function, 232
metaphors (user interface design), 471
methods, 74, 170-171
    Abandon, 286
    AddHeader, 280
    AppendToLog, 280
    BinaryWrite, 280
    calling, 169
    Clear, 280, 421
    COM/ASP integration, 370-371
    CreateObject, 290
    defined, 169, 205
    End, 280
    execute, 328-330
    Flush, 280
    get(), 331
    HTMLEncode, 290
    Lock, 288
    MapPath, 290
    navigate, 328-330
    Raise, 421
    Redirect, 280, 284-285

set(), 331
show(), 330
Unlock, 288
URLEncode, 290
Write, 280, 283-284
see also functions
Microsoft Development Environment, 17-19
    data connections, 190
    files, 50
Microsoft newsgroups, 521
Microsoft Scripting Components (scriptlets)
DHTML
    control interface, 322-324
    JavaScript public description objects, 322-324
    marking, 324
    user interface, 321-322
Server, 321
Microsoft Web site
    Data Access home page, 521
    IIS home page, 522
    SiteBuilder Workshop, 520
    VBScript home page, 520
    Visual Basic home page, 522
    Visual InterDev home page, 520
    Visual Studio home page, 520
MIN function, 232
models (ADO), 204-205
modes
    changing, 436-439
    choosing, 436
    Local mode, 434, 443
    Master mode, 14, 432-433, 443
    Offline mode, 14, 434-435
    setting, 435
MS SQL Server constraints, 243
multitier architectures, 141, 267

N

**n-tiered architectures
(DCOM), 368-369**
**NAME attribute (APPLET
tag), 159**
naming
columns (queries),
225-226
controls, 492
event procedures, 119
projects, 40, 45
servers, 46
**navigate method (page
object), 328-330**
navigating Web sites
design issues, 473
PageNavBar control,
487-490
**Netscape SSL connections,
46**
New Database Wizard, 35
**New HTML Page command
(Site Diagram menu),
476-478**
**New Project command (File
menu), 43**
New Project dialog box, 43
**New Web Project Wizard,
43**
directories, 44-45
isolated mode, 46
naming projects, 45
servers
connecting, 46
selecting, 45
SSL connection, 46
themes, 48
Web sites, 47
newsgroups, 521
Northwind case study
connecting database, 343
creating project, 343
database, 343
home page, 344
Order Details page,
350-355
Order Listing page,
347-350
Order Search page,
345-347

overview, 342-343
Web pages, 342

O

object model, *see* **COM**
**Object Remote Procedure
Calls (ORPCs), 366**
**<OBJECT> tag (HTML),
160**
ALIGN attribute, 162
CLASSID attribute,
161-162
HEIGHT attribute, 162
HSPACE attribute, 163
ID attribute, 162
VSPACE attribute, 163
WIDTH attribute, 162
objects
absolute positioning,
96-97
ActiveX controls, 160
adding to Web pages,
166-168
advantages, 164
aligning, 162
class IDs, 161
defining, 163
editing, 168-169
HTML markup,
160-163
limitations, 164-165
methods, 169-171
parameters, 163
security, 176
sizing, 162
ADO (ActiveX Data
Objects)
Command object, 205
Connection object, 205
Error object, 207
Field object, 206
Parameter object, 206
Property object, 207
Recordset object, 206
Application
accessing, 288
events, 289
methods, 288
ASPs, 12, 370-371

Client Object and Events
folder, 27-28
Client Scripts folder, 28
client-side scripting
DHTML, 318-320
document, 320
window, 320
customizing, 73-75
Data Environment Object
Model, 336-338
database objects
constraints, 243
diagrams, 250-255
indexes, 243
relationships, 240-242
tables, 240
viewing, 188-189
DCOM, 370-371
defined, 156, 205
design-time controls,
297-301
adding to Web pages,
303
compared to ActiveX
controls, 299
database-driven forms,
307-314
defined, 298-299
editing script, 306-307
Recordset control, 312
RecordsetNavBar con-
trol, 312
standard controls,
302-303
structure, 305-306
text view, 304-305
Textbox control, 312
editing
Design view, 255
Link View, 391
Java applets, 156-157
advantages, 165-166
aligning, 159
alternative text, 159
HTML markup,
158-160
limitations, 166
parameters, 160
running, 158
security, 176
sizing, 159
methods, 74

properties, 10, 74, 156
Request, 270
  Cookies collection, 271
  Form collection,
    272-276
  QueryString collection,
    278-279
  ServerVariables collec-
    tion, 276-278
Response, 279
  AddHeader method,
    280
  AppendToLog method,
    280
  BinaryWrite method,
    280
  Buffer property,
    280-283
  Clear method, 280
  ContentType property,
    280, 285
  Cookies collection,
    281-282
  End method, 280
  Expires property, 280
  ExpiresAbsolute, 280
  Flush method, 280
  methods, 281
  Redirect method, 280,
    284-285
  Status property, 280
  Write method, 280,
    283-284
scripting code
  Script Editor, 172-173
  statement completion,
    173
  Timesheet application,
    174-175
Server
  instantiating, 291-293
  methods, 290
  properties, 291
  referencing, 290
Session
  Abandon method, 286
  events, 287-288
  SessionID property,
    285
  storing variables in,
    286-287
  Timeout property, 286

snap-to positioning, 97
SOM (Scripting Object
  Model), 269
  VBScript, 420-421
ODBC
  data sources
    character set transla-
      tion, 195
    creating, 192-194, 197
    Database Connection
      Wizard, 193
    default databases, 194
    listing, 197-198
    security, 194
    selecting drivers,
      192-193
    testing, 195
  databases, 194-196
Offline mode, 14, 434-435
OLE DB, ADO, 209
one-to-many relationships,
  242
one-to-one relationships,
  242
onload event (window
  object), 320
On_Error statement
  (VBScript), 420
Open command (Link View
  shortcut menu), 391
Open Project dialog box, 18
Open With command (Link
  View shortcut menu), 391
opening
  files, 51
  Link View, 383-388
  projects, 43
operating systems
  architecture, 427
  choosing, 426
  development tools, 426
  mixed environments,
    430-431
  scalability, 426
  standards, 427
  Windows 95, 429-430
OptionGroup control, 302
Options command (Tools
  menu), 78
Options dialog box, 78
Order Report project, 45
ordering columns (queries),
  225

ORPCs (Object Remote
  Procedure Calls), 366
Other Windows command
  (View menu), 76
outer joins, 220-221
Outline windows
  Document Outline win-
    dow, 76-77
  editing source code, 76-77
  Script Outline window, 77
output
  buffering, 282-283
  content type, 285
  queries, 226
  sending to user, 283-284

P

page objects (Scripting
  Object Model)
  creating, 327-328
  methods, 328-330
  properties, 330-331
Page Transitions control,
  303
PageNavBar control, 302,
  490
  adding to Web pages, 487
  properties, 487-489
PageObject control, 303,
  327
pages, see ASPs; HTML;
  Web pages
paragraphs (HTML), 88-89
Parameter object (ADO),
  206
parameters
  ActiveX controls, 163
  ADO, 207
  Java applets, 160
  see also attributes
Parent Level pages (Site
  Designer), 488
Path property (Cookies collection), 281
physical database design,
  428
platforms
  architecture, 427
  choosing, 426

development tools, 426
mixed environments,
430-431
scalability, 426
standards, 427
Windows 95, 429-430
**plus sign (+), Link View
icons, 391**
positioning
absolute positioning,
96-97
dynamic positioning, 500
snap-to positioning, 97
**previewing (QuickView),
24-25, 56, 66, 79-80**
Primary Key constraint, 243
primary keys, 241
procedures
debugging, 418
JavaScript button, 112
procedure calls
LRPCs, 365
ORPCs, 366
sub procedures, 115
scope, 125
VBScript, 114-130
arguments, 114-115
event procedures,
119-120
functions, 116-119
HTML pages, 120
sub procedures,
114-116
variables, 121-125
processes, debugging, 419
Processes window (debugger), 419
**ProcessForm Active Server
page, 149**
processing
forms
ASPs, 273
server-side script,
146-150
HTTP requests, 278-279
producers (COM), 362
production, 393, 442
**programming support,
12-13**
programs, *see* **applications**
Project Explorer, 19
data connections, 190
files, 50

Project menu commands
Add HTML Page, 85
Add Item, 94
project model modes
changing, 436-439
Local mode, 434, 443
Master mode, 432-433,
443
Offline mode, 434-435
setting, 435
projects
ASPs
creating, 56-57
HTML page connection, 41-48
clients analysis, 50-51
creating, 42-43, 46-48
CSSs, 97-99
databases
creating, 244
Visual Data Tools, 43
directories
analysis, 52-53
default, 44
local, 53
servers, 49
subdirectories, 40
URLs, 41
virtual root directories,
40
working directories, 45
files
DSNs, 190-191
global files, 41
Project Explorer, 50
search files, 41
HTML
bookmarks, 94
dividers, 95
fonts, 89-90
hotspots, 94
images, 94-95
linking pages, 93
lists, 91
marquees, 95
paragraphs, 88-89
tables, 91-93
text color, 91
HTML pages
adding, 85-86
ASPs connection,
41-48

creating, 53-58
formatting, 86-91
properties, 86
IDE, 17
isolated mode, 46
layout, 55-56
naming, 45
New Web Project Wizard,
43
directories, 44-45
isolated mode, 46
naming projects, 45
naming servers, 46
selecting servers, 45
server connection, 46
specifying Web sites,
47
SSL connection, 46
themes, 48
Northwind case study
connecting database,
343
creating, 343
home page, 344
Order Details page,
350-355
Order Listing page,
347-350
Order Search page,
345-347
objects
absolute positioning,
96-97
snap-to positioning, 97
opening, 43
Order Report, 45
overview, 40-41
Sample Application
Wizard, 43
searches, 44
servers
analysis, 49
connecting, 46
directories, 49
folders, 49
naming, 46
selecting, 45
solutions relationship, 50
source control
adding files, 454
disabling, 454-455
enabling, 451-453
verifying, 453-454

specifying Web sites, 47
SSL connection, 46
system DSNs, 191-192
tables, 57
themes, 48
user DSNs, 191-192
viewing, 43, 56
Web Projects folder, 43
see also applications; files;
Web pages
properties, 74
ActiveX controls, 168-169
ADO, 207
column properties
diagrams, 246
tables, 253
COM/ASP integration,
370-371
Cookies collection, 281
database diagrams
column properties, 246
index/keys properties,
249-250
relationship properties,
248-249
table properties,
247-248
objects, 10
page object, 330-331
PageNavBar control,
487-490
Response object
Buffer, 280-283
ContentType, 280, 285
Expires, 280
ExpiresAbsolute, 280
Status, 280
Server object, 291
Web pages, 86
Property object (ADO), 207
**Property Pages dialog box,
86, 454**
protocols, SSL, 46
**public description objects
(JavaScript), 322-324**
Pubs database, 212-214

Q

queries (SQL), 187
columns, 221-223
adding, 224
deleting, 224
naming, 225-226
order, 225
customizing, 224-232
databases
adding new data,
235-236
changing data, 235
deleting data, 236
Delete query, 217
grouping results, 228-232
aggregate functions,
230-232
calculation method,
231
Insert query, 216
Insert Values query, 216
Make Table query, 217
output, 226
rows, 226-228
running, 223
Select query, 216
tables
joins, 218-221
selecting, 218-223
types, 216
update queries, 216
creating, 232-234
selecting tables to
update, 233
values, adding, 234
see also Query Designer
Query Designer
connecting to data
sources, 212-213
Diagram pane, 199-200
features, 199
Grid pane, 200, 226-228
Criteria column, 227
Or column, 228
Sort Order column,
227
Sort Type column, 227
overview, 33, 198
Results pane, 200-202,
214, 235-236

SQL pane, 200-201
toolbar, 215-217
Change Type button,
217
Remove Filter button,
217
Run Query button, 217
Show Diagram Pane
button, 215
Show Grid Pane but-
ton, 216
Show Results Pane
button, 216
Show SQL Pane but-
ton, 216
Sort Ascending button,
217
Sort Query button, 217
Verify SQL Syntax
button, 217
workspace, 199-201
see also queries
**QueryString collection,
278-279**
**QuickView, 24-25, 56, 66,
79-80**

R

**RAD (Rapid Application
Development), 11**
**Raise method (VBScript),
421**
**RDO (Remote Data
Objects), 203, 209**
**Recordset control, 302,
312-313**
**Recordset object (ADO),
206**
**RecordsetNavBar control,
302, 312**
recordsets, *see* **tables**
**Redirect method, 280,
284-285**
**referencing Server object,
290**
referential integrity, 241
**relationship properties
(diagrams), 248-249**

relationships, 240-242
    defining, 241
    many-to-many, 242
    one-to-many, 242
    one-to-one, 242
    referential integrity, 241
    tables, 255
Remote Data Objects, *see*
    RDO
remote debugging, 410
remote procedure calls
    LRPCs, 365
    ORPCs, 366
remote servers (DCOM),
    366
Remove Breakpoint com-
    mand (Debug menu), 416
Remove command (Site
    Diagram menu), 477
Remove Filter button
    (Query Designer toolbar),
    217
Reorder Pages command
    (Site Diagram menu), 477
reports (Broken Links
    report), 399
Request object, 270
    Cookies collection, 271
    Form collection, 272-276
    QueryString collection,
        278-279
    ServerVariables collection,
        276-278
requests
    HTTP, 278-279
    methods, 276-277
Response object, 279
    Cookies collection,
        281-282
    methods, 281
        AddHeader, 280
        AppendToLog, 280
        BinaryWrite, 280
        Clear, 280
        End, 280
        Flush, 280
        Redirect, 280, 284-285
        Write, 280, 283-284
    properties
        Buffer, 280-283
        ContentType, 280, 285
        Expires, 280

ExpiresAbsolute, 280
    Status, 280
Restart command (Debug
    menu), 416
robustness, IDE, 188
root directories (virtual root
    directories), 40
Rotate command (Site
    Diagram menu), 477
rotating site diagrams, 477
Run Query button (Query
    Designer toolbar), 217
Run to Cursor command
    (Debug menu), 416
running
    Java applets, 158
    queries, 223
    stored procedures,
        259-261
Running Documents win-
    dow (debugger), 418
runtime operations
    DTC, 13
    errors, debugging, 404

S

Sample Application Wizard,
    43
saving
    database changes (tables),
        254-255
    files, 51
    scraps, 75-76
    SQL scripts, 256-258
scalability (platforms), 426
scope (variables), 125
scraps, 75-76
Script Editor, 172-173
script library (Scripting
    Object Model), 331-333
Script Outline window, 26,
    76-77, 376
    Client Object and Events
        folder, 27-28
    Client Scripts folder, 28
    Client Server and Events
        folder, 30
    folders, 26-30
    Script Outline window, 26,
        76-77, 376

<SCRIPT> tags (HTML),
    105-106
scripting
    breakpoints, 409, 416-417
    client-side, 104-105
        advantages, 104
        DHTML DOM,
            318-320
        documents, 320
        HTML pages, 105-106
        limitations, 104
        server-side script inte-
            gration, 150-152
        Web pages, creating,
            108-113
        windows, 320
    color-coding, 23-24
    customizing, 73-75
    debugging
        breakpoints, 416-417
        err object, 420-421
        errors, 406
        execution, 414-417
        On_Error statement,
            420
        setup, 408-410
        syntax errors, 404
    editing, 76-77
    platforms (DTCs), 333
    scope, 125
    Script Editor, 172-173
    server-side script, 138-139
        capabilities, 139
        client-side script inte-
            gration, 150-152
        Hello, World example,
            144-146
        form-processing exam-
            ple, 146-150
    SOM, 269
        applications, 334-335
        DTCs, 13, 326-327
        enabling, 333-334
        overview, 325-326
        page objects, 327-331
        script library, 331-333
    see also ASPs; code;
        scripting languages/
        scripts

scripting languages/scripts, 73
ECMAScript, 142, 268
HTML pages, 105-106
JavaScript, 107-108
JScript, 107
Script Outline
Client Object and
Events folder, 27-28
Client Scripts folder, 28
Client Server and
Events folder, 30
folders, 26-30
Script Outline window, 26, 76-77, 376
SQL scripts, 256-258
VBScript, 106, 113
arguments, 114-115
Call keyword, 115-116
Case statements, 128-129
control structures, 125-127
Do loops, 130
enhancing Web pages, 131
event procedures, 119-120
For...Next loops, 130
functions, 116-119
procedures, 114, 120-121
Select Case statements, 127-129
sub procedures, 114-116
variables, 121-125
see also ASPs; code; scripting
Scripting Object Model (SOM), 269
applications, 334-335
DTCs, 13, 326-327
enabling, 333-334
overview, 325-326
page objects
creating, 327-328
methods, 328-330
properties, 330-331
script library, 331-333

scriptlets (Microsoft Scripting Components)
DHTML
control interface, 322-324
JavaScript public description objects, 322-324
marking, 324
user interface, 321-322
Server, 321
scripts, *see* **scripting languages/scripts**
ScriptTimeout property (Server object), 291
searches
files, 41
rows (queries), 226-228
Web pages, 345-347
Secure property (Cookies collection), 281
Secure Sockets Layer (SSL), 46
security
ActiveX controls, 176
Java applets, 176
ODBC, 194
Select Case statements (VBScript procedures), 127-129
Select Data Source dialog box, 190
SELECT statement (SQL), 187, 216
selecting
databases, 428
modes, 436
platforms
architecture, 427
development tools, 426
scalability, 426
standards, 427
Server object
instantiating, 291-293
methods, 290
properties, 291
referencing, 290
Server scriptlets, 321
server-side script, 138-139
capabilities, 139
client-side script integration, 150-152

debugging, 408-410
form-processing example
analysis, 150
ASP, 149
HTML form, 146-148
Hello, World example, 144-146
see also ASPs
servers
Client Server and Events folder, 30
code debugging, 14
connecting, 46
data sources, 192-193
domains, 40, 45
environment variables, 276-278
IIS Web site, 522
projects, 46, 49
remote servers, 366
selecting, 45
see also client/server model
ServerVariables collection, 276-278
SERVER_NAME variable, 276-278
Session object
Abandon method, 286
events, 287-288
properties
SessionID, 285
Timeout, 286
variables, 286-287
SessionID property (Session object), 285
Set Next Statement command (Debug menu), 416
set() method, 331
shortcut menu, Visual SourceSafe, 459-461
Show All Items filter (Links View), 389
Show Diagram Pane button (Query Designer toolbar), 215
Show Documents filter (Links View), 389
Show Executable Files filter (Links View), 389
Show External Files filter (Links View), 389

**Show Grid Pane button
(Query Designer toolbar),
216**
**Show HTML Pages filter
(Links View), 389**
**Show In Links filter (Links
View), 389**
**Show In/Out Links filter
(Links View), 389**
**Show Links Inside Pages fil-
ter (Links View), 389**
**Show Multimedia Files filter
(Links View), 389**
**Show Next Statement com-
mand (Debug menu), 416**
**Show Other Protocols filter
(Links View), 389**
**Show Out Links filter
(Links View), 389**
**Show Repeated Links filter
(Links View), 389**
**Show Results Pane button
(Query Designer toolbar),
216**
**Show SQL Pane button
(Query Designer toolbar),
216**
show() method, 330
**Sibling Level pages (Site
Designer), 488**
Site Designer, 15
    navigation bars, 487-490
    pages
        adding existing pages,
        481-484
        creating, 478-480
        icons, 485
        layouts, 490
        organizing, 485-487
        themes, 490-491
    site diagrams, 476-478
    see also designing
**Site Diagram menu
commands**
    Add Existing Page, 476,
    481
    Add Home Page, 477
    Add to Global Navigation
    Bar, 477
    Delete, 477
    Expand, 477
    New HTML Page,
    476-478

    Remove, 477
    Reorder Pages, 477
    Rotate, 477
    Zoom, 477
site diagrams
    creating, 476-478
    pages
        adding existing pages,
        481-484
        creating, 478-480
        deleting, 477
        icons, 485
        organizing, 485-487
    rotating, 477
    zooming in/out, 477
**SiteBuilder Workshop Web
site, 520**
sites, *see* Web sites
sizing
    ActiveX controls, 162
    Java applets, 159
**Snap to Grid command
(Tools menu), 97**
Snap to Grid tool, 97
**solutions/projects relation-
ship, 50**
**SOM, *see* Scripting Object
Model**
**Sort Ascending button
(Query Designer toolbar),
217**
**Sort Query button (Query
Designer toolbar), 217**
**source code control (Visual
SourceSafe), 20**
    component integration,
    455
    environment, 459-461
    IDE, 463
    installing, 449-451
    library functions, 455-456
        checking in files,
        457-458
        checking out files,
        456-457
        undoing changes, 458
    overview, 448-449
    shortcut menu, 459-461
    source control
        adding files, 454
        disabling, 454-455
        enabling, 451-453
        verifying, 453-454

    support, 14
    user access, 450-451
    version control, 448,
    461-462
    Visual SourceSafe
    Administrator, 450-451
Source view
    ASP, 53
    color-coded script, 23-24
    debugger, 407
    HTML pages, 86
    methods, 74
    properties, 74
    statement completion, 74
    tables, 67
    Visual InterDev editor, 66
speed, IDE, 187
**SQL (Structured Query
Language)**
    Database Designer, 34
    IDE, 187
    queries, 187
        columns, 221-226
        customizing, 224-232
        databases, 235-236
        Delete query, 217
        grouping results,
        228-232
        Insert query, 216
        Insert Values query,
        216
        Make Table query, 217
        output, 226
        rows, 226-228
        running, 223
        Select query, 216
        tables, 218-223
        types, 216
        update queries, 216,
        232-234
    Query Designer
        connecting to data
        sources, 212-213
        Diagram pane, 199-200
        features, 199
        Grid pane, 200,
        226-228
        overview, 33, 198
        Results pane, 200-202,
        214, 235-236
        SQL pane, 200-201
        toolbar, 215-217
        workspace, 199-201

scripts, 256-258
statements
    GROUP BY, 228
    SELECT, 187
Stored Procedure Editor,
    34
Trigger Editor, 34
SQL Server constraints, 243
**SSL (Secure Sockets Layer),
46**
**Start command (Debug
menu), 409**
**statement completion, 11,
74, 173**
statements
    SQL
        Database Designer, 34
        GROUP BY, 228
        Query Designer, 33,
            198-202
        SELECT, 187
    VBScript
        Case, 128-129
        On_Error, 420
        Select_Case, 127-129
**Status property (Response
object), 280**
**Step Into command (Debug
menu), 415**
**Step Out command (Debug
menu), 415**
**Step Over command (Debug
menu), 415**
Stored Procedure Editor, 34
stored procedures
    creating, 258-260
    errors, 260
    running, 259-261
style sheets (CSSs), 97-99
styles (dynamic styles), 499
sub procedures (VBScript)
    arguments, 114-115
    Call keyword, 115-116
    calling, 115
    Sub keyword, 114
**subtypes (VBScript vari-
ables), 122-123**
    changing, 124-125
    conversion functions, 124
SUM function, 232
support
    ActiveX controls, 25
    ASPs, 26

development teams, 14-15
DHTML, 15
DTC, 25-26
Java applets, 25
Master mode, 14
Offline mode, 14
programming, 12-13
Visual SourceSafe, 14
**syntax errors, debugging,
404**

T

**Table menu command,
Insert Table, 22, 67**
**table properties (diagrams),
247-248**
tables, 350
    Authors table (Pubs data-
        base), 214
    columns
        adding to queries, 224
        choosing for queries,
            221-223
        delete query column,
            222
        deleting from queries,
            224
        insert query column,
            222
        keys, 241
        naming, 225-226
        order, 225
        properties, 253
        symbols, 223
        update query column,
            222
    creating, 57
        database changes, sav-
            ing, 254-255
        database diagrams,
            251-255
    Design view, 67-68
    HTML, 91-93
    joins, 218
        inner joins, 219-220
        outer joins, 220-221
        relationships, 219
        types, 218

relationships, 240
    defining, 241
    many-to-many, 242
    one-to-many, 242
    one-to-one, 242
    referential integrity,
        241
    viewing, 255
rows
    grouping query results,
        228-232
    searching (queries),
        226-228
selecting
    for queries, 218-223
    for update queries, 233
Source view, 67
tabs (Toolbox), 68-69
**Tabular Data Control
(TDC), 512**
tags (HTML)
    <APPLET>, 158
        ALIGN attribute, 159
        ALT attribute, 159
        CODE attribute, 159
        CODEBASE attribute,
            158
        HEIGHT attribute, 159
        HSPACE attribute, 160
        NAME attribute, 159
        VSPACE attribute, 160
        WIDTH attribute, 159
    <BODY> tags, 106
    comment tag, 106
    <HEAD> tags, 106
    <OBJECT>, 160-161
        ALIGN attribute, 162
        CLASSID attribute,
            161-162
        HEIGHT attribute, 162
        HSPACE attribute, 163
        ID attribute, 162
        VSPACE attribute, 163
        WIDTH attribute, 162
    <SCRIPT> tags, 105-106
**TDC (Tabular Data
Control), 512**
testing
    applications, 393, 441
    ODBC, 195
    Web site usability,
        473-475

text
Design view, 66
dynamic content, 504-508
fonts (HTML)
color, 91
formatting, 89
size, 89
style, 90
scraps, 75-76
scrolling (marquees), 95
**text view (design-time con-
trols), 304-305**
Textbox control, 302, 312
**themes (Site Designer), 48,
490-491**
threads, debugging, 418
Threads window, 418
Timelines control, 302
**Timeout property (Session
object), 286**
Timesheet application
combo box, 171
Hours Worked field, 174
input, 174-175
methods, 169-170
properties, 168-169
toolbars
Debug, 410
HTML toolbar, 87
Query Designer
Change Type button,
217
Remove Filter button,
217
Run Query button, 217
Show Diagram Pane
button, 215
Show Grid Pane but-
ton, 216
Show Results Pane
button, 216
Show SQL Pane but-
ton, 216
Sort Ascending button,
217
Sort Query button, 217
Verify SQL Syntax
button, 217
Toolbox
controls
ActiveX, 69-70
adding/deleting, 68-69,
100

DTC, 72-73
HTML controls, 71-72
tabs, 68-69
customizing, 99-100
DHTML scriptlets, 324
scraps, 75-76
**Toolbox command (View
menu), 69**
tools
Database Designer,
243-244
database projects, 244
diagrams, 244-250
overview, 34
tables, relationships,
255
database projects, 43
RAD, 11
Site Designer, 15
Snap to Grid, 97
Query Designer
connecting to data
sources, 212-213
Diagram pane, 199-200
features, 199
Grid pane, 200,
226-228
overview, 33, 198
Results pane, 200-202,
214, 235-236
SQL pane, 200-201
toolbar, 215-217
workspace, 199-201
see also wizards
Tools menu commands
Customize Toolbox, 100
Options, 78
Snap to Grid, 97
View Links on WWW,
385
transactions, 268-269
Trigger Editor, 34
troubleshooting
broken links, 398-399
DLLs, 379
server connections, 46

U

underlined text, 90
Unique constraint, 243
Unlock method, 288
update queries
creating, 232-234
selecting tables to update,
233
values, adding, 234
Update query, 216
update query column, 222
URLEncode method, 290
**URLs (Uniform Resource
Locators), 41**
usability testing, 473-475
Usenet newsgroups, 521
user interfaces
designing
aesthetics, 472
design checklist,
492-493
goals, 468-469
layout, 472
metaphors, 471
navigation, 473
semantics, 473
user needs/expecta-
tions, 469
DHTML scriptlets,
321-324
usability testing, 473-475
**user preferences form (list-
ing), 273**
users
counting, 289
redirecting, 284-285
Visual SourceSafe access,
450-451
**Users menu command, Add
User, 451**

V

variables
debugging
editing values, 412
locally, 411-412
logic, 413

server environment,
276-278
Session object, 286-287
VBScript, 121-125
control structures,
126-127
data types, 121-125
defining scope, 125
subtypes, 122-125
variant data type (VBScript variables), 121-123
changing, 124-125
conversion functions, 124
VarType function (VBScript), 122-123
VBScript
control structures, 125-127
enhancing Web pages,
130-133
error-handling routines,
419-421
Hello World program
code, 112-113
HTML pages, 105-106
methods
Clear, 421
Raise, 421
On_Error statement, 420
procedures, 113-130
arguments, 114-115
Call keyword, 115-116
Case statements,
128-129
Do loops, 130
event procedures,
119-120
For...Next loops, 130
functions, 116-118
HTML pages, 120
Select Case statements,
127-129
sub procedures,
114-116
variables, 121-125
Web site, 520
VBScript button, 110
Verify command (Link View shortcut menu), 391
Verify SQL Syntax button (Query Designer toolbar), 217

version control (Visual SourceSafe), 20
component integration,
455
environment, 459-461
IDE, 463
installing, 449-451
library functions, 455-456
checking in files,
457-458
checking out files,
456-457
undoing changes, 458
overview, 448-449
shortcut menu, 459-461
source control
adding files, 454
disabling, 454-455
enabling, 451-453
verifying, 453-454
support, 14
user access, 450-451
View in Browser command (Link View shortcut menu), 391
View Links command (Link View shortcut menu), 391
View Links on WWW command (Tools menu), 385
View menu commands
Broken Links Report, 399
Debug Windows, 407
Other Windows, 76
Toolbox, 69
viewing
ASPs, 152
Debug menu, 407
object properties, 10
projects, 43
Script Outline, 376
table relationships, 255
Web pages, 58
views (Visual InterDev editor), 21, 64-66
Data view, 51, 188-189
Design view
adding HTML, 85-86
bookmarks, 94
color, 91
dividers, 95
drag and drop HTML,
22

fonts, 89-90
Format menu, 87
formatting, 86-91
hotspots, 94
HTML toolbar, 87
images, 94-95
linking pages, 93
lists, 91
marquees, 95
modifying objects, 255
overview, 84-85
paragraphs, 88-89
positioning objects,
96-97
properties (HTML), 86
tables, 67-68, 91-93
text, 66
Web page layout,
55-56
Link View
advantages, 401
features, 382-383
filtering, 388-389
object shortcut menu,
389-393
opening, 383-388
zooming in/out, 387
overview, 64-66
QuickView, 24-25, 66,
79-80
selecting for HTML
pages, 86
Source View, 53, 66
color-coded script,
23-24
debugger, 407
methods, 74
properties, 74
statement completion,
74
tables, 67
virtual root directories, 40
Visual Basic
components, 371-373
DCOM, 370
DLLs
compiling, 373
troubleshooting, 379
Web site, 522
Visual C++, 370

Visual Data Tools
Database Designer,
243-244
database projects, 244
diagram properties,
246-250
diagrams, 244-250
database projects, 43
Query Designer
connecting to data
sources, 212-213
Diagram pane, 199-200
features, 199
Grid pane, 200,
226-228
overview, 33, 198
Results pane, 200-202,
214, 235-236
SQL pane, 200-201
toolbar, 215-217
workspace, 199-201
see also queries
Visual InterDev editor, *see*
views
Visual J++, 370
Visual SourceSafe, 20
component integration,
455
environment, 459-461
IDE, 463
installing, 449-451
library functions, 455-456
checking in files,
457-458
checking out files,
456-457
undoing changes, 458
overview, 448-449
shortcut menu, 459-461
source control
adding files, 454
disabling, 454-455
enabling, 451-453
verifying, 453-454
support, 14
user access, 450-451
version control, 448,
461-462
Visual SourceSafe
Administrator, 450-451
Visual Studio Web site, 520

VSPACE attribute
<APPLET> tag, 160
<OBJECT> tag, 163

W-Z

Watch window (debugger),
412
Web applications
creating, 373-375
development, 446-448
integrating components,
376-378
Northwind case study
connecting database,
343
creating project, 343
database, 343
home page, 344
Order Details page,
350-355
Order Listing page,
347-350
Order Search page,
345-347
overview, 342-343
Web pages, 342
see also ASPs; projects;
Web pages; Web sites
Web pages
adding, 85-86
ASPs, 56-57
browsing, 58
client-side scripting,
104-113
CSS, 97-99
database-driven pages, 307
database connections,
308
design-time controls,
308-311
runtime scripts,
312-314
scripting platforms,
307
design-time controls, 303
DHTML project
base content, 501-502
data binding, 508-509

development guide-
lines, 514
dynamic text changes,
504-507
source code, 507-508,
511-513
title, 502-504
dynamic content, 500
external editors, 78-79
formatting
Design view, 86-91
Format menu, 87
HTML toolbar, 87
HTML
bookmarks, 94
creating, 53-58
dividers, 95
fonts, 89-90
hotspots, 94
images, 94-95
linking, 93
lists, 91
marquees, 95
paragraphs, 88-89
tables, 91-93
text color, 91
layout, 55-56
linking, 55, 93
Northwind case study
home page, 344
Order Details page,
350-355
Order Listing page,
347-350
Order Search page,
345-347
Web pages, 342
objects
absolute positioning,
96-97
snap-to positioning, 97
procedures (VBScript),
120
properties, 86
recordset pages, 347-350
tables, 57, 91-93
VBScript, 131
viewing, 56-58
see also ASPs; projects;
Web applications; Web
sites

Web Project menu com-
mand, Copy Web
Application, 395
Web Project Wizard, 43
    directories, 44-45
    isolated mode, 46
    naming projects, 45
    servers
        connecting, 46
        selecting, 45
    SSL connection, 46
    themes, 48
    Web sites, 47
Web Projects folder, 43
Web sites
    copying, 395-398
        benefits, 394
        child Webs, 396
        destination Web server,
        396
        security, 395
        source code control,
        401
    creating (Site Designer)
        existing pages, 481-484
        HTML pages, 478-480
        layouts, 490
        navigation bars,
        487-490
        page hierarchy,
        485-487
        page icons, 485
        site diagrams, 476-478
        specifying for projects,
        47
        SSL connection, 46
        themes, 490-491
        usability testing,
        473-475
    designing
        aesthetics, 472
        design checklist,
        492-493
        goals, 468-469
        layout, 472
        metaphors, 471
        navigation, 473
        semantics, 473
        user needs/expecta-
        tions, 469
    DHTML resources, 514
    Gamelan EarthWeb, 521

Java Boutique, 522
JavaSoft Home Page, 521
Macmillan Computer
    Publishing, 212, 519
Microsoft, 520
    Data Access home
    page, 521
    IIS home page, 522
    SiteBuilder Workshop,
    520
    VBScript home page,
    520
    Visual Basic home
    page, 522
    Visual InterDev home
    page, 520
    Visual Studio home
    page, 520
Site Designer, 15
World Wide Web
    Consortium, 522
see also ASPs; projects;
    Web applications; Web
    pages
WFC controls (Toolbox),
100
WHERE clause, 232
While keyword (VBScript
procedures), 130
WIDTH attribute
    <APPLET> tag, 159
    <OBJECT> tag, 162
windows
    client-side scripting, 320
    debugger
        Auto, 411-412
        Call Stack, 418
        Immediate, 413
        Locals, 411-412
        Processes, 419
        Running Documents,
        418
        Threads, 418
        Watch, 412
    Outline windows
        Document Outline win-
        dow, 76-77
        editing source code,
        76-77
        Script Outline window,
        77

Windows 95
    client/server model,
    429-430
    databases, 430
    Windows NT mixed envi-
    ronments, 430 431
Windows DNA (Windows
    Distributed interNet
    Applications
    Architecture), 367-368
Windows NT, 430-431
wizards
    Data Form Wizard, 35
    Database Connection
    Wizard, 190-198
    databases, 35
    New Database Wizard, 35
    New Web Project Wizard,
    43
        directories, 44-45
        isolated mode, 46
        naming projects, 45
        servers, 45-46
        specifying Web sites,
        47
        SSL connection, 46
        themes, 48
    Sample Application
    Wizard, 43
    see also tools
Working Mode menu com-
mand, Local, 437
working modes
    changing, 436-439
    choosing, 436
    Local mode, 434, 443
    Master mode, 14, 432-
    433, 443
    Offline mode, 14, 434-435
    setting, 435
World Wide Web
    Consortium Web site, 522
write event (document
object), 320
Write method, 280, 283-284
WYSIWYG editing, 12, 66

Z Order command (Format
menu), 95
Zoom command (Site
Diagram menu), 477
Zoom Link View option, 387

Active Server Pages Unleashed

—Stephen Walther

With many illustrations and real-world examples, this book shows you how to fully exploit the Active Server to create dynamic Web sites. You will create dynamic and powerful Web-based business solutions with Active Server Pages (ASP). ASP enables server-side scripting for IIS with native support for both VBScript and JScript. This book features in-depth explanations of the Active Server, BackOffice, and Visual Studio. It also covers data access, security, and Web page creation using Active Server Components. With timely solutions, *Active Server Pages Unleashed* allows you to explore the publishing, component-supporting capabilities of IIS 4; hone HTML skills for effective Active Server Pages programming; build interactive Web forms; use SQL to construct database queries that retrieve information from a database table, allowing you to design and create database tables of your own; work with the second set object to customize the properties for your needs; manage the communication between a browser and a Web server using discrete request and response pairs; distinguish between VBScript and JavaScript to determine which is the best language for your ASP scripting needs; create custom Active Server Pages components; and explore Visual InterDev and incorporate advanced features into your Web sites that use the best of Microsoft Active Platform technologies.

Price: $49.99 USA/$71.95 CAN   Intermediate–Advanced

ISBN: 1-57521-351-6   1032 pages

Special Edition Using Visual InterDev 6

—Steve Banick

Special Edition Using Visual InterDev 6 provides the reader with an easy-to-use reference to the newest version of Microsoft's Visual InterDev. This book teaches Internet application development with Visual InterDev in a steady, yet concise pace. After presenting foundational information for developing with Visual InterDev, this book quickly progresses into more advanced topics such as Dynamic HTML, scriptlets, ActiveX controls, database development, security, administration, optimization, and more. After only a year in release, Microsoft Visual InterDev is used by over 225,000 professional developers worldwide, making it the leading Web application development tool, with nearly twice as many users as its nearest competitor.

Price: $39.99 USA/$57.95 CAN   Intermediate–Advanced

ISBN: 0-7897-1549-X   750 pages

Sams Teach Yourself SQL in 21 Days, Second Edition

—Morgan, Perkins, Stephens, and Plew

Fully updated and revised to include coverage of PL/SQL and Transact-SQL, this easy-to-understand guide teaches you everything you need to know—from database concepts and processes to implementing security and constructing and optimizing queries. This book shows you how to create tables, modify data, incorporate security features, and tune the database for optimum performance. It emphasizes common database concepts, including SQL functions and queries. Q&A sections, step-by-step instructions, and review sections make learning easy and fun.

Price: $39.99 USA/$56.95 CAN   *Beginning–Intermediat*

ISBN: 0-672-31110-0   *624 pages*

Sams Teach Yourself Visual Basic 6 in 21 Days

—Greg Perry

In this book, Visual Basic programming techniques are presented in a logical and easy-to-follow sequence that helps you really understand the principles involved in developing programs. You begin with learning the basics of writing your first program and then move on to adding voice, music, sound, and graphics. After reading this book, you will be able to write your own DLLs, create ActiveX controls, use object linking and embedding (OLE), write Visual Basic programs that support multiple document interface, and much more. The various topics covered include properties, controls, and objects; graphics, controls, and methods; interfacing with Windows; arrays, OLE, and other topics; data control and SQL; multiple document interface; ActiveX-sound programming and DirectSound; building ActiveX controls; and all the latest features of Visual Basic. This book combines the proven *Sams Teach Yourself* format with the most popular programming language on the market and enables you to create and use ActiveX controls.

Price: $29.99 USA/$42.95 CAN   *Beginning–Intermediate*

ISBN: 0-672-31310-3   *800 pages*

Add to Your Sams Library Today with the Best Books for Programming, Operating Systems, and New Technologies

To order, visit our Web site at www.mcp.com or fax us at

1-800-835-3202

ISBN	Quantity	Description of Item	Unit Cost	Total Cost
1-57521-351-6		Active Server Pages Unleashed	$49.99	
0-7897-1549-X		Special Edition Using Visual InterDev 6	$39.99	
0-672-31110-0		Sams Teach Yourself SQL in 21 Days, Second Edition	$39.99	
0-672-31310-3		Sams Teach Yourself Visual Basic 6 in 21 Days	$29.99	
		Shipping and Handling: See information below.		
		TOTAL		

Shipping and Handling

Standard	$5.00
2nd Day	$10.00
Next Day	$17.50
International	$40.00

201 W. 103rd Street, Indianapolis, Indiana 46290   1-800-835-3202 — Fax

Book ISBN 0-672-31251-4